PLAYS FROM SOUTH COAST REPERTORY: HISPANIC PLAYWRIGHTS PROJECT ANTHOLOGY

BROADWAY PLAY PUBLISHING INC
56 E 81st St., NY NY 10028-0202
212 772-8334 fax: 212 772-8358
http://www.BroadwayPlayPubl.com

PLAYS FROM SOUTH COAST REPERTORY:
HISPANIC PLAYWRIGHTS PROJECT ANTHOLOGY
© Copyright 2000 by Broadway Play Publishing Inc

First printing: June 2000
I S B N: 0-88145-189-4

Book design: Marie Donovan
Word processing: Microsoft Word for Windows
Typographic controls: Xerox Ventura Publisher 2.0 PE
Typeface: Palatino
Copy editing: Michele Travis
Printed on recycled acid-free paper and bound in the U S A

CONTENTS

PREFACE

I remember fondly one night at Jerry Patch's office when he told me that South Coast Rep was beginning their Hispanic Playwrights Project and that my play, ONCE REMOVED, had been chosen for that year. It was an odd occurrence in the middle of all that pristine Anglo-Saxon Americana—where Latinos could be seen lurking in the shadows of hallways, picking up dishes in restaurants or handing out tickets in parking lots. In the middle of all this clean and polished Gringoism, the "other" was about to take center stage. (Even if only for two weeks.)

I remember the first year as a time full of camaraderie, mixed with jealousy and questions. Who is really Spanish? Should we write about magic realism? Should this only be for Latinos on the West Coast—i.e. Chicanos? Should we write in Spanish or in English? Do we want to be categorized as "Hispanic?" All of it troubling and enthralling and full of life. The work was eclectic and exciting. In the years I was there, José Cruz González was always generous and demanding.

I congratulate South Coast Rep for continuing to support Latino writers into the New century. This year one of my students, Jorge González, is part of the festival and for the past two years Rogelio Martinez, another student, has had reading workshops and commissions given to him. His reports have always been encouraging. So keep up the good work.

I know you will find this collection of plays moving, amusing and challenging. You will see that "Hispanic" covers a wide range of theatrical, political and social ideas—as diverse and colorful as America itself.

Eduardo Machado
Playwright
Columbia University
New York, New York

FOREWORD

South Coast Repertory's Hispanic Playwrights Project began in 1986 with the purpose of fostering and developing new plays by Latino playwrights for the American theatre. The need for such a program at that time was apparent; it was nearly impossible to find any published body of work by Latino playwrights, and although new play programs were springing up across the nation, few recognized the Latino community as a source for unique and contemporary work. S C R saw the potential for these artists and made the commitment. H P P was developed to provide the environment and professional support that these writers had previously lacked; to give them professional directors, actors, and dramaturgs and the opportunity to work in a low-pressure setting over several weeks, to experiment, cut, rewrite, and ultimately have their work read before a general audience. The initial vision became the springboard for fifteen years of developing plays by Latinos. More than a thousand manuscripts have been read and fifty eight have been workshopped, leading to eight S C R productions of plays by H P P writers; and along the way the program has also provided opportunities for dozens of Latino actors, directors and dramaturgs. Now an integral component of S C R's Pacific Playwrights Festival, H P P continues to thrive and to support innovative new work.

 The project has provided a vital boost for many of the artists who have participated. Many developed their early plays through H P P and have become important writers in the Latino and theater communities. Playwrights such as Edwin Sánchez, Octavio Solis, Edit Villarreal, Oliver Mayer and Lisa Loomer got their first mainstream professional theater experience through H P P and have gone on to make significant contributions . Others, such as Eduardo Machado, Cherríe Moraga and José Rivera, already forging important careers, were given visibility on a national level through their participation in H P P. By spotlighting the work of emerging and established writers, through readings, productions and publication, H P P continues to provide an example and an opportunity for future generations of Latino writers. We're proud to share with you these plays, which represent only a small fraction of the work H P P has helped develop.

We want to thank all the participants in the project, from the actors, to directors and dramaturgs. We also want to thank all the funders, without whom we wouldn't have been as successful. And of course, we must thank S C R's Artistic Directors, David Emmes and Martin Benson, who supported us even when the outside funding dried up. And finally, we would like to thank the playwrights for the gift of their words and stories. They continue to inspire us.

José Cruz González, *Project Director 1985-1996*
Juliette Carrillo, *Project Director 1997-present*

A NOTE FROM THE PUBLISHER

One of the things that we do as a publisher is take a play as it is given to us by the playwright and "massage" it into our house style. We endeavor to give a consistent form and look to all the plays that we publish. Two authors in this collection made specific requests that we deviate: José Rivera and Cherríe Moraga. So, just so you know that it is part of the plan: all the dialogue is in italics in ACT ONE and ACT FOUR of REFERENCES TO SALVADOR DALI MAKE ME HOT, and all of the Spanish is not in italics in WATSONVILLE: SOME PLACE NOT HERE.

Christopher Gould

Dedicated to Rubén Sierra
Actor, Director, Playwright and Maestro

BITTER HOMES AND GARDENS

Luis Alfaro

ABOUT THE AUTHOR

Luis Alfaro is a writer/performer who works in poetry, plays, short stories, performance and journalism. A multi-disciplined artist, he also works as a director, curator, producer and community organizer. A Chicano born and raised in the Pico-Union district of downtown Los Angeles, he is the recipient of a prestigious MacArthur Fellowship (1997-2002), N E A/T C G Playwrights Fellowship (2000-01), University of California Regents Scholar (2000) and a 1999 *Los Angeles Treasure* presented by the Los Angeles Central City Business Association. A highly anthologized writer, this year he is featured in the collections *Extreme Exposures* (Theater Communications Group), *Ciudad Hibrida/Hybrid City* (S C I-Arc Public Access Press), *Latino Heretics* (FC2 Press), *Out of the Fringe* (Theater Communications Group), *Urban Latino Cultures* (Sage Publications), *O Solo Homo* (Grove Press), *Twelve Shades Read* (Graphically Speaking LTD) and *Corpus Delecti* (Routledge). He is a member of New Dramatists (1998-2005). He is a resident artist at the Mark Taper Forum Theater in Los Angeles, where he is co-director of the Latino Theater Initiative since 1995. He has co-conceived, written and directed five special event shows for the Taper's Mainstage. He was a visiting artist at The Kennedy Center in Washington DC, where he created *Black Butterfly, Jaguar Girl, Piñata Woman and Other Super Hero Girls, Like Me.* He has toured his performance work throughout the United States, England and Mexico, and recently presented a new solo work, *CUERPO POLITIZADO*/POLITICIZED BODY, to a standing room audience at The Getty Center. His short film, *Chicanismo*, was produced by K C E T/P B S, nominated for a local Emmy award, won Best Experimental Film at the 1998 San Antonio *CineFestival* and was featured in San Francisco's *CineAccion '98.* A member of the Dramatist's Guild, he is the winner of the 1998 National Hispanic Playwriting Competition and the 1997 Midwest PlayLabs for his one-act play, STRAIGHT AS A LINE which was premiered at The Goodman Theater in Chicago and has subsequently been produced at New York's Soho Rep, Hennepin Center for the Arts in Minneapolis, Playwrights' Arena and The Actors Gang in Los Angeles. He teaches throughout the country including five years in the Writer's Program of U C L A Extension. He has been selected one of the "100 Coolest People" by *Buzz* magazine, "100 Most Influential Hispanics" by *Hispanic Business* magazine, "50 People to Watch" in *Variety* magazine, "25 Most Interesting People" by the *L A Weekly*. He was the subject of a cover article in the *Los Angeles Times* magazine and was recently selected as an important activist in *The Advocate* magazine.

BITTER HOMES AND GARDENS was first workshopped through H P P.
The cast and creative contributors were:

THELMA . . . . Anne Betancourt
RAY . . . . Rubén Sierra
JULIE . . . . .Laurie Woolery
ERIC . . . . Paul Saucedo

Director . . . . José Cruz González
Dramaturg . . . . .John Glore

CHARACTERS & SETTING

THELMA, *the mother*
RAY, *the father*
JULIE, *the daughter*
ERIC, *the son*

Scene: The living room of a house in East Los Angeles

Time: Present

Set: A living room, suspended. There are also window bars of various sizes suspended. At down stage left hangs a cello. There is an Altar of Memory. The altar can be a mound of dirt. Embedded in the altar are family photographs, religious artifacts, a T V Guide, a Kraft Macaroni and Cheese box, cigarette packs, etc. Upstage and behind the performing area hangs a scrim. Behind the scrim, and elevated from the set, sits the character of ERIC, behind bars. Next to him is a seventy-five pound punching bag that also hangs. ERIC is dimly lit throughout the whole play.

I'm the end of the line
The end of the family line
No baby pulled screaming
Out into this seething whirl
By chance or whim
(or even love?)
Our family tree hacked into decline
And I'm spared the pain
of ever saying
(goodbye)

Morrisey, *(I'm) The End Of The Family Line*

Scene One

(Lights out. The sound of the cello. A black and white home movie of the Martinez Family is projected onto the entire set. The four actors enter and assume a family pose down stage center. An extended camera flash. They are not smiling. Flash is over. The actors go to their positions. RAY sits offstage. ERIC assumes his position far up stage behind bars. JULIE is sitting on the couch reading a Soldier of Fortune *magazine. THELMA is standing down left, looking out, facing the audience, holding a cello. Sound out. Lights up. Camera flash)*

THELMA: Julie, I have something to show you.

JULIE: What is it?

THELMA: A cello.

JULIE: A what?

THELMA: A cello.

JULIE: What do I want a cello for?

THELMA: This cello, young lady, is going to save your life. Your father and I paid a pretty penny for it.

JULIE: Right.

THELMA: Now, I don't expect you to pick it up right away and just start playing it. That's why we're going to leave it in the closet. When you get tired of your girlfriends and grow less fond of the world, *like I did*, you can go into the closet and begin the cello.

JULIE: You shouldn't have bought it.

THELMA: Let me tell you a little something about the cello young lady, because the cello is a lot like the world. Are you listening to me?

JULIE: No.

THELMA: The world is *shit* Julie. Now I know you've heard me say this before, but it's true. Can you say that with me sweetie? *The world is shit.*

JULIE: *The world is shit.*

THELMA: Good. Don't tell your father we said that. I think the best way to deal with the world, as you grow older and more unhappy, is to play a musical instrument. A luxury I never had, need I remind you, and the cello is the most beautiful of all the instruments. Because the cello looks like a woman. Look at her big beautiful hips. We're gonna have hips like *these* one day. Now, I'm gonna put this cello away in the closet, but before I do, I want you to take a good look at this cello. One day you're gonna go into the closet, pull out this cello and say to yourself, *Oh freedom*.

JULIE: *Oh freedom*.

THELMA: The world is *shit* honey. Take it from me, I know. One day things are gonna get so nasty and ugly you're gonna need this cello.

JULIE: I don't believe this.

THELMA: People are gonna want to crucify you Julie. And believe me, they're gonna nail you once or twice. They always do. And when they do, you will say to them *"thank you asshole"*. Say that with me, won't you?

JULIE: *Thank you asshole*.

THELMA: Good. Don't tell your father we said that. The cross you carry, young lady, will weigh a lot more than Jesus' because you are a woman. And like Jesus you should look forward to a little crucifixion every now and then. It will build character. The sooner you learn the cello, the better.

JULIE: What about Eric? What's he gonna play?

THELMA: Your brother plays with his penis and it's perfectly acceptable. That's what I'm talking about here.

JULIE: What are you talking about, Thelma?

THELMA: Call me Mama. I'm talking about crawling, honey. You are a woman and in a few years people are gonna expect you to crawl.

JULIE: I don't mind crawling.

THELMA: Don't say that! Don't ever say that! You, Julie Martinez, are not like the rest of the girls on this block. *The crawlers*. You never were, you never will be.

JULIE: If you would just let me join the Girl Scouts...

THELMA: Absolutely not! Just look at that troop. You wanna know what they're gonna end up like? Look at their mothers. *Cows!* All of them. That's why they watch T V as much as they do. That's why they don't like us. That's why they don't talk to us.

JULIE: That's why they don't talk to *you*.

THELMA: Look at their hips Julie. Always trying to please their men, those Girl Scouts. I want something different for you. *(Sits on recliner.)* Cause the truth about it sweetie, is that once they marry you all they want you to do is shut up and get skinny. The thing they loved the most is the thing that scares them later. Because then they have to share power. And men, sweetie, equate power with penis. They think that if they give you power, they're cutting off their penises. And you know what a penis looks like?

JULIE: No, what?

THELMA: Military equipment. Every morning I wake up, I look down there, and I say to myself, "Oh dear, no penis. How much longer, Lord?" Powerless. We're completely powerless. *Membership has its privileges.* Never forget that.

JULIE: God.

THELMA: *You* are special. Your brother, on the other hand, is a *follower.* If that herd walked over a cliff, he'd jump right over with them.

JULIE: Leave him alone.

THELMA: You know what they're living with down there? Death. That's why none of them try. That's why their Spandex stretches. Doomed. I knew it the minute your father moved us to this desert, the suburbs. *(Gasps. Realizes thought)* Your father is trying to kill us!

JULIE: Well, I don't mind jumping off of a cliff if it means not having to play the cello.

THELMA: As soon as I become an executive assistant in the entertainment industry, I'm gonna save enough money and get you out of here.

JULIE: I like it here.

THELMA: Why are you so goddamned rebellious? Huh? Huh? Huh?

JULIE: *(Annoyed)* Oh shut up!

THELMA: Yes, right. Light me a cigarette sweetie.

(JULIE lights cigarette.)

THELMA: You look so sexy when you do that. You know, you should think about a career as a stripper. Better to plan ahead. I should have done that. But it's too late for me now. Well, that's what I get for marrying my childhood sweetheart, isn't it? But I'm not bitter. Did you hear me? I'm not bitter. *I'm miserable.* Big difference. The difference between being a woman and being a housewife. Never forget that. Anyway, you look beautiful. You should smoke.

JULIE: I hate it. It stinks up the whole house.

THELMA: We'll, I'm gonna stink it up so you might as well join me. *(Pause)* You know, at your age I did everything my mama asked me to.

JULIE: I thought grandma died when you were born?

THELMA: Oh don't ask me so many questions. Hey, let's hear old songs.

(Beat)

JULIE: Well?

THELMA: Well she did, but I could hear her.

JULIE: How?

THELMA: She talked to me. In all sorts of ways. The sound of the ocean. Through the furniture. The stove.

JULIE: The stove talked?

THELMA: Goddamnit Julie, you can be better than a Girl Scout. Opportunity is shining its light on you young lady. I invite you to be a musician.

JULIE: I hate the cello.

THELMA: No you don't. You think you hate the cello because there are more Girl Scouts than there are cello players. I know we all want to be on the winning side, but we can't. Being a winner. *Big fucking deal.*

JULIE: *Big fucking deal.*

THELMA: Good. Don't tell your father we said that.

(Lights out on living room. The sound of the cello.)

Scene Two

(Lights come up on ERIC in prison.
ERIC looks directly at audience.
He tries to speak and then stops.
ERIC begins to punch the boxing bag furiously.
He works up a sweat.
Stops.
Looks at audience.
He tries to speak.
Stops.
Starts crying.
Lights out on ERIC in prison.)

Scene Three

(Lights up on living room. JULIE is sitting on the couch reading Final Exit. *Lights up on living room. THELMA is on her knees looking for her pumps.)*

THELMA: Where the hell are those shoes of mine?

JULIE: Which ones?

THELMA: My pumps. My red pumps.

JULIE: Under the couch.

THELMA: Thanks honey. You know everything, you know that? *(She puts on red pumps.)*

JULIE: Where are you going?

THELMA: I'm gonna go see the ocean. I'm gonna take the orange Monte Carlo out to see the ocean.

JULIE: In your slip? Everybody's gonna see you.

THELMA: Good.

JULIE: Put on a dress. Please.

THELMA: It's too hot for dresses.

JULIE: You look nasty mom.

THELMA: Good. Can you see my tits?

JULIE: Too much.

THELMA: Great. Look out the window and tell me who's out there.

JULIE: *(Looks out window)* Mrs Santana and Mrs Chavez.

THELMA: Good. I'm gonna walk out there, let those cows watering their lawns get a good look at me, and then I'm gonna get in the Monte Carlo and run them over.

JULIE: *(Starts to cry)* Oh God, oh God.

THELMA: *(Nervous)* Listen honey, you ain't the only one whose been dreaming of ocean. I just need to float right now, that's all. I just need to float enough to get a grip.

JULIE: Just stop it Thelma! I hate this. You're just trying to scare me. I hate you.

THELMA: Aw, honey, is it something I said?

JULIE: *(Trying to regain composure)* I'm sorry, I'm sorry.

THELMA: Hey, let's stand on our heads like we used to?

JULIE: No! Don't. I hate it when you do that. It's okay. I'm all right now.

THELMA: Good. You scare me when you get this way.

JULIE: It's just that you make me so sad sometimes. So sad mama. Sometimes I wonder what's gonna happen to me?

THELMA: Nothings gonna happen to you sweetie. *(Waits, thinks)* Oops. I'm sorry. I didn't mean to say that! A *lot's* gonna happen to you! I can't lie about that stuff. Sorry. It's like those nuts that try to jump off buildings. You can't lie to them and tell them the world is fine and wonderful, cause it isn't. Trust me, I know. That's because I am the mother. I will always be smarter than you because I will always be older than you.

JULIE: Why do you do that?

THELMA: What?

JULIE: Ruin moments.

THELMA: Damnit Julie! People are gonna burn crosses. People are gonna shoot everybody at a Winchell's every now and then. People are gonna feed their babies to the Dobermans every once in a while. *(Looks at audience)* That's a true story by the way. I ain't saying it's good and I ain't saying it's bad, it just is. *(Looks at JULIE)* It's ugly. I know. But it's the way of the world. The other day at the market, the laser on the little conveyer belt wasn't working and the checker broke down, broke down sobbing, because she couldn't remember her numbers. She had to type them in and she couldn't remember her numbers any more. That's why they make operas. So that we can forget every once in a while. And they keep it expensive so that we can enjoy it, but not make it a drug. Oh honey, let's hear an opera.

JULIE: Only if you promise not to leave.

THELMA: Nope, I can't do that.

JULIE: Why not?

THELMA: Because that's negotiation. I'm a woman and I was born in the fifties. I can't negotiate. I'm no good at it. *(Pause. She stares intensely at JULIE.)*

JULIE: What? What are you looking at?

THELMA: Potential. I'm just looking for potential, that's all. Have I really been a bad mother Julie?

JULIE: Uh, huh.

THELMA: Good! I'm so afraid you're gonna turn out like the rest of the girls on this block. You need to be stronger. For the loss. All the men leave you. Your tits sag, you lose faith, you grow up, whatever the reason. They leave. Light me a cigarette sweetie.

(JULIE lights cigarette. Pause. THELMA stares at JULIE)

JULIE: Stop it.

THELMA: What do you know about sex Julie?

JULIE: Nothing. *(Thinks)* Everything.

THELMA: I want to talk a little bit about sex. Are you embarrassed?

JULIE: No, are you?

THELMA: No.

JULIE: Good.

THELMA: Watch this. This could save your life.

(THELMA *goes to a table and puts five Alka Seltzers in a glass with water. She puts a condom over the glass. The carbonation fills the condom as it expands. They both watch.* THELMA *in fascination,* JULIE *in horror. Condom pops off the glass like a balloon.* THELMA *laughs and bows to* JULIE, *waiting for her approval.* JULIE *slugs the couch in frustration.)*

JULIE: Damnit! *(She walks over to* THELMA, *as if to hit her. She lets out a deep breath and kisses her on the forehead and hugs her.)* Oh, my poor mother. What was it that made you this way? Is it the memory of the ocean? Dad dreams of fire and he can't get out of bed sometimes. Do you dream of the ocean? Is it quiet? Is it peaceful? Without the tidal waves and the undercurrents? I'm wondering if I'm ever gonna dream it mama. A quiet sea that I can float away on. Oh, mama, it's just that sometimes I feel like I can't breathe. Your life, your life is such a big responsibility for me. Sometimes I just need out. Out of this house of memory. All I dream are tidalwaves. I wake up drowning, choking, screaming. Drenched in sea sweat.

THELMA: Oh, honey...

JULIE: Wait! *(Composes herself)* Don't, don't say anything. I'm gonna put on an opera.

(Lights dim. The sound of the cello.)

Scene Four

(Lights come up on ERIC *in prison.*
ERIC *looks directly at audience.*
He tries to speak and then stops.
ERIC *begins to punch the boxing bag furiously.*
He works up a sweat.
Stops.
Looks at audience.
He tries to speak.
Stops.
Starts crying.
Lights out on ERIC *in prison.*
Sound out.)

Scene Five

(Lights up on Altar of Memory. THELMA *goes to Altar and kneels.* JULIE *walks to a special down stage left and begins to change into a nurse's outfit; shoes, cap and dress. This should take as long as* THELMA*'s monologue and be a rite of passage.)*

THELMA: I wanna talk a little bit about desire.
Desire is memory.
A time bomb that ticks with the kind of power that can blow up buildings. And one day it just fizzles out. Nothing. And you forget just when it blew or how. And it doesn't really matter because all that really mattered was that it was ticking.
Yesterday I turned forty.
I thought getting older meant getting wiser, but I'm not so sure anymore. When you're a housewife, nobody cares that you're smarter. Not your husband. Not the kids. Not the Betty Crocker Cake Mix. No one.
I thought that my body was changing in the way that it looked at the world, but I was wrong. The change is in the way the world looks at my body.
Well, I just want to say that somebody lied.
Somebody promised that being a housewife, being a mother, has its payoffs, but it doesn't.
I tried so hard not to be a *broad*, and now I can't wait to be one. Because the only women with real control in their lives are the *broads*. The women with the tube tops. The no make-up. The no pedicure. The no *Summer's Eve*. The broads who kick in the T V set when that idiot, that role model for all women, *Sally Jesse Raphael*, tells me I think too much, I haven't cared enough, I haven't cleaned enough. I haven't loved enough. And now they got that idiot *Cristina* telling it to me in Spanish. I'll bet you she's never made tortillas!
Well listen, *Sally fucking Cristina Jesse,* maybe you've got the pulse on how rotten your little life is, but you don't know shit about America.

(The sound of the ocean)

THELMA: Look at these hands. *(Raises both hands, palms facing audience)*
Look at these. Do you know what I've done with these?
I made a house with these. Did anybody notice? Not my father. Not my husband. Not my God. None of *those* men.
These hands have done a lot. The other day I took one of these fingers deep inside of me and gave myself a Fourth of July fireworks in the living room at four o'clock in the afternoon. Right in the middle of *Geraldo*. These hands made these tortillas.
(She reaches behind and grabs a dozen tortillas from the Altar of Memory.)
Do you know how hard I worked on these? Do you know how many dozens of these I've made in my lifetime? DID ANYBODY NOTICE

MY TORTILLAS? Just feel these things goddamnit.
(Tosses tortillas, like Frisbees, at the audience)
I've got nothing else to show for my life but these tortillas. Well, my kids,
but... never mind. Tortillas are my biggest accomplishment, and believe me,
I know that this body doesn't make them like she used to. Can you hear
the ticking time clock? *(Looks at woman in front row.)* What about you Miss
America? What are you going to do when it all starts to droop?
I got a son in prison. Do you know how many wrinkles that puts on a
mother? Do you? Yeah, I know what you're all thinking. Moralizing are
you? Well, he's guilty. Yeah, guilty. He shot his boss. The manager of a
7-11. Eric was never good at making Nacho sauce! A twenty-four-hour
convenience store drove him to murder. I'm glad the sum total of my son's
life didn't mean he was good at making fake cheese.
Well, I just want to say that I turned forty yesterday and my body is dying
to be a broad.

(Lights out on Altar of Memory. Sound out)

Scene Six

(The sound of the cello.
Lights up on ERIC in prison.
He is standing facing the audience.
He is holding a suitcase.
Lights out on ERIC in prison.
Sound out.)

Scene Seven

(In the dark we hear RAY's voice in the back of the auditorium.)

RAY: Hey where am I?

*(Lights up on living room. THELMA and JULIE are sitting on the couch. RAY enters
through the audience, carrying a shotgun, a black lunch box and wearing a hunting
cap. THELMA stands and looks out at audience.)*

THELMA: Oh dear, your father's walking through the audience with a gun
again. He's gonna wanna talk to everybody. I hope he ain't drunk. *(Shouts to
RAY)* You ain't drunk are you Ray?

RAY: No.

THELMA: Yes, right. Three weeks sober and now look what you've gone and
done. You're weak Ray. Weak. Don't you realize that we are here to support
you during your sobriety?

RAY: Yeah, that's why I'm drunk!

THELMA: Aw, well, it's probably better this way. *(To* JULIE*)* Make believe, see? Well, reason with him honey. *(She exits.)*

JULIE: *(To audience.)* Boy, you guys are lucky. In real time you'd have to wait an eight hour shift and a four hour overtime, but in the theater, fathers always walk in right on time.
Do you need help Ray?

RAY: No *mija*. Have you ever killed a moose with your bare hands?

JULIE: No.

RAY: Well, neither have I. Ain't that the darndest thing? Do you know where I grew up?

JULIE: On a ranch in *Mexico*.

RAY: That's right, and they don't have mooses over there. I don't even know what the hell a moose looks like.

JULIE: Do you want some coffee?

RAY: Coffee? What I want is a life! A purpose *mija*. Something to live for.

JULIE: Sorry, can't help you there. *(She exits.)*

RAY: *(To audience, pulls out paperback.)* Has anybody read this book? It's called *Iron John*. It's one of those men's books. I bought it because it's a bestseller. I wouldn't know what to buy if they didn't have those best seller lists.

*(*THELMA *enters.)*

THELMA: Ah ha! I knew it. You even have to read a book to learn how to cry.

RAY: Hey, give me a break here! You've been on stage practically every scene. Give me a chance to explain myself to these people. Look at this, you've got me sneaking around the audience just to get a word in edgewise.

THELMA: Well, make it quick. *(She exits.)*

Scene Eight

(Lights up on Altar of Memory. RAY *makes his way to the Altar while delivering monologue.)*

RAY: I just wanted to say that it's not my fault. Not my wife, not my kids, not that I seem so stiff in this scene. But, I refuse to paint myself the victim, cause, you know, I was born in the forties, and that's just not acceptable. I'm having a tough time here, so bear with me.
(He is now at Altar of Memory, kneeling.)

I've been having dreams about this book.

I'm killing this moose with my bare hands. The moose is just a moose. One of the many stupid mooses in the wilderness, you know, and I am killing it with my bare hands. And standing behind me are those ethical animal people and they're all white. And so, of course, I pay them no mind, cause, you know, I work at Sears and that's all I got on my back all day is white people.

I ain't saying white people are bad, I'm just saying that all the Mexicans at work got white people on their backs. And maybe it's just coincidence, but you just don't pay them no mind.

So I'm tearing the moose apart and standing there in front of all the ethical animal people are John Bradshaw and Robert Bly. People healers. White Indians. They're just standing there watching me and they're crying. Sad tears rolling down their cheeks. And Bly looks at me and say's "Boy, you've really changed Ray." And Bradshaw says, "Yes, you're a different man, Ray." And I feel real guilty for a few minutes there, but I finish killing the moose anyway. Cause, the truth of it is, you have to make choices.

So I don't know if the moose is the environment or white people or what. But what I do know is that things have changed. I mean, when did it happen? How did we get here? Is the Bicentennial over? What do I do? I got a son in prison. Do you know how many *canas* that puts on a man? Yes, *changed.* The woman I married is not the same woman I live with now. *Changed.* The house I built, built it with my own hands. *Changed.* And this world, this world is changing. I don't know where I belong in it. I don't understand it and I most certainly don't agree with it, but I have to live with it one-day-at-a-time. So why do I feel so lousy?

But I'll tell you something. I can see it, okay? I'm alive, and I know what's going on. I may not know what to do about it, but I'm alive. I can see it and I know what's going on.

(The sound of the cello. Lights dim on Altar of Memory. RAY *goes over to the couch and lays down on it, face up.)*

Scene Nine

(Lights up on living room. JULIE *enters adjusting a Girl Scout sash around her torso.)*

JULIE: I know you can't get up.

RAY: Yeah, how do you know that?

JULIE: Cause sometimes I wake up with that train rolling through me too.

RAY: This has nothing to do with trains Julie.

JULIE: Sometimes I wake up and I've got the ocean memory in me. I can't breathe and I feel like I'm choking. I'm so scared, I'm frozen stiff. I know how you feel.

RAY: Yeah?

JULIE: Yeah.

RAY: You should relax.

JULIE: *You* should relax. Yeah, sometimes I wake up and I'm soaking wet.

RAY: What about the therapy? I'm still paying for the therapy, are you going?

JULIE: I'm still going. It's good. You should go sometime.

RAY: One is all I can afford.

JULIE: It's family counseling Ray, we're *all* supposed to be going. I keep having to make excuses. The other night I finally said to the therapist that my mom couldn't come cause she was crazy, my brother was in prison, and my dad couldn't get out of bed.

RAY: Jesus, Julie! Do you have to run around telling the world about our problems?

JULIE: Nice Ray, real nice.

RAY: Where are you going?

JULIE: Girl Scout meeting.

RAY: Aren't you a bit old for that?

JULIE: You're never too old Ray. I'm gonna learn how to talk like Ozzie and Harriet if it kills me.

RAY: You talk fine honey.

JULIE: Don't bullshit me dad.

(Pause)

RAY: Do you think I'm a drunk?

JULIE: Think? No, why?

RAY: Well, I'm not. Drunks don't know their drunks. I know.

JULIE: Good, I'm glad.

RAY: Glad I'm a drunk?

JULIE: No. Just glad. You know, when I was a little girl I used to stay up all night looking out the window, so afraid you wouldn't come home. Then, I'd look down and there you'd be, passed out on the lawn, and somehow everything was okay and I'd be able to go to sleep.

RAY: That's sweet.

JULIE: Yeah...

RAY: I drink for a reason you know. I'm not like those bums out in front of Frank's Liquor. Those guys are what's wrong with this country. No *verguenza*. Sitting around all day, none of them work.

JULIE: No jobs.

RAY: That's no reason to drink. I drink *cause* I got a job! Those guys got nothing to worry about. Me? I got plenty to worry about. Plenty to drink about. Those guys lost all hope. I'm drinking cause I got hope.

JULIE: Hm.

RAY: I remember when you were a little girl, barely learned to talk, you used to run around the house asking me, *(Mimics her as a baby)* "What time is it? What time is it? What time is it?" And I used to say to you, "What do you care? You've got nothing to worry about! You're four years old. Ask me that question when you get a job."

JULIE: Nice Ray, real nice.

RAY: Well, I got hope. I got hope.

(The sound of the cello. Lights out. RAY *slumps down on the couch and* JULIE *exits.)*

Scene Ten

(Lights up on prison cell.
It is empty.
Lights out on prison cell.)

Scene Eleven

(The sound of the ocean.
Family home movies of the Martinez' are projected onto the stage.
Lights come up on the Altar of Memory.
ERIC *is standing in front of the Altar, facing the audience, holding a suitcase.*
RAY *is still lying down on the couch.*
THELMA *is standing directly in front of the large frame, facing the audience,*
as if she is looking through it. She is smoking a cigarette.
Film out.
Sound out.)

ERIC: I was Twelve. Twelve years old.
Boxing champ of my neighborhood.

Carried my titles like medals on a war veteran.
Each muscle,
dripping off of me like a Roman statue.
My stomach.
Flat.
Tight
Lean.
Featherweight belt wrapped around me
like a custom fit.

And one day I heard her.
Thelma.
Mother figure.
Stranger to me.
Since birth.
Tried.
Tried to stop me.
Said boxing was too dangerous.
Her son was too beautiful to get his nose broke.
Her son was too special for sports.

In this world you are only successful if you deal in violence.
Boxer.
Police man.
Car salesman.

She said I was too special for violence.
I had better things to do.
Bigger fish to fry.
The choices were my own,
but I had to choose from *her* menu.

Said they wanted a Newscaster.
A personality to entertain and inform at backyard barbecues.

One Day I went to the Rec Center,
and my coach told me it was over.
Technical knock-out.
Courtesy of mom.
Oh mom.
Apple pie mom.

Next morning I woke up
and I looked out the window.
And I saw a wounded sparrow.
Had fallen off of a tree.
Was lying on the pavement.
"Get up", I screamed.
"Get up."

"You gonna let her get away with this?
Huh?
You gonna let her get away with this?"

Sparrow sat there.
Unable to decide.
Helpless.
Pathetic.

"You've got choices in this world Eric."
Yes, right.

Thelma's driving out to see the ocean.
"Move," I scream.
And she runs over the broken sparrow.
"Move, move, move."
And I can't be sure,
but I think I saw her aim and smile.

That night I dreamt of a broken sparrow.
When I woke up in the morning,
I could feel,
I could feel,
a space between my shoulders and my arms,
that was missing.
Where my wings had been clipped.

I can't fly,
I can't move.
"Eric, is everything okay?", she says.
I can't speak.
"Eric?"
I've got a broken wing, I've got a broken life.
"Eric?"
Don't you come in that door mom.
Don't you come in that door.
Cause I'll kill you.
I'll kill you mom.

Dad says, "You got choices Eric.
Live up to your potential.
'Be all that you can be',
but within reason, of course."

Yeah?
Well I did.

You want to make a change?
You want to cut out a roadblock?
You want things just like they were,

nice and simple?
You want to live in the past
with the perks of the future?
Well, then kill your boss!
That's right. Kill your boss.
If he gets in your way, kill your boss.
K O that nine to five right out of here.
If they get in your way,
get them out of your way.
That's right.
Get them out of your way.
(Points to a woman in the audience)
"Oh god", she's saying. This woman here. In that row. That woman right
there just said, "Oh god". That's what she said, "Oh god", and just shook
her head. Shook her head like this. *(Does a nod of disapproval)* "Oh god",
what, ma'm? Yes, you, there. "Oh god" what? You shouldn't talk in the
theater. This is my story. This is my time. If you feel like you're being held
hostage, it's because you are. That's the theatre for you. Don't "Oh god"
while I'm talking.

The only thing that's true
is that it's a world without end.
And I'm a broken sparrow.
On the pavement.
On the street.
In front of the house that I grew up in.
And my mother.
Is on her way to the ocean.
And she's gonna run me over.
Cause I can't move.
Cause she clipped my wings.
Cause she clipped my wings.
Cause she clipped my wings.

So I made a choice.
A choice I wasn't too happy with.
A convenience store murder.
It's cheap.
Unoriginal.
As common as the sun rising.
But I made a choice.
I made it myself.
I grabbed at the straws.
I went for broke.
I ran the extra mile.
I went all ten rounds.

Cause it's a world,
It's a world without end.

(The sound of the cello.
Lights out on Altar of Memory.
ERIC *exits.)*

Scene Twelve

(Lights up through bars projected on the living room. RAY *sits on recliner and pulls out a remote control from his shirt pocket and turns on the television. The sound of the television.* THELMA *is seated on the couch reading a magazine. Lights up on living room.)*

THELMA: You look good Ray. That suit fits you real nice.

RAY: It's a uniform. I'm warning you, I'm real tired, so don't start.

THELMA: That uniform fits you real nice Ray. What does the tag say, Sears?

RAY: I'm serious Thelma, give it a rest.

THELMA: Uh, huh, you look good Ray. Real good. A real model of labor is what you are.

RAY: You're making me very angry.

THELMA: How do I look? You like these earrings? They're little bowls of fruit.

RAY: I'm not gonna look at you until you put on your robe.

THELMA: Aw, come on Ray, you've seen it all before, remember honey?

RAY: I'm going to bed, good night.

THELMA: Who put the bars on the windows?

RAY: I don't know, who did? Did you see who did that Thelma?

THELMA: Why'd you put them up Ray?

RAY: Security.

THELMA: You son of a bitch! You're trying to kill me, aren't you? You like this? You like this Ray? You want blood on your hands, is that what you want? Look at me goddamnit! Look at me. What are you afraid of? What are you afraid of, you coward? You afraid to look at my pussy? *(Runs to window and flashes the neighbors.)* You afraid the neighbors are going to look at my pussy? DO YOU KNOW WHAT KIND OF POWER I HAVE DOWN THERE? DO YOU?

RAY: I'm going to bed. What you need is a nap.

THELMA: Oh, is that what I need? You know what you need...

RAY: Go to bed Thelma! Good night.

THELMA: Yes Raymond, run to your room. Put up a fight for once, goddamnit. Look at you, like a scared little boy. You little faggot! I'm sorry. Too mean. *(Pause)*
I heard a cello last night Ray. Not the one we bought Julie, not the cello of freedom. A real sad one, full of death and loneliness.

RAY: It's okay Thelma, let's put on your robe.

THELMA: Take the bars off Ray. Please. Take the bars off. I'll start wearing my clothes, just take the bars off.

RAY: I can't do that.

THELMA: Why not?

RAY: It's too late, we can't negotiate.

THELMA: What kind of animal am I that needs bars, huh? Am I a dog Ray? *(She barks.)* Am I a pig? *(She squeals.)* Am I a snake? *(She gets down and starts slithering on the shag.)* I'm trying to tempt you Raymond.

RAY: Get up. Thelma please, get up.

THELMA: *(She slithers around him and wraps herself around one of his legs.)* Here I am on the floor Ray. This snake wants to seduce you. Perfect opportunity to negotiate. Take off your clothes Ray. Look at me. I'm dripping Ray. I'm dripping for you.

RAY: Stop it. The rug's dirty for Christ's sake.

THELMA: I'm dripping for those bars to come down, so come on down Raymond. *(She bites her lip.)* I bit my lip. I'm bleeding. *(Bites some more. Starts crying. Starts wailing)* Help me Ray. I'm gonna bleed to death. I'm a real damsel in distress here. You like it. I can see it.

RAY: I'm going to bed.

THELMA: *(Cuts the act)* Aw, alright, alright, alright. Shit. Damnit. Help me up at least.

RAY: I'll get something for your lip. Where's the first aid kit?

THELMA: I used it up, I've been very violent lately. Help me put on my robe.

(RAY comes over and helps THELMA put on robe. She leans over and kisses him on the lips. He doesn't resist.)

THELMA: Thank you Raymond. I don't mind your not sleeping with me, just don't deny me your kisses. You got blood on your lips. You know what that means, we're together for life.

RAY: *Oh, great.*

THELMA: We just sealed it with blood. Dance with me honey.

(Sleepy Lagoon *comes on. She puts her arms around him and they begin to slow dance.*)

THELMA: Do you remember this song? We played this at your mom's funeral. What is that, a trumpet?

RAY: Uh, huh.

THELMA: They shoulda used a cello. Kiss me again. Oh Ray, this is just like old times. You happy?

RAY: No, not really.

THELMA: Good, neither am I. I'm sorry about all this Ray.

RAY: I understand Thelma.

THELMA: No you don't. You really don't Ray.

RAY: Don't talk honey, just dance.

THELMA: I don't mind that you sleep with other women.

RAY: Aw, Thelma, come on.

THELMA: Really, I don't. I've had a few stiff ones myself, you know. It just makes for a well rounded personality.

RAY: You gonna keep talking.

(*They keep dancing.*)

THELMA: You can't keep those bars up forever Ray. One day I'm gonna be dead and you're gonna want that freedom yourself.

RAY: We'll talk about it when that day comes.

THELMA: You can't keep the world away from me. It's all in here. Traces of America everywhere in this house.

RAY: Honey, we're having such a good time, ssh.

THELMA: The Taco Bells, they're here Ray. Infomercials and T V evangelists, they're all here. Deeply woven into the fabric of this house. News-at-Eleven is sitting on the love seat. (*Pause*) Moon glow.

RAY: What?

THELMA: Moon glow. Isn't that the name of this song?

RAY: No, I don't think so.

THELMA: Damn, I shouldn't have peeled all the labels off the records. How could I have thought I'd remember all these songs? See what happens when you're in this house all day?

RAY: Don't think about it.

(They continue dancing. Pause)

THELMA: I saw the gun Ray.

(Sound out)

RAY: *(Silence)* Yeah?

THELMA: Yes, dear. Were you going to shoot me with that gun? Were you going to put me out of my misery?

(RAY starts to cry.)

THELMA: I'm not miserable Raymond. I'm kind of happy. I'd be happier if you took the bars off the windows. I'd be happier if no one wore clothes, but I'm happy. Do you love me honey?

(RAY nods yes.)

THELMA: Good, cause I sold the gun. Don't buy a new one okay? You don't need it. Don't kill me okay?

RAY: Uh, huh.

THELMA: I know what you're feeling Ray. The loss. You wish it was all like it used to be. I felt that way when the kids grew up. Everything I lived for, every moment of my life was those kids. I lived for them. I lived through them. What they don't tell you in those goddamn Lamaze classes is that they're gonna leave you! They leave you and that's supposed to be natural. Maybe this is something that only a mother can understand, I don't know. You spend your life teaching them to be independent so that they can be on their own, and then, whatever time you have left, is spent trying to get them back. Do you understand?

RAY: Uh, huh.

THELMA: Yeah, well, it never is like you think it was. *(Pause)* I miss you Raymond. I miss the dog, I miss the bake-offs, the tortilla contests. Don't think I don't remember. I remember it. All of it. But I saw the signs Raymond. I looked for them. I kept my eyes open and I saw the world change, and I changed with it. You, you walk around with blinders on. You numb yourself with whatever they got on the shelves at Frank's Liquor. You know what would happen to you, if once, you really saw this neighborhood, this side of the border for what it really is? You'd give up the booze, you'd get that hunting rifle of yours and you'd go down to that dead end existence you call a job and you'd shoot everyone wearing a Sears name tag. That's what you'd do. Start with the managers and the supervisors and hopefully you run out of ammunition by the time you get to the reformed *cholas* selling the lipstick and popcorn. Sure it's scary, but you can't, you can't float struggling for the breath the way that you are.

RAY: Uh, huh.

THELMA: Everything, everything they told us was a commercial Ray. And all I'm saying is that I'm not buying it anymore. I'm gonna go have myself a coming out. I'm gonna go get me one of those *quinceanera* dresses with the lace and the hoop. I'm gonna rent it from the place with the mural on Broadway. It'll be my coming out, just like the guys in the Gay bars. I'm gonna call my mom and everybody on this block and say, "Hey, you guys, guess what, I'm back. I went to somewhere like hell, like the corner of Hollywood and Western, and I'm back." I lived to tell.

(The sound of the ocean)

THELMA: I saw the women with the tummy tucks and the new noses and the new chins. I saw the twenty-four hour cable shows and the drug addicted former child T V stars. The Winchell's beggars and the Bob's Big Boy massacre. I saw it all. *(She begins to cry.)* I saw the pain and I saw the misery. Housewives hunched over from carrying the weight of their cultures. Pretending they were climbing pyramids while they were digging spiritual graves. I saw anger and loneliness. Sadness. Ooh, the sadness... I saw desperation and isolation. I saw America. I saw it all over the place. I saw my cunt. The power that is my cunt. I reached down there and I tasted a force of nature, and it opened itself up to a pain. Something bigger and more painful than those kids of ours that raced through me. I saw an interview with the top ten serial killers on *Hard Copy*. I did. They were celebrities and we were *nobody*. I saw this house of ours with its carved wood and drooping arches. This house with it's rooms full of memories and that attic full of sadness. I looked in the den and I saw our first kiss. Holding hands on the porch. Walking in the backyard. I saw you making love to me in the kitchen. That beautiful round ass of yours. Your body on top of mine in the breakfast nook. I saw our son and he was *smiling*. God, do you remember that? How long has that been? I saw it. All of it. Do me two favors Raymond. This is all I ask. Will you? Will you please?

RAY: What?

THELMA: Don't kill me and take the bars off the windows.

(RAY stops crying and takes out his handkerchief, blows his nose.)

RAY: I can't do that Thelma.

THELMA: Which one Ray? Which one?

RAY: The bars. I can't take them down. It's too late. I can't negotiate.

THELMA: Sure you can. We can negotiate Ray, for old times sake. Let's negotiate, just like we used to.

(They stare at each other in silence. RAY turns away.)

(The sound of the cello. Lights out on living room, leaving the shadow of the bars projected onto the stage.)

Scene Thirteen

(Lights up on Altar of Memory. JULIE *is standing in front of the Altar filling a hypodermic needle with a liquid from a medicine jar. She is slow and deliberate in her duty.* ERIC *walks to a special downstage left and begins to take off his prison outfit. There should be something innocent and sensual about this ritual. It is also a rite of passage.* THELMA *sits on the recliner, in a low lamp light, cigarette in hand. Looking at* ERIC. *Sound out)*

JULIE: There are unfortunate things that happen in the world. Really. Things beyond our control. That's why I chose nursing and Eric chose prison. The nice thing about nursing is that it leaves time for other things, like playing the cello for instance. The nice thing about prison is that it's just like home without your parents. I want to say something about the world, and nursing, that my parents don't seem to understand. It's not that they're slow, they're just hopeful.... America is not Ozzie and Harriet. America is fat ass K-Mart shoppers. America is not Cotton. America is Rayon. America is not Guccis. America is Seven-Eleven. Now, I'm not saying this because I'm some bitter anti-American or anything. Not because I was raised on beans and tortillas. Hell, I'm just as embarrassed about Maria Conchita Alonso as anyone else. I'm saying this because it's *true.* As true as the word of God. He says things and I say things and we say these things because we know these things. It's a mystery, but that's religion. So accept it and go on living little lamb.

(The sound of the ocean)

JULIE: Sometimes the world looks like it's gonna burst. A cut so deep you can't stop the bleeding and it's rushing at you in torrents. At those times, all you can do is put to rest the broken legged horse, the distempered dog, the overfed sheep. You can not heal the wound, so you must silence the scream, otherwise, you will hear it the rest of your life. That's why I chose nursing as a profession. Because nurses open their ears. They listen for the pain. They want to hear the scream and do something about it. The rest of us are deaf.
Well, I strangled someone yesterday down at the hospital. Yeah, I know. I felt that way at first too. But I like to think of that someone as America. I strangled America because it was drowning in a sea of its own blood. It was choking. Can you hear it? *(Pause)* Of course not, you're all deaf sons of bitches.

THELMA: Well, I can hear it. I've been swimming in this ocean all of my life. You think I've been floating because I don't say anything. Because I'm *funny.* Because I'm *interesting.* But I've been struggling for the breath since the day I was born. You think you got problems, you should try living in

here. *(Points at her head)*
Julie can hear it. Sometimes I look at her hearing the pain of the world. You
can see all the sadness and the hurt. But more than that, you can see that she
is drowning in her own ocean. My whole family is drowning. Helpless with
the tidal waves and the undercurrents. Is yours? Yes, right. She just listens
and reacts. When she can still the water and calm the storm, this is what she
does. This is her calling, mercy killings! That's exactly what they are. What
a *beautiful* word for that strange thing. I know she's in a lot of trouble down
at the hospital and I don't want to implicate her any more than she already
is, but it's just that I'm so *damn* proud of her. She's a perfectionist. So I know
she knew exactly what she was doing.

(Lights dim on Altar of Memory and on THELMA. *Silence)*

Scene Fourteen

*(Slides appear on both sides of the theater. They are slides of the Martinez family.
In some, the whole family is together, others can be individual shots. About twelve.
The final photo is of* JULIE *and* ERIC, *arms over each other's shoulders, smiling.
As the slides fade a film of* JULIE *as a little girl is projected during the following
scene. The film traces, very slowly,* JULIE's *body including her face. The film is very
deliberate and* JULIE *is not speaking or emoting. She is simply looking at the camera.
Lights up on living room.* ERIC *is lying on the couch, face up. He is wearing a white
Hanes tank top T-shirt, boxer shorts and white gym socks.* JULIE *is standing over
him, behind the couch and looking down at him.)*

JULIE: I know you can't get up. That's okay, you don't have to. You don't
know how much I missed you Eric.

(He rolls over, facing away from her. She rolls him back.)

JULIE: Hey, come on now. You've been away too long. Don't hide from me.
Besides, I got a little surprise for you. *(She holds up syringe.)* Don't worry,
I can see your veins from here. I can see all the way inside you Eric. It's a
little welcome home boost. Give me your arm.

(He stretches out his arm, she gives him the shot.)

JULIE: Count to a hundred.
Remember Pepe, our chihuahua?

(He jerks in a little spasm.)

JULIE: Just relax, don't worry.
Well, Pepe got run over about a year ago. Some man, some power-dick guy
in one of those red Corvettes was racing down the street and he accidentally
hit Pepe.

*(*ERIC *spasms again.)*

JULIE: Yeah, it was bad. The Corvette guy looked back, saw Pepe and just kept on going. Pepes and women don't mean a thing in this world, do they? Well, I walked out to the middle of the street and Pepe was lying there in a pool of blood. He was trying to move and he just looks up at me, and he stops.

(ERIC *starts breathing hard.*)

JULIE: He looks at me with this look, as if to say, "I know it's over, don't make this ugly, just do it." Yeah, that's what he was saying, "I'm feeling all the pain and misery of this world. I ain't a fighter, so just take me out". So, I did. I leaned down and I kissed our little Pepe on the nose and I just hugged him. I don't know if I suffocated him or if he just did it himself. Whatever it was, it was peaceful. Peaceful and right.

(ERIC *starts to jerk.*)

JULIE: Don't you agree?
Listen Eric, you have to forgive now. It's okay. You're gonna feel a little numb. Don't worry. You know, Thelma and Ray think the world of you. They just come from a different place. A place where people think of different things to say for what they feel.

(*He starts convulsing.* JULIE *ignores him.*)

JULIE: You were the most beautiful baby when you were born Eric. You had that beautiful brown skin, all soft, just like Grandma Consuelo.

(ERIC *grasps at her hand.*)

JULIE: It's okay, hold my hand. Don't worry, I'm a nurse. (*Looks at audience*) I do this all the time. (*To* ERIC) Just relax and try to enjoy it. Think about how smart Pepe was. Believe me, it will be a lot easier if you just forgive them now. You don't need them anymore.

(ERIC *starts to contort more violently and falls off the couch and onto the floor.* JULIE *pulls a wallet out of her pocket and sticks it in his mouth.*)

JULIE: I remember the first time I held you Eric. You were naked and your skin was so soft, and I asked Thelma what you had between your legs and she said, the *future family tree.* Isn't that sweet?

(*She giggles, he is choking.*)

JULIE: You do Eric, you know that?

(ERIC *tries to crawl to the little table. He tries to grab at phone.* JULIE *steps on his hand.*)

JULIE: She's right, you know. I will never, ever have a child. You can count on that. But you, you could keep this family going forever if you wanted. Hopeful, are you? How are you doing down there? Keep counting. Now, I ask you Eric, really, what's the point? I have memories of you that are as strong as my memory of the ocean. And they will always be with me. Do you hear me? *(Shouts down at him)* THEY WILL ALWAYS BE WITH ME.

(ERIC goes unconscious. The sound of the ocean)

JULIE: Picture this house Eric. Picture this house and it's memories. It's carved wood and drooping arches. Running in the living room. Grandma Consuelo on the rocker. Look, it's kitty. What about the plum tree? *(Trying to retain her composure.)* Ray cutting the grass, the cook-offs, the fig trees. This house Eric. Walk through it. Each room is a memory. A memory that takes you back. You wanna run through it? Hold my hand. Eric? Eric?

(Sound out. JULIE kneels down and checks his pulse. She leans forward and kisses his cheek, whispers in his ear.)

JULIE: Say hello to Grandma Consuelo.

(The sound of the cello. Lights dim on the living room. JULIE begins to drag ERIC's body off stage. Lights come up on the Altar of Memory and slowly start to dim.)

Scene Fifteen

(Sound out. Lights up on living room. THELMA runs in and looks out of window. JULIE enters, looking disheveled, trying to regain her composure. She sits on couch.)

THELMA: *Uh, oh.* Light me a cigarette sweetie.

(RAY storms in. He is wearing a baseball cap and glove. He kicks the couch and looks at THELMA.)

RAY: Goddamnit, Goddamnit, Goddamnit!

JULIE: What's the matter?

RAY: No more. Do you hear me? No more. That was the last straw!

JULIE: What's going on?

RAY: This time you went too far. I can't take it anymore. *(Looks at JULIE)* Tell her, I can't take it anymore. I'm breaking. *(Looks at THELMA)* You're making me break Thelma. Is that what you want? Now think about it. You want me to crack? Is that what you want me to do, crack? And wipe that shit eating grin off of your face!

JULIE: Did little league lose again?

RAY: Aaagh! *(He storms out.)*

JULIE: He's gotta stop this. *(Yells to him off stage)* You gotta stop this Ray. *(To THELMA)* He can't be doing this every week. This is not the way families communicate. *(Yells to him)* You can't do this Ray. It's just little league, Christ!

(RAY *enters with a can of beer in hand.*)

THELMA: It's the Knights of Columbus that are doing this to him.

RAY: You shut up! *(He sits on recliner. Pause)* Your mother was flashing the little league game.

JULIE: Mom! God. And this is National Family Week. Isn't anything sacred to you?

THELMA: My pussy.

JULIE: Oh God, Mom, please.

RAY: Everybody saw her. She had a group of boys in the outfield watching her show. We lost the game on account of your mother.
You gotta watch her. I thought you were gonna watch her? Where were you? What's the point of being a nurse if you can't watch her?

JULIE: I was watching *Jeopardy*. I can't watch her every five minutes.

RAY: You said you were gonna be responsible for her. If you can't handle her, you gotta let me know.

THELMA: I don't need anybody to watch me.

RAY & JULIE: *You shut up!*

RAY: Now, are you gonna watch her or what?

JULIE: I was watching *Jeopardy* damnit! America watches *Jeopardy* and so am I. She's not gonna take the last of life's little pleasures from me. *(Looks at* THELMA*)* You are not. Do you hear me? You are not. All I got left is nursing and *Jeopardy*, and you are not going to take them away from me.

THELMA: You got the cello. That's one of life's big pleasures.

JULIE: FUCK THE CELLO! Listen to me Thelma, I'll kill you before you make me give up *Jeopardy*. It's my half hour, my own special time. Do you hear me? It's *Alex* and Julie, not Thelma and Julie, get it?

RAY: They're gonna take it all away from us. All of it. I don't know what it is you want, Thelma. They're gonna take that Family of the Year plaque away from us, the Ideal Citizens award, the Role Models trophy. They're gonna take Honorary Mayor away from me. They're not gonna let me help at mass. Is that what you want? You know, the guys at the hall are gonna give me a lot of shit for this, but I'll take it. You know why I'll take it? You know why? CAUSE I LOVE YOU HONEY! Do you hear me? I LOVE YOU HONEY. But I'll tell you one thing, and mark my word, if I'm not in that Fourth of July parade this year, you're dead. Your ass is mine.

THELMA: Oh honey...

RAY: So stop! Just stop.

THELMA: Stop what?

RAY: Stop showing your body around like it's some kind of trophy, a prize, a work of art or something.

THELMA: But it is.

RAY: Shit. *(To* JULIE*)* Do something.

THELMA: A power force is what it is.

RAY: *(To audience)* Do you hear her? Can you hear this? Is it just me? Am I the only one in this house who can hear it? *(He breaks down crying.)*

JULIE: It's alright Ray. Go to your room, I'll handle it.

(RAY takes out a handkerchief, looks out at the audience and starts bawling. He turns and exits the room.)

Scene Sixteen

(JULIE pulls out a syringe from her pocket and sits on the couch. She motions THELMA over to the couch. In the following sequence, JULIE preps THELMA's arm and injects her. They sit on the couch.)

JULIE: Oh Thelma, Thelma, Thelma. You have to listen very carefully now because I am going to say this only once. No pretend please. I am as co-dependent as I can get right now. The next step is suicide. I want to let you know something. If I go, you go. This isn't a threat, it's information. Puff if you understand.

(THELMA takes a drag off cigarette and puffs.)

THELMA: Did you hear him? Hates to see my body. Those little boys were practically dissecting and labeling me like some biology frog. Your father should think of this as community service.

JULIE: Do you know how much this upsets him? Do you want him to leave?

THELMA: When I was a little girl...you got a minute?

JULIE: I'm warning you, this better have a point.

THELMA: When I was a little girl I used to drink too much Coke, and you know, back then it had real coke in it.

JULIE: I know, go on.

THELMA: Well, I was completely addicted. I was always nervous, too excited. My father would slap me hard across the face in the evenings just to make me stop talking.

JULIE: Yeah, so?

THELMA: The worst part was that it screwed up my metabolism. I had breasts at the age of nine. I mean breasts! My hormones were raging, and I really think that it was because of the coke. I wore these little girl outfits that I just loved, but I was busting out all over. I looked like some cheap kiddie porn.

JULIE: Go on.

THELMA: My mother, my mother Julie, was beautiful. She never cut her hair and it went past her knees. It took her hours to comb. When it got tangled it was just horrible. A mood came over her that was something terrible. But, we all have crosses to bear and that was my mother's.

JULIE: The point Thelma, the point.

THELMA: Yeah right. My mother's name was Esperanza. Hope. But you know what my father used to call her? Hopeless. You know why? It scared him. Too much power. The long hair, the breasts, the skin, the lips the color of blood. But, *(To audience)* and this is the point here, *(To* JULIE*)* my mother never touched herself. At mass with her long black flowing veil over her head, she would make the sign of the cross without touching herself. The most beautiful body my mother had and she didn't even know it. Absolutely no sparks. Electricity and my mother never knew it.

JULIE: I'm still waiting Thelma.

THELMA: Well, because my mother never touched herself, we never touched her. You know, I never really knew my mother. One day she walked into the ocean, and, they say, that an undercurrent...an undercurrent...in the ocean.

JULIE: *(Pause)* It's okay Thelma.

THELMA: When I touch myself, I'm a little girl again. I'm young, I have the body I used to have, I'm a *broad*. But, I'll tell you what I'm not, a mother! I failed. Failed. I should have drowned the both of you in that ocean. Don't you see? We live in a desert. This whole city is a desert. Dry, and burning up. I don't care what they think, because I don't know what my mother feels like. *(Begins to sob)* I don't know what my mother feels like. I don't know what my mother feels like...

(THELMA *passes out on* JULIE's *lap.*)

JULIE: Your mother died when you were born Thelma.

(The sound of the cello. Lights out on living room.)

Scene Seventeen

(The sound of loud salsa music.
Traffic noise.
People talking and laughing in Spanish.
RAY *appears in a pool of light.*
He is standing, looking out, facing the audience.
He is eating a taco dorado (hard shell taco).
The sound of gunfire.
RAY *is being shot.*
He falls, still holding the taco in his hand.
Lights out.
Sound out.)

Scene Eighteen

(Lights up on living room. THELMA *is sitting on the recliner, holding a phone receiver to her ear.)*

THELMA: Oh, It was awful. Drive by shooting. That's city life for you. Uh, huh. King Taco. Yeah, I know. He had a fondness for hard shells. Yeah, terrible, terrible... Well, he's not dead yet, technically speaking. It's a coma. Well, I suppose it's just a matter of signing a little paper and pulling some silly plug. Thanks for the suggestion. Well, If it's any consolation, you're his favorite sister. Flowers? Fruit? Oh what a kind offer, to even think of us. But what about, uh... cash? *(Disappointed)* Yes, of course. I understand.

(JULIE walks in in her nurse's outfit.)

THELMA: Well, I gotta get going. If he lives, I'll tell him you called. Goodbye. *(She hangs up.)* There's very little to worry about. It's a coma.

JULIE: A coma?

THELMA: A state of some sort. Bottom line is we'll have to take care of him. Take care of him like a baby.

JULIE: A baby?

THELMA: Yes, a baby. He'll be a blithering little baby and we'll have to take care of him. But we always have, haven't we?

JULIE: *I'm* not taking care of him.

THELMA: What?

JULIE: You heard me. I'm not taking care of him. My whole life has been taking care of this family. I'm tired of taking care of this family.

THELMA: Well, you might not want to take care of your father, you disrespectful awful person, but you're going to have to take care of somebody. You know, in Mexico...

JULIE: You're not from Mexico! You've never been to Mexico. You've been to Tijuana. You don't know what the hell Mexico looks like and you don't know what they do down there. So stop acting like you know what's happening *globally*, because you don't.

THELMA: What's wrong with you? You're not acting like a caretaker at all. You haven't been climbing those twelve steps again, have you?

JULIE: I'm through taking care of people. (*Breaks down sobbing.*)

THELMA: Oh, dear, you have. Listen sweetie, you're going to have to take care of somebody. That's human nature. It's in our bodies. I may complain about it. But I never stopped taking care of your father. And this will be no different. It will be easier actually.

JULIE: I just hurt so bad.

THELMA: Aw, honey, we're all hurt and uncomfortable, it's a fact of our lives.

JULIE: I lost my job.

THELMA: No!

JULIE: Yes, I've lost my job.

THELMA: But why?

JULIE: They say I've been giving my patients *unnecessary medicine*.

THELMA: *Unnecessary medicine*? All medicine is unnecessary. But we keep taking it. Did you tell them that?

JULIE: I didn't get a chance.

THELMA: Well, do you want me to call them?

JULIE: It doesn't work that way.

THELMA: I can, you know.

JULIE: Yes, I know.

THELMA: Well who cares? We're going to get so much insurance money from your comatose father we won't know what to do with it.

JULIE: It's not the money.

THELMA: I know. Hey, couldn't you work for Mother Theresa's charity? Now there's a country that could really use your help. They got people with living rooms on the street. Kids selling Chiclets wholesale.

JULIE: Stop it.

THELMA: Oh, god! Oh, god! Here it comes again.

JULIE: What? What is it.

THELMA: I'm getting a memory. Hold my hand honey.

(JULIE *holds her hand. It passes. She relaxes.*)

THELMA: Whew. Gone.

JULIE: Are you okay?

THELMA: Yeah, It was just a thought. But, oh Julie, what a thought it was! Wait here. I got something that will keep you occupied forever.

JULIE: Oh, god.

(THELMA *goes to wall and retrieves cello.* JULIE *sees it.*)

JULIE: Oh, my god.

THELMA: Look at this cello. Look deep into the heart of this cello and tell me you're not saying 'Oh Freedom'.

JULIE: Oh, god. Oh, god.

THELMA: Freedom from it all Julie. Play it and forget. Let's forget all of this crazy world and it's pain. This cello has been sitting here waiting for this day. The men, they leave you. They always leave you. But we find ways. Ways to mend the loss.

JULIE: I'll kill myself.

THELMA: Oh no you won't! You Julie Martinez are not going to do what every other woman on this block has done. We're not the dying kind. We Martinez' have all lived well into our nineties.

JULIE: *Oh, great...*

THELMA: This is the family line.

JULIE: The end of the family line!

THELMA: You shut up. You scare me when you get this way. Light me a cigarette honey.

JULIE: I don't care Thelma.

THELMA: What about your brother? Who'll take care of your brother?

JULIE: My brother's been taken care of....

THELMA: We've got to make his return as smooth and easy as possible. He's a man Julie. A creature of habit. They're not easily adaptable. He just got out of a cage. We've got to give him a little familiarity.

JULIE: Familiarity?

THELMA: We've got to make things easy for him. Bring him back into the world.

JULIE: He ain't coming back to the world.

THELMA: I made us name tags with six digit prison numbers. I chained up all the appliances. I took the mattress off his bed and I spray painted the frame gray. Familiarity.

JULIE: You don't get it do you?

(THELMA *reaches under the couch and pulls out a Sears power drill.*)

THELMA: You know what I'm going to do tonight? I'm going to take the bars off the windows. All of them. The bars on the windows. The bars on the bike. Even the wet bar. Anything with the word 'bar' in it goes. Tonite this neighborhood is going to hear the drill of freedom. Because sweetie, a woman's work is never done. Never, never, done. Your brother needs the best of both worlds. He needs a woman's world: slavery and freedom.

JULIE: What do you know about Eric's needs?

THELMA: I know lots. I'm his mother.

JULIE: Yes, and what kind of mother are you Thelma?

THELMA: What?

JULIE: What kind of mother are you?

THELMA: What do you mean?

JULIE: I'll tell you what kind of mother you are.

THELMA: Don't say anything you'll regret.

JULIE: No regrets. An absent mother. Did you hear me? An absent mother. Not bad, not good, not there. Not present.

THELMA: Stop it.

JULIE: You're not his mother. You're Thelma. Hello Thelma, I don't think we've ever met.

THELMA: Don't.

JULIE: I don't know how you could possibly know about what Eric needs.

THELMA: Time out.

JULIE: Yes, that's right. That's what you took. A time out. You weren't there Thelma. You weren't there. You refused to hold him, refused to nurse him, refused to feed him. Do you know who did that? Do you know who did that Thelma?

THELMA: Time-out.

JULIE: I was there and I did that. I did that. Look at my tits. He used *these* tits. Look at me godamnit! These should have been your tits. These should have been yours. But you took a time out.

THELMA: I took a time out.

JULIE: It's okay you took a time-out. Really. It's okay. Just don't try to romanticize the past. The past is boring. It's done. Let's just forget it.

THELMA: I can't forget it.

JULIE: I'm the end of the line. The end of this line. I'll take care of you and you'll take care of me. We know how to do that, take care of each other.

THELMA: Yes, but what about your father?

JULIE: I'll take care of that.

THELMA: What about Eric?

JULIE: It's been taken care of. Let's do it right this time. The way it should have always been.

THELMA: Yes, right. The way it should have always been. *(Long pause. She begins to cry. Lights a cigarette instead)* Well, take off your crown sweetie.

JULIE: No. I don't want to. Nostalgia.

THELMA: Yes, nostalgia. Hey, you know what? I'm gonna write a book.

JULIE: About what?

THELMA: About all of this. Oh, I know not much has happened to us, but somebody should write it down, for nostalgia's sake. We'll keep it in place of pictures. Where's the typewriter?

JULIE: Under the couch with everything else.

THELMA: Why is that?

JULIE: We're a one act.

THELMA: Yes, right. *(She pulls the typewriter from under the couch.)* Let's see now, this shouldn't be too difficult to work. Geez, if only I had become that secretary in the entertainment industry, I wouldn't be having this problem now. Listen honey, why don't you play the cello while I type? It'll help with my concentration.

JULIE: Really? I still only know one song.

THELMA: Still? After all this time? *(To audience)* Isn't that sweet? *(To* JULIE*)* It must be a good song.

*(*JULIE *picks up the cello.)*

THELMA: Okay. Ready.

(Pause)

JULIE: *(Laughs)* Where's the paper?

THELMA: No paper. I'm typing for memory.

(JULIE *hugs the cello.*)

(The sound of the cello. Lights out on the living room.
An extended camera flash.
JULIE *and* THELMA *are standing in a family pose.*
They are smiling. The family home movie resumes.
The Altar of Memory is lit.
The sound of the ocean over the cello.
The actors exit. Lights out)

END OF PLAY

CLAUDIA MEETS FULANO COLORADO

Joann Farías

ABOUT THE AUTHOR

Joann Farías studied playwriting with Edward Albee and Denise Chavez at the University of Houston. Her play CLAUDIA MEETS FULANO COLORADO was workshopped at South Coast Repertory Theater's Hispanic Playwrights Project 1997 and read at Brava! for Women in the Arts's Winter Reading Series 1998. She has also done radio drama: *The Witch Dentist*, produced by Shoestring Radio Theater and *Primavera*, produced by Jack Straw Productions as part of the 1998 Artists Support Program.

She currently resides in Seattle, Washington, where she is active in the local arts community. She co-authored an original production for The Immediate Theater entitled BLOOD ORANGE, and did an adaptation of Arthur Schnitzler's REIGEN, entitled THE ROUND GAME. She and Chuck Hudson co-authored a translation of Molière's GEORGE DANDIN for Cornish College of the Arts. She has written two outreach plays for Seattle Opera's Education Program, entitled LA CASA VERDI and ORPHEUS SINGS OF LOVE. She is a member of Los Norteños writers group, and has participated in several readings. She participated in the Women Playwrights Festival, sponsored by A Contemporary Theater, and Hedgebrook Writers Retreat.

In Houston, she served for five years on the Board of Directors of No Encontramos, a not-for-profit theater company that produced Shakespeare and children's theater in Spanish, classic Spanish theater, works by contemporary Hispanic playwrights, and multimedia collaborations with DiverseWorks.

She holds a B A and M A in English from Brigham Young University, with emphasis in theater and classics, and did extensive postgraduate work in theater at the University of Houston.

CLAUDIA MEETS FULANO COLORADO was first workshopped through H P P in August 1997. The cast and creative contributors were:

CLAUDIA . . . . .Vanessa Marquez
ABUELA . . . . Miriam Tubert
BUTCHER . . . . Michael Manuel
WIFE . . . . .Laurie Woolery
FULANO COLORADO . . . . Armando Molina
ENSEMBLE . . . . .Edna Alvarez, Catarina Maynard, Thom Rivera,
Winston J Rochat

Director . . . . Paulo Nuñes-Ueno
Dramaturg . . . . .Kim Euell

CHARACTERS & SETTING

CLAUDIA, *an orphan girl, ten*
ABUELA, *grandmother of* CLAUDIA, *sixties*
BUTCHER, *a man in his thirties, married to* WIFE
WIFE, *a woman in her thirties, married to* BUTCHER
FULANO COLORADO, *a Mephistophelean character who always wears something red, ageless.*
OLD WOMAN CORO 1, *a woman in her sixties*
OLD MAN CORO 2, *a man in his sixties*
YOUNG WOMAN CORO 3, *a woman in her twenties*
YOUNG MAN CORO 4, *a man in his twenties*
FELINA, *a cat who appears primarily in voice and dead at the end*

Scene: a small Hispanic neighborhood in Texas.

Time: the 1950s.

A NOTE ABOUT STAGING

The entire play is performed in one act with a playing area that includes the BUTCHER's shop, the cemetery, the home of CLAUDIA and ABUELA, and a central playing area representing the town. The CORO appears unmasked in all scenes except those pertaining to the ABUELA, in which they wear masks covering the top half of their faces and represent the ghosts of the past.

There are twenty-three separate scenes, some short, some long, that move quickly and smoothly with no set changes to form a continuous whole. Significant props include a butcher knife, packages wrapped in butcher paper to resemble meat, a nylon grocery bag, a comb, a washboard and piece of bar soap, the horns of a bull, and at the end, a dead cat. Significant costume changes include a wedding dress and wedding coat, a sports coat with carnation, mourning finery, bloody shirts, and masks.

Scene One

(The setting is the same throughout the play. Upstage center is a butcher shop, where the BUTCHER *and* WIFE *work. It is represented by a butcher block with knife, counter, glassed case with meat, hanging sausages, chickens, and the head of a cow. They live in quarters immediately upstairs from the shop but never seen. The shop is on a platform with steps, where people can sit and congregate, and opens onto the central playing area.)*

(Upstage right is the cemetery, where CLAUDIA *and* ABUELA's *family lie buried, along with the rest of the town's dead.)*

(Far left, and distant from the other areas, is an area with a table and chair representing the home of CLAUDIA *and* ABUELA.)

(Downstage center is the central playing area, representing the town square or the place where people gather.)

(At rise: BUTCHER *is in his shop serving customers.* WIFE *is helping him and chatting with the customers.* CORO *is in and out of the shop.* FULANO COLORADO *is listening and observing.)*

(Enter CLAUDIA, *at cemetery.)*

CLAUDIA: *(Placing it on her mother's grave)* Here's a rose for my Mami.
She was very beautiful, my Mami. She had long black hair. When I grow up, I'm going to have long hair, too.
It's been so long since my Mami died I can't even remember her. I just know I had a Mami, and she was real pretty. And she was nice, too, and I had a Papi and a family, like the other people. I was like the others, but I can't remember how it felt. It didn't feel like nothing because I didn't know it was going to go away. Now I know, but I can't change it.
So I come here, to remind myself of the others, the others that I remember only a little, by their voices and the way they felt, like my Mami's hair.
Para tì, Amà, una flor. (She runs off.)

BUTCHER: What would you like, Leticia?

YOUNG WOMAN CORO 3: Milanesas.

OLD MAN CORO 2: I was telling Concha here.

OLD WOMAN CORO 1: *Ay, Viejo.*

YOUNG MAN CORO 4: Where's the money I gave you?

YOUNG WOMAN CORO 3: I don't know. I don't know what happened to the money.

BUTCHER: *No milanesas.*

YOUNG WOMAN CORO 3: *¿No milanesas?*

OLD WOMAN CORO 1: You know what she did then?

BUTCHER: No. We ran out.

YOUNG WOMAN CORO 3: Oh.

YOUNG MAN CORO 4: Oh, we know what she did then.

BUTCHER: Can I get you something else?

YOUNG WOMAN CORO 3: Well, you know what they say, *Si no hay lomo, de todo como.*

OLD WOMAN CORO 1: A daughter is still a daughter.

YOUNG MAN CORO 4: Woman, all you do is spend.

YOUNG WOMAN CORO 3: Well maybe if you worked a little more.

BUTCHER: *Si no hay lomo, de todo como.*

YOUNG WOMAN CORO 3: All right, I'll go with the *carne para guisar.*

YOUNG MAN CORO 4: A daughter is still a daughter.

BUTCHER: It's real good.

YOUNG WOMAN CORO 3: Is it?

YOUNG MAN CORO 4: *(Exiting)* I work all day, Leticia. All day.

OLD MAN CORO 2: A daughter is still a woman.

BUTCHER: Yeah. Here you go, Leticia.

YOUNG WOMAN CORO 3: Thank you, José.

OLD WOMAN CORO 1: A daughter is still a woman.

BUTCHER: How easy it is to cut things up. Ya! They're gone. I wonder why people don't cut each other up. I mean, really cut each other up. Oh, once in a while somebody goes for a stab, but then they see all the blood coming out and they get scared and stop. People don't know what's inside themselves. They can't deal with the truth of the fluid. They don't know what they're eating.
I'd know how to do it right. I'd know how to handle the muscles, the joints, the bones. I'd know how to lift the body onto the table. I'd know how to hang it.
You gotta have the right tools. You gotta have cleavers, cutters, a saw. A strong, level surface. You gotta know how to move those arms and legs and get them around. Slice those hams, those giant hams the humans have.

And I'd know how to deal with the eyes. They're not much different, cows' eyes and people's eyes, especially when they're dead. Don't be afraid of the eyes.

(ABUELA, *holding nylon grocery bag, and* CLAUDIA *enter.* YOUNG MAN CORO 4, *masked, follows them, with blood on his garments, blood on his mask. The sound of a train and train whistle. He attempts to stand in front of the* ABUELA.)

ABUELA: No! *(She turns away from him, and he leaves.)*

(The sound of a cat's meow.)

CLAUDIA: She followed me.

ABUELA: She smells the meat.

BUTCHER: What would you like, Mariana?

ABUELA: Bones.

BUTCHER: I got you some meat, too.

ABUELA: Good.

OLD MAN CORO 2: She has your eyes, Mariana.

ABUELA: That's what they tell me.

OLD MAN CORO 2: Bright as candles.

ABUELA: That was a long time ago.

OLD MAN CORO 2: *(Flirting with* CLAUDIA) I remember. I knew your *abuela* here when she was young. *Qué chula*. She had big eyes, that one. Big eyes that looked. I used to wink at her, and she'd run away, but then she'd look back. That's gonna get her in trouble, I thought. That looking back.

(BUTCHER *dons a wedding coat over his apron. The wedding march begins.*)

OLD MAN CORO 2: I was at her wedding, sitting in the side for the bride. I knew them both, but I wanted to sit on her side. I had my wife with me. She was a friend of the *novia*.

(WIFE *enters dressed as a bride. She joins* BUTCHER. *They face the audience as if the altar.*)

OLD MAN CORO 2: We all smiled when she came in, *vestida de blanco*. We love a wedding. It makes the world good. Pretty soon there's sons and daughters, and we see them in the town, with the children. And then we go to their children's wedding, and their children's children are born and are called after the names of their fathers, and we say, They look like you. We're tied by our names and our faces to each other, so we don't have to be alone. She was real shy at the wedding. She didn't look up. But we could feel her eyes. It was like she was sad. To be a bride and be sad. *Qué vergüenza*. But we understood. We were all sad. Everyone's sad at a wedding, because you know that's the way it's gotta be. *Así es la vida.* But her sadness made her beautiful.

(BUTCHER *and* WIFE *make a promenade, and the entire town promenades with them. The couple exits, and the others remain.*)

OLD WOMAN CORO 1: Well, another happy couple.

OLD MAN CORO 2: *(Sarcastically)* Yeah. I remember when I got married.

OLD WOMAN CORO 1: You were drunk when you got married.

OLD MAN CORO 2: Why do you think I did it?

OLD WOMAN CORO 1: I thought you were dying for love.

OLD MAN CORO 2: I was dying for something.

YOUNG WOMAN CORO 3: Hector brought the mariachis to sing at my window.

FULANO COLORADO: He won them in a card game.

YOUNG WOMAN CORO 3: You won the mariachis?

YOUNG MAN CORO 4: I won five songs. I would have brought them anyway.

OLD MAN CORO 2: Were you lucky in love? You know what they say—unlucky in cards, lucky in love.

CLAUDIA: What does that mean, lucky in love?

ABUELA: Nothing, *mihija.*

FULANO COLORADO: Maybe the mariachis got lucky.

YOUNG WOMAN CORO 3: My father was standing there the whole time.

ABUELA: What'd the mariachis sing?

YOUNG WOMAN CORO 3: *Solamente una vez.*

FULANO COLORADO: *(Exiting)* I hate that song.

YOUNG WOMAN CORO 3: *(Singing) Solamente una vez*
Amé en la vida
Solamente una vez
Y nada más.

OTHERS: *(Singing) Y cuando ese milagro*
Realiza el prodigio de amarse
Hay campanas de fiesta que cantan
En el corazón.

ABUELA: That's a pretty song.

YOUNG WOMAN CORO 3: It was a pretty night.

YOUNG MAN CORO 4: There'll be another pretty night.

OLD MAN CORO 2: I bet the *novios* are having a pretty night.

ALL: Yeah.

OLD MAN CORO 2: I'm ready for a beer.

MEN: Yeah!

(The men leave. The women remain.)

(End of scene)

Scene Two

(Setting: Central playing area)

(At rise: This picks up immediately from previous scene. Men have just left to drink beer. WIFE enters in her wedding gown.)

(ABUELA, OLD WOMAN CORO 1, AND YOUNG WOMAN CORO 3 undress her as a bride and redress her as a wife during the following dialogue.)

CHILD'S VOICE: ¡Amá! ¡Amá! Where are my shoes?

YOUNG WOMAN CORO 3: Under the bed, where you left them.

CHILD'S VOICE: I can't find them.

OLD WOMAN CORO 1: You're not looking.

CHILD'S VOICE: I am looking.

ABUELA: If I have to come in there...

CHILD'S VOICE: I found them.

WIFE: You better be getting ready for school.

CHILD'S VOICE: I am.

OLD WOMAN CORO 1: Oh, the virgin stuff gets over with quick.

ABUELA: The first month.

YOUNG WOMAN CORO 3: After that, you get to know what's going on with your own ass. You let him, sure, but you don't really need it. That's his thing.

WIFE: Why do we let them?

YOUNG WOMAN CORO 3: We could run.

OLD WOMAN CORO 1: Real far.

ABUELA: You could lock yourself in the bathroom, and have him pounding there all night:

MAN'S VOICE: Leticia, come out! You're keeping me up all night. I gotta go to work in the morning.

WIFE: You could keep it from him.

OLD WOMAN CORO 1: He'd just go to a whore.

YOUNG WOMAN CORO 3: And give her all your money.

WIFE: Who thought this up?

ABUELA: They say God.

WIFE: God.

OLD WOMAN CORO 1: Ha!

YOUNG WOMAN CORO 3: He must be a man.

ABUELA: But you know, it's kind of nice. When he gets that look. You know, the look.

YOUNG WOMAN CORO 3: The look.

OLD WOMAN CORO 1: The look.

YOUNG WOMAN CORO 3: And it's you he needs. He'll do anything for you.

OLD WOMAN CORO 1: For a few minutes.

ABUELA: But in your heart, you know that this is the way it has to be. This is what you were born for, and it's good to be what you were born for.

YOUNG WOMAN CORO 3: You get used to him.

OLD WOMAN CORO 1: After a while.

YOUNG WOMAN CORO 3: If he went away, you know you'd miss him. You'd miss his smell. You'd miss his chest with black hairs on it. You'd miss his demands. You'd even miss his stinky breath.

ABUELA: Then one day you feel something different. You look at the man and you know he's made you pregnant. And there he is sleeping, as if nothing ever happened. "You," you say to the man, but he keeps on sleeping.

OLD WOMAN CORO 1: Men are such babies. They have their macho, sure, but they don't know. They can go on and on, and it doesn't touch them at all. Only women know.

ABUELA: Then you tell them, "*Tu vas a tener a un hijo.*" And they're so happy. They bring you flowers. They treat you real sweet.

WIFE: It's themselves they're bringing flowers, only they have to do it through you. It's themselves they're treating sweet, in the person of their child.

YOUNG WOMAN CORO 3: Mother. Now that's sweet. How can it be? Yesterday I was just a person.

OLD WOMAN CORO 1: For that reason, because they don't know, because they go on and on not knowing, in your heart you have to call your husband a *tonto*. For not knowing.

ABUELA: But how could he know? He'd have to be a woman. How can you teach a man what it's like to be a woman? He's so busy being On Top, he can't stand to Come Down to where you are:
So this is what it's like from the other side. Not bad.

OLD WOMAN CORO 1: But, you know, they never do.

ALL: *Tontos.*

OLD WOMAN CORO 1: My husband is a *tonto*. I got tired of his *tonto* ways of running everything. Whenever I tried to do something, he would come along and make it the other way. Everything I did, he undid. Then he would say that was just The Way It Was.
I ran away once.

YOUNG WOMAN CORO 3: You did?

WIFE: Where did you go?

OLD WOMAN CORO 1: California.

ALL: Aaaaahhhh!

OLD WOMAN CORO 1: Not with another man, just with myself. That was what I wanted, just to be with myself and my children. My mother wouldn't take me:

ABUELA: Go back to your husband.

OLD WOMAN CORO 1: Mami, I don't like him.

ABUELA: Why not?

OLD WOMAN CORO 1: He's mean to me.

ABUELA: No, he's not.

OLD WOMAN CORO 1: He doesn't let me do anything.

ABUELA: That's the way it is. Go back home. It's no good to see you running away like this. What if everyone ran away?

WIFE: What IF everyone ran away?

OLD WOMAN CORO 1: I took the children to California to pick fruit. There he was, running after me, trying to get his family back. When he got to where we were, he didn't say nothing to me. He just kissed the babies and brought in the food: *frijoles, cebolla, carne.* Then he came and lay down with me.
He held me real tight. I couldn't breathe. I thought he was gonna cry, but he

didn't. I was afraid he was gonna beat me, but he didn't. When he fell asleep, he was breathing real hard, like panting: Hu-hu, hu-hu. I thought, "He's scared".

WIFE: Scared?

OLD WOMAN CORO 1: Yes, scared. I thought, "He could die, of a heart attack." I felt sorry for him. So I stayed, and I didn't run away again.

(During the following, the women exit one by one.)

MAN'S VOICE: Leticia, where are my shoes?

YOUNG WOMAN CORO 3: Under the bed, where you left them.

MAN'S VOICE: I can't find them.

OLD WOMAN CORO 1: You're not looking.

MAN'S VOICE: I am looking.

ABUELA: Do I have to come in there?

MAN'S VOICE: I found them.

WIFE: You're gonna be late for work.

MAN'S VOICE: No, I'm not.

(All exit.)

(End of scene)

Scene Three

(Setting: The Butcher shop)

(At rise: The BUTCHER is alone in his shop, FULANO COLORADO listening from afar, unbeknownst to BUTCHER.)

BUTCHER: There's something of the stink in us all. See this—it's an intestine. It's where the stink is. But it's also where the food is. Without the stink, we got no food. Without the food, we die.
Here's the cow's stinky part. It's filled with grass. And the human stinky part? It's filled with cow.
Does that make us better than the cows? I've been trying to figure that out—all my life I've been trying to decide.
The cow eats grass. It is bad for a cow to eat grass? I don't think so.
What's grass? It grows on the ground. It's everywhere.
The human eats cows. It is bad for the human to eat a cow? I don't know.
They're not everywhere like the grass, but really they are. I see cows all the time. And they're *tontos*, except when they want to hurt you, then they're real smart. But they're more like us than the grass. They have eyes. That's

the thing that makes the cow different from the grass. The grass don't look at you when you go to eat it. That's why we ask, why I ask, when I'm lying in bed at night—is it bad to eat a cow? I wonder.

But really I don't, because if I didn't eat a cow it might eat me. Or something would. An alligator. Or a lion. Lions eat humans. Are they bad? I don't think so, except when they're eating a human. And if that human is me, they're real bad. They're beautiful, the lions, with their grand heads. If they eat another animal, that's okay with me, for the sake of the beauty. If I were anything but a human, I'd be a lion. A lion eats what it wants and doesn't worry about the rest. And if a lion stinks, well, that's just part of being a lion.

FULANO COLORADO: *(Entering)* I'm not so sure, José.

BUTCHER: What do you mean?

FULANO COLORADO: I think there is some pretty good evidence to the effect that cows have souls.

BUTCHER: Cows have souls? Like the souls of men? I don't remember that from catechism.

FULANO COLORADO: I saw it in a book somewhere. St Francis, I think it was. So when you kill a cow, you really are committing a sin.

BUTCHER: What about the grass? Does the grass have a soul, too?

FULANO COLORADO: What's grass? It grows on the ground. It's everywhere. But a cow. That's different.

BUTCHER: Oh.

FULANO COLORADO: Maybe you should think about a different line of work.

BUTCHER: Oh.

FULANO COLORADO: Just something to think about.

BUTCHER: I see what you mean.

FULANO COLORADO: Adios. *(He exits.)*

BUTCHER: St. Francis wasn't one of the better saints. At least that's what the padre says.

(Exit BUTCHER.)

(End of scene)

Scene Four

(Setting: The empty home of CLAUDIA *and* ABUELA.*)*

(At rise: Enter CLAUDIA, *alone, singing.)*

(During this song, FULANO COLORADO *enters and listens to her singing, hating her.)*

CLAUDIA: *(Singing)* My cat is named Felina
I got her when I was small
She came *piu piu* to our door
Oy she was so sad

I asked my *abuela*
Can we keep her?
Abuelita told me no
We have no *carne* for a cat

She'll eat my *carne*
She'll sleep with me in bed
She won't make no noise
I promise she'll be good

Green eyes and yellow feet
Long whiskers and a tail
She licks herself all over
She's a clean-minded cat

When I'm asleep she's there
Humming her song to me
I'm always happy inside
Cause I know I have a friend

*(*ABUELA *enters and sits.)*

ABUELA: *(To* CLAUDIA*)* Come here, *mihija*. I have to comb your hair.

*(*CLAUDIA *sits in front of her, and* ABUELA *begins combing her hair and braiding/ arranging it. In the middle of this,* YOUNG MAN CORO 4, *masked, enters, in a blood-stained shirt, to the sound of a train and train whistle.* ABUELA *drops the comb and abruptly pushes* CLAUDIA *away, and turns from him. He pursues wherever she turns.)*

YOUNG MAN CORO 4: *(Masked) ¿Amá?* Will you look at me, *Amá?*

ABUELA: No.

CLAUDIA: *Abuelita?*

YOUNG MAN CORO 4: *(Masked) ¿Amá?* Will you look at me, *Amá?*

ABUELA: No.

CLAUDIA: *Abuelita?*

YOUNG MAN CORO 4: *(Masked)* *¿Amá?* Will you look at me, *Amá?*

ABUELA: Go!

(CLAUDIA picks up the comb and starts to leave, distressed.)

CLAUDIA: *Felina! Felina! Vente p'acá!*

(The sound of a cat's meow.)

CLAUDIA: Come here, *mihija.* I have to comb your hair.

(CLAUDIA exits. The sound of Solamente una vez *by Trio Los Panchos.* BUTCHER, *masked, in a sport coat and carnation, approaches her.)*

BUTCHER: *(Masked. Shyly)* I saw you at the dance.

ABUELA: You saw me at the dance?

BUTCHER: *(Masked)* I saw you.

ABUELA: And you didn't dance with me?

BUTCHER: *(Masked)* No. But I saw you.

(Exit BUTCHER, *as* ABUELA's *suitor, with* ABUELA. *Enter* CLAUDIA, *at cemetery.)*

CLAUDIA: *(Placing a rock on her father's grave)* Here's a rock for my Papá, to make him strong.

(Exit CLAUDIA.*)*

(End of scene)

Scene Five

(Setting: The Butcher shop.

(At rise: WIFE *is in shop alone, making feints with the* BUTCHER's *knife.* BUTCHER *enters, sees her antics, and is alarmed.)*

BUTCHER: What are you doing?

WIFE: Nothing.

BUTCHER: Don't play with that. It's not a toy.

WIFE: I'm not playing with it. I'm practicing.

BUTCHER: Practicing for what?

WIFE: I don't know.

BUTCHER: Give it to me. Let's go upstairs.

WIFE: It's not fair.

BUTCHER: What's not fair?

WIFE: Why do you get to have the knife?

BUTCHER: Because I'm the Butcher. It's my job.

WIFE: I think it's more than your job. I think you like it.

BUTCHER: I'm a butcher. I cut people meat. That's my job. What's wrong with that?

WIFE: Nothing's wrong with that. *(Pause)* You've always got blood in your socks.

BUTCHER: I'm a butcher. You knew that when you married me.

WIFE: I didn't know about the socks.

BUTCHER: Did you want me to show you my dirty socks?

WIFE: You could have told me.

BUTCHER: I didn't think about it.

WIFE: What did you think about?

BUTCHER: I thought about you, and how nice it would be if you were my wife.

WIFE: Oh.

BUTCHER: What do you want me to do?

WIFE: I don't know.

BUTCHER: What do you want me to do about my bloody socks?

WIFE: I'll wash them.

BUTCHER: Okay.

WIFE: That's my job.

BUTCHER: Can we go upstairs?

WIFE: Of course.

(BUTCHER and WIFE go upstairs.)

(End of scene)

Scene Six

(Setting: Central playing area.)

(At rise: CLAUDIA *is sitting alone.* COROS 1 *and 2 enter and walk by. They greet her without breaking stride. She watches.* BUTCHER *and* WIFE *enter and walk by; the same. She watches again.* COROS 3 *and 4 enter and pass her; the same.)*

CLAUDIA: What's gonna happen to me?

COROS 3 & 4: You're gonna grow up.

BUTCHER & WIFE: And get married.

COROS 1 & 2: In the town.

CLAUDIA: But who will marry me?

ALL: Don't worry.

YOUNG WOMAN CORO 3: There'll be somebody.

OLD MAN CORO 2: There always is.

WIFE: A nice young man

OLD WOMAN CORO 1: From a good family.

ALL: In the town.

CLAUDIA: Who will give me away?

OLD MAN CORO 2: Oh, there'll be somebody.

BUTCHER: Somebody in the town will give you away.

YOUNG MAN CORO 4: To somebody in the town.

YOUNG WOMAN CORO 3: You'll live right here.

ALL: Next door to us.

WIFE: You'll be okay.

CLAUDIA: Really?

(They all pause.)

ALL: That's the way it is.

OLD MAN CORO 2: Your mother and father did.

*(*CORO *exits.* CLAUDIA *is left alone.)*

CLAUDIA: My mother and father died.

FULANO COLORADO: What about California?

CLAUDIA: What?

FULANO COLORADO: California.

CLAUDIA: California?

FULANO COLORADO: You could always go to California.

CLAUDIA: How would I get there?

FULANO COLORADO: You father could take you there. He could take you away to California.

CLAUDIA: But I don't have a father.

FULANO COLORADO: You could.

CLAUDIA: How?

FULANO COLORADO: You could be adopted.

CLAUDIA: Who would adopt me?

FULANO COLORADO: I know a millionaire who wants to adopt you. He saw you in church, and he fell in love with you. He asked me, "Who's that beautiful girl?" I said, "That's Claudia the orphan". He said, "I want to adopt her and take her back to California with me".

CLAUDIA: But what about my grandmother?

FULANO COLORADO: She'd be glad to get rid of you. She's happier with her ghosts than she is with you.

CLAUDIA: What should I take?

FULANO COLORADO: You don't have to take anything. He'll buy you all new things.

CLAUDIA: Like what?

FULANO COLORADO: Anything you want. A blue dress with white shoes. A pair of gloves.

CLAUDIA: When?

FULANO COLORADO: Right now.

CLAUDIA: No.

FULANO COLORADO: I thought you wanted a father.

CLAUDIA: I'm not ready.

FULANO COLORADO: He loves you so much, Claudia. He's been waiting so long for a beautiful daughter, and now he's found you. There are so many things he wants to do for you, so many wonderful places to show you. It hurts him to wait.

CLAUDIA: I have to think about it.

FULANO COLORADO: I'll tell him. He'll be sorry, but he only wants you to be happy.

(CLAUDIA *exits.*)

(*End of scene*)

Scene Seven

(*Setting: The Butcher shop*)

(*At rise:* WIFE *in shop, alone, cleaning up.*)

BUTCHER: (*Entering*) Here you are. I didn't know where you were.

WIFE: Do you love me?

BUTCHER: (*Coming to her and putting his arms around her*) You know I love you.

WIFE: No.

BUTCHER: No?

WIFE: You just want you know what.

BUTCHER: You asked me if I loved you.

WIFE: Do you? Don't touch me.

BUTCHER: What's wrong with you?

WIFE: You just want me for that.

BUTCHER: You're my wife.

WIFE: I want you to want me for more than that.

BUTCHER: I want you for everything.

WIFE: Oh.

(*Exit* WIFE *and* BUTCHER. FULANO COLORADO, *who has been listening, enters.*)

FULANO COLORADO: I don't understand how they can do that. He sticks it in her and they go on and on and pretty soon she's screaming ah! ah! and he's grunting uh! uh! It's a nasty business. I've done it. Plenty of times. I've even done it with men, down by the railroad tracks.
You can do it by yourself, and you don't even have to take off all your clothes in front of somebody you don't know. That's the part I hate—taking off my clothes. I don't have an ugly body, but I don't want some woman looking at it. When a woman looks at your body, she kind of owns you. She knows you got a hairy mole on your *culo* and then she thinks she's better than you. But it's more than that. It's that you're familiar to her. When she sees you on the street, she remembers how you looked. You can

see the memory of your body cross her face for just an instant. Right there in broad daylight, your body is exposed in memory for all the world to see. I just want to slap a woman when I see her remembering me in that way. The same with a man. And the shame. There's always shame. Her shame. His shame. But not my shame. I don't regret what I did. It was okay for the minute that it lasted. It's the memory I hate. The memory they have of you is a part of you they steal from you, and there's no way to get it back. You'd have to kill them to wipe it from the earth. Then their soul would still remember. Down in hell, there would be echoing through the infernal chambers a memory of you making love.

That's why I don't do that anymore. Not with nobody but myself. That way I keep my memory of me to myself.

(End of scene)

Scene Eight

(Setting: The home of ABUELA *and* CLAUDIA.*)*

(At rise: CLAUDIA *and* FULANO COLORADO *enter, in serious conversation.)*

CLAUDIA: If we go, can I take my little cat?

FULANO COLORADO: What little cat?

CLAUDIA: Here, I'll show you. Felina! Felina! *Vente p'acá!*

*(*CLAUDIA *goes offstage to get cat. The sound of a cat snarling.)*

CLAUDIA: Felina, what's wrong with you? We're going to California. There's lots of mice in California. *(She returns to* FULANO COLORADO *onstage.)* She won't come.

FULANO COLORADO: I'm allergic to cats.

CLAUDIA: Looks like cats are allergic to you, too.

FULANO COLORADO: We'll do something about it.

CLAUDIA: I have to bring Felina. I can't leave her here. She'll die without me.

FULANO COLORADO: Don't worry. I'll take care of everything. You just get ready.

CLAUDIA: Okay.

(Exit CLAUDIA *and* FULANO COLORADO.*)*

(End of scene)

Scene Nine

(Setting: The Butcher shop)

(At rise: BUTCHER *and* WIFE *are working in shop.* CLAUDIA *runs by. They wave her in.* WIFE *hands her a package of scraps.)*

WIFE: *(Fixing* CLAUDIA's *hair with her hand)* How's your little kitty?

CLAUDIA: Oh, she's fine.

BUTCHER: I gave you something for her.

CLAUDIA: *Gracias.*

WIFE: Come inside, *mihija.* Let me comb your hair.

*(*CLAUDIA *and* WIFE *exit.)*

BUTCHER: She's the one I love most. Ever since I was a kid I loved that girl. There's something uppity about her. She was always a little too good. I wanted to prove to her that I was somebody, that I was a man. I wanted to see that uppity proud look go away. And I did. When I bought her the house, she was happy. She didn't want to show it—she's too proud—but I could tell. When we had our first baby, I saw so much softness in that woman, behind the look. Who is that woman behind the look? I go crazy wanting to know. And I know. Sometimes. Then I don't. I don't know what else to do. We're in it for real. We have a house. That makes it real. We have babies. That makes it really real. But is it? I look at her sometimes, and I see something else behind the look. A doubt. I want to break through the look and strangle that doubt. But I can't.

(Enter YOUNG WOMAN CORO 3 *and* YOUNG MAN CORO 4.*)*

BUTCHER: I can't do nothing but what I do. I work. I come home. I give her everything. That's all.

YOUNG MAN CORO 4: That's all.

(End of scene)

Scene Ten

(Setting: Central playing area)

(At rise: BUTCHER, WIFE, *and* YOUNG MAN CORO 4 *in shop, chatting. Enter* FULANO COLORADO *and* OLD MAN CORO 2, *holding a bottle of wine,* OLD WOMAN CORO 1 *trailing them, keeping an eye on her drunk old man.)*

OLD MAN CORO 2: Sometimes I think it's written in the sky in invisible letters:

OLD MAN CORO 2 & FULANO COLORADO: *It ain't gonna happen.*

(YOUNG MAN CORO 4 *steps out of the shop to listen.*)

OLD MAN CORO 2: I keep dreaming someday I'm gonna have enough money and I'm not gonna have to work till my back hurts. Every day I come home and I tell Concha, Someday I'm not gonna have to work no more.

OLD WOMAN CORO 1: *Ay, viejo.*

OLD MAN CORO 2: I tell you, someday.

FULANO COLORADO: It ain't gonna happen.

OLD MAN CORO 2: (*To* YOUNG MAN CORO 4) You see that pretty girl?

YOUNG MAN CORO 4: What pretty girl?

OLD MAN CORO 2: The one with the little bitty here (*Waist*) and the real big here (*Bust*).

YOUNG MAN CORO 4: Yeah?

OLD MAN CORO 2: Someday that girl is gonna fall in love with me, and we're gonna run off together. When old Concha hears about it, she's gonna drop dead of a heart attack.

YOUNG MAN CORO 4: Whoa!

(BUTCHER *and* WIFE *step out of the shop to listen.*)

OLD WOMAN CORO 1: That beautiful girl ain't gonna fall in love with an old goat like you.

OLD MAN CORO 2: I know, I know.

WIFE: What's all the racket?

OLD WOMAN CORO 1: Mando's drunk again.

BUTCHER: Why you drunk, Mando?

OLD MAN CORO 2: I'm trying to forget.

BUTCHER: What you trying to forget?

OLD MAN CORO 2: I can't remember.

BUTCHER: Then it worked.

OLD WOMAN CORO 1: Oh, it worked.

OLD MAN CORO 2: Someday I am going to be the man my father was. When I build a cabinet the corners will be perfect, level and true. The angles will be right the first time. I'll get it right the first time. And when I finish I won't have to keep going back again and again and have people saying *Está tueco, que mal.* No, they'll walk by and touch the carvings and they'll say how beautiful it is, how beautiful. Just like your father used to do. You're just like your father.

FULANO COLORADO: You'll never be the man your father was.

OLD MAN CORO 2: I know.

FULANO COLORADO: Concha knows it.

OLD WOMAN CORO 1: *Ay, Viejo.*

FULANO COLORADO: You can see it in her eyes.

OLD MAN CORO 2: I just want my life to be good. I want it to be golden. I want my woman to be happy...

BUTCHER: Don't we all.

OLD MAN CORO 2: ...and my children to look at me the way I looked at my father, and say

YOUNG MAN CORO 4: I want to be the man my father was.

FULANO COLORADO: Do I have to say it?

OLD MAN CORO 2: No. I know. It ain't gonna happen.

(FULANO COLORADO *exits.* ABUELA *wanders in.*)

OLD WOMAN CORO 1: Doesn't he remember? I was that girl with the little bitty here and the real big here. I was that girl.

ABUELA: You were.

OLD WOMAN CORO 1: And I did fall in love with that old goat, back when he was a handsome young goat, and we ran away together. Doesn't he remember? (*She exits.*)

ALL: We remember.

(*Enter* YOUNG WOMAN CORO 3.)

YOUNG WOMAN CORO 3: (*To* YOUNG MAN CORO 4) What are you doing here?

YOUNG MAN CORO 4: Nothing.

OLD MAN CORO 2: Concha, my wife. She was a very beautiful girl, and her father, he didn't like me. So we had to run away. We ran away and spent three days in the desert. We ate nothing but jackrabbit—*conejo.* After that, Concha don't want to eat rabbit no more. She said, I'll die before I eat another rabbit. Ah, but that was good, the rabbit days. There we were, just Concha and me, like rabbits in the desert.

(OLD MAN CORO 2 *exits.* CLAUDIA *enters.*)

ABUELA: We went with her father to look for you.

BUTCHER: I didn't want to find them.

YOUNG MAN CORO 4: I did. I wanted to see them, like rabbits.

CLAUDIA: I like rabbits. They run fast.

BUTCHER: I said, Let them go. *Así es la vida.*

WIFE: Her father took his anger to his grave.

BUTCHER: What a fool.

WIFE: A daughter is still a daughter.

BUTCHER: A daughter is still a woman.

YOUNG MAN CORO 4: Like rabbits.

ABUELA: Come on, *mihija.*

YOUNG WOMAN CORO 3: There's never enough money. There's never enough.

CLAUDIA: But I want to hear about the rabbits.

YOUNG MAN CORO 4: I work all day, Leticia, all day. What do you do with the money?

ABUELA: There aren't any more rabbits.

(ABUELA *and* CLAUDIA *exit.)*

BUTCHER: His father was a good carpenter. Built his own coffin.

WIFE: That's too much.

BUTCHER: He wanted to get it right.

WIFE: That's still too much.

BUTCHER: It was all carved. Mahogany. Inlaid with velvet. It was a beautiful coffin.

WIFE: Did he dig his own grave, too?

BUTCHER: He left instructions.

WIFE: He's taking business away from the undertaker.

YOUNG WOMAN CORO 3: How much does it cost to get buried?

YOUNG MAN CORO 4: *(With loving mockery)* Too much for you, Leticia. You can't afford to die.

YOUNG WOMAN CORO 3: I was only asking.

BUTCHER: He was a proud man.

YOUNG MAN CORO 4: I'm glad he's not the man his father was.

BUTCHER: Why?

YOUNG MAN CORO 4: His father took me.

YOUNG WOMAN CORO 3: How?

YOUNG MAN CORO 4: It's a long story. I can't prove anything, but I know.

BUTCHER: Everybody knows.

WIFE: Everybody knows everything. I want other people to pick my flowers for me when I go.

YOUNG WOMAN CORO 3: What kind of flowers do you want?

YOUNG MAN CORO 4: *(Derisively)* Flowers.

WIFE: Gardenias.

BUTCHER: What are gardenias?

WIFE: My favorite flower.

YOUNG WOMAN CORO 3: I'll remember.

YOUNG MAN CORO 4: Come on, Leticia.

(YOUNG MAN CORO 3 *and* YOUNG WOMAN CORO 4 *exit.*)

BUTCHER: I didn't know that was your favorite flower.

WIFE: You don't know anything about me.

BUTCHER: That's the truth.

(WIFE *returns to the shop.* BUTCHER *follows.*)

(*End of scene*)

Scene Eleven

(*Setting: The Butcher shop*)

(*At rise:* BUTCHER *and* WIFE *are working in their shop.* ABUELA *enters with nylon grocery bag.*)

BUTCHER: What would you like, Mariana?

ABUELA: I saw you at the dance.

BUTCHER: You saw me at the dance?

ABUELA: Yes.

BUTCHER: Oh.

ABUELA: But you didn't dance with me.

BUTCHER: Oh.

(BUTCHER *and* WIFE *exchange glances.* ABUELA *exits.* BUTCHER *and* WIFE *follow her out, protectively.*)

(End of scene)

Scene Twelve

(Setting: Central playing area)

(At rise: FULANO COLORADO *enters and looks around. No one is there. He makes as if to speak, but nothing comes out. He goes to the empty* BUTCHER *shop. He inspects the knife, the cutting board, the cow's head with boredom. He makes as if to speak, but nothing comes out. He goes to the cemetery. Again, empty. He goes to the central playing area. No one. He sits on the ground. He tries to speak, but nothing comes out. He sits in emptiness for one minute. He hears* CLAUDIA *singing far away. Her voice grows nearer, and the nearer she is, the more animated he becomes.)*

*(*CLAUDIA *enters, singing.)*

FULANO COLORADO: Claudia, I've got something for you.

CLAUDIA: What?

FULANO COLORADO: The shoes.

CLAUDIA: What shoes?

FULANO COLORADO: The white shoes. The shoes the millionaire's gonna get you when you go to California to be his daughter.

CLAUDIA: White shoes? Real white shoes?

FULANO COLORADO: And lacy white stockings to match.

CLAUDIA: Give them to me. When I see those shoes, I'll know he's my father.

FULANO COLORADO: *(Taking out a page of the Sears catalog)* Here they are.

CLAUDIA: Where?

FULANO COLORADO: Here.

CLAUDIA: That's just a page of the catalog. I've got that at home.

FULANO COLORADO: These are the ones.

CLAUDIA: Oh.

FULANO COLORADO: He just doesn't know your size.

CLAUDIA: Okay. I'm size ten.

FULANO COLORADO: Okay, I'll circle size ten, and take it back to him.

CLAUDIA: Okay.

FULANO COLORADO: I'll be back.

CLAUDIA: With the shoes.

FULANO COLORADO: And stockings.

CLAUDIA: Okay.

(CLAUDIA *and* FULANO COLORADO *exit.*)

(*End of scene*)

Scene Thirteen

(*Setting: The Butcher shop*)

(*At rise:* BUTCHER *working in his shop.* ABUELA *comes in to order meat,* FULANO COLORADO *carrying her grocery bag.* YOUNG MAN CORO 4, *masked, follows her, unseen by* BUTCHER *but seen by* FULANO COLORADO.)

BUTCHER: What would you like, Mariana?

ABUELA: I want the best.

BUTCHER: The best.

ABUELA: My son is coming home today. I want to make the best for him.

BUTCHER: The soldier comes home.

ABUELA: Yes.

BUTCHER: He survived the war.

ABUELA: Yes.

BUTCHER: Well, the best, Mariana, the very best part of the beef is the heart. That's where the love is in the cow and in the person, too. Since this is a fiesta made for love, we'll give you the heart.

ABUELA: I'll be glad.

FULANO COLORADO: You're lying, Josá.

BUTCHER: What do you mean?

FULANO COLORADO: If the best is the heart, why do you charge so much money for the loin? The most money is the best. Count on it.

ABUELA: Well, I don't know.

BUTCHER: She can't afford the loin.

FULANO COLORADO: Then you admit the loin is the best.

BUTCHER: Well...

FULANO COLORADO: He's trying to give you less than the best.

ABUELA: I want the best for my baby.

BUTCHER: I'm trying to make her happy. Be happy, Mariana. Your son is coming home. The happy part is the best.

ABUELA: The happy is the best. Yes. I'll take it. The happy part. See you later, Pancho.

(*Exit* ABUELA, *followed by* YOUNG MAN CORO 4, *masked.*)

FULANO COLORADO: The happy part.

(FULANO COLORADO *takes out a beer, opens it, and offers one to* BUTCHER, *who refuses.* FULANO COLORADO *sits nearby, watching him work and drinking the beer.* WIFE *enters.*)

WIFE: I kept your supper. Aren't you coming up?

BUTCHER: I got a lot to do.

WIFE: The children want you to say good night. They won't go to sleep.

BUTCHER: I'll be up in a while.

WIFE: What's wrong?

BUTCHER: Nothing. I just got a new side of beef in. I gotta take care of it.

WIFE: Can't you do that tomorrow?

BUTCHER: People gotta eat tomorrow, Felicia.

WIFE: Oh.

BUTCHER: Tell the children I'll kiss them in their sleep.

WIFE: Okay.

BUTCHER: I'll be up in a while.

WIFE: You're going out.

BUTCHER: I said I'll be up in a while.

WIFE: Don't make a lot of noise when you come home. I don't want the whole neighborhood to see you falling on your face.

BUTCHER: Don't tell me how to run my business, woman.

WIFE: I wish I could go out. You never take me anywhere.

BUTCHER: I'll take you to the movies.

WIFE: The movies. I want to go out like you do.

BUTCHER: Only whores go out on the street. What would the people say?

WIFE: I wish I weren't a woman.

BUTCHER: What?

WIFE: Nothing.

BUTCHER: Go upstairs. I have to finish my work.

WIFE: Your work.

BUTCHER: Felicia.

WIFE: Good night.

(BUTCHER *removes apron, puts down tools, and exits with* FULANO COLORADO, *who hands him a beer on the way out.* WIFE *exits.*)

(*End of scene*)

Scene Fourteen

(*Setting: The Butcher shop*)

(*At rise:* YOUNG MAN CORO 4, *masked, bloodied, is wearing the* BUTCHER's *apron and working in the shop as though he were the* BUTCHER. ABUELA *enters with nylon grocery bag.*)

YOUNG MAN CORO 4: (*Masked*) What would you like, Mariana?

ABUELA: (*Screaming in fright*) Time has stopped. I can hear the clock ticking, but I know now it's just a machine.
They tell me my son is dead.
I can't believe them. They took me to look at his body. That's not him, I said. My son is a little baby. He's not that large thing with blood everywhere. There are places on him where the meat shows through. I thought, That's not my baby. That's a piece of meat with a human face and blood beneath the skin.

(*Enter* CLAUDIA, *with a comb.*)

ABUELA: And this child is not his daughter. How can a living child come from a piece of meat?

(ABUELA *exits,* YOUNG MAN CORO 4 *following her, leaving* CLAUDIA *alone, holding the comb.*)

CLAUDIA: There's a sadness growing in me. I don't know what it's from. They say you're sad with your eyes, that you cry.
It's not in my eyes that I feel it. Sadness has settled in my mouth; it has the taste of iron.

(FULANO COLORADO *joins her, still holding his beer.*)

FULANO COLORADO: What are you doing?

CLAUDIA: Listening.

FULANO COLORADO: To what?

CLAUDIA: Stuff.

FULANO COLORADO: What stuff?

CLAUDIA: Crickets. The wind. The train far away.

FULANO COLORADO: I don't hear anything.

CLAUDIA: When I close my ears I can hear my own blood swishing through my veins. Life. I'm listening to life. I'm looking real hard at everything, trying to make a picture in my heart of the way it all is, today. I'm ten years old. This is how it is today. And it'll never be like this again, because I'm leaving.

FULANO COLORADO: This place is a shithole. You're better off leaving.

CLAUDIA: The dirt, the sky, the crickets, the train. This is my home.

FULANO COLORADO: There's nothing here for you.

ABUELA: Claudia! *¡Vente p'acá!*

CLAUDIA: *¡Ya estoy, Amá! ¡Ya vengo!*

(CLAUDIA *leaves.* FULANO COLORADO *puts down the beer, closes his eyes, and strains to listen.*)

FULANO COLORADO: I still don't hear anything.

(*End of scene*)

Scene Fifteen

(*Setting: The Butcher shop*)

(*At rise: The sound of children playing.* WIFE *is sweeping the shop and occasionally calling to them.* FULANO COLORADO *enters and begins sharpening the knife, with periodic sharpening noises throughout the following scene. There is a heavy tread, then a slam of the door.* BUTCHER *enters, drunk.*)

BUTCHER: *¡CALLATE!*

(*The children's voices suddenly hush.*)

WIFE: José, what are you doing?

BUTCHER: They're making too much noise

WIFE: They're children. Children make noise.

BUTCHER: Not my children. Not in my house.

WIFE: Children, go outside. *¡Ahorita!*

(*The door slams. The couple is alone. It's the dread alone. She tenses.*)

BUTCHER: What are you doing?

WIFE: I'm doing my work.

BUTCHER: And what would that be?

WIFE: Fixing the clothes.

BUTCHER: Whose clothes are those?

WIFE: Yours. Don't you recognize them?

BUTCHER: They look like mine. But they could be somebody else's.

WIFE: What are you talking about?

BUTCHER: That shirt. It's not so special. It could belong to anybody.

WIFE: This shirt is yours. I bought it for you. I wash it for you. I fix it for you. I'm your wife. This is your shirt.

BUTCHER: That shirt could belong to another man.

WIFE: What other man?

BUTCHER: That's what I want to know. What other man?

WIFE: There is no other man.

BUTCHER: But you said there was.

WIFE: I said nothing.

BUTCHER: You said what other man.

WIFE: You asked me what man the shirt could belong to.

BUTCHER: And you said what other man.

WIFE: I was asking you.

BUTCHER: I want to know.

WIFE: *There is no other man.*

FULANO COLORADO: What about those children?

BUTCHER: Are those my children?

WIFE: You know they are.

BUTCHER: How do I know?

WIFE: Look at them. Look at that boy's face. He's just like you.

BUTCHER: He could be my brother's.

WIFE: I'm not your brother's wife.

BUTCHER: Whose wife are you?

WIFE: You know whose wife I am.

BUTCHER: *Whose wife are you?*

WIFE: *I'm your wife and there is no other man. You are my only husband. You are the only father of my children.*

BUTCHER: You better be telling the truth.

WIFE: You know I am.

BUTCHER: Or you know what.

WIFE: *(Looking at* FULANO COLORADO *holding the knife)* Yeah, I know what.

BUTCHER: What?

WIFE: I know.

BUTCHER: Well.

WIFE: I got to get dinner.

BUTCHER: You get dinner. I'm gonna go look at those children again.

*(*BUTCHER *exits, slamming the door.* WIFE *makes the sign of the cross.)*

FULANO COLORADO: I could have had a child, but the screaming kids puking sticky stuff all over made me sick.

*(*FULANO COLORADO *exits.)*

WIFE: You forget about the sticky stuff when you see them smile.

(End of scene)

Scene Sixteen

(Setting: Cemetery)

(At rise: CLAUDIA *is at cemetery, visiting the family.)*

CLAUDIA: *(Placing it on her sister's grave)* For my sister, Dolores, a taco. She was always bugging our mother for food. *(She exits.)*

FULANO COLORADO: The body when alive maintains itself in a state of medium wetness. If it's too wet, it's bleeding to death, like in a gunfight or a stabbing, or it's drowning itself, like pneumonia, or it's shitting itself to death, like in cholera. The body can't get itself too wet, or all the living wetness leaks out, and soon it dies. On the other hand, if it's too dry, the sap don't flow, and the parts can't all partake of the vital moisture. So the body, living, is medium wet.
Then the medium wet gets *muy* wet or *muy* dry, and it stops working. Then it gets really wet, cause all the dry dividers between the various types of wetness break, and now it's a terrible swamp of wetness. But that passes, and the dryness soon sets in. A dry carcass, then dry bones, then dry dust,

muy, muy dry.

By this time her family will be in the carcass state. I love thinking of her here above the ground, in a perfect state of medium wet, doing all these nice things for these bodies in a state of medium dry.

Someday, Claudia, you'll be down there, too, and your wetness will gradually pass into a dryness, like your family, and all these gifts you bear will be an irony.

(End of scene)

Scene Seventeen

(Setting: Central playing area.)

(At rise: CORO *and* ABUELA *are visiting in and out of butcher shop.* BUTCHER *and* WIFE *are in shop.* FULANO COLORADO *is mingling with everyone.* OLD MAN CORO 2, *as Wanderer, enters with suitcase.)*

OLD MAN CORO 2: I'm back! I'm back! *Mi pueblo*, I kiss you. *(Kisses the ground)* I can't believe it. I can't tell you how long it's been, how many things have happened. I've seen this town in my dreams, I swear it. That porch, oh, that porch—look at it. It's still there. I'm so happy! I'm gonna sit down on that porch like I did when I was a kid. Now, tell me everything. What's happened since I've been gone?

YOUNG MAN CORO 4: Well, where do we start?

YOUNG WOMAN CORO 3: Chucho's wife got the cancer and died, and he was so sad he lost a foot.

OLD MAN CORO 2: How did he lose a foot from being sad?

YOUNG MAN CORO 4: He was a diabetic.

YOUNG WOMAN CORO 3: He got sad and didn't take his medicine.

ABUELA: I told him to eat *nopalitos*. They're good for the diabetes. They cured my uncle.

FULANO COLORADO: A pretty young nurse cured your uncle.

ABUELA: Same thing.

BUTCHER: By the time we found him grieving it was too late for his foot.

YOUNG WOMAN CORO 3: So now he's walking around without a foot.

CLAUDIA: How can he walk without a foot?

ABUELA: He don't go far.

OLD MAN CORO 2: *¡Ay, que terible!* Chucho without a foot. And he was the best dancer. Man, we used to tear up the dance floor.

OLD WOMAN CORO 1: I remember dancing with you. Do you remember dancing with me?

OLD MAN CORO 2: How could I forget, Mariquita?

(They dance.)

OLD MAN CORO 2: She's not as skinny as she used to be.

OLD WOMAN CORO 1: What happened to his hair?

BOTH: I wish (I'd/he'd) never come back. Better to remember (her/him) the way (She/he) was.

WIFE: He never married.

YOUNG MAN CORO 4: People don't get married in California. They just live together.

BUTCHER: I wish we'd just lived together.

WIFE: You wouldn't have lived long.

BUTCHER: Why not?

WIFE: My father would have shot you.

BUTCHER: Oh, yeah. I would have had a short life—but happy.

ABUELA: The happy's the same if it's short or long.

BUTCHER: I wouldn't know.

OLD MAN CORO 2: *Ay, Dios mio. Ya me voy.*

YOUNG MAN CORO 4: Where you going? You just got here.

OLD MAN CORO 2: Back to California. This place is falling apart, and the people, too.

YOUNG WOMAN CORO 3: And California isn't?

OLD MAN CORO 2: It's not the same.

WIFE: Why not?

OLD MAN CORO 2: California's not my home. I wasn't born there. When the earthquake comes and the mountain falls, if I'm not under it, I don't care.

(FULANO COLORADO takes his suitcase and leads him off. The others follow.)

(End of scene)

Scene Eighteen

(Setting: The cemetery)

(At rise: CLAUDIA *enters and approaches the family plot.)*

CLAUDIA: For my brother, Jaime, I give you a hit, because you were always hitting me. *(She hits the ground.)* Then I give you a hug, because Mami always made you hug me after. Now the whole family's here but me. *(Lying on an empty space near the family)* And here is where I'll be when my train comes.

(End of scene)

Scene Nineteen

(Setting: The butcher shop)

(At rise: BUTCHER *alone in shop, drunk)*

BUTCHER: You can always tell when the meat's not good, before it gets bad. It has a kind of smell, a kind of look. It's not a happy look.
Meat usually cooperates in being meat. A cow knows it's a cow, and it knows it's got to be killed. That's how cows are. That's how they die. And the meat they make, it knows it's meat for you to eat.
Now a *zorillo*, a raccoon, that isn't like a chicken or a cow. It doesn't know it's gonna be meat. So generally the meat's not good. You gotta train a thing to be meat, so it knows, so it understands, and it grows itself right for you to eat it.
But some things, they know they're supposed to be meat, and they don't grow right just to hurt you. You cut them open, and they're bad inside. How did this thing get bad? I just killed it. It must have been bad from the beginning. From the beginning of its life, it took food from you, it drank your water, it lived in your barn, on your land, and when its time came to pay you back by being meat, it won't be right. That makes me mad. Bad meat makes me very mad.

(End of scene)

Scene Twenty

(Setting: The cemetery. The entire CORO *is present and masked, as monuments, whom* ABUELA *will visit, one by one.)*

(At rise: Enter ABUELA, *arrayed in finery.)*

ABUELA: *(Laying flowers on a grave)* Here's my first stop. My first *muerto.* Papá.

OLD MAN CORO 2: *(Masked)* Thank you for the flowers, *mihija.* They're beautiful. Your mother will be pleased.

YOUNG MAN CORO 4: *(Masked)* ¡Ama!

ABUELA: How soft their voices are, like the petals of a rose. I remember when his voice cracked like thunder, and his eyes were flashing fire. I was so afraid.

OLD WOMAN CORO 1: *(Masked) Mihija,* why do you disturb our sleep?

ABUELA: I wanted to talk to you. I have questions for you that I never got to ask when you were alive.

OLD WOMAN CORO 1: *(Masked)* Why didn't you ask me then, when I might have cared about your little problems? Now I'm dust, and all the children of the flesh are the same to me, and their problems are all alike.

YOUNG MAN CORO 4: *(Masked) ¡Ama!*

ABUELA: I didn't know.

OLD WOMAN CORO 1: *(Masked)* The same I didn't know.

ABUELA: What is it that causes my unhappiness?

OLD WOMAN CORO 1: *(Masked)* Blood, *mihija.* The trouble's in the blood. Women have more of it than men. That's why we have more troubles.

ABUELA: But what can I do?

OLD WOMAN CORO 1: *(Masked)* Die. Then you won't have no more troubles.

YOUNG MAN CORO 4: *(Masked) ¡Ama!*

ABUELA: Oh.

OLD MAN CORO 2: *(Masked)* Thank you for the flowers, *mihija.*

OLD WOMAN CORO 1: *(Masked)* Take away the flowers, *mihija.*

ABUELA: *(Taking the flowers)* Okay, Mami. I don't bring you flowers no more.

(ABUELA *gently takes leave of all her dead, including her son. End of scene)*

Scene Twenty-one

(Setting: The home of CLAUDIA *and* ABUELA.*)*

(At rise: CLAUDIA *and* FULANO COLORADO, *contemplating a vial.)*

FULANO COLORADO: It's easy. All you have to do is put it in her food. She goes to sleep. You put her in the little bag, and we all go to California.

CLAUDIA: Will it hurt her?

FULANO COLORADO: Of course not. Would your millionaire father hurt your little cat?

CLAUDIA: Of course not.

FULANO COLORADO: Well?

CLAUDIA: I'm not sure.

FULANO COLORADO: Tell me about it.

CLAUDIA: About what?

FULANO COLORADO: About why you're not sure.

CLAUDIA: I don't know if I want to leave my *abuela*. Won't she miss me when I go away?

FULANO COLORADO: Does she miss you now? I mean, you're gone all the time, and she hardly cares.

CLAUDIA: I know.

FULANO COLORADO: Look. You can come back anytime you like.

CLAUDIA: How would I get back?

FULANO COLORADO: On the train. *(Pause)* Your father would buy you a first class ticket to come see your old town. And when the people found out, they'd have a parade.

CLAUDIA: Why?

FULANO COLORADO: Cause you'd be a millionairess. You'd be *muy importante*. You'd be riding in the back of a big white car, and waving to all the people. They'd have a big sign that said WELCOME HOME CLAUDIA. And at the very end of the parade would be a house, a big beautiful mansion that your millionaire father will buy for your *abuela*. That's where they'll take you, and when you get there, she'll be waiting with a big hug for her Claudia, the millionairess, who got her that beautiful house with all the beautiful things.

CLAUDIA: All the things in the Sears catalog!

FULANO COLORADO: Everything she wants. A washing machine. A great big fan to blow the air when she gets hot. Furniture. Clothes. Everything. And all because of you. If you don't go be adopted, you'd be robbing her of everything she could have had.

CLAUDIA: Oh.

FULANO COLORADO: And a beautiful golden bed for your little cat to sleep in. A golden bowl for her to drink milk. She'd have the best meat, the very best meat. The butcher will come and personally deliver the biggest steak for the millionairess cat.

CLAUDIA: Oh.

FULANO COLORADO: Look at what you have here. Look at what you could have in California Which is better?

CLAUDIA: California.

FULANO COLORADO: Well?

CLAUDIA: What happened to the shoes you promised to give me?

FULANO COLORADO: They're waiting for you in California.

CLAUDIA: They are.

FULANO COLORADO: In your room.

CLAUDIA: I get my own room?

FULANO COLORADO: Yes, but only if you go.

CLAUDIA: Okay. (*Calling to the cat and taking the lid off the vial*) Felina! (*To* FULANO COLORADO) I'll do it.

FULANO COLORADO: Good. I'll go send a telegram to your father.

(CLAUDIA *exits to find the cat.* FULANO COLORADO *watches her eagerly.*)

(*End of scene*)

Scene Twenty-two

(*Setting: The butcher shop*)

(*At rise:* BUTCHER, *sober, in his shop, mopping up.* WIFE *enters, pulls a bloody rag out of the mop bucket, and with a mocking shriek, throws it at him, hitting his chest.*)

BUTCHER: What the hell?

WIFE: Your sock. It's your bloody sock from last night.

BUTCHER: Felicia, the health department's gonna close us down.

WIFE: They're gonna close you down. They done closed me down a long time ago. *(She picks up a bucket of bloody mop water, and throws it on him.)*

BUTCHER: Woman, you're crazy! *(He picks up two severed cattle horns, and putting them to his head, assumes the identity of a bull.)*

BUTCHER: I'm gonna get you, *señorita.* I'm gonna get you with my horns.

(WIFE shrieks and runs. BUTCHER chases her around the shop. FULANO COLORADO enters and hands her the knife, which she brandishes, deliriously.)

WIFE: I'm gonna cut you, Mister Toro. I'm gonna cut you with my knife.

BUTCHER: I'll gore you.

(Run and dodge)

WIFE: How easy it is to cut things up!

(Run and dodge)

WIFE: Ya! They're gone.

(Run and dodge)

WIFE: They're not much different, cow's eyes and people's eyes.

(BUTCHER chases WIFE, who slips and falls, on her front. BUTCHER leaps on her from behind. She squirms away and runs offstage. He charges, roaring, after her. FULANO COLORADO follows them. She screams. He howls—a howl which could either be pain or ecstasy. The knife clatters to the ground.)

(End of scene)

Scene Twenty-three

(Setting: Central playing area)

(At rise: ABUELA in her home. BUTCHER and WIFE working in shop. CORO in and out of shop. There is a cry of anguish offstage. Everyone comes running. CLAUDIA comes in with the dead cat in her arms. ABUELA looks at her for the first time.)

WIFE: What's wrong, *mihija*?

CLAUDIA: Felina. She won't wake up.

BUTCHER: What happened?

WIFE: She ate some bad meat.

CLAUDIA: No.

ABUELA: A train hit her and killed her, like my son.

CLAUDIA: No.

BUTCHER: Those boys got her. *Ay*, I'm gonna kill them.

CLAUDIA: No.

YOUNG WOMAN CORO 3: All things die, *mihija*. It was her time to go. She's with God now.

CLAUDIA: No. I killed her.

BUTCHER: What?

CLAUDIA: It's my fault.

WIFE: What happened?

CLAUDIA: Fulano Colorado...

BUTCHER: What'd he do to you?

CLAUDIA: He told me there was a millionaire in California who wanted to adopt me and be my father. But Felina wouldn't go, so he gave me some medicine to make her sleep so I could take her. I put it in her milk, but she won't wake up, and now she's not breathing. I think she's dead.

BUTCHER: Let me see.

(CLAUDIA *hands her over.* WIFE *and* ABUELA *both check. The town assembles and gathers around.* BUTCHER *hands the cat to* OLD WOMAN CORO 1.)

BUTCHER: I'm sorry, *mihija*.

OLD WOMAN CORO 1: Ay, Claudia.

OLD MAN CORO 2: Fulano Colorado, he's a liar.

YOUNG WOMAN CORO 3: He lent me money, but I couldn't pay. I didn't know what else to do.

BUTCHER: He kept telling me if I didn't hit her, I wasn't a man.

OLD MAN CORO 2: I never should have sold my tools. Fulano Colorado told me, What's the use? You're no carpenter, not like your father.

YOUNG MAN CORO 4: Don't worry, *mihija*. We'll get you a new cat.

CLAUDIA: I don't want a new cat.

YOUNG WOMAN CORO 3: She killed her cat.

OLD WOMAN CORO 1: Fulano Colorado killed her cat.

OLD MAN CORO 2: A millionaire in California.

YOUNG MAN CORO 4: Man, I've heard that before.

WIFE: There's nothing for you in California.

BUTCHER: You know what they do to little girls in California? Sell them to the camps. Honey, you be picking fruit.

WIFE: Better stay home.

OLD WOMAN CORO 1: With your family.

CLAUDIA: My family's dead.

YOUNG MAN CORO 4: This whole town is your family.

BUTCHER: I'm your *compadre, mihija*. Haven't I always taken care of you?

CLAUDIA: Felina's dead. My baby.
We all lose our babies. That's the shame of life.

OLD MAN CORO 2: Better a cat than a little girl.

BUTCHER: Where is he?

YOUNG MAN CORO 4: Over here.

BUTCHER: What'd you do to this little girl?

FULANO COLORADO: Nothing.

BUTCHER: She says you killed her cat.

FULANO COLORADO: What cat?

CLAUDIA: You gave me medicine for Felina, to put her to sleep, so we could take her.

FULANO COLORADO: How much did you give her?

CLAUDIA: All of it.

FULANO COLORADO: You're not supposed to give her all of it. It's too much. Just a few drops.

CLAUDIA: You didn't tell me.

FULANO COLORADO: Didn't you read the little paper?

CLAUDIA: What little paper?

FULANO COLORADO: This one.

CLAUDIA: *(Grabbing paper)* Aaaahhh!

(The men try to grab him, and they all run off after him, but he eludes their capture. The BUTCHER takes his knife and follows. The women follow behind him, leaving ABUELA and CLAUDIA alone on the stage.)

ABUELA: *Mihija...*

CLAUDIA: You didn't want me.

ABUELA: *Mihija...*

CLAUDIA: You want my daddy who died.

ABUELA: *Mihija...*

CLAUDIA: You think I should have died in that accident. Why was I left, when all the good ones were taken?

ABUELA: You were with me when the accident happened.

CLAUDIA: Everyone who ever loved me is taken from me.

ABUELA: That was a sign.

CLAUDIA: My Mami, my Papi.

ABUELA: You're my consolation.

CLAUDIA: Now Felina's taken, too.

ABUELA: You're God's gift to me in place of my son.

CLAUDIA: What am I gonna do?

ABUELA: The only thing you can do, *mihija*, is remember.

(The town carries in Felina, on a pillow arrayed with flowers. They all go to the cemetery. They place her on the family plot, with a feast.)

(End of scene)

END OF PLAY

ILLUMINATING VERONICA

Rogelio Martinez

ABOUT THE AUTHOR

Rogelio Martinez was born in Sancti-Spíritus, Cuba, and came to this country in 1980 on the Mariel boatlift. His work has been developed and presented at South Coast Repertory, Manhattan Theater Club, Oregon Shakespeare Festival, Mark Taper Forum, the Group Theater in Seattle, the Playwrights' Collective, INTAR, Lincoln Center Director's Lab, and the Flea Theater. Mr Martinez is currently under commission to write a new play for South Coast Repertory. His screenplay, *Journey Through Havana*, was commissioned by Fox Searchlight and Goat Cay Productions. WHEN IT'S COCKTAIL TIME IN CUBA, a new play, was part of this year's New Work Now Festival at the Public Theater. Mr Martinez is a graduate of Syracuse University and the Columbia University School of the Arts. He is a member of New Dramatists.

ILLUMINATING VERONICA was first workshopped through H P P in
June 1999. The cast and creative contributors were:

VERONICA . . . . Marissa Chibas
MANUEL . . . . Vic Trevino
ROSARIO . . . . Ivonne Coll
PEPIN . . . . John Vargas
SOFIA . . . . Adriana Sevan
ERNESTO . . . . Joseph Della Sorte

Director . . . . Lisa Portes
Dramaturg . . . . Amy Freed

CHARACTERS & SETTING

VERONICA, *early thirties*
MANUEL, *her husband, thirties*
ROSARIO, *her former maid, fifties*
PEPIN, *Minister of Culture, forties*
SOFIA, *early twenties*
ERNESTO, *seventies*

Place: Havana, Cuba

Time: 1960-1961

ACT ONE

Scene One

(Havana, Cuba. December 1960)

(A room off the entrance to the house. There are several giant bookcases overflowing with books. To the side there is a large window with its curtains pulled closed. The window faces the street.)

(A classical painting hangs on the back wall. The painting is in the rococo style. In it a pair of young lovers find each other alone in a sumptuous flower garden. It is both erotic and frivolous.)

(The centerpiece of the set is a very old chandelier. Probably one of the first models to be powered by electricity.)

(Evening. ROSARIO is standing on a chair trying to dust the chandelier. A piece falls off and breaks. Unaware that ROSARIO is there, VERONICA enters reading a book.)

VERONICA: What are you doing here? Get down immediately.

ROSARIO: I'll go see if Carlito can put it back together.

VERONICA: Carlito left six months ago.

ROSARIO: I forgot.

VERONICA: You don't work here anymore.

ROSARIO: I miss you.

VERONICA: I've invited you over for *café* three times.

ROSARIO: I don't miss your *café*.

VERONICA: Please. Rosario. Get down.

ROSARIO: You can't make me not work.

VERONICA: There's no work for you here. I do all the cleaning now.

ROSARIO: You're not very good at it.

VERONICA: I can't let you do this.

ROSARIO: It's the only thing I'm good at.

VERONICA: No. It's the only thing you know.

ROSARIO: The first day it was brought in it was sparkling clean but your father insisted I get up on a chair and dust it anyway.

VERONICA: Get down. I want to show you something.

ROSARIO: You're not going to frighten me as you did when you were a child.

VERONICA: No. Look what I have. *(She shows* ROSARIO *the book.)* Lenin!

ROSARIO: AHHHHHHHH!

VERONICA: What's wrong?

ROSARIO: It's because of that bald headed communist I don't work here anymore.

VERONICA: Doesn't Lenin look like Yul Brynner. I'm in love with him.

ROSARIO: Oh, please.

VERONICA: The two of them together. Passion and intellect.

ROSARIO: Impossible to find that mix in a man.

VERONICA: Fidel!

ROSARIO: Too hairy. What are you doing?

*(*VERONICA *is up on a chair dusting the chandelier.)*

ROSARIO: What if you fall?

VERONICA: I'll get up again. Sometimes I think you're ridiculous.

(Pause)

ROSARIO: You're pregnant.

VERONICA: How did you know?

*(*ROSARIO *smiles.)*

ROSARIO: Take advantage of it. Use it as an excuse to lie down whenever you get a chance.

VERONICA: For someone who's worked her whole life you sometimes say lazy things.

ROSARIO: You're not dusting very well.

VERONICA: Read the book.

ROSARIO: I can't. I don't know how.

VERONICA: Of course you can.

ROSARIO: What is it exactly?

VERONICA: Letters from Lenin to Gorky.

ROSARIO: You read anything nowadays.

VERONICA: Are you reading?

ROSARIO: I'm trying to.

(VERONICA *gets down from the chair.*)

ROSARIO: The floor is dirty.

VERONICA: Stop walking with your head down. There's a lot more going on than dirty floors.

ROSARIO: You need me.

VERONICA: Yes. As a friend.

ROSARIO: No. You can't live without me. Do you get lost when you leave the house?

VERONICA: I try not to go anywhere.

ROSARIO: You were raised to have me always at your side.

VERONICA: The other day I was gone for four hours. My husband had to go and find me. I was three blocks away but I didn't know how to get back.

ROSARIO: You have to ask directions.

VERONICA: I don't know east from west.

ROSARIO: Just have them point.

VERONICA: Havana seems so purposeful nowadays. Everyone is walking with a purpose. I don't want to get in the way.

ROSARIO: If I was still working for you you would have no problems.

VERONICA: It's for the best.

(ROSARIO *looks around the room.*)

ROSARIO: I can't believe I lived here once. This was my home.

VERONICA: You can come back any time you want but as a friend.

ROSARIO: You can't let this house fall apart.

VERONICA: I won't. I've watched you my whole life. I know how to take care of this house.

ROSARIO: If your father could see you now he'd fall over and die. You never picked up a broom in your life and now you even wash clothes.

VERONICA: I didn't know washing clothes could be so fulfilling.

ROSARIO: I didn't know it either until Fidel told us it was.

VERONICA: Are you reading?

ROSARIO: I told you. I don't know how.

(VERONICA *grabs the book from* ROSARIO.)

VERONICA: "Without work and without struggle, book knowledge of communism is absolutely worthless, for it would continue the old separation of theory and practice."

ROSARIO: Lenin is criticizing you.

(*She has returned to dusting.*)

VERONICA: Yes. I was society but not anymore. Here. Let me dust.

(VERONICA *gets up on the chair almost knocking* ROSARIO *over.*)

ROSARIO: Is there anything you want me to do?

VERONICA: Just sit and watch me work as I used to watch you work.

ROSARIO: You'd fall asleep.

VERONICA: And when I woke up everything would be new again.

ROSARIO: That's why you don't know what you're doing. You never stayed awake long enough to learn.

VERONICA: My eyes are open now. (*She works.*)

ROSARIO: It's hard to go home every night. I liked living here.

VERONICA: It's only normal to go home to your own family.

ROSARIO: When you take care of another family your whole life your own family forgets you.

VERONICA: How is your husband?

ROSARIO: He has a girlfriend. Petuca is her name.

VERONICA: Have you told him you know?

ROSARIO: She cooks almost every night. And we all—like a family. I sit at one end of the table, Petuca at the other and he between us. In the center.

VERONICA: That's terrible.

ROSARIO: Petuca is very polite. She even does his wash. There was a time girlfriends had sex with other woman's husbands while the wife stayed home and cooked and cleaned. Now all that is unclear. Petuca not only has sex with him but does his laundry as well. That's a revolution for you.

VERONICA: You get along with her?

ROSARIO: It's not her fault that she's half my age and prettier.

VERONICA: You're very pretty.

ROSARIO: When you look at me you only see the past.

VERONICA: I used to want to look like you when I was young. I thought you were the most glamorous woman I knew.

ROSARIO: I was the maid.

VERONICA: You did it with such flair.

ROSARIO: Now I work in a tobacco factory with hundreds of other women. I miss your father. I miss working for him. I miss running this house. Now I'm just a cog in a wheel.

VERONICA: But what a wheel!

ROSARIO: What?

VERONICA: Communism.

ROSARIO: Your father is in Miami making another maid feel special.

VERONICA: Do you still have sex with your husband.

ROSARIO: VERONICA!

VERONICA: I don't know how you can put up with not having him there. I demand it every night.

ROSARIO: Silly.

VERONICA: No. No. It's true. The revolution has given us the right to demand sex from our husbands.

ROSARIO: As long as you're young.

VERONICA: That will change.

ROSARIO: No.

VERONICA: It will. Even if I have to go up to Fidel and tell him about it. He understands our place in this society.

ROSARIO: In bed or in the kitchen.

VERONICA: You're hopelessly cynical.

ROSARIO: I've lived through too many promises.

(VERONICA *reads from the book.*)

VERONICA: This is Fourier.

ROSARIO: Who is he?

VERONICA: Very important man. "In any given society the degree of woman's emancipation is the natural measure of the general emancipation." One of these days I'm going to throw out my father's old books and replace them with books like this.

ROSARIO: It's just words in a book.

VERONICA: Fidel reads all the time. He's probably already read this one. If only you could read. Communism can't thrive under cynicism.

ROSARIO: Veronica—

VERONICA: Have your husband's girlfriend read it to you.

ROSARIO: Will it get me back my husband?

VERONICA: It will teach both of you how to survive without him.

ROSARIO: I already do.

(MANUEL *enters carrying a stack of books.*)

MANUEL: Rosario.

VERONICA: About time.

(VERONICA *is still standing on the chair.* MANUEL *walks over to her.*)

MANUEL: I can see up your skirt.

ROSARIO: Oh, how long it's been since a man has wanted to look up my skirt.

MANUEL: So much promise under this skirt.

VERONICA: Naughty.

(VERONICA *kisses her husband. Some of the books drop to the ground. All three get on the floor and begin to pick them up.*)

ROSARIO: All these books—

MANUEL: I have a lot of work.

ROSARIO: I should go.

VERONICA: Why don't you come with us on Saturday.

ROSARIO: Where?

VERONICA: Didn't you see Fidel on T V asking for help?

ROSARIO: When I see him I turn the sound down.

VERONICA: How do you understand him?

ROSARIO: If he doesn't make sense with it down then it isn't important.

VERONICA: I turn the sound down when Manuel is sleeping and I understand everything Fidel says.

ROSARIO: You allow your wife to watch Fidel while she's in bed.

MANUEL: I'm there next to her.

ROSARIO: But her eyes are not on you.

VERONICA: Oh, nonsense. Fidel says the Yankees will attack at any moment. I want to be ready.

ROSARIO: Good night.

VERONICA: Are you coming on Saturday?

ROSARIO: Where?

MANUEL: To help cut cane.

VERONICA: Fidel's counting on all of us.

ROSARIO: You're going too?

VERONICA: Yes. I have Papi's old machete.

ROSARIO: You can't lift that old thing.

VERONICA: I do already. Every night before I fall asleep I lift it several times—and when I wake up it's the first thing I do. Whenever I can steal a moment I practice my machete swing. Do you want to see?

ROSARIO: I should go.

VERONICA: No. Stay. Have dinner with us.

ROSARIO: I have to be loyal to my husband's girlfriend. She gets very angry when I don't come home for dinner. I'll come by tomorrow after work. I'll walk you around the block and show you where you live.

(The two women kiss and ROSARIO *exits.)*

MANUEL: You have to let go.

VERONICA: What do you mean?

MANUEL: She wanted to go home.

VERONICA: I hadn't seen her in months.

MANUEL: And you think you're friends?

VERONICA: The best of friends.

MANUEL: She worked for you.

VERONICA: We can't be friends?

MANUEL: No.

VERONICA: I let you marry me and you were a bellboy in my father's hotel.

MANUEL: That's different.

VERONICA: How?

MANUEL: Love.

VERONICA: Yes. It does complicate things. *(She kisses him.)* What happened today?

MANUEL: Later.

VERONICA: No. I want to know now. I've waited all day for you to come home. What's it like out there.

MANUEL: Everyone has—importance. I go to work and everyone around me is running around doing their own thing—but with a goal. All of us have the same goal. Survival. Of course there are terrible things too.

VERONICA: Like what?

MANUEL: They shot several men today.

VERONICA: What?

MANUEL: At the stadium. All of us in the office went during lunch.

VERONICA: You saw the men shot? What was it like?

MANUEL: We booed and yelled and ate our lunch. Ordinary and extraordinary —

VERONICA: No. What was it like when they—BANG! *(She laughs.)*

MANUEL: I closed my eyes.

VERONICA: Oh, what good are you!

MANUEL: I'll keep them open next time.

VERONICA: There isn't going to be a next time.

MANUEL: Yes. The day after tomorrow.

VERONICA: Can I go?

MANUEL: Of course not. I don't want you having nightmares afterwards. *(He notices the broken glass.)* What happened?

VERONICA: I broke it.

MANUEL: Everything is falling apart. I should take it down before it falls on top of us.

VERONICA: It's part of my family.

MANUEL: Where are they now?

VERONICA: That's not the point.

MANUEL: They left you and the chandelier.

VERONICA: Not for lack of trying. If my father could have stuffed it in his suitcase he would have taken it with him.

(He kisses her.)

VERONICA: Longer.

(He kisses her longer.)

VERONICA: No. This. I want you to grow it longer. *(She grabs his beard.)*

MANUEL: You don't like the way I look.

VERONICA: It's too short.

MANUEL: I'm not doing this because of Fidel.

VERONICA: That's what all the men say.

MANUEL: I want—

(*She kisses him again. Slowly she reaches into his pocket and takes out a letter.*)

VERONICA: What is this?

MANUEL: Why are you always sneaking into my pockets?

VERONICA: How else can I find out what you're hiding from me.

MANUEL: I was going to show you.

(*She looks at the letter.*)

VERONICA: From my father.

MANUEL: Yes.

VERONICA: You read it.

MANUEL: I didn't think you'd mind.

VERONICA: I like to open my own letters.

MANUEL: It was already open. Someone brought it by work.

VERONICA: I don't understand.

MANUEL: They have their eye on you.

VERONICA: Who?

MANUEL: The secret police. It's nothing to worry about—

VERONICA: They read the letter?

MANUEL: Yes.

VERONICA: Why?

MANUEL: It's from your father in Miami. Telling you how life there is—he has a new Cadillac.

VERONICA: As if that's what life is. (*She reads the letter.*)

(*Pause*)

MANUEL: That's not the first letter you've received.

VERONICA: I don't write back.

MANUEL: They can't understand why you stayed. Your whole family—all your friends left.

VERONICA: I was married.

MANUEL: You married me after.

VERONICA: I want to be part of this.

MANUEL: They don't trust you.

VERONICA: Why?

MANUEL: They think you're a spy.

(She laughs.)

MANUEL: Everyone is spying on everyone else. The C I A and the K G B are here. A cigar Fidel gave away exploded. If he had lit it himself—you do see their point.

VERONICA: No. I don't. Do you?

MANUEL: I'm just trying to make you understand.

VERONICA: Understand what?

MANUEL: You don't belong here.

VERONICA: Where do I belong?

MANUEL: With your father.

VERONICA: Do you think that?

MANUEL: It doesn't matter what I think.

VERONICA: It does. To me it does. *(She takes out a check.)*

MANUEL: A thousand dollars. Every month the check gets fatter.

VERONICA: When will he draw the line between sentiment and his wallet. The man puts a price on everything. *(She puts the check in a little box on one of the bookshelves.)*

MANUEL: You're not going to cash it. What if we need the money—

VERONICA: I like to remember why I stayed.

MANUEL: With the babies on their way—

VERONICA: Tell me everything that happened to you today—and start with the executions. *(She laughs and he kisses her.)*

MANUEL: If you were a spy I'd still love you.

VERONICA: A spy. *(She laughs.)* If Fidel walked through that door I'd still choose you.

(They kiss.)

MANUEL: I have good news.

VERONICA: You do?

MANUEL: I have all sorts of news, Veronica.

VERONICA: Good.

MANUEL: How are the babies? Can they take the shock.

VERONICA: They're tough. Just like their mother.

MANUEL: When are you going to stop acting as if you can do everything?

VERONICA: When you finally realize I can.

MANUEL: Do you want to hear the news or not?

VERONICA: YES!

MANUEL: The Minister of Culture himself—I didn't think he knew me—shakes my hand and tells me my work is exceptional.

VERONICA: Really.

MANUEL: We get talking. About baseball mostly. How the Yankees just lost the World Series to the Pirates. He thinks they should come here during the off-season and have Fidel work with them. Of course all the time I'm shaking my head Yes! Yes! I want a promotion. And as he turns to go he tells me there's a chance—more than a chance I'm going to get promoted to the archival department.

VERONICA: What will you do there?

MANUEL: I will no longer be just a lowly censor. No. My job will be to go through all the books published in the last fifty years and put them in a socialist context.

VERONICA: Rewrite them?

MANUEL: If necessary.

VERONICA: All the books—

MANUEL: Every single one of them. It's a long term project.

VERONICA: Oh.

(MANUEL *walks over to the stack of books he carried in.*)

MANUEL: The whole lot of them—counterrevolutionary! My reports have to be in by the end of the week. You take half.

VERONICA: I can't wait to get started.

MANUEL: We're going to have to spend extra time going over the ones you read.

VERONICA: I always find everything that's counterrevolutionary in them.

MANUEL: I don't want them to find out.

VERONICA: That your wife is intelligent.

MANUEL: That she does half my work.

VERONICA: I'd do so well there.

MANUEL: I know.

VERONICA: How many women work there?

MANUEL: Three. Four.

VERONICA: What do they do?

MANUEL: One is a secretary.

VERONICA: And the others?

MANUEL: I'm not sure what they do. We have so many people on the payroll.

VERONICA: Fidel is going to put an end to all that.

MANUEL: Corruption.

VERONICA: Having women sit home and watch life pass them by.
He wants us to participate in the experiment.

MANUEL: What experiment?

VERONICA: Communism. That's how he referred to it on the radio this morning.

MANUEL: As an experiment?

VERONICA: Yes. He wants women to work. Rosario works in a tobacco factory.

MANUEL: She worked before the Revolution.

VERONICA: Are you saying I can't?

MANUEL: You'll have your hands full with the twins.

VERONICA: I want a job at the Ministry of Culture with you.

MANUEL: It doesn't happen overnight.

VERONICA: Have you asked him about it?

MANUEL: I'm going to. As soon as I get this.

(She looks at one of the books.)

VERONICA: Proust.

MANUEL: Oh, yes. A new translation.

VERONICA: I loved Proust growing up. All the talk about madeleines. I had Rosario make me madeleines one afternoon. But they didn't taste the way Proust told me they would—

MANUEL: I never read him.

(She puts down the book and walks over to one of the bookshelves. She gets a book.)

VERONICA: Here it is. Volume One. I must have read this same section over and over again.

MANUEL: You have a copy of it?

VERONICA: My father's copy. He gave it to me when I turned fifteen.
(She reads.) "As soon as I had recognized the taste of the piece of madeleine soaked in her decoction of lime-blossom..." I can't read on. Let's have madeleines tonight.

MANUEL: I don't even know what they are.

VERONICA: All of a sudden I miss home.

MANUEL: You are home.

VERONICA: Yes. I know. Isn't that silly.

(MANUEL is looking at the book.)

MANUEL: *Remembrance of Things Past.*

VERONICA: Yes.

MANUEL: This one's easy. The title alone is counterrevolutionary.

VERONICA: Why?

MANUEL: The past is not worth remembering. All the injustice and favoritism—all that is in the past. We can't stop to think about it when we're making our own way in the world.

(VERONICA is reading the book.)

VERONICA: He writes with beauty and grace.

MANUEL: And uses too many words. Look at this. There are two more volumes. No three. FOUR! Why wasn't this man stopped.

VERONICA: Let's have madeleines tonight and forever after ban him from Havana. If that's what Fidel wants.

MANUEL: Good.

(VERONICA puts her copy of Proust back on the bookshelf.)

MANUEL: Veronica?

VERONICA: What?

MANUEL: Why was Rosario here today?

VERONICA: She thinks this is her home.

MANUEL: You don't know what side people are on.

VERONICA: You're paranoid.

MANUEL: I'm not.

VERONICA: Then why do you keep a knife by our bed?

MANUEL: I know how much it excites you to think I protect you.

VERONICA: They're teaching women how to fire AK-47s. That's more exciting than a knife.

MANUEL: Alright. I wasn't going to show you this.

VERONICA: What?

MANUEL: Shh. *(He takes out a handgun from his bag.)*

VERONICA: My God.

MANUEL: They gave it to us at work today.

VERONICA: They did.

MANUEL: We've already practiced with them.

VERONICA: Why?

MANUEL: They want everyone prepared for an American attack. I was the best shot. There's already rumors at work that I fought with Fidel.

VERONICA: You did fight.

MANUEL: I never met Fidel.

VERONICA: It doesn't matter. When you told me that I knew you were the man for me.

MANUEL: Most women shy away from violence.

VERONICA: There are all types of violence.

MANUEL: You're reading again.

VERONICA: How do you know?

MANUEL: What you just said. Dogmatic—something Marx would say.

VERONICA: Marx is not dogmatic.

MANUEL: Boring.

VERONICA: He dazzles me.

MANUEL: I've left you alone all day and I come home and you can't stop talking. *(He puts the gun away.)*

VERONICA: I read all day. I want you to know I'm not wasting my time.

MANUEL: I want to take a bath before dinner.

VERONICA: Alright.

MANUEL: Then after dinner to work.

VERONICA: Yes. We'll get started immediately after dinner.

MANUEL: Good.

VERONICA: Thank you.

MANUEL: Why?

VERONICA: I don't know. I suddenly felt like saying that.

(He kisses her.)

VERONICA: Sweet.

(Suddenly an air raid siren is heard. They panic.)

MANUEL: Get the lights. *(He looks outside.)*

VERONICA: Do you see anything?

MANUEL: All the lights are out.

VERONICA: Hurry.

(The lights are off. The siren is still heard.)

VERONICA: Are they bombing us? Get under here.

(They get under a table.)

MANUEL: Do you think getting under this table will protect us from Yankee bombs.

VERONICA: This is what Fidel tells us to do. I saw him demonstrate it on T V. He got right under the table and took his gun out—

MANUEL: I don't want you to watch so much television.

VERONICA: Why not?

MANUEL: It seems all that's on is Fidel.

VERONICA: That's all I'm interested in.

MANUEL: Maybe you should switch the channel next time he's on.

VERONICA: When Fidel comes on both stations carry him.

MANUEL: Then just turn it off.

VERONICA: Was that a bomb?

MANUEL: No. Are you listening to me?

VERONICA: Are they bombing us yet? Take out your gun, Manuel.

MANUEL: No.

(She takes the gun from the bag.)

MANUEL: You don't know what you're doing.

VERONICA: Point. And shoot.

MANUEL: Put it down.

VERONICA: I just want you to know. I have the courage to follow through with things. *(She puts the gun down.)*

MANUEL: I bet it's a false alarm.

VERONICA: The lights are out.

MANUEL: Yes.

VERONICA: Maybe you want to make love to me.

MANUEL: It's a false alarm every day.

(Pause)

VERONICA: I want color.

MANUEL: What?

VERONICA: I want color television, Manuel.

MANUEL: That doesn't exist.

VERONICA: Nixon showed one to the Russians a couple of years ago.

MANUEL: You're going to believe Richard Nixon.

VERONICA: My father has one in Miami.

MANUEL: Then maybe that's where you belong.

VERONICA: You must get one for me.

MANUEL: I'll try.

VERONICA: Promise me.

(The siren stops.)

MANUEL: Another false alarm.

(Blackout)

Scene Two

(Two weeks later. PEPIN, *in a military uniform, is on stage. His back is to us. He studies the bookcase.)*

(After a moment VERONICA *enters and offers* PEPIN *a glass of rum.)*

VERONICA: There you are. My husband will be back soon. Would you like to sit.

PEPIN: I don't have much time.

VERONICA: You're early.

PEPIN: Yes. My timing isn't always the best. I hope it's alright. *(He drinks.)* Thank you, Mrs Santiago.

VERONICA: Veronica.

PEPIN: Mrs Santiago if it's alright.

VERONICA: No one ever calls me that anymore.

PEPIN: I have a hundred and eighty men working for me. Half of them are married. I can't remember the names of all their first wives.

VERONICA: What?

PEPIN: Sorry. The first names of all their wives.

VERONICA: Is my husband taking on another wife?

PEPIN: You'd be the last to know.

VERONICA: I'm locked up in here all day.

PEPIN: Then you must get out more often, Mrs Santiago. At least to find out what your husband is doing.

VERONICA: I was hoping we'd become friends and you'd tell me.

PEPIN: A snitch.

VERONICA: A spy. It's more romantic.

PEPIN: Your spy.

VERONICA: Yes. Every woman should have one.

PEPIN: You don't trust your husband.

VERONICA: Fidel says we must keep alert at all times and have our eyes wide open.

PEPIN: For Yankee imperialism not adultery.

VERONICA: Adultery is alright?

PEPIN: It has its virtues. There are other things you should be worried about, Mrs Santiago.

VERONICA: I don't understand.

PEPIN: The United States possesses weapons that can wipe us out of existence. When you put adultery next to that you see just how small your concerns are.

VERONICA: Yes. Small.

PEPIN: Tiny.

VERONICA: Would you like more rum?

PEPIN: No.

VERONICA: I didn't expect you in uniform.

PEPIN: I have trouble taking it off. It commands such respect. Just got this little red star the other day.

VERONICA: What did you do to get it?

PEPIN: I saved Fidel's life when we fought together in the Sierra.

VERONICA: You did?

PEPIN: He thinks I did. During the war it was my job to sneak around at night breaking into bookstores and stealing for him. He is a very serious reader.

VERONICA: I thought you were about to say.

PEPIN: What?

VERONICA: Never mind.

PEPIN: What?

VERONICA: That Fidel is a very serious thief.

PEPIN: Yes. He is that too.

VERONICA: He is?

PEPIN: A thief with a conscience.

VERONICA: Certainly an ideology to back up robbery.

PEPIN: You can look at it that way.

VERONICA: I don't.

PEPIN: Good.

VERONICA: You go from a thief to Minister of Culture.

PEPIN: I was very good at it. I left little I O Us for the merchants.

VERONICA: Did Fidel pay them back?

PEPIN: Yes. He became president.

(She smiles.)

(Pause)

VERONICA: I like your uniform.

PEPIN: Most women do.

VERONICA: I didn't—

PEPIN: Of course not, Mrs Santiago. It comes easy to you.

VERONICA: What?

PEPIN: Flattery. You were taught to make strangers feel welcomed.

VERONICA: Yes.

PEPIN: Whores are taught a similar skill. Of course they take it to a different conclusion—or not so different.

VERONICA: My husband—

PEPIN: I'm making you uncomfortable.

VERONICA: No. I'm quite familiar with the word whore.

PEPIN: You are?

VERONICA: It appears several times in the Communist Manifesto.

PEPIN: Yes. It does. *(Pause)* My children love the uniform. They can't believe it's daddy wearing it. I raise my voice and they do everything I ask them to do. My own barracks. Even my wife falls into line.

VERONICA: Do you wear it to bed?

PEPIN: As a matter of fact I often do—only out of alertness. When the Yankees attack all I will have to do is jump out of bed and—

VERONICA: Go steal books.

PEPIN: I'm quite useless really. When will they figure that out. *(Pause)* You're pregnant.

VERONICA: Two months. Maybe when they get in trouble my husband can borrow your uniform.

PEPIN: They?

VERONICA: Twins.

PEPIN: Isn't it too early to tell.

VERONICA: I broke an egg and there were two yokes in it.

PEPIN: Superstition.

VERONICA: Knowledge passed down from generation to generation.

PEPIN: Congratulations.

VERONICA: I have names picked out for them. Fidel and Che.

PEPIN: What if they're girls?

VERONICA: Girls?

PEPIN: Yes. No one thinks of girls.

VERONICA: You do.

PEPIN: I have a couple of my own.

VERONICA: Fidel and Che. It doesn't matter what they are. They're communists.

PEPIN: You know that for a fact.

VERONICA: Why are you surprised?

PEPIN: They're not even out of the womb and they're communists. It took Fidel almost thirty four years to admit he was one.

VERONICA: The world moves at a different pace.

PEPIN: How do you keep up? You no longer have three servants to help you.

VERONICA: I do with less. How did you know that?

PEPIN: When your husband went to work for us we did an extensive background check.

VERONICA: I stayed.

PEPIN: Yes.

(Pause)

VERONICA: I don't know where he is.

PEPIN: What?

VERONICA: What's taking him so long. He should be here.

PEPIN: It's not six yet. I'm early.

VERONICA: He just stepped out. He was extremely excited. He thinks— I shouldn't say this.

PEPIN: What?

VERONICA: Did he get the promotion?

PEPIN: That's between your husband and me. Did he say where he was going?

VERONICA: No.

PEPIN: I can't stay long. That's why I dropped by early. Maybe I should do this later.

VERONICA: I'm sure if you wait five more minutes.

PEPIN: You love your husband very much.

VERONICA: Yes.

PEPIN: I'll give you five more minutes.

VERONICA: He'll be happy you waited.

PEPIN: I want to make you happy.

VERONICA: Would you like more rum?

PEPIN: Just five more minutes.

(Pause)

(PEPIN studies the painting.)

VERONICA: Do you like it? It belongs to my aunt.

PEPIN: I suppose she is in Miami.

VERONICA: Yes.

PEPIN: It's too bad she didn't take the painting with her.

VERONICA: She tried. The *milicianos* at the airport thought it was a work of art. They sent me back home with it.

PEPIN: So it hangs proudly in your house. Lenin says, "It is not enough for revolution that the exploited should demand changes; what is required for revolution is that the exploiters should not be able to live and rule in the old way."

VERONICA: I'm sorry it has such an effect on you.

PEPIN: My advice is to take it down.

VERONICA: Why?

PEPIN: It will only get you in trouble.

VERONICA: It's art according to the *milicianos* at the airport.

PEPIN: They have no taste—what's left of Yankee influence.

VERONICA: And you do?

PEPIN: I don't have to. I read Marx.

VERONICA: What are you saying?

PEPIN: Everything must have a purpose, Mrs Santiago.

VERONICA: Love.

PEPIN: Romantic love. They are obsessed with each other.

VERONICA: Is that wrong?

PEPIN: Obsession put to such a frivolous purpose is always wrong.

VERONICA: When is obsession right?

PEPIN: Whenever it's directed toward myself because I am not a frivolous man and therefore know what to do with such affection.

VERONICA: You do believe in romantic love?

PEPIN: No. I believe in making the most out of what's thrown my way.

(She laughs.)

VERONICA: It's just a painting.

PEPIN: With very little use in revolutionary society.

VERONICA: The end of romance.

PEPIN: The end of sentimentality, Mrs Santiago. Art is secondary to purpose.

VERONICA: I'll take it down. Will you help me?

PEPIN: Of course.

(They take the painting down.)

VERONICA: I'm so lucky.

PEPIN: Why?

VERONICA: The Minister of Culture is redecorating my house.

*(*PEPIN *takes out a knife.)*

PEPIN: I've had this knife since I was five. I used to carve my name on everything. This need of mine.

VERONICA: What?

PEPIN: To mark where I've been. *(He gives her the knife.)* Go ahead.

VERONICA: What happens when she returns.

PEPIN: Your aunt?

VERONICA: Yes.

PEPIN: Why would she return?

VERONICA: They say —

PEPIN: Who?

VERONICA: My father says this won't last.

PEPIN: And you believe him?

VERONICA: No.

PEPIN: You're afraid to destroy the painting because you think they're going to march back in.

VERONICA: I didn't say that.

PEPIN: You can't live in two worlds.

VERONICA: I need to sit down.

PEPIN: Are you alright.

(She sits.)

VERONICA: I don't feel well.

PEPIN: Here. Have a glass of water.

VERONICA: Thank you.

PEPIN: Can I—

VERONICA: Do you ever get—do you ever remember things from your past. Things you had forgotten. Like a painting has the—to remember what you were like.
It happens sometimes when I'm alone. I go into my older sister's room— she has this little music box that I open and Schumann plays. And just as it gets—I think she's going to walk through the door. I wait and I wait but she never comes back.

PEPIN: She isn't returning.

VERONICA: I've spent my whole life in this house. Do you think they have similar memories?

PEPIN: Who?

VERONICA: My family. Do they remember? It takes a hundred and eighty-six steps from my room to the front of the house. I just did that again the other day. Do they remember that?

PEPIN: Find yourself something else to do than count steps from your room to the front of the house.

VERONICA: I'm trying to.

(Pause)

PEPIN: Your husband is about to come back.

VERONICA: Maybe you should go.

PEPIN: I have bad news for him.

VERONICA: You can't—

PEPIN: He didn't get the promotion.

VERONICA: Why?

PEPIN: I didn't think he was trustworthy enough.

VERONICA: He is.

PEPIN: My concern has more to do with you. A wife can have the wrong kind of influence on her husband.

VERONICA: I want this more than anything.

PEPIN: I don't think you have any idea what you want.

VERONICA: You don't know me.

PEPIN: I'll break the news to him tomorrow. It's best I do it at work. I was curious to see you with my own eyes.

VERONICA: Curious?

PEPIN: He hasn't brought you by work. No one knew what you looked like. *(He gets up to go.)*

VERONICA: Don't go.

PEPIN: Mrs Santiago. *(He is eye to eye with her. He kisses her.)* That kiss just now proves to me there's a revolutionary in you just aching to get out.

VERONICA: What are you doing?

PEPIN: You can't live in two worlds.

VERONICA: What do you mean?

PEPIN: Lenin, Mrs Santiago.

VERONICA: Lenin?

PEPIN: "It is not enough for revolution that the exploited should demand changes; what is required for revolution is that the exploiters should not be able to live and rule in the old way."

VERONICA: I love my husband.

PEPIN: You can't have revolution under the values taught to you by your father.

VERONICA: What do you want?

PEPIN: For you to prove to me that you can let go of everything you come from.

(She cuts the painting with the knife.)

VERONICA: Is that enough?

PEPIN: That and more. *(He gently takes the knife from her hand.)* It is your decision to make.

VERONICA: What?

PEPIN: Whether he gets the promotion or not. I'll stand by your decision, Mrs Santiago.

(He exits. VERONICA is restless. She looks out the window to see if anybody was looking at her. She closes the curtains. ROSARIO enters. VERONICA jumps.)

ROSARIO: The door was open.

VERONICA: You scared me.

ROSARIO: I have good news. I came straight here to tell you.

VERONICA: You saw a man on your way in?

ROSARIO: No.

VERONICA: Of course you did. What did he say?

ROSARIO: There was no one.

VERONICA: I think you should go.

ROSARIO: AS OF NEXT WEEK I'M YOUR NEIGHBOR.

VERONICA: What?

ROSARIO: I'm moving into Mrs Busto's home just down the block.

VERONICA: And where is she going?

ROSARIO: Veronica.

VERONICA: What?

ROSARIO: She is in jail.

VERONICA: It's her house.

ROSARIO: I thought you'd be happy for me.

VERONICA: This is not your neighborhood.

ROSARIO: I've lived here almost half my life.

VERONICA: Working for my father. Not the same thing, Rosario.

ROSARIO: Too good for me?

VERONICA: It's not your house.

(Pause)

ROSARIO: They warned me about you.

VERONICA: Who?

ROSARIO: The secret police.

VERONICA: What are you doing talking to them?

ROSARIO: I'm in charge of this block. I work for them.

VERONICA: You do?

ROSARIO: I spy on everybody. I report the comings and goings of the entire block.

VERONICA: You already do that. Everybody knows you're the biggest gossip around.

ROSARIO: Fidel has raised gossip to the level of national security. It is my responsibility to gossip. I love the job. It's called the Committee to Defend the Revolution.

VERONICA: Why wouldn't they let me do that.

ROSARIO: They don't trust you. Look at how you live. There is enough room here for three families.

VERONICA: What do they want? For me to give it away.

ROSARIO: They can make you do that.

VERONICA: They can?

ROSARIO: Yes.

VERONICA: I was born in this house.

ROSARIO: You're too sentimentally attached.

VERONICA: To what?

ROSARIO: To the way things used to be.

VERONICA: You know that's not true.

ROSARIO: Your head is in those books but everything else—the rest of you is somewhere else.

(Pause)

VERONICA: I'm happy for you.

ROSARIO: You're not.

VERONICA: I will be.

ROSARIO: You've always wanted me close by. I will protect you.

VERONICA: From what? I don't understand.

ROSARIO: I know everything. From the kitchen to the bedroom. I know all the women who are having affairs.

VERONICA: You do?

ROSARIO: The secret police showed me photographs. I knew the moneyed classes were kinky but I wasn't prepared for what I saw.

VERONICA: What?

ROSARIO: This little block is jumping with secret rendezvous and lies—who knew there were that many different uses for a four post bed.
And that's as much as I'll tell you.

VERONICA: Did you ever have an affair?

ROSARIO: Everyone did. There was no television and reading could only get you so far.

VERONICA: I didn't think women did that back then.

ROSARIO: The men couldn't do it all by themselves.

VERONICA: I was told today that I have to be an adulteress to be truly revolutionary.

ROSARIO: I know the Revolution wants to take credit for everything but adultery was part of Cuba long before Fidel.

VERONICA: A woman like myself would never have done that years ago.

ROSARIO: You don't know anything about human character.

VERONICA: I guess I don't.

ROSARIO: Are you going to?

VERONICA: You'd be the first to find out.

ROSARIO: Yes.

VERONICA: Are you having one now?

ROSARIO: I've tried three times but men no longer want to commit to anything. They want it over and done with before any sentiment is involved. And besides I don't have time. I work all day and clean all night. The women who have time are women like you—the old bourgeoisie—who still haven't gone to work.

VERONICA: I've never heard you use that word before.

ROSARIO: What word?

VERONICA: The B word. Bourgeo—it's not a nice word when you use it to refer to me.

ROSARIO: It's the truth.

VERONICA: You don't always have to tell the truth.

ROSARIO: I do now that I work for the government.

VERONICA: Why are you doing this?

ROSARIO: You have faith, Veronica. When you were little and you prayed in church I was jealous of you because I really thought you were talking to God. The way you squeezed your eyes shut and put your little hands together. All your life you've had faith. It makes no difference to you whether it's Fidel or God. Or whoever will come along after him. Don't you understand? I get to be first in line. I've never had a chance to be first in line.

(MANUEL *enters with a bottle of champagne. He pops it.*)

MANUEL: Here we are. (*He gives glasses to his wife and* ROSARIO.)

ROSARIO: What are we celebrating?

MANUEL: Yes. Tell us the news.

VERONICA: What?

MANUEL: Veronica.

ROSARIO: Oh, forget it. There's plenty to celebrate. Let's just drink.

VERONICA: Why are you looking at me like that?

ROSARIO: Champagne at six in the afternoon. What a life we're headed for. Can I have some more.

(*He pours her some more.* MANUEL *stares at his wife.*)

MANUEL: A few blocks down I ran into Pepin.

VERONICA: Pepin?

MANUEL: He was just here. The man who had rum in my house— who told me how much he liked you.

VERONICA: He did?

MANUEL: He went on about how gracious and kind you were— how comfortable you made him feel.

VERONICA: It was the rum that made him comfortable.

ROSARIO: Can I have some more? I feel great.

MANUEL: Anyway he started to walk away—I asked. I had to know. Did I get the promotion? He said, "Ask your wife". And with that he was on his way again.

VERONICA: He said to ask me.

MANUEL: Tell me now. I can't wait any longer.

ROSARIO: Tell him already.

(*Pause*)

MANUEL: What did he say?

VERONICA: He told you I knew.

MANUEL: Why are you making me wait?

VERONICA: Manuel. I'm sorr—

(MANUEL drops the glass accidentally as he grabs his wife.)

MANUEL: JUST TELL ME.

(Pause)

VERONICA: You got it.

(He hugs VERONICA. Then he dances wildly.)

MANUEL: Of course. Of course I got it. Of course. I wanted you to say it—to say the words.

(ROSARIO pours herself another glass of champagne.)

ROSARIO: Congratulations.

MANUEL: Sometimes I don't understand you.

VERONICA: I want to understand myself.

(MANUEL pushes ROSARIO out.)

MANUEL: Take the bottle—the glass. Take it with you. Good night.

ROSARIO: I'll come and see you—

MANUEL: I want to be alone with her.

ROSARIO: Good night.

VERONICA: Rosario. Is there work for me at the tobacco factory?

MANUEL: You don't have to go to work.

ROSARIO: Nothing right now.

VERONICA: I didn't think so. I thought I'd ask.

ROSARIO: I'll let you know.

VERONICA: I've been reading about tobacco.

ROSARIO: You're always reading.

VERONICA: I can't jump into something without having read up on it first.

ROSARIO: You don't need to read books to roll tobacco. *(She exits.)*

MANUEL: Tobacco, Veronica? You don't have to—

VERONICA: I want to.

(MANUEL looks at the painting.)

MANUEL: I can't leave you alone. You tear up the house like a hurt puppy dog.

VERONICA: I didn't like it anymore.

MANUEL: You said it was your favorite.

VERONICA: Oh, well. I fell out of love with it.

MANUEL: You didn't have to tear it with a knife.

VERONICA: Two years ago my father would have bought you that job.

MANUEL: It doesn't work that way anymore.

VERONICA: Oh. How does it work?

MANUEL: Hard work gets you somewhere.

VERONICA: Is that it?

MANUEL: Why are you angry?

VERONICA: I don't know.

MANUEL: You have something on your mind.

VERONICA: Forget it.

MANUEL: You're envious. That I actually can do this without the help—not your father. Or you. Or anyone. On my own.

VERONICA: On your own.

MANUEL: Yes. I know your father is over there starting a business—telling you I'm not any good.

VERONICA: I don't care.

MANUEL: I know you don't—after a while though you start to believe him.

VERONICA: No.

MANUEL: This is the first time I feel I deserve you. *(He walks over to the bookshelf and gets the box with the checks. He rips the first check.)*

VERONICA: What are you doing?

MANUEL: We don't need him.

(He rips a second check. She grabs the box away from him.)

VERONICA: Don't do that.

MANUEL: Why not?

VERONICA: I like to remember.

MANUEL: What kind of man he is?

(She takes the box.)

VERONICA: I'm still a housewife with two kids on the way.

MANUEL: We both wanted—

VERONICA: Did we? Every day I sit at home. In the morning after you go I do the wash. Or clean the silverware. And with the dusting and the mopping it isn't until noon that I realize I'm not going anywhere. That this is it.

MANUEL: What do you want?

VERONICA: To be taken seriously.

MANUEL: I take you seriously.

VERONICA: Why can't you tell them I do half your work? *(Pause)* I'm going to the movies. I haven't left the house all day.

MANUEL: Sure. Let me go wash up—

VERONICA: Alone.

MANUEL: I can call Rosario and see if she'll go with you.

VERONICA: She's no longer my keeper.

MANUEL: I'll let Pepin know you want to work.

VERONICA: Good. I think he is going to start coming around more often.

MANUEL: He said that?

VERONICA: In a way.

MANUEL: I hope you're right. *(Pause)* Veronica. How will you know how to get back?

VERONICA: I'll ask directions. *(She exits.)*

(Blackout)

Scene Three

(A month later)

(There is a picture of Fidel Castro where the painting used to hang. Under it, in block letters, the word Vigilance)

(VERONICA enters nervously. She closes the curtains. She looks back at the picture of Fidel. She walks right up to it.)

VERONICA: I suppose you're going to stare the whole time. I say No. You can't watch us have sex. This is none of your business. Call me old fashioned but I don't like to be watched. *(She turns Fidel's picture over.)*

(PEPIN enters in uniform.)

VERONICA: I don't know why you bother to wear a uniform. You're just going to take it off.

PEPIN: Formality.

VERONICA: For this?

PEPIN: I imagine a day when we just talk.

VERONICA: You do?

PEPIN: Yes. I walk in and we sit drinking *café* and chatting about politics. My uniform doesn't always have to come off.

VERONICA: Let me go make some *café* then.

PEPIN: I said I imagine a day. I left it open for the possibility of us having something other than sex.

VERONICA: Not today.

PEPIN: No. I'm afraid today the uniform comes off.

VERONICA: When then? When I'm old and gray. When you've moved on.

PEPIN: You have a lot of questions for me.

VERONICA: You have no answers.

PEPIN: I can't think until after sex.

VERONICA: Is that what you tell your employees at work.

PEPIN: They wouldn't understand.

VERONICA: My husband would. He tells me the same thing. Then he falls asleep afterwards and never lets me in on the thinking.

PEPIN: What do you want?

VERONICA: I'm almost three months pregnant.

PEPIN: Yes.

VERONICA: My mother warned me if I had sex after three months the children would have psychological problems.

PEPIN: Why?

VERONICA: All that bumping and banging—the children would feel unwanted.

PEPIN: Luckily this is a scientific age we are living in. Your mother was wrong. *(Pause)* We haven't had a conversation like this since we first met.

VERONICA: No.

PEPIN: I come in. The curtains are either closed or you close them. And then.

VERONICA: I woke up wanting to talk.

PEPIN: Talk to your husband.

VERONICA: He works now more than ever. I guess he has to take up the slack now that his boss comes over to his house and screws his wife.

PEPIN: This conversation is not going the way I expected it to go.

VERONICA: You didn't expect a conversation.

PEPIN: Should we just give up and try again next Tuesday.

VERONICA: You wouldn't be able to think for an entire week. It would paralyze the Ministry of Culture. The country would have no culture for an entire week just because I didn't lie back and do my duty.

PEPIN: Good bye, Mrs Santiago.

VERONICA: In the throes of passion you call me Veronica.

PEPIN: This isn't exactly the throes of passion.

VERONICA: You can't stand the fact you're having sex with someone like me.

PEPIN: What?

VERONICA: Old society.

PEPIN: Why do you say that?

VERONICA: You don't even look at me afterwards. You can't stand me.

PEPIN: You're reading too much into my selfishness in bed. You're not the first one to complain. I'll come around next Tuesday.

VERONICA: I'm not the kind of woman the communists want to see have sex with their Minister of Culture. For one thing I always light your cigarette afterwards and then I get up and get you a shot of rum.

PEPIN: So?

VERONICA: I'm still bound to my sex.

PEPIN: Yes. You are.

VERONICA: I don't want to be. That's why I want to come work—

PEPIN: What?

VERONICA: I want a job at the Ministry.

PEPIN: You do?

VERONICA: Yes. Hasn't my husband told you?

PEPIN: I see you more than I see him.

VERONICA: He tells me he asks you every day.

PEPIN: You shouldn't believe everything your husband tells you.

VERONICA: Are you sure he hasn't asked you?

PEPIN: Yes.

VERONICA: I'm asking you now.

PEPIN: I have to consider this.

VERONICA: What's there to consider?

PEPIN: No more Tuesdays I suppose. This would have to end.

VERONICA: You're not taking me seriously.

PEPIN: The Ministry is not the right place for you.

VERONICA: I want to work. Just to have someone let me work.

PEPIN: You wouldn't feel comfortable.

VERONICA: You promised this would free me. All it did was get my husband a job. I am still home. Waiting.

PEPIN: Listen to me. You're going to wait a long time. The truth is that you're neither of this society nor the last.

VERONICA: What are you going to do with me?

PEPIN: I should go.

VERONICA: What's going to happen to me?

PEPIN: Society evolves. Every day there are fewer of you.

VERONICA: You're going to watch me rot in this house—some kind of punishment for crimes I didn't commit.

PEPIN: This is not a bad house to rot in.

VERONICA: This isn't even my house. Everything in it belongs to my father. Is it too much to ask to be taken seriously? Papi thought it was. Then I read Marx and quickly learned everything Papi had taught me was wrong. Submission. Grace. Weakness. They were nothing but antiquated beliefs. Now there are new ideas. Fulfillment. Equality. Strength. Ideas that have taken hold of me. That have filled me. And I don't ever see me letting them go.

PEPIN: You have really missed the point.

VERONICA: I don't understand.

PEPIN: You have made this Revolution all about yourself. What you want. What you need. Do you really want to understand Marx? There is only one question you have to ask yourself. What purpose do I serve? (*He turns to go.*)

VERONICA: I do half of my husband's work

PEPIN: What?

VERONICA: I do—

PEPIN: Before you say another word understand that I will have to react accordingly. You don't want to do this to your husband.

VERONICA: He lied to me.

PEPIN: Don't destroy both your lives. He's your only connection to this new society—the only one keeping you alive around here.

VERONICA: I don't care.

PEPIN: Mrs Santiago, let me just walk away.

VERONICA: You think he has the intellect to understand this society. Not a chance. My husband is not smart enough. Or cruel enough to send artists away—to censor literature. To do what needs to be done. I can be cruel, Pepin. It's just that up to now I've used my husband to do it. Do you want me to be cruel.

PEPIN: I asked you not to tell me the truth. I like you. I liked coming here. You had one purpose in this revolution. You've just betrayed your only purpose.

VERONICA: I'm coming to work with you.

(PEPIN *opens the curtains and the window. For the first time in the play the outside world is heard.*)

PEPIN: When we fuck it always feels like the middle of the night. Then I go out into the day and I'm thrown off. Particularly on a day like today. As I walk down the street people salute me. They don't know I'm just a bureaucrat. They think I'm some soldier who fought some terrible war and deserves all these little gold stars and honors. When I leave your house I feel complete. And I walk out into the street and I think they're saluting me for just having fucked you. As if this house has remained impenetrable to them until now. I guess that's what a revolution is. Opening doors. Walking in and doing whatever the hell you want. (*He begins to kiss her in front of the window.*)

VERONICA: What are you doing?

PEPIN: When they stormed the Winter Palace they had dinner with silverware so heavy it made their hands sore.

(*She backs away.*)

VERONICA: Not in front of the window. (*She begins to undo her dress.*)

PEPIN: No. I don't want that. I've already had that.

VERONICA: What?

PEPIN: I asked you to stop. (*He goes over to the bookshelf and looks at the books.*) Proust.

VERONICA: Yes. It's my father's—what are you going to do?

PEPIN: You want adventure. You're going to get real adventure.
(He throws books out as—)

(Lights fade to black)

END OF ACT ONE

ACT TWO

Scene One

(Three months later. Late April 1961. After the Bay of Pigs)

(All the books are gone. The chandelier has been taken down, put to one side, and covered with a white sheet.)

(A very pregnant VERONICA *is looking out the window.* MANUEL *sits to one side.)*

MANUEL: Is that them?

VERONICA: No. Another army truck.

MANUEL: I've seen so many these past two weeks.

VERONICA: I feel protected.

MANUEL: Do you?

VERONICA: Yes. If the Yankees attack again I'm going down to the beach with your gun and I'm going to start shooting them as they come off the boat.

MANUEL: They wouldn't let you near the beach. We're in trouble, Veronica.

VERONICA: They still need volunteers.

MANUEL: Not us.

VERONICA: Why not?

MANUEL: I lost my job.

VERONICA: Lots of people lose their job.

MANUEL: They found counterrevolutionary books in my house. It was my job to ban those books.

VERONICA: It was all a misunderstanding. I think that's them.

MANUEL: Now we have strangers moving in with us.

VERONICA: Go help them with their luggage.

*(*MANUEL *goes to the window.)*

MANUEL: They got here on their own.

VERONICA: Go.

MANUEL: They took away my gun.

VERONICA: They did?

MANUEL: They asked me to come in last week—they wanted the gun.

VERONICA: Why?

MANUEL: After the Yankee attack they are cracking down on everyone they suspect. *(He exits.)*

(After a moment he returns followed by SOFIA *and* ERNESTO.*)*

VERONICA: *Compañeros! (She embraces* SOFIA *and* ERNESTO.*)* Welcome. How was your trip?

SOFIA: Rotten.

VERONICA: I'm sorry.

*(*SOFIA *looks around the room.)*

SOFIA: But worth it. This is our house now?

MANUEL: Well. It's not all—

ERNESTO: I saw another living room on the way in.

VERONICA: We like this room because it faces the street. Less private but more light.

ERNESTO: Enough rooms to get lost in.

MANUEL: The house is not all yours.

ERNESTO: I know.

*(*MANUEL *takes out a blueprint.)*

MANUEL: I think we should look at the blueprint they sent us.

VERONICA: Let me make *café.*

MANUEL: Let's get this settled first.

SOFIA: There's no need to hurry. We're not going anywhere. I do love the neighborhood.

(They are all looking at the blueprint. The lights go out.)

SOFIA: Blackouts. How exciting.

MANUEL: Get used to it. *(He gets candles.)*

ERNESTO: Do the lights always go out?

MANUEL: It's been this way for the last two weeks. Almost every hour. They don't know when the Americans will attack again.

VERONICA: Fidel turns off the lights so Yankee planes can't hit their targets.

SOFIA: I didn't know we were moving into a target.

VERONICA: If my father was flying his own plane he'd attack this house first.

(MANUEL *lights a candle.*)

ERNESTO: Your father left?

VERONICA: That surprises you.

ERNESTO: No.

VERONICA: That I stayed.

SOFIA: You were in love.

VERONICA: You're very clever.

MANUEL: What does the map say? I'm tired of holding this. Ahhh.

VERONICA: Hot wax.

MANUEL: Yes.

VERONICA: Too bad.

SOFIA: Do you want me to hold it?

VERONICA: My husband has a lot to make up for. Let him hold it.

(SOFIA *wanders over to the chandelier. She peeks under the white sheet.*)

SOFIA: Like a ghost.

VERONICA: What?

SOFIA: I'm afraid of ghosts. It's so hard to get rid of them.

MANUEL: A glass of water near your bed.

SOFIA: Yes.

MANUEL: Most of the time they're just thirsty.

ERNESTO: Or hungry.

VERONICA: I wouldn't know.

SOFIA: You've never been haunted.

VERONICA: No.

SOFIA: Am I frightening you?

VERONICA: You're a child.

SOFIA: I want to protect you from whatever ghosts might be haunting you.

VERONICA: I told you—

SOFIA: We'll start tomorrow. A glass of water in every room of the house. Why isn't it up?

VERONICA: We were afraid it was going to fall on our heads.

ERNESTO: What happened to all the books?

VERONICA: I threw them out. Who has time to read?

(ERNESTO *points to the map.*)

ERNESTO: These are our rooms.

SOFIA: That's not half the house.

MANUEL: You're not getting half.

VERONICA: This one should be theirs too.

SOFIA: What about those two rooms in the back?

VERONICA: Yours.

ERNESTO: Thank you. You have a very nice home.

MANUEL: It was an order.

SOFIA: Who gets this room?

VERONICA: It's for all of us to share.

SOFIA: Good. I was afraid we weren't going to have a reason to run into each other.

VERONICA: I think everything is clear now. Oh, and that kitchen next to the nursery is yours.

ERNESTO: We don't want any trouble.

VERONICA: Of course not.

(*The lights come back up.*)

VERONICA: There it is. We're not under attack. It would be terrible if on your first night here my father and friends decided to come back and claim their property.

SOFIA: They already tried and they failed.

VERONICA: That's not going to stop them from trying again.

MANUEL: I'll help you bring your bags to your room.

VERONICA: He was a bellboy at my father's hotel.

MANUEL: Yes. I was.

VERONICA: You were very good.

(MANUEL *picks up two suitcases but hurts his back.*)

MANUEL: I don't have the back of a young man.

SOFIA: Have you ever had someone walk on your back?

MANUEL: Intentionally?

SOFIA: I read it in a sex manual. It works for back pain as well. Lie down.

MANUEL: Are you sure?

(*Even before he has time to think about it,* SOFIA *has pushed him to the ground.*)

VERONICA: I'm afraid he's weak. Other women on the block have assured me it's a condition all men go through. I'm not convinced.

ERNESTO: She won't hurt him.

VERONICA: I don't care.

(SOFIA *walks on* MANUEL's *back.*)

MANUEL: Ahhh.

SOFIA: How do you feel?

MANUEL: Better.

SOFIA: You're holding a lot in.

MANUEL: You can tell.

SOFIA: A lot of anger wrapped up in knots.

MANUEL: Yes.

SOFIA: You're angry we're moving in and taking away half your house.

MANUEL: That's enough.

VERONICA: Do you feel better?

MANUEL: You read this in a sex manual?

SOFIA: Actually I don't read. I learned by having it done to me.

ERNESTO: Sofia got in a lot of trouble when she was young.

SOFIA: Life in the provinces.

VERONICA: What about it?

SOFIA: Not much to do.

VERONICA: In Havana there's something to do every minute of the day.

SOFIA: I'm sure of it.

VERONICA: Outside this house there's plenty for you to do.

ERNESTO: Sofia always finds too many things to do.

SOFIA: I'm not dull.

VERONICA: Good. I can use the excitement.

ERNESTO: Is that what you want, Mrs Santiago.

VERONICA: I haven't been excited in a while.

ERNESTO: You have a child on the way—

VERONICA: Twins.

ERNESTO: That's a good deal of excitement.

SOFIA: How many months?

VERONICA: Ask their father he did all the dirty work.

MANUEL: Six.

VERONICA: Seven. Now I'm starting to think it wasn't you that night.

MANUEL: Stop it.

SOFIA: Can I listen to your babies?

VERONICA: I don't think you'll hear anything.

SOFIA: You're happy?

VERONICA: It's going to turn out alright for them.

SOFIA: Has it not turned out alright for you?

VERONICA: I've done fine.

SOFIA: You haven't moved up like we have.

VERONICA: No. I guess if you're looking at it that way—

SOFIA: What other way is there?

VERONICA: I think there's another way.

SOFIA: I can hear kicking. They're restless Cuban boys. I want to be your friend.

VERONICA: You can come watch T V in my side of the house if you'd like.

SOFIA: I would love that.

VERONICA: When my husband is away. It's not color. He promised me color.

MANUEL: I've tried.

SOFIA: Color television.

VERONICA: Yes. Another broken promise.

(ROSARIO *is heard offstage.*)

ROSARIO: Anyone home. *Compañeros.*

(*She enters holding a basket full of mangos.*)

ROSARIO: Welcome, *compañeros.* My name is Rosario Cruz and I am—

MANUEL: The neighborhood spy.

ROSARIO: Fidel's eyes and ears. So he may go to bed at night—and do whatever he does very well I'm sure—and not fear a Yankee surprise attack.

MANUEL: Like the last one.

ROSARIO: Fidel wasn't surprised. Why do you think we won? I'd like to think it was because of people like me.

ERNESTO: I'm Ernesto and this is my granddaughter Sofia.

ROSARIO: The Communist party welcomes you to Havana with open arms.

(She hugs SOFIA.*)*

ROSARIO: Please accept our condolences for the grave loss you have suffered. You are the daughter of martyrs. Their blood rushes through the arteries of our country. They strengthen us through their heroism. Their ultimate sacrifice never to be forgotten.

(She gives SOFIA *the mangos.)*

SOFIA: Thanks.

VERONICA: I'm sorry.

SOFIA: So am I.

ROSARIO: You have arrived at the start of Carnival. The next few days will be very exciting.

SOFIA: Is Carnival still on?

ROSARIO: We have blackouts but Fidel never cancels a party. Go out tonight and have fun.

ERNESTO: She's planning to.

ROSARIO: That basket is a gift from the Housing Authority and Fidel Castro.

MANUEL: Fidel Castro himself. When does he have the time?

ROSARIO: I picked the juiciest, tastiest, most succulent mangoes for you, Sofia. The same ones he would have picked.

*(*ERNESTO *and* MANUEL *pick up the suitcases and exit.)*

VERONICA: My husband does not want you around.

ROSARIO: I didn't cost him his job.

SOFIA: What happened?

ROSARIO: Her husband thinks I got him fired. You should tell him the truth.

SOFIA: No. Definitely not. Men don't know what to do with the truth. They either get really quiet or react violently.

ROSARIO: Women process it first then react violently.

VERONICA: Not all women.

ROSARIO: More and more nowadays. The Revolution has given us an outlet for our anger.

VERONICA: What do you mean?

SOFIA: She's right. I can challenge the authority of the husband.

VERONICA: You're not married.

SOFIA: I've been around enough marriages to know what it's like.

ROSARIO: All the women on the block are no longer afraid of their husbands.

VERONICA: I've never feared Manuel.

(SOFIA *eats a mango.*)

SOFIA: Hmmm. Delicious.

VERONICA: How old are you?

SOFIA: Twenty two.

VERONICA: You talk like you were forty.

SOFIA: I haven't lived a protected life.

VERONICA: You suppose I have.

SOFIA: You trust him.

VERONICA: I don't trust you.

SOFIA: Why are women always willing to trust the husband and never the other woman.

ROSARIO: We all know what we're capable of.

VERONICA: What do you mean?

ROSARIO: If the opportunity arose I'd take it.

VERONICA: What opportunity?

SOFIA: To sleep with Manuel. *(Pause)* I feel like I've been naughty and I'm being sent to my room. *(She takes the rest of the mangos with her. She takes a bite out of the one she has in her hand.)* It does taste just like one Fidel would pick.

(She exits. The two women look at each other. ROSARIO *opens her arms but* VERONICA *walks away.)*

VERONICA: Do you want something to drink?

ROSARIO: You don't have to be polite.

VERONICA: Why are you here?

ROSARIO: To welcome them. Are you scared of me?

VERONICA: You don't come around.

ROSARIO: When the secret police raided your house I thought you'd blame me for it.

VERONICA: The more you stayed away—

ROSARIO: I didn't want them to think I was—

VERONICA: A friend.

ROSARIO: Every day I'd look for an excuse to come in and just as I'd get to the door I'd turn around.

VERONICA: I saw you at the market.

ROSARIO: Yes. I saw you. Those avocados you're picking are not very good.

VERONICA: You look at what I buy.

ROSARIO: Out of my concern for you.

VERONICA: You're spying on me.

ROSARIO: No.

VERONICA: How do you like your work?

ROSARIO: I've sent nineteen people to jail. Even by their standards I'm a success. *(He is standing by the poster of Fidel.)* Everyone on the block has a picture of him up on some wall.

VERONICA: My husband is jealous of him.

ROSARIO: If I were a man I'd be too.

VERONICA: Why?

ROSARIO: Look at his eyes. He makes you believe you're the only one in the room. Men don't know how to do that. They're always looking this way and that.

VERONICA: After the *milicianos* took away the books and Manuel lost his job—I felt I was a liar—a fraud. That he could see that.

ROSARIO: Fidel?

VERONICA: Yes.

ROSARIO: Fidel is blind. You know he needs to use glasses.

VERONICA: Why doesn't he?

ROSARIO: Would the world be in love with him if he did.

VERONICA: I wouldn't care.

ROSARIO: Veronica. In this neighborhood I'm the only one you have to fear and I happen to like you.

VERONICA: I had sex—

ROSARIO: You don't have to.

VERONICA: I had sex with Pepin to get him work.

ROSARIO: That's not the official story.

VERONICA: No one admits to anything anymore. Everyone is afraid of everyone else. Who's working for whom—who's turning who in. Who's a spy. Who isn't. Who's a fool. No. That I know.

ROSARIO: How was he—the Minister of Culture— in bed?

VERONICA: Believe me it had no literary value. It was just sex.

ROSARIO: Awful.

VERONICA: Not that awful.

ROSARIO: Did you like him?

VERONICA: I don't know. My husband was happy—I thought he was. I was expecting to go to work—nothing goes the way you expect it to go.

ROSARIO: No.

(Pause)

VERONICA: How do you like your new home.

ROSARIO: It's good but not the prettiest on the block. It doesn't quite have the—the grandeur of this house. In my house there is no room in the ceiling for a chandelier—how I used to love that chandelier. I want one just like it. I don't know why you took it down. You're letting this house fall apart.

VERONICA: I'm beginning to understand how it all works.

ROSARIO: Do you? I got promoted. I read now. The newspaper—or books. At the tobacco factory. They tell me I have a voice for radio.

VERONICA: You just started taking classes and you already know how to read—

ROSARIO: Of course not. It doesn't make any sense. That's what I'm trying to tell you.

VERONICA: I know.

ROSARIO: I've missed you, Veronica.

VERONICA: I've missed you.

ROSARIO: Why can't we be friends again?

VERONICA: Friends?

ROSARIO: Yes. There was a time we were—

VERONICA: We were never friends. I realize that now.

ROSARIO: I felt close to you.

VERONICA: You felt responsible for me. Not the same thing. Are you willing now to be my friend?

ROSARIO: What about your husband—

VERONICA: It doesn't matter what he thinks.

ROSARIO: I didn't do anything to get you in trouble.

VERONICA: I believe you.

ROSARIO: Good.

VERONICA: Rosario. Will they ever trust me?

ROSARIO: Yes.

VERONICA: How?

ROSARIO: I don't know yet.

VERONICA: I want them to trust me.

(MANUEL enters.)

MANUEL: You can visit them in their side of the house if you want.

ROSARIO: I'll check in on them and then I have to go change for Carnival. This year I'm dancing the mambo with a Soviet engineer on a float constructed completely out of tobacco leaves.

VERONICA: Let's hope your passion doesn't set it on fire.

ROSARIO: No. Let's hope it does. (She exits.)

MANUEL: They're dragging your grandmother's cherry chest out into the patio to make room for their things.

VERONICA: Did you stop them?

MANUEL: The cherry chest has no value to them. Who understands that kind of thing anymore?

VERONICA: Antiques?

MANUEL: Yes.

VERONICA: You certainly didn't when I married you. You wanted to throw it away. At least they want to exile it to the patio.

MANUEL: I've learned the value of things.

VERONICA: You have?

MANUEL: Yes. There is an inherent value to things old. They contain within them years and years of survival.

VERONICA: There is great value in survival.

MANUEL: Yes.

VERONICA: You mean your own survival.

MANUEL: Ours. I don't want them in our side of the house.

VERONICA: She lost her mother and father. You haven't had that kind of loss happen to you.

MANUEL: You understand her?

VERONICA: Yes.

MANUEL: And Rosario? You can't trust anyone.

VERONICA: Can I trust you?

MANUEL: We have to.

VERONICA: What is marriage without trust.

MANUEL: Yes.

VERONICA: I'll go see how they're doing.

MANUEL: Veronica?

VERONICA: Yes?

MANUEL: I can't live here—I want to go.

VERONICA: Where? *(Pause. She laughs.)* Oh, yes, my father would love that. Do you know what they would do to us in Miami? Have you read those letters? They'd take us to the Catholic church to rid us of all communist dogma—exorcise the beast out of us.

MANUEL: I'm serious about this.

VERONICA: You think I'm not.

MANUEL: I work seventy hours a week pouring cement. This isn't what I bought into.

VERONICA: Sacrifice, Manuel.

MANUEL: And there's a man across the street watching us almost every day.

VERONICA: That will pass.

MANUEL: No one thought it would turn out this way. Not even you.

VERONICA: I gave up my family.

MANUEL: I've paid a man. He's agreed to smuggle us out.

VERONICA: What?

MANUEL: Next week—

VERONICA: You have?

MANUEL: Yes.

VERONICA: You didn't tell me—

MANUEL: You would of convinced me not to do it.

VERONICA: You go behind my back—with what money?

MANUEL: Your father's checks.

VERONICA: I never wanted to take that money.

MANUEL: There are strangers moving in.

VERONICA: His money.

MANUEL: I'll pay him back.

VERONICA: Why did you do this?

MANUEL: I lost my job and I can't get—nothing. It's backbreaking work for what—because you read books that tell you life should be a certain way. It isn't, Veronica. I've lived in the real world. You haven't. In here. Locked up with books—theories and ideals and and—this is not what life is.

(VERONICA *sits down.*)

VERONICA: It's already dark.

MANUEL: What?

VERONICA: I never went out after dark. How does my father go from protecting me to leaving me behind?

MANUEL: I don't know.

VERONICA: Right up to the last moment I never thought he'd leave. I've never been very smart about those things.

MANUEL: What?

VERONICA: Judging character.

MANUEL: I had to get us out of here.

VERONICA: I thought you were another man.

MANUEL: I lied only to protect you.

VERONICA: Is that why you didn't ask him.

MANUEL: What?

VERONICA: Pepin. I would have done anything to work.

MANUEL: I know you would have but—

VERONICA: Why didn't you ask him?

MANUEL: I did.

VERONICA: You never did.

MANUEL: Of course—

VERONICA: He said you didn't.

MANUEL: He was lying.

VERONICA: Why would he lie to me?

(Pause)

MANUEL: It's so easy.

VERONICA: Yes. It is.

MANUEL: I don't want to see you go out there and get hurt.

VERONICA: A man's world.

MANUEL: Not your world.

VERONICA: Oh.

MANUEL: Rosario's world. Sofia's.

VERONICA: Yours.

MANUEL: Yes.

VERONICA: What was I going to do here?

MANUEL: You couldn't even find your way home.

VERONICA: All I wanted was for you to show me. Do you understand that everything I valued in you—your politics—if you ever had any real politics—your honesty. Your ideals. All that is gone. Even your looks. I don't find you attractive anymore. You are a fraud.

(Pause)

MANUEL: I didn't want you to work. I had a chance to take care of you. Fully. You were mine.

VERONICA: You are a profoundly naïve man. I had to have sex with Pepin to get you that job.

MANUEL: Why?

VERONICA: Did you really think you could get anything on your own?

MANUEL: While I was working—

VERONICA: Yes. Right here. On our floor. You're standing in the middle of it.

MANUEL: You couldn't even do that well.

VERONICA: That's not why you lost the job.

MANUEL: No?

VERONICA: I told him the truth.

MANUEL: What?

VERONICA: I told Pepin that I did your work—that you weren't smart enough to do it all by yourself.

MANUEL: Why?

VERONICA: You don't know me as well as you think you do.

(MANUEL *sits down.*)

(*Pause*)

(*After a moment several loud explosions are heard.* MANUEL *hits the floor.*)

VERONICA: My father.

MANUEL: Get down.

VERONICA: He's come back.

(MANUEL *pulls a lamp down. It breaks. Semidarkness. Another explosion*)

MANUEL: They're attacking.

(*He gets* VERONICA *down on the floor next to him.*)

VERONICA: Go out there.

MANUEL: No.

VERONICA: Go.

MANUEL: I don't even have a gun.

VERONICA: You said you'd protect—

MANUEL: Stay down.

VERONICA: You weren't afraid—

MANUEL: I am.

VERONICA: Coward.

MANUEL: I can't take this anymore.

(SOFIA *enters. She runs up to the window and looks through the curtains.*)

SOFIA: Come and look.

MANUEL: Get away from the window.

VERONICA: My father—

SOFIA: What are you doing? Get over here.

VERONICA: He's come back.

SOFIA: It's beautiful.

MANUEL: They're shooting at us—

SOFIA: Explosions.

MANUEL: Get down.

SOFIA: It's Carnival! They're lighting fireworks.

MANUEL: What?

SOFIA: They're celebrating.

VERONICA: Oh.

SOFIA: Look at the fireworks.

(VERONICA *looks out the window.*)

VERONICA: Red. And more red. And some more red. The color this year is red.

(VERONICA *goes to exit.* MANUEL *is sitting on the floor.*)

MANUEL: Where are you going?

VERONICA: I always thought that all those books would change the way people think. That people would look at me not as a woman with a wealthy family but as one with no past. That you would look at me not as your wife but as your equal. That all of you would trust I'd find my way home—it might take me hours but I would eventually come home.

(VERONICA *exits. Several more explosions are heard. A carnival is heard outside.*)

SOFIA: Makes my heart pound.

MANUEL: Loud noise.

SOFIA: Anticipation. (*She walks up to him.*) Neutral territory.

MANUEL: What?

SOFIA: This room. Communal. Your wife doesn't trust me.

MANUEL: My wife is a very insecure woman.

SOFIA: She has reason to be.

MANUEL: Why?

SOFIA: She has to make sure a man stays around—not just for her but for the baby.

MANUEL: What do you know about pregnancy?

SOFIA: I've called it quits after three months. The father would not own up. You would, wouldn't you?

MANUEL: Own up. Yes. Of course.

SOFIA: A gentleman.

MANUEL: I take responsibility for my actions.

SOFIA: Sex is not an action one should take responsibility for. It's just an instinct.

MANUEL: I take responsibility for my instincts.

SOFIA: Why? Does the lion feel remorse after killing his prey?

MANUEL: I think it's the lioness that does most of the killing.

SOFIA: I don't know much about wildlife.

MANUEL: You're from the country.

SOFIA: Yes. I was told all the wildlife was here in Havana.

MANUEL: Havana is tame nowadays.

SOFIA: And Carnival?

MANUEL: Just a distraction.

SOFIA: I missed all the fun.

MANUEL: Yes.

SOFIA: B C.

MANUEL: What?

SOFIA: We have an expression in the provinces. B C—Before Castro.

MANUEL: History begins with Fidel.

SOFIA: Yes. I suppose it will end with him as well. *(Pause)* How did you meet Veronica?

MANUEL: I saw her at the hotel one afternoon and followed her home.

SOFIA: And what an impressive home.

MANUEL: Those were impressive times. Everyone was trying to outspend everyone else.

SOFIA: And you were picking up the crumbs until she fell in love with you.

MANUEL: Do you always try to get ahead of the story?

SOFIA: I like finishing other people's thoughts. It comes in handy when you're around people who don't like to speak their mind. I do it for them.

MANUEL: What am I thinking right now?

SOFIA: How can I stop myself from seducing her. What other kinds of thoughts are there? Tell me, Manuel. I heard now all the fun is indoors.

MANUEL: I wouldn't know. I'm married.

SOFIA: Oh, you would know. To tell you the truth I prefer it inside. I'm not much of an exhibitionist. I hate scandal.

MANUEL: Your grandfather seemed to suggest you caused a great deal of scandal where you came from.

SOFIA: I've come to the city for anonymity. You can't do anything in the country without having everyone know about it.

MANUEL: You can't do anything in this country without having Rosario know about it.

SOFIA: She likes me.

MANUEL: It doesn't mean she won't turn you in.

SOFIA: My scandal is of a more private matter.

MANUEL: She doesn't care.

SOFIA: I kissed Rosario in my room.

MANUEL: What are you talking about?

SOFIA: Her lips offered no resistance. It's good to have something on someone. Now I can get on with the business of setting Havana on fire.

MANUEL: This is how it all works now.

SOFIA: Yes.

MANUEL: You have it all figured out. My wife has yet to understand it.

SOFIA: As long as you do.

MANUEL: What do you want?

SOFIA: I haven't made up my mind yet.

MANUEL: About what?

SOFIA: Whether I want you or your wife. I'll let you know when I decide.

MANUEL: My wife is not the kind of woman—

SOFIA: Everything is up for grabs now. It's not the same. Not what you're used to.

(Offstage we hear a sewing machine.)

MANUEL: What is that?

SOFIA: My grandfather found your sewing machine.

MANUEL: It makes a lot of noise. It's very old. Does he sew?

SOFIA: He doesn't. Whenever he's confused he turns it on. It comforts him.

(They listen to the sewing. Lights fade to black)

Scene Two

(A week later)

*(*ERNESTO *and* VERONICA *are on stage drinking* café. *They clink their little cups together.)*

ERNESTO: Are you sure you should be drinking *café*?

VERONICA: The babies like it. Whenever I do I feel them shake and rattle inside me.

ERNESTO: When Sofia was eight months old she used to love for me to dunk her pacifier in my *café*. She couldn't get enough of it. She'd just lie there trying to squeeze as much of the *café* out of it as possible. When she could speak it was a whole different thing—then she'd demand her cup in the morning. That's when it started.

VERONICA: What?

ERNESTO: Her demands. And I gave into every single one of them.

VERONICA: Including moving here?

ERNESTO: You can see that I'm not a happy man.

VERONICA: You didn't live your whole life in a city—it must be difficult.

ERNESTO: She wanted to come live in Havana. Few people have said no to Sofia.

VERONICA: When I was growing up my life was one no after another.

ERNESTO: And now?

VERONICA: I've stopped asking.

ERNESTO: You're an adult.

VERONICA: Thank you. To maturity.

ERNESTO: I'd rather toast to youth.

VERONICA: Youth you toast with wine; maturity with *café*.

(They clink their cups together.)

ERNESTO: You're nervous today.

VERONICA: I see an end to this.

ERNESTO: Your pregnancy.

VERONICA: Yes. That as well.

*(*ROSARIO *enters.)*

ROSARIO: Good morning, *compañeros*.

ERNESTO: Would you like some *café*?

ROSARIO: I can't say no. Is he here?

(VERONICA *takes* ROSARIO *aside.*)

VERONICA: What have I done?

ROSARIO: Where is he?

VERONICA: In the bedroom.

ROSARIO: They're on their way.

VERONICA: Have I done the right thing?

ROSARIO: Yes. Yes.

VERONICA: What is he going to say?

ROSARIO: It doesn't matter.

ERNESTO: *Compañera.*

(ROSARIO *takes a sip of* café. VERONICA *walks over to the curtains and peeks outside.*)

ROSARIO: Mmmm. Put a little zip in my life.

ERNESTO: I make it stronger than most people.

ROSARIO: You do.

ERNESTO: I'm a widower. *Café* is the only excitement I get all day.

ROSARIO: You feel the blood rush all through your body.

ERNESTO: Yes.

ROSARIO: I'm going to make it my business to find you something more exciting.

ERNESTO: A wife?

ROSARIO: Don't be silly. All the women on the block are married. I'm going to find you a mistress.

VERONICA: Rosario.

ROSARIO: I'm trying to make an old man happy.

ERNESTO: I'm old? It has never occurred to me that I'm old. (*He sits in a chair.*)

VERONICA: Do you think I did the right thing?

ROSARIO: You did what was necessary. Whether it's right or wrong—what a silly question. You're a strong woman.

VERONICA: Yes.

ROSARIO: Your father will never accept you as you are.

VERONICA: I know.

ROSARIO: And if your husband left on his own you'd end up in jail. They already think you're a spy.

VERONICA: This is what they want. They're going to have to trust me after this.

ROSARIO: What do you think of Ernesto?

VERONICA: For what?

ROSARIO: Anyone on this block—

VERONICA: I can't think right now.

ROSARIO: Veronica. Do you remember when your father left? At the airport. All of us were there.

VERONICA: Yes. Why?

ROSARIO: You didn't want to kiss him good bye but I gently pushed you forward until you had to.

VERONICA: That kiss is all I have left.

ROSARIO: I want you to kiss your husband good bye so you can get on with your life.

(ERNESTO *has fallen asleep*).

VERONICA: He fell asleep—and so proud of how strong his *café* is.

ROSARIO: Veronica.

VERONICA: He has no idea what's going on.

ROSARIO: It's nice to be old.

VERONICA: Is it?

ROSARIO: Not to have to worry about how it's all going to turn out.

(SOFIA *enters.*)

SOFIA: There's a crowd outside.

VERONICA: It's alright. Everything's going to be alright.

SOFIA: Two men want to have a word with your husband.

VERONICA: Yes. Alright. (*She doesn't move.*)

ROSARIO: Do you want me to go get him?

VERONICA: No. No. Of course. I'll go.

(VERONICA *starts to exit just as* MANUEL *enters.*)

MANUEL: What's going on?

VERONICA: Just go talk to them. I'm sure—

MANUEL: Sofia.

SOFIA: They're holding signs. Yankee lover. Worm.

MANUEL: What have you done?

VERONICA: Nothing.

MANUEL: You told them I wanted to leave.

(She walks up to him.)

VERONICA: I'm always kissing the men I love good bye.

MANUEL: You love me?

(She kisses him.)

MANUEL: Do you have any idea what's going to happen to me?

VERONICA: I think so.

MANUEL: This isn't going to get you what you want. *(He exits.)*

VERONICA: Rosario.

ROSARIO: Yes. *(He exits.)*

(The crowd is heard outside.)

(SOFIA pours herself a cup of café. VERONICA stands quietly.)

(After a few seconds the crowd subsides. ERNESTO wakes up and picks up the newspaper. He reads a moment.)

ERNESTO: This is going to go on for another five years at the very least. It says here—

SOFIA: Stop pretending you know how to read.

ERNESTO: Alright. I heard it on the radio. It's the same news, isn't it?

SOFIA: Put it down.

ERNESTO: Fidel introduced a five year plan. That means he intends it to go on.

VERONICA: The Revolution.

ERNESTO: Yes. There are plans for it to continue.

SOFIA: We can consider it a five year lease on our side of the house.

ERNESTO: A five year stay in the city—away from the country. Away from where I belong.

SOFIA: Don't be so melodramatic. You're old. The old belong wherever there are people willing to take care of them.

VERONICA: You have my father's room. I suppose my two sisters are taking care of him now. When I was young I used to cut across the patio so that Rosario wouldn't see me—right across the patio to his room. I'd wake him up every morning. Then after the kisses and the hugs I'd march back across the patio all sleepy eyed and back to my bed. I felt it was my duty to wake up my father. *(Pause)* My husband will get five years as well. Everyone is getting a five year extension on this life.

ERNESTO: If I make it that long. *(He gets up to go.)* I sleep on the floor out of respect to your father's property—his bed.

VERONICA: You don't have to do that.

ERNESTO: What if he were to come back and find a stranger in his bed?

SOFIA: Goldilocks and the Three Bears. I used to love that story when I was young.

ERNESTO: What did the bears do when they found Goldilocks?

SOFIA: I don't remember. Did they eat her?

VERONICA: That's Little Red Riding Hood.

SOFIA: That was the wolf.

VERONICA: Yes.

ERNESTO: Goldilocks had tasted all three porridges and tested all three beds searching for what she liked best, but I don't know what happened when the bears came home. I imagine they were mad as hell. Wouldn't you be? *(He exits.)*

VERONICA: Isn't it funny how you can forget something that meant so much to you growing up.

SOFIA: Goldilocks.

VERONICA: No. Waking Papi up every morning. Duty. The duty towards my family. I haven't felt that way in a long time.

SOFIA: Do you miss them?

VERONICA: I didn't for a long time. Maybe I should move out. Let someone else live here.

SOFIA: This house is big enough for Fidel's ego.

VERONICA: Yes. Funny thing is growing up I didn't want to be here.

SOFIA: You wanted to move?

VERONICA: I saw a postcard of a town covered in snow. Salt Lake City—Mormon Capital of the World. And I knew that's where I belonged. In all that snow. With the little houses and the chimneys. I ran to my father and told him I wanted to leave. Big mistake.

SOFIA: How old were you?

VERONICA: Five. I told him I wanted to go to a place where everyone walked on clouds. I showed him the postcard. He said it wasn't a cloud they were walking on but water. And I said, Even better. He smiled and took me to a lake, threw me into the water and yelled for me to walk. And as much as I tried I couldn't. At that time my father was incredibly nationalistic. Nothing was better than Cuba and he was going to prove it to me.

SOFIA: He did.

VERONICA: This is it. I either sink or swim.

SOFIA: You swam.

VERONICA: My father must be senile. He now believes in things he once told me were false.

SOFIA: Senility runs in families.

VERONICA: It does?

SOFIA: Unfortunately. Every morning right after I wake up I go through all the names of the men whose life I've ruined. I test my memory with a list I have—I'm already trying to ward off the effects of old age.

VERONICA: Your grandfather seems in good enough health.

SOFIA: He couldn't remember what happened to Goldilocks.

VERONICA: None of us could.

SOFIA: I know. We're all in trouble.

(VERONICA *turns to go.*)

SOFIA: I told your husband you were planning to turn him in.

VERONICA: How did you know?

SOFIA: Rosario.

VERONICA: Then why didn't he run away?

SOFIA: He didn't believe me.

VERONICA: You can't dismiss gossip in this country. It will kill you.

SOFIA: He's not coming back.

VERONICA: I know. Do you think—

SOFIA: What?

VERONICA: Do you think it's enough for them?

SOFIA: The secret police?

VERONICA: Yes.

SOFIA: They won't leave you alone forever.

VERONICA: Next time around it might be you they come for.

SOFIA: They might come for me but they will end up taking you.
I'm not as easy as your husband.

VERONICA: I didn't think you were.

SOFIA: And I thought we could be sisters.

VERONICA: Sisters?

SOFIA: Family. I don't want to give up the chance to have something
genuine.

VERONICA: Thank you but—

SOFIA: The children are going to need an aunt. Let me be their aunt.
My grandfather and I will take you into our family. You can even take
our last name if you'd like.

VERONICA: Why would I want to do that?

SOFIA: I'm giving you a chance to take our name—we were the ones Fidel
fought for—we're the ones who are going to get what we want.

VERONICA: And politics.

SOFIA: Something you read in a book.

(VERONICA *walks over to the window.*)

VERONICA: He's still there.

SOFIA: Who?

VERONICA: The man watching the house.

SOFIA: Did you really think turning in your husband would make him
disappear. Nobody trusts you. It's your choice. The house doesn't have
to be divided by this room.

(ERNESTO *enters.*)

ERNESTO: I couldn't fall asleep thinking about Goldilocks. Finally I
remembered what happened. In fact no one knows what happened to
Goldilocks. The story ends with her jumping out the window and whether
she broke her neck or got lost in the woods or maybe even made it out of
the woods, nobody knows. All that's certain is the three bears never saw her
again. *(Blackout)*

Scene Three

(Five months later)

(PEPIN is on stage no longer in uniform. He peeks under the white sheet to look at the chandelier. There are a few books on the bookshelves. After a moment VERONICA enters.)

PEPIN: I let myself in.

VERONICA: Haven't you always.

PEPIN: You knew I would come.

VERONICA: I can't say I'm surprised.

(He looks at the chandelier.)

PEPIN: Beautiful.

VERONICA: That old thing.

PEPIN: There's nothing in the law that says we don't accept beauty.

VERONICA: What do you mean?

PEPIN: Put it up. Let it light the room.

VERONICA: People will talk.

PEPIN: Yes. It's hard to get past pettiness.

VERONICA: You didn't come here to tell me that.

PEPIN: No. Obviously not. I see you're reading once again.

VERONICA: Yes. Trying to build up a library. Marx. Engels. Lenin. No Proust.

PEPIN: Anything interesting?

VERONICA: It used to be you who would quote me Lenin.

PEPIN: I'm ready to listen.

VERONICA: Alright. Marx says, "Our bourgeois, not content with having the wives and daughters of their proletarians at their disposal, not to speak of common prostitutes, take the greatest pleasure in seducing each other's wives."

PEPIN: Marx said that?

VERONICA: It seems Marx would consider you bourgeois.

PEPIN: You're taking it out of context, Veronica.

VERONICA: That's what this whole thing is. Taking an idea that is pure and corrupting it until it gets you what you want.

PEPIN: That has to change.

VERONICA: Would you like something to drink?

PEPIN: You're hopelessly polite.

VERONICA: I've learned to poison drinks.

PEPIN: Then I'll pass.

VERONICA: It's quite easy really. All you need is trust.

PEPIN: What?

VERONICA: The trust of the person you're poisoning.

PEPIN: Trust is so hard to come by nowadays.

VERONICA: I heard rum is even harder to come by.

PEPIN: Vodka?

VERONICA: Don't care for it.

PEPIN: I adapt.

VERONICA: I try to.

PEPIN: I should compliment you.

VERONICA: On what?

PEPIN: Triplets.

VERONICA: Yes. I was expecting twins.

PEPIN: I know. What did you name the third one? I remember you said Fidel and Che, but you didn't expect a third one.

VERONICA: I named him Ernesto.

PEPIN: Do the three of them get along?

VERONICA: What do you think? Fidel is pushy in the crib. They fight a lot. Three boys are tough.

PEPIN: Daughters would be more difficult. I have two.

VERONICA: Why do you think that is?

PEPIN: It's easier to break their heart.

VERONICA: I see that the Revolution hasn't made you any less sexist.

PEPIN: Tolerance is an acquired taste.

VERONICA: Like vodka.

PEPIN: Vodka goes down smoother.

VERONICA: I have—

PEPIN: Yes?

(*Pause*)

VERONICA: I should get back to them. If I don't keep my eye on them they're liable to start their own revolution.

PEPIN: With more success than this one I hope.

VERONICA: What do you mean?

PEPIN: I'm sorry that your husband had to go to jail.

VERONICA: Don't start with the apologies—my children will be grown men by the time you finish.

PEPIN: I just want to tell you I feel responsible for what happened.

VERONICA: Is that all?

PEPIN: No. Obviously not. Your application for work at the Ministry found its way to my desk. You impressed a lot of people.

VERONICA: I changed my name.

PEPIN: Yes. The address looked familiar. I drove by and I put it all together.

VERONICA: I wanted to work doing what I thought I was good at.

PEPIN: Did you think you could get a job at the Ministry without me finding out?

VERONICA: I wanted to see you again.

PEPIN: You could have come to my office.

VERONICA: I wanted you to come here.

PEPIN: Why?

VERONICA: I wanted you to see that you couldn't stop me.

PEPIN: I know.

VERONICA: Life around here continues.

PEPIN: I know that.

VERONICA: Why did this have to happen? I was on your side.

PEPIN: I couldn't accept that.

VERONICA: You didn't have to try and destroy our lives.

PEPIN: We do things with enthusiasm.

VERONICA: I should get back to my children.

PEPIN: I approved you come work for us.

VERONICA: You did?

PEPIN: Part of a Revolution is learning—growing.

VERONICA: I can't believe—really?

PEPIN: Yes. I wanted you to come work for us.

VERONICA: What—what do you mean?

PEPIN: It cost me my job. That among other things. Certainly my involvement with you—I'm afraid neither of us has a job with this government.

VERONICA: I didn't—

PEPIN: They investigated everything—a very thorough investigation. None of us can survive that kind of scrutiny.

VERONICA: You didn't fight back.

PEPIN: No use. I just have to wait.

VERONICA: For what?

PEPIN: We're slowly learning. Once again I'm sorry. We haven't yet learned what to do with those of us who are genuine. It's a lesson we'll have to learn if this is going to work. *(He exits.)*

(VERONICA uncovers the chandelier. She is fascinated by it. It's as if she's looking at it for the first time. SOFIA enters and VERONICA is startled.)

VERONICA: Where are the babies? Did they take the babies? What happened—

SOFIA: Shh. They're asleep.

VERONICA: Oh. I thought—

SOFIA: No one is going to take them away.

VERONICA: I had a nightmare last night. It was so real. The man across the street had come over and taken my babies.

SOFIA: Mariano. I found out his name.

VERONICA: The man across the street.

SOFIA: He has a name. Mariano. I flirt with him every day.

VERONICA: How could you talk to him.

SOFIA: He's harmless really. He doesn't even know why he's standing there. The secret police just told him to look for any suspicious activity. He doesn't know anything about us.

VERONICA: Just another gossip.

SOFIA: Yes.

VERONICA: My grandmother used to watch the neighbors make love from her room.

SOFIA: She did.

VERONICA: She watched everything they did.

SOFIA: Your grandmother would have done well working for this government.

VERONICA: Not much difference.

SOFIA: When I was walking home from the doctor's yesterday with the babies I caused a great scandal. People thought I was a single mother. They stared at me trying to make me ashamed of myself. Do you think Havana will change?

VERONICA: What do you mean?

SOFIA: That perhaps one day women will be allowed to be women. That we'd get to do what we want.

VERONICA: And I didn't even think you were a revolutionary.

SOFIA: It's so easy.

VERONICA: I don't think so.

SOFIA: No. It is. It's not giving a damn what people think. For now I'll continue to cause scandals.

VERONICA: What is your next scandal?

SOFIA: The seduction of Mariano. He's married so I know the type.

(Crying is heard off stage.)

VERONICA: Is someone trying to take them?

(VERONICA goes to exit, but ERNESTO walks in holding all three babies.)

ERNESTO: I passed quietly by their crib but they heard me and demanded I pick them up.

VERONICA: You give easily into other people's demands.

SOFIA: They need to take their nap.

ERNESTO: I couldn't resist.

SOFIA: They're so cute. Oh, before I forget. Here. *(She takes out a letter.)*

VERONICA: From my father. It's opened.

SOFIA: Mariano read it.

VERONICA: He did.

SOFIA: Did you know he didn't read a sentence till last year and now he's spying on you? If that's not a testament to the success of the Revolution I don't know what is.

ERNESTO: What does it say? Is he coming back? Do we have to move out?

SOFIA: I don't think our half of the house is his anymore.

ERNESTO: He'll get a lawyer and try to claim it.

VERONICA: How could he. He just got up and left.

ERNESTO: What does it say? Is he coming to kick us out?

SOFIA: You can't worry. If he comes back Fidel will kick him out again.

ERNESTO: You put too much faith in Fidel.

VERONICA: Read me the letter, Ernesto.

(She gives ERNESTO the letter. The lights change.)

ERNESTO: "Every day Havana fades so that the streets I played in when I was a child are now alleys. Memory either narrows a place to the point of disappearing or causes it to grow in your imagination. I can tell you that in the memory of most of my friends Havana has grown in scope and stature. They want Havana. I've decided to let go because for me Havana is a house on a quiet street—a house that no longer belongs fully to me. Street by street or room by room they've taken Havana from me. Last night I forgot what you look like and though the thought of forgetting you rattled me a little I soon decided that you were like the house that no longer belonged to me. With love, your Father. P S. This is my last letter to you. I have grown sentimental and I am embarrassed by everything I say or do in respect to Cuba."

(Pause)

VERONICA: I love you, Father.

ERNESTO: Yes.

VERONICA: Do you love me, Father?

ERNESTO: Yes.

VERONICA: With all your heart.

ERNESTO: Yes.

VERONICA: Say it, Father.

ERNESTO: With all my heart.

VERONICA: You are my family.

SOFIA: Of course.

(The babies begin to cry. The lights change back.)

VERONICA: Invite him in for *café*.

SOFIA: Who?

VERONICA: Mariano from across the street.

SOFIA: I don't know if he can cross the street.

VERONICA: If he can read I'm sure he can cross the street.

SOFIA: I don't know if he's allowed to.

VERONICA: Why not try? Let's have a party.

SOFIA: What are we celebrating?

VERONICA: Let's just have a party. After a while we'll know exactly what we're celebrating.

(VERONICA *plugs in the chandelier. For the first time it's on. A brilliant light covers the entire stage.*)

SOFIA: Beautiful.

VERONICA: Enchanting.

ERNESTO: Like a fantasy.

VERONICA: Yes. It's like that, isn't it.

SOFIA: Warm.

ERNESTO: Let the babies see it.

(*They show the babies the light.*)

VERONICA: The man who wrote that letter and his friends. When they come back we will turn off all the lights and close all our doors and then we will hope they don't recognize their old homes. That they have forgotten them. We will hope they go away.

(*The babies stop crying. Everyone laughs.*)

(*Lights fade to black.*)

END OF PLAY

LANDLOCKED

Cusi Cram

ABOUT THE AUTHOR

Cusi Cram is of Bolivian and Scottish descent. She grew up mostly in New York City, but has lived and worked in London, Rome, Greece, and Bolivia. She has written and performed two solo shows, BOLIVIA and EURIPIDAMES, both produced by New Georges. She also co-wrote and performed two shows of absurdist sketch comedy with her sister, Kate Mailer, THE SISTER COLLAGE and THE SISTER COLLAGE RETURNS. Cusi has acted in numerous plays in and out of New York and has been in several independent films, as well as originating the role of Cassie Callison on ONE LIFE TO LIVE. Her other plays include THE END OF IT ALL (a commission from South Coast Rep), LUCY AND THE CONQUEST, THE DIGNITY OF MARTYRS, MARSALA FOR TWO, and DOT SINGS OUT LOUD. Cusi's work has been produced and developed by South Coast Rep, the Williamstown Theater Festival, Naked Angels, the Ensemble Studio Theater, the Miranda Theater, the Women's Project, New Georges, Ubu Rep, Here, P S 122, and at the Dag Hamarskjold Theater at the United Nations. She is the recipient of a Nickelodeon New Brain grant, the Le Comte du Nouy grant from the Lincoln Center Theater Foundation, a playwriting residency at Marymount College and a fellowship from the Lila Acheson Wallace American Playwrights Program at Juilliard. Cusi is a graduate of Brown University. She lives in Greenwich Village with her husband Peter Hirsch.

LANDLOCKED was first workshopped through H P P in June 1998. The cast and creative contributors were:

ANNA . . . . .Svetlana Efremova
REPORTER/CAMILLA . . . . .L Scott Caldwell
CONSTANZA/LINDA . . . . .Kadina Halliday
PIERRE LUIGI . . . . .Richard Coca
ALDO . . . . Mikael Salazar
DR BOB . . . . .Jeff Allin

Director . . . . .Juliette Carrillo
Dramaturg . . . . .José Rivera

LANDLOCKED premiered at the Miranda Theater (Valentina Fratti, Artistic Director) in New York City, opening on 11 November 1999. The cast and creative contributors were:

ANNA .... Helen Wassell
REPORTER/CAMILLA ....Kate Mailer
CONSTANZA/LINDA ....Amy Wilson
PIERRE LUIGI .... Matt Servitto
ALDO ....Michael Port
DR BOB .... Peter Hirsch

Director .... Jim Gaylord
Set .... Warren Karp
Lighting .... Chuck Cameron
Costumes .... Polly Byers
Sound .... Crispin Freeman

CHARACTERS & SETTING

ANNA, *a Swiss German artist*
REPORTER, *a reporter of indefinable European descent*
CONSTANZA, *an art dealer from anywhere who could be any age*
PIERRE LUIGI, *a Bolivian restaurant manager*
ALDO, *an ex-garbage man from Rhode Island*
CAMILLA, *an English sculptor,* ANNA's *sister-in-law*
DR BOB, *an American dentist*
LINDA, *an American underwater archaeologist*

Setting: Zurich, Rome, and an island in Greece

it is always ourselves
we find
in the sea and
the deep blue
dream of sky

e e cummings

Things like to get lost and be
found again by others. Only
human beings love to find themselves....

Yehuda Amichai

for Peter

ACT ONE

Scene One

(Darkness. The sound of ocean waves. Lights fade up to reveal ANNA, *a Swiss-German woman in her late twenties. She has a light Swiss-German accent. The walls of the stage are covered with meticulously ordered garbage, the kind of garbage that could wash up on a beach.)*

ANNA: I collect things. I collect things that wash up on beaches. I collect dolls heads, sea glass, sea shells, rubber boots, wood shaped like arthritic fingers, rusted metal—I am particularly fond of the of the color and texture of rust—and plastic bottles so torn to pieces by waves that they can no longer contain. I recreate these beaches in places far from the sea, Paris, Basil, Vienna, and most recently Zurich. I collect lost things. Lost things feel different in the hand.

(Blackout)

Scene Two

(Darkness. The sound of ocean waves. Lights up on a gallery opening in Zurich. People are milling about looking at the walls covered with the meticulously organized garbage. A reporter approaches ANNA, *she wears large thick, black framed glasses. She has an accent that could be from anywhere.)*

REPORTER: Fabuluous show Anna, fabulous. Are you in contact with other people in the found art movement? You and Peter Specht have a very similar sensibility.

ANNA: I am in contact with very few people. Most of the time I spend at the beaches where I collect lost things. I like the sea, perhaps because I grew up by a lake. If there was a movement of people who grew up by a lake but dreamt always of the sea, I would be part of such a movement. I have never heard of Peter Specht.

REPORTER: Are you espousing an anti-lake platform?

ANNA: What?

REPORTER: Are you against lakes?

ANNA: Of course not.

REPORTER: Well, many of Europe's lakes are filled with rubbish. What exactly is your position on the lakes? (*Getting aggressive*) What about the lakes, Anna?

ANNA: Perhaps I will leave the lakes to Peter Specht. Excuse me, I wish to try some of the hors d'oeuvres.

REPORTER: Are you aware there are plans to start a museum of found objects in Utrecht?

ANNA: I have never been to Utrecht. Right now I feel hungry.

(ANNA *crosses away from the reporter.* ANNA *is intercepted by* CONSTANZA *the gallery owner. She wears a turban. She is from everywhere.*)

CONSTANZA: Anna, Anna, *carissima*, Anna, everyone is saying that you are a *vraiment* genius. I put my thinking cap on, and I have an idea, a *fabuloso* idea. You're gonna flip.

ANNA: Really?

CONSTANZA: You need an agent.

ANNA: Why?

CONSTANZA: Because everyone needs an agent, *amore*. We have to think of a fucking way to sell these beaches. *Scusa mei*, I smell money and I get a dirty mouth.

ANNA: You can't buy a beach. It's one of the reasons I like them.

CONSTANZA: Anna—I want to be your agent, let me be your agent, *leibshein* please.

ANNA: Constanza you don't know anything about being an agent.

CONSTANZA: What's to know, schmooze, schmooze, kiss, kiss, sign on the dotted line, time to go to the bank. I'm a natural.

(PIERRE LUIGI, *a Bolivian man in an Armani suit, stands transfixed in front of a pair of dentures glued to the wall. He looks at them from all sides. He opens and closes his mouth.*)

ANNA: Excuse me.

CONSTANZA: Right, right, circulate, work the room, *leibshein*. I'm going to find someone very important to introduce you to.

(ANNA *crosses toward* PIERRE LUIGI. CONSTANZA *adjusts her turban.* ANNA *tilts her head to one side observing* PIERRE LUIGI *squatting beneath the dentures searching for something.*)

ANNA: Hello.

PIERRE LUIGI: Oh, hello. Very beautiful painting. Not painting, beautiful garbage. I've never seen anything like this. It really speaks to me.

ANNA: And what does it say?

PIERRE LUIGI: It says...that one of these lost things alone you would not even notice—but together they make something beautiful.

ANNA: Interesting.

PIERRE LUIGI: Yes, it is. Do you like the sea?

ANNA: Very much

(PIERRE LUIGI *and* ANNA *stare at each other transfixed.*)

PIERRE LUIGI: Then why are you in Switzerland?

ANNA: I try to leave as much as possible. The mountains give me a headache.

PIERRE LUIGI: Me too. And my country has higher mountains that Switzerland. I am always dizzy there.

ANNA: What country is that?

PIERRE LUIGI: Bolivia, you know Bolivia?

ANNA: I know of it. I've never been there. But I've always been interested in countries that have no coast.

PIERRE LUIGI: Excuse me, I must correct you, it is my duty to correct you. Bolivia once had a coast, not a big one, but once, once my country had a port, a beautiful port. My family is originally from that port, you know the name of that port?

ANNA: No.

PIERRE LUIGI: I will tell you—the name is Antofagasta. My country lost this port in a war with Chile a long time ago in the War of the Pacific. Chile has so much coast, but she must also have my port. There are many songs in my country which speak of this. You know Zulma Yugar?

ANNA: No, I'm afraid I don't.

PIERRE LUIGI: She is like Barbara Streisand, but Bolivian. Zulma sings one song that makes all Bolivians cry—the song is *Busco el Mar*, you never heard it?

ANNA: No.

PIERRE LUIGI: You want me to sing it?

ANNA: Not right now.

PIERRE LUIGI: Of course not. I am just so angry at my country. How can a country loose a coast? Only in Bolivia. *Busco el Mar* means I look for the sea, well you can spend all your life in Bolivia looking for the sea, and you never find it. I come from a family of fisherman.

ANNA: You don't look like a fisherman.

PIERRE LUIGI: No, I manage a fish restaurant.

ANNA: Here in Zurich?

PIERRE LUIGI: No, I live at sea level. I must live at sea level for my health. I came to this exhibition because I woke up queasy, you know? My house is on the beach of Rome, Ostia.

ANNA: You live in Rome?

PIERRE LUIGI: Yes. *La citta eterna.* Of course I would prefer to live on the *spiagga eterna,* the eternal beach, but a job is a job. I am here on business, a conference of seafood restaurants. Can I take you to dinner for fish, or what you prefer.

ANNA: Maybe.

PIERRE LUIGI: You know what, I give you my card, when you come to Rome you will eat plenty of fish.

ANNA: I'm sorry, I never go to Rome.

PIERRE LUIGI: But now you must come. You have a reason that likes you very much.

ANNA: I don't think so.

PIERRE LUIGI: Please take my card. Maybe dinner tonight, I have a beautiful voice.

ANNA: Maybe. Excuse me, someone said the cheese was good.

PIERRE LUIGI: Sure, sure, we chat later. My name is Pierre Luigi. Funny name. French and Italian. But I am from Bolivia. I will tell you the story of my name, maybe later. What's your name?

ANNA: Maybe I will tell you that later too.

(ANNA *crosses away from* PIERRE LUIGI. PIERRE LUIGI *watches her and shakes his head, his attention shifts back to the dentures.* ANNA *is intercepted by* CONSTANZA *who is with* ALDO, *a tall muscular man from Rhode Island.*)

CONSTANZA: There you are, *amore mio.* Look at this big American I found, not bad huh, he loves what you do with garbage. Go on, tell her, big guy. Come on, go, go.

ALDO: Yeah, I guess. I mean, I've never seen anything like it, that's for sure.

CONSTANZA: You two must *charlar, parler,* shoot the shit, so to speak. (*Whispering loudly to* ANNA) Americans always have a little extra *dinero* to spend on a souvenir of their trip, if you know what I mean, *amore mio?*

ANNA: But they're not for sale. And I don't need an agent Constanza.

CONSTANZA: You do, you just don't know it yet.

(CONSTANZA *crosses up stage.* ANNA *and* ALDO *smile politely at one another. A pause.*)

ALDO: Wow. I mean, wow.

ANNA: In response to what?

ALDO: I mean...um these things on the wall. How'd you think them up?

ANNA: Well, I find things and then it's a lot of hard work with an occasional moment of inspiration.

ALDO: Wow. I, well...I didn't think I'd be saying this much. Actually, I thought I came to Switzerland to stop saying this, but I used to work in sanitation.

ANNA: Oh.

ALDO: I was um... a garbage carrier, you know, a garbage man.

ANNA: *(Intrigued)* How interesting.

ALDO: Well, actually it was pretty interesting. So, all this...um...I never thought garbage could be so um...attractive, if that makes sense?

ANNA: Yes it does. I want people to see things that normally they would ignore, throw away even, to see them as something attractive, as you say. I have always been attracted to things we overlook.

ALDO: Wow. I could tell you some stories.

ANNA: Interesting. Are you in Zurich for some time?

ALDO: Oh yeah, I'm not going anywhere.

ANNA: Good. Are you working here also in sanitation?

ALDO: Oh no, that's all behind me. Mostly, I'm skiing. I love the mountains.

ANNA: Well, there are many of them here.

(CONSTANZA *pops her head out.*)

CONSTANZA: Anna come quick. Pronto. There is a very important collector at the cheese table.

ANNA: O K Constanza. Will you excuse me, I believe there is some good *chevre.*

ALDO: Chever?

ANNA: Goat cheese, the soft white one.

ALDO: Oh, it is good, superior. I don't know anything about cheese, but I know what I like. See you later...maybe?

ANNA: Maybe.

(ANNA *crosses away.* ALDO *drains his drink shakes his head.* PIERRE LUIGI *is gingerly trying to remove the dentures from the wall. He pulls, pushes, trying not to be noticed.* ALDO *stands next to* PIERRE LUIGI, *taking in the beauty of the garbage. He notices* PIERRE LUIGI.)

ALDO: Hey, mister, I don't think this is interactive art work. I think you're just supposed to look at it.

PIERRE LUIGI: Please mind your own business.

ALDO: Excuse me, I um...happen to know the artist and I don't think she would appreciate you making off with her work.

PIERRE LUIGI: You could never understand.

ALDO: If you don't stop it. I'm going to have to make you stop.

PIERRE LUIGI: Look, Mr America, something here belongs to me. I hear there is good cheese, perhaps now might be the moment to try it.

ALDO: I'm not trying any cheese.

(PIERRE LUIGI *gives a last tug to the dentures, they fall off. He puts them in his pocket.*)

PIERRE LUIGI: Excuse me, there is a young lady here who was very beautiful and I need to find her to make dinner arrangements.

ALDO: You are not going anywhere. Give me the dentures.

PIERRE LUIGI: No.

ALDO: Give me the dentures, man.

PIERRE LUIGI: No.

ALDO: I am going to make you give me the god damn dentures.

(ALDO *shoves* PIERRE LUIGI. PIERRE LUIGI *shoves* ALDO.)

ALDO: GIVE ME THE TEETH BEFORE I KNOCK THE ONES IN YOUR MOUTH OUT.

PIERRE LUIGI: Impossible!

(ALDO *takes a swing at* PIERRE LUIGI. PIERRE LUIGI *groans and begins to yell loudly.*)

PIERRE LUIGI: I must speak to the artist. Help, I can explain. I MUST SPEAK TO THE ARTIST BEFORE THIS MAN KILLS ME. I AM HONORABLE. I AM AN HONORABLE MAN.

(CONSTANZA *and* ANNA *move toward* ALDO *and* PIERRE LUIGI.)

CONSTANZA: *Che succeso?* Please stop the man screaming please, screaming's not good for selling.

ALDO: This man is trying to steal the art work.

CONSTANZA: O K, Mr Honorable, you have drunk enough of the free wine. I think it's time to say *arrivederci*.

PIERRE LUIGI: I must speak to the artist. I am not stealing.

CONSTANZA: If you don't leave now, you will tell your story to the police, *capice*?

PIERRE LUIGI: I MUST SPEAK TO THE ARTIST!

ANNA: I am the artist.

PIERRE LUIGI: No. Not you?. *Dios Mio*. May I speak to you in private.

ALDO: Give her back the friggin teeth first. He's got the dentures in his pocket.

PIERRE LUIGI: Here. *(He hands her the teeth.)* This is very private matter, you understand ?

ANNA: I'm not sure I do.

ALDO: Be careful. He's a nut job. I know a nut job when I see one.

PIERRE LUIGI: Am I talking to you? No, I am talking to the beautiful artist. This is a matter between the two of us, O K Mister Man?

ANNA: *(To* ALDO*)* Thank you for your help.

CONSTANZA: O K *tout le monde*, everything is peachy. Back to drinking. Look at the pretty pictures. Anna, I have it all under control. No problem. *Bene. Bene. Bene.* Fun. Fun. Fun

(CONSTANZA *and* ALDO *cross away from* PIERRE LUIGI *and* ANNA.)

PIERRE LUIGI: This is difficult for me. Sometimes I feel I have no luck, sometimes I feel I have all the luck.

ANNA: And what do feel now?

PIERRE LUIGI: No luck. I think the life of Pierre Luigi is the hardest in the world and that you cannot escape the curse of a family. My family is known as the unluckiest family in Cochabamba. Tonight, I met woman who is so beautiful and talented and then I must tell her immediately the most painful thing in my life. This is no luck.

ANNA: And what is the most painful thing?

PIERRE LUIGI: Those teeth you are holding are mine.

ANNA: But you have teeth. I noticed them right away.

PIERRE LUIGI: They are not mine, the ones in my mouth now. I mean they belong to me, but they are false, very good no?

ANNA: You do have a strange smile.

PIERRE LUIGI: I know.

ANNA: How do you know these ones are yours?

PIERRE LUIGI: I know, believe me I know. I wish I didn't know. I wish I could take you to a fish dinner, sing for you and never speak of my teeth. Every time I come close to something beautiful, I loose it.

ANNA: How did you lose your teeth?

PIERRE LUIGI: I lost them in the sea on that Greek beach that you also visited. Life is always easy for me at the sea, or so I thought. I have false teeth. I cannot tell you why, not now. It's too much. That day, I ate kalimari, it was not fresh, it was like rubber, my teeth felt a little loose. I took a swim in the sea, it was a day with wind, the water was rough, and a wave hit me in the face and kaput, I loose my teeth. I also lost the woman I loved. She was on the beach. She said she could not love a man without teeth. There is more. Not now. Perhaps in Rome.

ANNA: I'm afraid it won't be in Rome. That is a lost city for me. As lost as your teeth.

PIERRE LUIGI: Perhaps I can help you find it again?

ANNA: I don't think so. But, we could still have dinner tonight. You could sing.

PIERRE LUIGI: You are very kind but I've lost my appetite. I couldn't sing tonight. *(Pause)* May I take the teeth?

ANNA: No. I'm afraid that is not possible.

PIERRE LUIGI: But they have a value of great sentiment for me.

ANNA: Yes of course, but they are very important to the ambiance of that particular beach. In my mind they are the centerpiece. You can have them back after the show closes.

PIERRE LUIGI: All right, I don't want to mess up your beautiful garbage. You make very magical things. I would be grateful for the teeth, I don't actually need them, but they are in my family for some time.

ANNA: Are they from Bolivia?

PIERRE LUIGI: Yes.

ANNA: Wow, Bolivian dentures on a Greek beach. I always hate it when people say the world is small because there is so much of it I will never get to see, but the distances have become shorter. Don't you think? *(Pause)* I've enjoyed talking to you.

PIERRE LUIGI: You know where I am. If you would like to talk more.

ANNA: I like what you said about my work.

PIERRE LUIGI: I meant it. You've got something good going on here. You must keep doing it, no matter what.

ANNA: Really?

PIERRE LUIGI: Yes, really. O K, I go now.

ANNA: Good-bye, Pierre Luigi, I promise to send them.

PIERRE LUIGI: Good-bye.

(PIERRE LUIGI *exits quickly.* ANNA *holds the teeth and looks at them. She shakes her head.* ALDO *approaches her.*)

ALDO: Strange guy, huh?

ANNA: Not really.

ALDO: I'm sorry, I didn't mean to cause a scene or anything.

ANNA: I don't mind. I like scenes. So much of life is avoiding scenes. It is quite a relief when one actually happens.

ALDO: I don't know scenes seem to follow me like flies.

ANNA: I never did get to the cheese.

ALDO: Hungry?

ANNA: Yes.

(*Blackout*)

Scene Three

(ANNA's *studio/apartment later that night.* ANNA *and* ALDO *in bed.* ALDO *sleeps like a baby.* ANNA *sits on the edge of the bed she is awake, but in a dream state.*)

ANNA: Tell me anything. Tell me my teeth are bad, they are. I've smoked since I was twelve. Tell me that you have loved better than this, that all this, the years, the waiting, the tears, the hushed phone calls, the letters, the secrets, the meetings during siesta, the afternoons on your desk, tell me it means nothing. Tell me you don't think about it. Discourage me. Tell me once again that you will never leave her. I am just a diversion. I have diverted you in front of statues, fountains and Renaissance palaces. I go home to stone, and clay and work till my hands ache and I think, I think if I can make something beautiful, you'll stay, you'll stay through the night. Tell me anything. I can't live waiting. Don't promise. Don't speak about the future. Don't call me in the middle of the night. Don't wake me with your voice, that sounds so intimate. It is not intimate. Tell me anything, as long as its bad.

ALDO: Hey Anna, um... you're laughing or crying or something. Are you awake or asleep, or what?

ANNA: I'm not sure.

ALDO: Bad dream.

ANNA: Sort of.

ALDO: Don't you just hate that. Life's hard enough, right?

ANNA: Yes.

ALDO: Well, I feel wide awake.

ANNA: I'm sorry. Would you like a coffee?

ALDO: Why would I want a cup of coffee?

ANNA: Because it's hot, because it is dark, because usually when I'm awake I want a cup of coffee.

ALDO: I don't drink coffee.

ANNA: What a shame. (*She moves to get up.*)

ALDO: It'll keep you up.

ANNA: Exactly. I'll get more rest if I'm awake. *(She exits offstage to make coffee.)*

ALDO: Hey, um, I'm skiing Mount Uetliberg tomorrow, you wouldn't want to come?

ANNA: *(Off-stage)* No I wouldn't.

ALDO: I don't get it. Here you are in this country with the best skiing in the world, and you just met a devil of a skier who would be tickled to get you on skis, and you want to spend all day arranging garbage. *(He gets out of bed and begins to do sit ups.)* Don't get me wrong, I told you that you have an uncanny knack for making garbage look attractive. I might even start investing in art, I like it so much.

ANNA: It's not for sale.

ALDO: How do you get by Anna, if you won't sell?

ANNA: I don't need much. *(She enters.)* What are you doing Aldo?

ALDO: Oh...a set of sit ups. I feel awake. You drink coffee, I usually do sit ups or watch cable T V. No matter how many I do my stomach never gets hard. I want abs of steel, but mine are more like play dough.

ANNA: What is play dough?

ALDO: Something soft. *(He finishes sit ups, comes over to ANNA. He strokes her arm.)* I think I like you.

ANNA: I think I like you too.

ALDO: Give me a reason.

ANNA: Because you have abs of Playdough. Stomachs are not meant to be hard.

ALDO: Hit me again.

ANNA: You have good teeth.

ALDO: I need another one, Anna.

ANNA: Because you were once a garbage man.

ALDO: Those are the strangest reasons I've ever heard. But I like them. The question is do you think you can like me now that I am no longer a garbage man? Kick me, if I'm not living the life of Riley.

ANNA: Why are you living Riley's life and not your own?

ALDO: Because of a startling combination of good and bad luck.

ANNA: What do you mean?

ALDO: Well, Anna I have a knack.

ANNA: A knack?

ALDO: An ability, I have an ability to find things, like you I guess. Only sometimes what I find gets me into trouble.

ANNA: Are you a criminal? A garbage man with a past?

(ANNA *begins to see* ALDO *as a possible canvas for her work. She begins to pick up objects to place on him.*)

ALDO: No, no, of course not. I don't think I am. Not technically speaking. O K. Basically, Rhode Island where I come from, is heavily controlled by the Mafia, the government of Rhode Island is not unlike the government of Italy, except smaller and more corrupt.

ANNA: Is the food as good?

ALDO: My guess is no. So, over the years, doing my rounds I've picked up various , let's call them items, items of trash that belong to the Mafia. Which I really should not have seen, but by chance, fate, or what you will, I did.

ANNA: What kind of items?

ALDO: I think it's better not to be too specific. Let's just call them items.

ANNA: O K.

ALDO: *(He removes stuff from his head and neck.)* Is this stuff clean? It smells funny. So, one day I found a very incriminating item and I felt like I should go to the police, even though I knew that could mean some big trouble for me.

ANNA: What did you find Aldo?

ALDO: Let's just say, it wasn't good, Anna. Let's just say that. So I go home to wash up before going to the police and right inside my door is a brown paper bag with more money than I've seen my whole life and a brief, but to the point note, that said get out of the country fast.

ANNA: Wow.

ALDO: So I did. I figured it was my safest bet. *(Referring to objects)* This is kinda weird.

ANNA: Why Switzerland?

ALDO: Because I could go anywhere. Because Switzerland is clean and uncorrupt, or at least all the corruption takes place in the safety of a nice big bank, which now that I have something to bank, is all right by me. I also love to ski.

ANNA: *(She sculpts ALDO's face.)* Aldo, please tell me what the incriminating item was.

ALDO: *(A little uncomfortable)* A very hairy left arm with a wedding band on the ring finger.

(Blackout)

Scene Four

(A dentist's office in Rome. Lights up on PIERRE LUIGI in a dentist's chair. DR BOB, an American dentist, is looking in PIERRE LUIGI's mouth.)

DR BOB: They look good Pierre Luigi. You say that bully was an American?

(PIERRE LUIGI tries to answer, but cannot. He clenches his fist.)

DR BOB: They are sticking very nicely. That extra-emollient gum seems to do the trick. All in all, I'd say your mouth is a pleasure to behold. And if I don't say so myself, displays some of my finest work to date.

(PIERRE LUIGI still with various dental equipment protruding from his mouth, nods and gurgles in agreement.)

DR BOB: You are welcome, my friend. You were a fascinating case. The most complicated and intricate bridgework I have ever done. If I were back home, you might make the cover of Dental America, but here in Italy these things are not important. The tooth in all its complexity, is not as cherished as in the States. American dentists, Pierre Luigi, are artists in their own right, and don't you forget it.

(PIERRE LUIGI spits and sits up.)

PIERRE LUIGI: I am very thankful to you Dr Bob. These new dentures you make for me remind me of my old teeth. They fit with my face, it's not like I am wearing someone else's smile.

DR BOB: Exactly! I'd like you to buy a rotary brush, Pierre Luigi, with elmo florescence.

PIERRE LUIGI: Yes, of course, Dr Bob. May I ask you a question Dr Bob? Something in confidence.

DR BOB: Pierre Luigi, of course...if it has to do with teeth, I may very well be able to answer it. If its something else, I'm probably less qualified, and most likely won't give you good advice. Shoot!

PIERRE LUIGI: Dr Bob, have you many younger patients who wear dentures?

DR BOB: Not many, but a few. There's the odd accident that knocks a mouth full of teeth out, certain trauma-related incidents. In Italy most commonly auto and Vespa accidents. But in this line of work you see everything. Why do you ask Pierre Luigi?

PIERRE LUIGI: I came to you Dr Bob, so I could forget my past, all the things that happend to me in Bolivia, that brought me to Rome. I spend so much money, but you must pay a lot to forget a past.

DR BOB: Pierre Luigi, my rates are reasonable, perhaps a little higher than the Italian rates, but that all pays for the shipping and handling of American dental products. Now what was it you wanted to ask, I have a complicated root canal at three and I like to focus before I go in.

PIERRE LUIGI: Have you ever had a *colpo di cuore*, Dr Bob, you love someone the second you see them?

DR BOB: Yes.

PIERRE LUIGI: You have?

DR BOB: Yes.

PIERRE LUIGI: Your wife Giuseppina?

DR BOB: Nope.

PIERRE LUIGI: So you know when you have it, something in your heart goes ba-ba-boum.

DR BOB: Ba-ba-boum, yes.

PIERRE LUIGI: Tell me of this love, *Dottore*?

DR BOB: No, not now. Not before a root canal.

PIERRE LUIGI: Maybe one day, I buy you dinner at the restaurant. And you will tell me over fish and wine about your *colpo di cuore*?

DR BOB: I don't know about that.

PIERRE LUIGI: Well, I had ba-ba boum last week.

DR BOB: Really?

PIERRE LUIGI: Yes. I met a woman at an exhibition. She was something else. And the art was something else. It spoke to my soul, Dr Bob. Each wall is covered with garbage from a different beach. And then I notice there is garbage from a beach I spent my vacation on last summer. And then Dr Bob, I see my teeth!

DR BOB: The teeth you lost before you came to me?

PIERRE LUIGI: *Claro que si!* I am thinking! I must find the artist to talk to them or maybe I just take them because they are mine. So I tried to take them and the American man hits me on the mouth and I scream for the artist. And the artist, Dr Bob, is the ba-ba-boum!

DR BOB: Ba-ba-boum found your teeth?

PIERRE LUIGI: Yes. So, I am now in love with someone who already knows my secret. I wanted to leave. I wanted to run, but...

DR BOB: Ba ba boum!

PIERRE LUIGI: Yes, ba-ba-boum. She was very beautiful to me. Perhaps no matter how much money you pay, your past is in your smile. Yes, *dottore*?

DR BOB: I don't know if I'd put it quite like that, not good for business.

PIERRE LUIGI: We were supposed to have dinner, but I was afraid that man did something to my mouth when he punched me. When I first met her I was like O K here we go, but then I felt so afraid of her, Dr Bob, I wanted to run away. But I'm not going to be a wuss anymore. So the question I ask you Dr Bob is, can this woman love me, knowing that all but five teeth in my mouth are from plastic?

DR BOB: Not plastic, Pierre Luigi, a hybrid of cyberplastocine treated at a high temperature....

PIERRE LUIGI: Yes, yes, I told her about my hot plastic teeth. So, can a beautiful woman with a vision, because she has a vision *dottore*, can she love a manager of a fish restaurant with no teeth? Can she?

DR BOB: Easy, easy, hot sauce. Did she seem to like you?

PIERRE LUIGI: Yes.

DR BOB: Did she have a husband?

PIERRE LUIGI: I didn't see one.

DR BOB: Well, it was a ba-ba-boum, right? Not just a ba or a boum?

PIERRE LUIGI: *(Over excited)* Ba-ba boum! Dottore, Ba-ba boum!

DR BOB: Well, I don't see why not. I'm all for people chasing the ba-ba boums! Holding onto them, because they don't happen every day, Pierre Luigi.

PIERRE LUIGI: I have your blessing, you know of teeth, and surprisingly, you know the heart, so you say yes!

DR BOB: Yes! yes! yes! I'll do my best to keep what you got in there! All right, pal?

PIERRE LUIGI: Ba-ba-Boum!

(*Blackout*)

Scene Five

(ANNA *'s studio/ living space.* CAMILLA, *an Englishwoman in her thirties, puts the finishing touches on a clay beetle, she is sculpting. She is* ANNA*'s sister-in-law.*)

CAMILLA: Anna, I've just finished the most hideous dung beetle! You must have a look!

(CAMILLA *finesses the beetle.* ANNA *enters. She is holding a mauled yellow rubber boot and a rusted tin can. She approaches the clay beetle and looks at it from several angles.* CAMILLA *nervously awaits her approval.*)

ANNA: It is very ugly. I congratulate you.

CAMILLA: (*A little disappointed*) Well, I always say, not all of us can make beautiful things. So why not make something truly hideous and scary? Mind you, I get a good price for them at the shop. Tourists somehow think they're very Swiss.

(ANNA *places the boot and can on a large canvas and looks at them.*)

ANNA: You have a knack, Camilla. You married a rich man, and your hobby makes you richer.

CAMILLA: (*A little hurt*) It's not really a hobby is it? I mean if you're geting paid?

ANNA: Of course not. I'm sorry, I didn't mean anything.

CAMILLA: Of course you did. You're right and it irritates me. (*Pause*) We all pay in different ways. Your brother is no picnic in Provence. Ernst is difficult to the core. Rich and difficult. Most rich men are.

ANNA: I never understood my brother.

CAMILLA: The dung beetle's tentacles are very hard to sculpt. They're terribly thin! Ernst was the tidiest man I'd ever seen. I know that doesn't seem like a very romantic thing, but I thought "That man could make me—the unruliest, wildest of wenches—ordered, calm and correct." Oh damn, this tentacle is too thick!

(ANNA *is meticulously moving the boot and can around the canvas, placing them in different areas around the canvas, and removing them as she tries to find the perfect spot.*)

ANNA: What do you think, like this? (*As she moves the boot*) Or like this?

CAMILLA: The first, definitely the first. (*She works for a second and stops suddenly*) Here I am going on about dung beetles and your tidy brother and you haven't said a word about IT.

ANNA: About what?

CAMILLA: The show, your Zurich debut. How was it, darling, tell me everything. Ernst insisted we go on ski weekend which nobody enjoyed. Sorry, the show, you, every last word. I'm silent with anticipation.

ANNA: I think it went well.

CAMILLA: And? And...I need a little more Anna. A morsel

ANNA: People seemed to like it. I was surprised.

CAMILLA: Surprised my foot, of course they liked it, you're oozing talent. My question for you is: are they going to pay you? When is the green going to grow, darling? I hate you living on cous-cous and meusli and tiny government grants.

ANNA: I don't need much. I just want people to see the sea as I see it.

CAMILLA: As a big rubbish bin?

ANNA: No, as a place where everything converges—a place where things are redefined, or as someone at the show said, a place where lost things you would never have noticed come together and are somehow newly beautiful.

CAMILLA: And who said this?

ANNA: Someone.

CAMILLA: Is that the American someone who phoned earlier?

ANNA: No.

CAMILLA: Sometimes, I look at you Anna and I wonder what it must be like to be you. I have no mystery, I'm not an enigma, that's my charm.

ANNA: Yes. Your face is wide open. You don't say anything and I know your thoughts.

CAMILLA: And what am I thinking now?

ANNA: The American—I met him at the show. He used to be a garbage man, he's from Rhode Island. He came to Switzerland to ski and to get away from the mafia.

CAMILLA: How thrilling, Is he lovely and brutish?

ANNA: He has very good teeth. Americans have such big teeth.

CAMILLA: Yes they do, they certainly win out over the English. Most of my family can't even close their mouths, because everything is so crisscrossed and fang-like. Thank god I had an American Grandmum who insisted on teeth braces.

ANNA: I met someone else at the show, but he has no teeth.

CAMILLA: An old man? Maybe a toothless sugar-daddy?

ANNA: He's quite young. He really understood my work. Camilla, it was as if he was explaining it to me. I felt very comfortable with him and terrified at the same time.

CAMILLA: Sounds exciting.

ANNA: Yes and no. Anyway, he lives in Rome. But, I'm not sure I could love a man with no teeth. Is that shallow of me?

CAMILLA: Of course not, darling. But who knows, a toothless Italian could be Mr Right?

ANNA: He's not Italian. He's from Bolivia. He sent a smoked salmon to the gallery yesterday with a note that said, "I am in Rome now, but my heart is swimming upstream to you."

CAMILLA: Ah, a toothless poet, I knew one of those once. You lived in Rome, didn't you?

ANNA: Yes I did. (*Silence*)

CAMILLA: All right, I'll be very English and keep my distance. I can't bear to look at this beetle another second. I have to get back home. The nanny has a bad foot, and she's taking some sort of water therapy at the clinic. I'm off. Dinner Sunday, little Ernie is so fond of you. You bring him such treasures. I often find him with his ear pressed to a seashell you've given him, laughing.

(CAMILLA *kisses* ANNA *and exits.* ANNA *looks at the beetle and picks up a piece of clay. She holds it in her hands for a few seconds, puts it to her cheek and then quickly puts it down.*)

(*Blackout*)

Scene Six

(*Half-lights come up on* ALDO *and* ANNA; ALDO *is sleeping like a baby.* ANNA *sits at the foot of the bed. She is in a dream state.*)

ANNA: I'm leaving. You can't stop me. All day I've been walking, walking on marble steps the Campidoglio, the Spanish steps, up and down, smooth ancient steps. I'm packing. Don't look at me sideways. Don't say you're sorry, because you're not sorry. Along the Pincio, in to Villa Borghese, down the Via Veneto, to Piazza del Tritone. The fountains, all the fountains. I'm taking everything. Everything I taught you to see. Your eyes will be dead and lonely like when I met you. I had never seen such a handsome dead man before. I thought, "Maybe there is something moving in the gray of his eyes". You had forgotten what it was like to laugh with your whole body. You will forget again, because I am leaving this city; this city which persists in living. This city which I love more than you, this city which I'm learning to hate.

(ANNA *snaps out of her trance-sleep.* ALDO *also stirs.*)

ANNA: I'm sorry. I don't know what's happened to me. All I do is wake you up.

ALDO: I can't think of anybody I'd rather have keep me up. Coffee?

ANNA: Sit-ups?

(*Blackout*)

Scene Seven

(*A table in the restaurant* PIERRE LUIGI *manages in Rome.* DR BOB *is sitting with him.*)

PIERRE LUIGI: You ate good fish, Dr Bob?

DR BOB: Yes indeedy, I haven't had such a variety of fish in years.

PIERRE LUIGI: You must remember to floss, Dr Bob.

DR BOB: Right you are, Pierre-Luigi. Usually I carry floss, but this afternoon I felt impetuous. Giuseppina and the kids are visiting their aunt in Frascati. I had a difficult appointment today, the end of a very complicated capping job, a young American woman, an underwater archeologist, lost her two front teeth and four on the upper left; an on the job accident, something involving a large amphora.

PIERRE LUIGI: Ouch. Poor woman, but these things happen all the time.

(DR BOB *nods in agreement*)

PIERRE LUIGI: So, this is where I live, Ostia, the beach of Rome. Not so beautiful, but for me it's O K. I wake up, I smell the sea. Sometimes it smells more like a bathroom. This O K until I am saving up enough to have my own very good fish restaurant.

DR BOB: And where will you have that, Pierre-Luigi? In Bolivia?

PIERRE LUIGI: No, no, Dr Bob. There is no sea in Bolivia. Bolivia lost her coast a hundred-twenty-nine years ago. I will never return to Bolivia until she has her own port. For now, I find the most beautiful beach in Europe and there I make my restaurant.

DR BOB: You certainly are fond of the sea. Well that's good, Pierre Luigi. Every self-respecting man has to have a passion outside of his profession, something that takes his mind off the day to day chores; the strain of bringing home the bacon.

PIERRE LUIGI: And Dr Bob, what is your passion? Maybe a little ba-ba-boum?

DR BOB: I'm a married man, Pierre Luigi. I cherish those vows. My family comes first, before dentistry even.

PIERRE LUIGI: Of course, Dottore, only the other day in your office you said you knew about ba-ba-boums. I asked if it was Giuseppina, your beautiful wife and receptionist. Because I could understand Dr Bob if it was. Giuseppina, *entre nous*, Dr Bob, is a very sexy lady.

DR BOB: Yes she is. She has kept her figure and her teeth intact. She has good genes, and even better gums.

PIERRE LUIGI: So tell me *Dottore*, tell me of your ba-ba-boum. It is Saturday. The restaurant is no busy. We ate fish. We floss later.

DR BOB: Do you like sculpture Pierre Luigi?

PIERRE LUIGI: Yes, *Dottore*. Michelangelo, the Davide, beautiful naked people, what's not to like?

DR BOB: Well, Pierre Luigi, what brought me to Rome in the first place, was a love of sculpture. Now you may find this hard to believe, but as a young man of twenty-two, just having finished college, I wanted to be a sculptor. Now my family, they are just about the sweetest people you ever met, but they are professionals, lawyers, doctors, accountants, one of my uncles is a judge. In Indiana, people just don't lose their head for Italian Baroque sculpture. They are reasonable in Indiana, Pierre Luigi, reasonable to THE POINT OF UNREASONABLENESS. Well, I came over here with my graduation money and looked at sculpture. Mostly I just stared. I was mad for Bernini. He could make marble seem like it was moving. Do you know how hard that is? I would look at his work and weep.

PIERRE LUIGI: Like me and the sea. I cry like a baby.

DR BOB: Yes, infantile, Pierre Luigi, I had an infantile response to the sculpture of the Baroque period. And then I met Giuseppina.

PIERRE LUIGI: This is the part I am waiting for.

DR BOB: She was lovely, just lovely. In bloom. I met her in Piazza Navona. Both of us were staring at the Fountain of the Four Rivers. Well actually, I was staring at the fountain, and Giuseppina was staring at me.

PIERRE LUIGI: *Claro que si!* I bet she was.

DR BOB: Well, she was lively and full of sex appeal—and I left Rome determined to come back, marry Giuseppina, and become a sculptor

PIERRE LUIGI: You devil. This is *muy romantico!*

DR BOB: Well, that's when the romance ended. My family was appalled at both ideas. My mother threatened to throw herself under a train; my father said he would never speak to me again; my grandparents, they just looked confused. And Pierre Luigi, I am not a brave man. My parents' approval, the love of my family, I couldn't turn away from that.

PIERRE LUIGI: This is hard—I know this—it is hard for a man.

DR BOB: So I agreed to go to dental school. It seemed the closest profession to sculpture I could find. It seemed there was some artistry involved. I wasn't dedicated enough to medicine to become a surgeon. I considered architecture, but that was even too out there for my parents. It all seems silly now, but I was desperate then.

PIERRE LUIGI: *Ay, porbrecito,* I think you are a artist Dr Bob. I say this all the time.

DR BOB: And I appreciate that Pierre Luigi, more than you could ever know.

(DR BOB *begins to cry.*)

(*Blackout*)

Scene Eight

(ALDO *is doing sit ups.* ANNA *reads a large book entitled* Bolivia.)

ALDO: Fifty eight, fifty nine, sixty. (*He stops.*)

ANNA: I don't see it doing anything. Perhaps you eat too much cheese.

ALDO: Well—I'm a big guy—I'm not like you. I need to put a lot in to keep the motor running. Where's Bolivia?

ANNA: In South America, between Peru and Chile. It has no sea—I want to go there.

ALDO: Is it clean?

ANNA: Not like Switzerland. I like the landscape. (*She holds up a picture.*)

ALDO: Bleak.

ANNA: Yes.

ALDO: I don't get you. I like you. But I don't get you. Why you want to go there...what's there? I'm here, why would you want to go anywhere else?

ANNA: Sometimes I just need a trip.

ALDO: Oh.

ANNA: I met someone from there at the opening, He reminded me that I wanted to go there.

ALDO: You liked him that much, huh.

ANNA: He had a friendly face. You don't find so many friendly faces in Switzerland.

ALDO: Do you have anything nice to say about your country? I think it's pretty amazing.

ANNA: The mountains are very beautiful, but I don't want to have anything to do with them.

ALDO: But you'd go half way around the world to see some other mountains, which are most likely pretty similar, if not inferior to the ones outside your back door.

ANNA: But I know the ones here already.

ALDO: So?

ANNA: I get excited by the puzzle of places.

ALDO: I don't get it.

ANNA: What don't you get? I want to go to Bolivia because it's a country with no sea and high mountains, like Switzerland—but half-way around the world. I want to know what's different there. I want to talk to people who have never seen the sea and ask them what they think it's like. I want to visit the highest place in the country and the lowest, and compare their garbage.

ALDO: Sounds pretty good, except for the garbage part. Can't we do that here?

ANNA: You can't do that in your own country. Even if you don't have a map—you have one in your head.

ALDO: I see. Anna, I mean I like the garbage, I like it just fine, but what does it all mean?

ANNA: I can't tell you that Aldo.

ALDO: What do you mean?

ANNA: I shouldn't have to explain it to you.

ALDO: No need to get all hoity toity with me.

ANNA: I don't know what that means.

ALDO: It means, tell me what this *(Referring to garbage round him)* is all about.

ANNA: Fine. I think that we are more what we have lost than what we have—what we throw away, leave behind, lose—tells us more about who we are than what we hold on to.

ALDO: So what did you lose Anna?

ANNA: Everyone has lost something they really regret. Maybe you haven't yet.

ALDO: Look, I understand you. I've lost more than I care to remember. I'm not an idiot just because I used to haul trash. I could tell you some stories.

ANNA: When?

ALDO: When you tell me why you wake up screaming every night.

(Blackout)

Scene Nine

(DR BOB and PIERRE LUIGI an hour later in the fish restaurant. Much brandy has been drunk.)

DR BOB: I was the best dental student Indiana had seen in years. My bridge work, my dentures, extraordinary!

PIERRE LUIGI: You are the Michelangelo of dentistry, *senza dubbio.*

DR BOB: I insisted on marrying Giuseppina. I married her to annoy my parents. I'll be candid with you Pierre Luigi, that is not a good reason to marry someone.

PIERRE LUIGI: For other things yes, but not marriage, because *you* live with the wife, not your parents.

DR BOB: Giuseppina was miserable in Indiana. She couldn't eat anything. She refused to learn English properly. We had to move back to Rome. Giuseppina was pregnant with Bobby and I was certain she would lose the baby because the only thing she could eat were Frosted Flakes.

PIERRE LUIGI: They are very good.

DR BOB: Well yes, I've always enjoyed them myself. But I was not happy back in Rome, it was a place so filled with everything that I had not become—the difference between a sculptor and a dentist is large, Pierre Luigi.

PIERRE LUIGI: Hey, you got a job, many people have no jobs. I don't want to rush you, but you came here, I think you came to tell me the story of your ba-ba-boum. Soon the Saturday night rush, you know, it doesn't look like I am working, but I am working.

DR BOB: Of course, of course, excuse me. I get long winded with brandy. Well, Lierre Puigi, I met someone.

PIERRE LUIGI: Here we go.

DR BOB: She was a patient of mine. She came to me with a cracked tooth. Her mouth was a mess. She was a smoker. She needed a root canal, ten cavities, as I recall, and advanced gingivitis.

PIERRE LUIGI: Ah, the dreaded gingivitis.

DR BOB: She was an art student.

PIERRE LUIGI: And very beautiful with yellow teeth?

DR BOB: Well not beautiful, or exactly full of sex appeal in the way Giuseppina is, she was the kind of pretty that every time you looked at her you would notice something new. Her beauty was shy, it didn't reveal itself all at once.

PIERRE LUIGI: A shy beauty—the best.

DR BOB: Besides being lovely to behold, she also was a sculptress. She had talent. Boy, oh boy, did she. (He gets lost in thought.)

PIERRE LUIGI: And?

DR BOB: And I fell head over heels, knock your socks off, take your breath away in love with her. I loved her pretty much the first time I looked in to her mouth. I think it took her some more time. I was never exactly sure what she felt until the end.

PIERRE LUIGI: She loved you. You shared sculpture, a love of stones is very strong, like my ba-ba-boum and me, we love the sea. These loves bring people together. Can I tell you what my ba-ba-boum made for me? She wrote me a letter on sea shells, thanking me for the fish I sent her. Each shell has a word in it. How did she think that up? I'm sorry, go on.

DR BOB: Well, she somehow managed to make all the dead stones of Rome come alive for me again. For the first time in years, I was happy to be where I was. She was enough Pierre Luigi, she was enough.

PIERRE LUIGI: Why are you not with her?

DR BOB: Because I'm from Indiana, Pierre Luigi and you don't leave a wife and two small children for a twenty-two-year-old sculptress when you're from Indiana. I am many things Pierre Luigi, but I am not brave.

PIERRE LUIGI: Nonsense. You are a big brave American dentist. *Dottore,* great love requires great courage. I will make you brave. You must see this lady again. I insist. One ba-ba-boum on the house.

(Blackout)

Scene Ten

(ANNA's studio. ANNA holds a pair of dentures. She looks at them. She cleans them. ANNA looks at the dentures again. She puts them down. She exits. CAMILLA enters with a bottle of wine. She suddenly sees the dentures and screams.)

CAMILLA: Anna! What on earth are you doing with someone's teeth? Are you trying to kill me with terror? I've had a beastly fight with your brother. He's having an affair. That's why he's so bloody awful to me—because he feels so bloody awful. He better not be in love. I married Ernst because he was rich and tidy. Some young, long-legged thing would be messy.

(ANNA enters holding sea shells to her ears. She has heard nothing CAMILLA has said.)

ANNA: I didn't know you were here.

CAMILLA: Open this. I can't. What are those? *(Pointing to the teeth)*

ANNA: The Bolivian's teeth.

CAMILLA: Now that is a rather primitive expression of love!

ANNA: I'm sending them back.

CAMILLA: Of course darling, I'm sorry. I've had a hell of a day. Little Ernie has impetigo. And Big Ernie is a mother fucker. He's fucking some skinny banker from Torino. I don't want to talk about it and if you're kind and sympathetic, I'll kill you.

ANNA: All right, what's the best thing to pack these teeth in? I also want to send this shell, and a message in a bottle.

CAMILLA: Packing things are in my cupboard. Let's go out to dinner and charge it on his card. Better yet, I feel a shopping spree coming on. I need something cashmere, something big and cashmere. You wrap up your teeth in peace. I'll just sit here and polish off this Mouton de Rothschild. I took it from Ernst's god damn wine cellar. That filthy, tight-fisted, fucking bastard! I'm sorry Anna, I know he's your brother.

ANNA: I much prefer you to him.

CAMILLA: Now that's loyalty. So the teeth are going to Rome. But you of course, are not.

ANNA: No, but I want to go somewhere soon. Listen to this shell, it always soothes me when I feel upset.

CAMILLA: Do you think you love the toothless man in Rome? I so used to love being in love.

ANNA: I liked him very much the minutes we spoke. But he's not here.

CAMILLA: And the skiing garbage man is. Be careful of convenience my dear, it can wind up being very inconvenient. What does your message say, read it to me. Distract me, darling.

ANNA: *(Reading)* "Here are your teeth. I will miss them. They were one of my best finds. Perhaps you are another one. Anna"

CAMILLA: I think that's very romantic, but I'm not sure because it's all about false teeth. What about the garbage man? Is it sex? They say the sex doesn't last, but I wish I had found out for myself, because it might not last, but it must make everything much easier while it does.

ANNA: He is very physically able. He surprises me. I'm going to the post. Would you like something?

CAMILLA: Yes, something a little stronger than this. I'll just lie here. *(She lies on the floor and listens to a sea shell).*

ANNA: Are you sure you're all right?

(No reply. ANNA exits. CAMILLA snoozes on the floor with a seashell to her ear. ALDO enters carrying a huge broken mirror.)

ALDO: Anna! Anna! I've got the mirror. It gave me a gash you wouldn't believe. I was bleeding down the Keltenstrasse. I don't think people bleed very often down the streets of Zurich. The looks I was gettin'! Hey Anna!

(CAMILLA gets up.)

ALDO: Oh!

CAMILLA: Oh is right! Anna has exquisite if impractical taste. I am Camilla.

ALDO: Oh yeah, the sister in law. Nice to meet you. I'm Aldo.

CAMILLA: Well, I'd offer you a drink, but Anna doesn't even have Pernod.

ALDO: Well, I don't know what that is anyway. What I'd really like is some first aid.

CAMILLA: Of course, of course. I'm an expert at this sort of thing. I'll just get some gauze.

(CAMILLA exits. ALDO looks at the empty wine bottle and tries to pronounce it.)

ALDO: Motown dee rothschild?

(CAMILLA returns with a huge roll of gauze, tape, scissors, disinfectant.)

CAMILLA: You just sit right down here.

ALDO: I think some of that pink stuff and a Band-Aid would do the trick.

CAMILLA: Nonsense, it's very deep. It requires a dressing.

(CAMILLA *wraps a huge amount of gauze around* ALDO's *thumb.*)

ALDO: Anna saw that mirror lying against some fence in the suburbs. She kept on talking about how beautiful broken mirrors were. I thought it might make her happy. Strange things make her smile, you know?

CAMILLA: Yes.

ALDO: It's funny, I moved to Switzerland to get away from garbage, but now I'm picking it up for free.

CAMILLA: I moved to Switzerland to clean up my act. And look at me...

ALDO: Can I ask you something? I mean you know Anna pretty well, right?

CAMILLA: Yes, of course.

ALDO: Do you know if something bad happened to Anna, some trauma? I mean, an accident, a sudden death, something in her family?

CAMILLA: Well, her brother is a truly horrible human being, and I can say that because I am his wife. But they barely speak. How thankful I am for her. It's been lovely having a place to escape to...to do a little work. I'm a sculptor, you know. I used to be quite good, but one gets distracted from the things that one is really good at. I'm not a very good mother. I'm terribly impatient. I'm not a good wife. Oh dear, it's all so sad.

ALDO: So, you don't know if anything happened to her?

CAMILLA: Well, she doesn't reveal much. Wait, I know she hates Rome. Something happened there.

ALDO: Rome, huh?

CAMILLA: Yes. It must have been an affair, a liaison of some sort.

ALDO: You think so?

CAMILLA: Don't worry. Darling, whatever it is, it's long over, and now you're here to carry her garbage, what a blessing!

(*A knock at the door.* CONSTANZA *enters breathless, holding a letter.*)

CAMILLA: Who could that be? It's open.

CONSTANZA: O K, *allora.* Big News. Where's Anna? I'm so excited I don't know what to do with myself. Where's Anna? I need to talk to her, *pronto.*

CAMILLA: I'm sorry, do I know you?

CONSTANZA: I'm Anna's agent, sort of. She doesn't have an agent, but if she did it would be me, if I were an agent. I want to be an agent.

ALDO: What she talking about?.

CONSTANZA: O K, *entre nous*, bottom line, we have a helluva an offer on the table. I'm talking big money.

CAMILLA: How big is big?

CONSTANZA: So big, I'm all jumpy and crazy inside. *(To* ALDO*)* You look familiar?

ALDO: We met at Anna's show.

CONSTANZA: Right, looks like you've become an art lover. That Anna, she gets all the breaks. O K time is money, *bene, bene*, where is Anna?

*(*ANNA *enters.)*

ANNA: I'm here, Constanza. What do you want?

CONSTANZA: *Leibshein*, we have to talk. Time for a *tete a tete*. I've been working for you, all I do is work for you. Currently, you are my only client.

ANNA: That's too bad because I'm not your client.

CONSTANZA: That's what you think. I'm here to talk money, *mi amor, soldi, dinero*, a lot of it. The Museum of Found Art in Utrecht, they are crazy about you, *loco, cocoo,* basically they can't get enough of you. The man there, Ono somebody, I forget his name, he's like Anna, blah blah blah genius, Anna blah blah blah virtuoso, like cool your jets Ono...But the bottom line is...they want three pieces. Am I a pro or what? Time to pat Constanza on the back. So maybe now you're my client?

ALDO: Wow.

CAMILLA: It's about time.

ANNA: A museum wants to buy my work? Are you sure?

CONSTANZA: Yes I'm sure. It's too good. I know you have principles, I love principles—I don't understand them, but this is a museum, *leibshien,* say it after me a museeeumm.

ALDO & CAMILLA: Museeeumm.

ANNA: I feel uncomfortable selling, everything belonged to someone else before. I see myself as the host of a big beach party. You can't charge for a party.

CAMILLA: Oh, yes you can. Right Aldo?

ALDO: Best parties I've ever been to had a cover charge.

CONSTANZA: I won't go to a party unless I have to pay for it.

ANNA: But it would be nice to know that people could always look at my beaches if they wanted to.

ALDO: This is the big time, baby.

CONSTANZA: Big is not the word.

CAMILLA: And it means you could travel to any beach, anytime you wanted.

ALDO: You've been talking about needing a trip.

CAMILLA: You barely survive on those tiny grants.

ANNA: I don't feel ready. *(Pause)* I'll think about it.

CONSTANZA: O K, O K, *no capisco*. Can't get my head around this. Elaborate, *amor*. I want to be on the same page with you.

ANNA: I'll let you know, Constanza.

CONSTANZA: You'll let me know? Fuck, this is a hard job. Does this mean I'm your agent?

ANNA: I don't know.

CONSTANZA: O K. I go. *Je vais*. I tried. I'm going home and putting two bottles of Don Perignon on ice, because I hope to be celebrating very soon. Anna, you say no enough people stop asking.

(CONSTANZA exits.)

ALDO: She's a piece of work.

CAMILLA: She certainly is. I would like to propose a toast. *(Toasting)* To museums and taking the motherfucker to the cleaners. Now, I'll put my head under the tap and then I'm taking everyone to an exorbitant dinner. I insist. *(She exits.)*

ALDO: Hey baby, you happy?

ANNA: I feel strange. A part of me doesn't want to let these beaches go.

ALDO: But think about it, you could go wherever you want. You could leave Switzerland.

ANNA: It seems too easy.

ALDO: I got that mirror for you. I was wounded in action. I think I just needed a Band-Aid, but Camilla seemed to think it was a war wound.

ANNA: Thank you. It 's beautiful.

ALDO: No, you're the one who's beautiful.

ANNA: I am not beautiful. You are beautiful. Beautiful people are always trying to tell the normal people that they are beautiful—it's sort of a consolation prize.

ALDO: I think you're beautiful. I like everything about you. It's pretty simple. I like the way you drink coffee in the middle of the night, I like the way you try to hide your smile, I like the way you didn't give that crazy woman what she wanted. I like you, Anna.

ANNA: You're being silly.

ALDO: I even like the way you refuse to take a compliment. So, you want someone to spend that money with, if you decide to take it?

ANNA: What do you mean?

ALDO: I mean I like you to the point of following you to every beach in Europe. And I don't even swim, but I'll learn. I like you enough to pick up any piece of garbage you find. Anna, I would like to carry your garbage for a long, long time.

ANNA: How long is a long, long time?

(Blackout)

END OF ACT ONE

ACT TWO

Scene One

(Dr Bob's office, Linda, a young enthusiastic American is in the chair. Dr Bob is finishing up.)

Dr Bob: So I think you should really invest in a rotary brush with elmo-fluorescence. I always say there's no investment like an investment in your teeth.

Linda: Well, I'll take a look. I already use a rotary brush and I know how expensive they can run. As much as I'd like to—I appreciate your consideration and kindness Dr Bob—but underwater archeologists don't make a lot of money.

Dr Bob: All right Linda—I understand your predicament. So, how long are you in Rome?

Linda: Well, I'm working off the coast of Ostia for at least another month. Unless of course there are any more accidents.

Dr Bob: I'm sure that won't be the case.

Linda: If only you knew, Dr Bob—if only you knew. I'm not sure if there's a tooth in my mouth that's mine. All my life I've been getting accidentally "hit in the mouth". I have yet to have someone actually punch me, but in some way that would be a relief.

Dr Bob: Well, Linda, I've had experience in that arena and let me tell you, its not fun at all. If I can be candid with you, because I feel I can, three of my own teeth are not my own. I lost them in the line of fire, so to speak.

Linda: Well, I know the feeling. I've been popped in the mouth by a tennis ball, a Frisbee, a large rock, a squash racket, a skate board, and most recently a third century Roman amphora. Someone up there doesn't want me to have teeth.

Dr Bob: But you still have one of the nicest smiles I've come across.

Linda: Thanks, Dr Bob. I've been fortunate enough to work with some of the finest Doctors of Dentistry, like yourself.

(Pierre Luigi enters.)

PIERRE LUIGI: *Scusa-mei* Dr Bob, Giuseppina said I could come in; she said you are running late.

DR BOB: Yes, of course Pierre Luigi, you know me—I get distracted. Everyone has such interesting stories. Ah, Pierre Luigi, this is a fellow countryman of mine, Linda; Linda, this is a friend and patient, Pierre Luigi. If you are looking for a good fish dinner, Pierre Luigi manages a terrific restaurant specializing in seafood.

LINDA: *(Quite taken with* PIERRE LUIGI*)* Great, I love seafood. I'm there.

PIERRE LUIGI: And I love beautiful women who love seafood. You and Dr Bob, and of course the sexy Giuseppina will be my guests tonight.

LINDA: Excellent.

DR BOB: Oh dear, I can't. I have a previous engagement. Perhaps I could join you for a drink after....

PIERRE LUIGI: Of course. I am at the restaurant all night.

LINDA: Well, I better go. I need to get back to Ostia and do some work.

PIERRE LUIGI: But I live and work in Ostia. Why do you stay there?

LINDA: I am an underwater archeologist. I'm diving for a third-century bath house off the coast.

PIERRE LUIGI: Wonderful. You love the sea?

LINDA: Yes...I'm usually in it.

PIERRE LUIGI: Here is the card of the restaurant. After ten there are fewer people.

LINDA: Cool. See you next week Dr Bob.

DR BOB: Yes of course. Make an appointment with Giuseppina.

*(*LINDA *exits.)*

DR BOB: You have a flair Pierre Luigi—a flair for the ladies—I didn't realize.

PIERRE LUIGI: Nice smile.

DR BOB: Not a tooth in her mouth is her own.

PIERRE LUIGI: Interesting.

DR BOB: What about your ba-ba-boum?

PIERRE LUIGI: What about her? She never comes to Rome. I can't leave because the restaurant is so busy. It seems like if it is meant to be, it should be easier. In short, the ba-ba is not very booming. So, I've been trying to find your old ba-ba-boum. There is no Clara Springer listed in Lucerne, Zurich, Basil, or Lugano.

DR BOB: Well Pierre Luigi, thank you for your help...perhaps we should just let it rest.

PIERRE LUIGI: No, Dr Bob—I want you to be happy in this life. I want you to see this woman again.

DR BOB: But Giuseppina—I have Giuseppina.

PIERRE LUIGI: Yes you do—but this is not enough. I have a friend in Zurich. I'll make him do investigations. Don't you worry I find your ba-ba-boum Dr Bob. What's the girl with no teeth's name again?

DR BOB: Linda.

PIERRE LUIGI: Linda, nice name. Dr Bob. I must find Clara.

DR BOB: You certainly are head strong, Pierre Luigi.

PIERRE LUIGI: You think so? You're right. I can be unstoppable, if I want to. I must remember this.

(DR BOB *goes into* PIERRE LUIGI's *mouth. The sound of a dentist's drill.)*

(Blackout)

Scene Two

(Half light up on ANNA *and* CAMILLA *in bed in* ANNA's *studio.* CAMILLA *snores.* ANNA *sits bolt upright in bed.)*

ANNA: I can't. I can't.

CAMILLA: What darling?

ANNA: I can't marry Aldo. Not that he really asked me. I think he did last night, but I can't anyway.

CAMILLA: All right darling, I will. Now go back to sleep.

ANNA: Camilla, he said he would carry my garbage for a long long time. What does that mean, exactly? *(She gets up and exits.)*

CAMILLA: God, I've got a helluva a hangover. Maybe you should just shoot me, or if guns make you squeamish, hang me—I feel unafraid of death. What are you doing?

ANNA: *(Off stage)* Coffee...

CAMILLA: Make me one too. I suggest marrying someone you love. I didn't, and it's not much fun. I don't know if love conquers all, but it makes the bloody mess that life is more palatable...lots of milk, no sugar. Maybe love is a panacea, maybe it isn't; it's terribly pleasant as I recall with really horrid bits. I was in love with a painter from Sweet Home, Oregon. I met him at art school. He was lovely, full of talent. He mostly painted breasts, very large breasts, mostly my breasts. But he smoked marijuana all the time. He wanted me to go back to Sweet Home with him, and you know I really wanted to. I was such an idiot, I just couldn't imagine having a family with him. I had this notion that you weren't a woman, a real proper bona fide woman without houses, babies, husbands.

(ANNA *enters.*)

CAMILLA: Now I know it's all just something that one can do. I wish I'd known that when I said I couldn't go to Sweet Home.

CAMILLA: Do you love him?

ANNA: I'm not sure.

CAMILLA: One usually knows.

ANNA: I think I've only known once.

CAMILLA: Who was it?

ANNA: An American dentist in Rome.

CAMILLA: Oh, how unlikely.

ANNA: Yes, he was just that.

CAMILLA: And...

ANNA: And...I know I loved him.

CAMILLA: How did you know?

ANNA: He felt...he felt like home to me. After I met him, everything made sense, at least for awhile. I didn't want to be anywhere else. He was enough. I loved him, but....

CAMILLA: Oh god, don't say it.

ANNA: He was married....

CAMILLA: So...your home had other tenants. How did you meet this two timing Yankee dentist?

ANNA: I was studying sculpture in Rome and went to him for some cavities. He had wanted to be a sculptor. I think he actually had talent. He was a very good dentist. His bridge and denture work were exquisite. He was a good person, except for the wife. He seemed like someone you should love, except for the wife.

CAMILLA: And it didn't end well.

ANNA: No, not at all—I punched him—knocked out his three bottom teeth. I just got so angry that I had found this...home and it wasn't really mine. I left Rome after that. He didn't even know my real name.

CAMILLA: Really? Why not?

ANNA: In Rome I used a different name. I thought I would be a better artist if I disassociated myself with my past, as I never felt very connected to it. After I left, I stoppped doing sculpture, I took back my old name...And I cut off that part of my life. Rome, I've never loved a place like that. In the last few weeks I have these dreams about him and the city. Last night I dreamt I was a stone, and on the outside I was one shape, but inside I was a completely different shape. I need to find out more about that shape

CAMILLA: Only one thing to do. Go to Rome. Go, Anna. And while you're there look up the toothless man you talk about all the time.

ANNA: I'm not sure if I can. Rome, was so many things to me.

CAMILLA: Go to Rome. See the city you love again. See them both.. Find out if you love either of them. Get it all straightened out. Run away with one or the other of them or stay there and do sculpture again, or come back and marry that lovely garbage man, or not. There are so many things that you can do. Anna, go to Rome. Please go. Go for me.

ANNA: Should I tell Aldo?

CAMILLA: Leave that to me. I might stay here for a few days—get Ernie—until I'm sorted out.

ANNA: Of course.

CAMILLA: Time to pack. You've got to look smashing. I'm giving you Ernst's platinum card to tide you over.

ANNA: Thank you Camilla. Thank you. I'm scared.

CAMILLA: Nonsense, *la citta eterna* awaits you.

(*Blackout*)

Scene Three

(*The fish restaurant.* PIERRE LUIGI *and* LINDA *are sitting over wine.*)

PIERRE LUIGI: So—how did you happen to choose a profession where you are always losing your teeth?

LINDA: Oh—probably because I have four older brothers.

PIERRE LUIGI: What do you mean?

LINDA: Well—they were always forcing me to do scary things. You know—dive from high places, walk along steep precipices, jump between wide gaps. It seemed like those were the only things that ever got any respect from them. So when I was thinking about what I wanted to be— I chose something that I knew would impress them. I've also always liked finding things, I feel like a detective—an underwater detective.

PIERRE LUIGI: Oh, I like this—sounds mysterious.

LINDA: Can I ask you a question? Not to be forward, but I find it easier to be up front about these things. In most of the countries I've worked in, very charming interesting men take me out to dinner and I'm charmed and interested until a wife or fiancée or a live-in girlfriend surfaces a week or sometimes a month or two later. That is not so charming or interesting to me.

PIERRE LUIGI: No, no—this is not charming. I will be frank.

LINDA: Please.

PIERRE LUIGI: I do not have a *ragazza* or a wife or a fiancée.

LINDA: Great.

PIERRE LUIGI: Yes, great... but...

LINDA: Here we go...

PIERRE LUIGI: I have a situation, yes a situation. I have a correspondence with a woman who lives in another city.

LINDA: You write letters?

PIERRE LUIGI: Yes. But she never comes to Rome. It's difficult.

LINDA: Well, *(She thinks for a minute)* I guess I'm O K with that.

PIERRE LUIGI: Good.

(They lean in to kiss, DR BOB enters.)

DR BOB: Oh, Gosh. Three's a crowd, excuse me. I better go. It's late. Giuseppina will get in a temper.

PIERRE LUIGI: No, no *Dottore*, please. I bring out the grappa. Linda and I are just becoming friends.

LINDA: You bet.

(PIERRE LUIGI exits.)

DR BOB: Good fish?

LINDA: Oh, yes. Fried, boiled, in a risotto, why there was even some sort of a fish mousse.

DR BOB: Well... Pierre Luigi is fond of fish.

LINDA: Yes he seems very fond of fish indeed.

(Silence)

DR BOB: I think the world of Pierre Luigi.

LINDA: So, I have your blessing Dr Bob?

DR BOB: Well its none of my business. But you're a fellow countryman, and foreign men often don't always have the best motives.

LINDA: I can take care of myself Dr Bob.

(PIERRE LUIGI *enters with grappa.*)

DR BOB: Now doesn't that look yummy!

LINDA: Certainly does. Will you excuse me for a second?

(LINDA *exits.*)

PIERRE LUIGI: *Fantastico* Dr Bob—To Dr Bob.

DR BOB: Linda is a swell girl. She's the real thing. I hope your intentions are um...honorable. I know there was that garbage collector artist woman...just reminding you.

PIERRE LUIGI: And I thank you Dr Bob. But I've been thinking maybe we are not supposed to be with the ba-ba-boums in our life, maybe the best we can hope for is to find a ba or boum and settle down. I feel comfortable with Linda. She lost her teeth so many times. I want to thank you Dr Bob.

(PIERRE LUIGI *kisses* DR BOB *on both cheeks.*)

DR BOB: Now, now.

(LINDA *enters.* PIERRE LUIGI *stands.*)

LINDA: I'm back.

DR BOB: So you are.

PIERRE LUIGI: And the grappa is waiting. I would like to make a toast. To new and old friends.

(LINDA *lunges at* PIERRE LUIGI *and kisses him.* ANNA *enters.*)

DR BOB: Clara! Oh my God.

PIERRE LUIGI: Anna?

(ANNA *looks from person to person.* PIERRE LUIGI *untangles himself from* LINDA. ANNA *runs offstage.* DR BOB *and* PIERRE LUIGI *follow.* LINDA *stands alone. She drains her glass of grappa as well as the other two glasses.*)

(*Blackout*)

Scene Four

(ANNA *runs on stage. She stops to catch her breath.* DR BOB *enters running.*)

ANNA: I didn't come to see you.

DR BOB: I didn't think you did.

ANNA: I came to see Pierre Luigi. I'm thinking about a trip to Bolivia.

DR BOB: I wish I could explain how good it is to see you.

ANNA: I'm not sure why I came. I think I really came to see Rome again. That's really why I came.

DR BOB: You look as exactly as I remember you.

ANNA: I don't ever change. It's a problem. People should change. You got new teeth?

DR BOB: Um, why yes I did.

ANNA: They look good, almost real.

DR BOB: Thanks.

ANNA: I spent the whole day walking. When I lived here, I was inspired by every stone. I wanted so much to make something as beautiful as this place.

DR BOB: And have you?

ANNA: I'm not sure. I got a lot of ideas today. I shouldn't have stayed away so long.

DR BOB: Rome's a good place for ideas. A lot of people seem to have them here.

ANNA: It was the first place I learned about inspiration. The city inspired me to be greater than myself, to reach up. Well, it wasn't just the city.... I never understood why you had so much confidence in me. I had so little.

DR BOB: You had plenty, you just didn't know it. Scared people can see confidence from a mile away.

ANNA: I went to Piazza Mattei today, to the Fountain of the Turtles.

DR BOB: You always liked that one. The turtles are very nicely executed.

ANNA: Remember the story about the fountain, it's probably not true. You know the one about the beautiful Mattei princess that had many suitors, but one of them, who was not really a contender, decided to build the Fountain of the Turtles outside her window in the middle of the night. So, the Princess woke up the next morning to the sound of running water. She looked out her window and the suitor was standing in the *piazza* with the fountain he had made her. And he looked up at her and said he had tried to make something as beautiful as her. And she married him.

DR BOB: In some accounts she didn't. But I like it better your way.

ANNA: I'd have married him, for something that beautiful. I kept on thinking today, who I wanted to be more in that story the princess or the suitor, I couldn't decide.

DR BOB: You know, I always wanted to make something for you. I thought about it a lot. I even did some sketches. But, I was shy. I mean you were the real McCoy. I remember watching you in your studio and you had this assurance, this naturalness, which...well it knocked my socks off. I'm not sure I've ever loved anything so much as watching you work. It inspired me, it was as if all of a sudden someone turned the lights on. I miss that feeling.

ANNA: I do too.

DR BOB: Really?

ANNA: I don't feel like anything I've made has been as good as when I lived here. It's strange, because recently I've been getting a lot of attention for my work, but I don't feel I deserve it. I know I've done better. I lost something when I lost you. Sometimes, I think you were my muse.

DR BOB: I never knew. *(Pause)* Look, would you like to get a hot chocolate and...do you still like hot chocolate?

ANNA: I told you I never change.

DR BOB: *(He looks for his wallet.)* Damn, I left my wallet, my jacket, at the restaurant. We could walk back over there then go somewhere...catch up.

ANNA: I don't want to go back to the restaurant.

DR BOB: Please, let me buy you a hot chocolate. I'll just go get my jacket. *(He begins to leave.)* You'll be here?

ANNA: Be quick.

DR BOB: I'll run all the way.

ANNA: Good, I haven't had a *cioccolato caldo* in seven years.

(DR BOB runs offstage. ANNA waits a minute. She begins to walk off-stage and then runs.)

Scene Five

(The restaurant. LINDA sits drinking grappa. DR BOB enters.)

DR BOB: Hello Linda. I forgot my jacket.

LINDA: Yup.

DR BOB: Quite an evening. Full of surprises. Well, I better be going!

LINDA: Uh huh.

DR BOB: Is Pierre Luigi here?

LINDA: Nope.

DR BOB: Oh, I'm sorry.

LINDA: Yup.

DR BOB: Well....I best be going.

LINDA: Home to your wife?

DR BOB: Right.

(DR BOB exits. LINDA exits through a door to get some more grappa. ALDO enters.)

ALDO: *(Reading from a piece of paper)* Da Silvano's, this is it. *(Calling)* Anna, Anna are you here?

(He moves toward the kitchen, he pushes the door open. LINDA is on the other side. He somehow manages to hit LINDA in the mouth.)

LINDA: Aw, God!

ALDO: I am so sorry.

LINDA: It's all right, it happens to me all the time.

ALDO: Did I get you in the nose?

LINDA: No, no, the mouth, where else? That'll teach me to walk through swinging doors drinking a bottle of grappa. Am I bleeding? Any cracked or missing teeth?

ALDO: Not that I can see.

LINDA: Phew. *(She smiles in disbelief.)* Woow!

ALDO: You have a great smile.

LINDA: Well it's fake. Not one of my teeth is real. Impressive huh? I'm not violent or anything. I'm just unlucky. I'm not sure where everybody went. I was being kissed, skillfully, I might add, and my dentist yelled Clara and my date yelled Anna.

ALDO: Anna was here?

LINDA: I guess so. I only saw one person, but whoever she was ran out, and my dentist and my date followed them or her.

ALDO: Do you always travel with a dentist?

LINDA: No but I should, it might end up being cheaper. I think one of my caps is loose.

ALDO: So you're sure Anna was here?

LINDA: I'm not sure of anything. Who is she, anyway?

ALDO: The first woman I ever volunteered to carry garbage for anytime, anywhere in the world, for as long as she wanted.

LINDA: O K, that's enough for me, I'm leaving. *Buena sera.*

ALDO: I think she said no.

LINDA: How do you know?

ALDO: She skipped town in the middle of the night.

LINDA: That is a bad sign, take it from me, I know all the bad signs.

ALDO: I shouldn't have asked her. I knew that I shouldn't have while I was doing it. I just really like her. I shouldn't be here even, Italy was the last place I wanted to come to, let me tell you. But her sister-in-law told me she might be here, so here I am, like an idiot. It's like, I thought she was my fresh start, my sign that I was finally in the right place, at the right time, doing the right thing.

LINDA: What do you mean?

ALDO: Got an hour or three.

LINDA: Yup.

ALDO: You don't want to hear this. I should try and find Anna. God knows what she's up to, I probably don't want to know. You've got better things to do, with your time.

LINDA: I wish that was the case.

ALDO: Geeze, I dunno. All my life I've been trying to keep my nose clean. But I'm always in the wrong place at the wrong time, finding things I don't want to find. And that's the least of it.

LINDA: Elaborate.

ALDO: I am always the guy who gets punched by mistake in a bar, some idiot mistakes me for someone else, or I'm coming out of the bathroom at the wrong time, or someone just doesn't like my face.

LINDA: I hear you, pal. Go on

ALDO: I've eye witnessed three murders, found a thumb, an index finger, and eventually a hairy left arm with a wedding band on the ring finger, that one was my ticket out. I figured if someone was going to pay me to leave town, maybe I would stop seeing things I wasn't supposed to. I did the wrong thing, because I thought maybe it was right. And then I meet Anna. I felt like I was in the right place for the first time in my life. Wow, did that feel good. She was opening up a whole new world for me. Now it's lost. Maybe it was never there. Or it wasn't mine to have.

LINDA: Look, I don't know your name, and I've drunk a bottle of Chianti and several glasses of this dreadful Grappa, which tastes like a combination of turpentine and mouth wash, but I want to tell you something stranger, Anna/Clara, whatever her name is, didn't open up any world for you—she just brought out something that was already there. You chose to see what she showed you, you wanted to see something new. It's all still yours. And you can still make a fresh start. I'm making one right now. Would you like to join me? *(She winces.)*

ALDO: Are you O K?

LINDA: I'm fine. My mouth hurts, I have the beginning of a migraine and my hopes are dashed yet again. But when you've been hit in the mouth as many times as I have, you learn to smile through excruciating pain. Otherwise, people would just feel so sorry for you all the time.

ALDO: Maybe you should just stop trying to smile so much.

LINDA: But I've paid so much for this smile. So, what about you? Are you going to chase this woman from city to city, hoping for a glimpse, waiting for the final rejection that will set you free?

ALDO: I have no idea what I'm going to do.

LINDA: Would you like to see the beach of Rome?

ALDO: Why?

LINDA: Because that's where I live. I'm not proposing anything, but my couch. I've had my weekly dose of rejection and humiliation. Do you like the water?

ALDO: I am more of a mountain person.

LINDA: Oh.

ALDO: But I always seem to be on a beach these days. I came to Europe to ski and stop finding limbs....

LINDA: I came to Europe to stop being hit in the mouth, but....

ALDO: Hey, you said it, fresh start. Right here, right now.

LINDA: Right. To new beginnings and being in the wrong place at the wrong time, but somehow it's right.

ALDO: I should get some ice for your mouth. Your upper lip is swelling.

LINDA: Don't worry, I can't feel a thing. I'm sort of self anesthetized.

ALDO: I should get some ice, anyway. *(He gets up.)*

LINDA: Get a glass for yourself and we can toast and toast the night away.

ALDO: I'd like that. I'd really like that.

(Blackout)

Scene Six

(DR BOB, *holds his jacket.*)

DR BOB: Clara? Anna?

(PIERRE LUIGI *enters.*)

PIERRE LUIGI: What did you do with my ba-ba-boum?

DR BOB: Listen you, she also happens to be my ba-ba-boum. And you've scared her off. Do you have to have every interesting woman in Western Europe? You've already left one tonight, drinking herself in to a stupor.

PIERRE LUIGI: You trying to make me feel guilty, Mr Married man? Well, what is the sexy Giuseppina doing this evening? Huh? And your two boys?

DR BOB: You're the one who told me I needed my own ba-ba-boum. You opened the whole can of worms.

PIERRE LUIGI: I did not tell you that could take mine.

DR BOB: You toothless gigolo.

(PIERRE LUIGI *moves to punch* DR BOB. DR BOB *ducks, he moves to punch* PIERRE LUIGI, *he suddenly stops. He holds* PIERRE LUIGI's *jaw.*)

DR BOB: Close. Open. I can't punch you. It's like taking a hammer to the David. My greatest work to date Pierre Luigi, is your mouth. I don't want to hit you. Aw gosh, I don't know what I want. (*A pause*)

PIERRE LUIGI: I know what I want.

DR BOB: What?

PIERRE LUIGI: I want Anna. I told you great love requires great courage, Dr Bob, but I was scared like a baby. I am ready now, to dive off this cliff, take the plunge, come what may. I don't care if she hits me in the face and knocks out every tooth in my head. Anna. She is the only thing I want.

DR BOB: We've lost her. She doesn't want either of us, pal

PIERRE LUIGI: I don't care. I want her Dr Bob.

(PIERRE LUIGI *runs offstage.* DR BOB *follows.*)

(*Blackout*)

Scene Seven

(ANNA's *studio a day later.* CAMILLA *sits and sculpts a devil. There is a knock at the door.*)

CAMILLA: Oh god its impossible to ever get anything done. Impossible. It's open.

DR BOB: Does Clara or umm...... I mean Anna live here?

CAMILLA: Who wants to know?

DR BOB: Her friend, her former dentist.

CAMILLA: Oh yes, you. What are you doing in Zurich?

DR BOB: Well, there was a conference of.... No actually I am lying, there was no conference. I came to see Anna. I've been to every gallery in Zurich asking about an artist named Anna who works with garbage. The last one I went to gave me this address.

CAMILLA: She's not here. I am not expecting her back any time soon. I suggest you phone next time, maybe when your wife goes out for milk?

DR BOB: You know about Giuseppina?

CAMILLA: I know, oh yes I know. You are talking to the wrong person if you want sympathy, or anything resembling compassion. I've just left my husband because he's been having an affair with his Italian co-banker. This is a bust of him. I don't know when Anna will be back. She wouldn't tell me because I can't keep a secret. If you'll excuse me, I've got some work to do. I used to be a very good sulptor and then it became a hobby. I am trying to remedy that. Sorry if I am rambling on. I haven't seen a grownup in days, just my son. He's at the daycare. I sacked the nanny. She was too pretty.

DR BOB: Could I ask a favor? It may sound a little strange.

CAMILLA: I'm not into anything strange, particularly with somebody who has a wife.

DR BOB: Can I just watch you work, maybe hold a piece of clay? I think I'd like to. I used to work with clay. I haven't allowed myself the pleasure in over twenty years.

CAMILLA: Are you all right?

DR BOB: I'm fine, just fine. Everything is upside down, but I'm doing fine. Here I am in Zurich and seems I came here just to see you make something out of nothing. I thought I would come here and have something to say to Anna. I thought I might tell her that I miss her and that I know I will always miss her. I didn't come to Zurich to win her back or promise her anything, it's too late for promises, just to tell her that I miss her. She has scarred me, but I am grateful for the scars, if that makes sense?

CAMILLA: It makes a lot of sense. It's what we do with those scars that's so difficult. I'll tell her.

DR BOB: Thank you. Could I just watch you work for a little while? Pretend I'm not here.

CAMILLA: I'm not much good at that sort of thing.

DR BOB: All right. I'm sorry. I'll leave.

CAMILLA: No, no please stay. But if you stay I'll have to chat. I just can't pretend you're not here.

(CAMILLA *hands* DR BOB *some clay.* CAMILLA *continues to work with the clay.*)

CAMILLA: I like Americans. I should have married an American. A painter. I wanted something safe. Now I know nothing is safe. He was from Sweet Home, Oregon. It seemed so far away. Now nothing seems far away. New Zealand seems close.

(*Blackout*)

Scene Eight

(*Greece. The stage is cleared. Blue Light is reflected on the back walls covered in garbage. The sound of the sea and Greek Bouzouki music.* ANNA *sits with a sketch pad, sketching a large sea shell.* PIERRE LUIGI *enters, he is out of breath.*)

PIERRE LUIGI: Anna! I knew you would be here. I knew you would be in Greece. I just knew it. I went to the hotel and asked for you, I said have you seen the pretty Swiss lady artist and the man said...

(ANNA *holds up her hand, for* PIERRE LUIGI *to be quiet and continues sketching.*)

ANNA: Not bad. I've been finding things I like and drawing them. I think next I'll sculpt them and then maybe put them all together, in a sort of three dimensional collage.

(PIERRE LUIGI *looks over* ANNA'*s shoulder at the sketch.*)

PIERRE LUIGI: I like the sea shell. It looks powerful.

ANNA: It is powerful. (ANNA *sketches some more.*)

PIERRE LUIGI: I found you.

ANNA: You seem to find a lot of things.

PIERRE LUIGI: What do you mean?

ANNA: You found me, you found that pretty girl in Rome, maybe you found another one on the ferry coming here, who knows. You're such a finder.

PIERRE LUIGI: It was nothing Anna, believe me.

ANNA: You said your heart was swimming upstream to me.

PIERRE LUIGI: It was, it is. It's just a long way up, you know? That girl was just a distraction.

ANNA: Well, I had a distraction of my own in Zurich.

PIERRE LUIGI: I see.

ANNA: He offered to carry my garbage for as long as I wanted.

PIERRE LUIGI: Oh, did he? That's a good line.

ANNA: But I realized I didn't want anyone else to carry it. And that maybe I should stop thinking about lost things and think about what I have.

PIERRE LUIGI: You have me, Anna. You have me. (*He leans in to kiss her, but then pulls away*) I can't. I want to, I really want to, but I can't. I have some problems.

ANNA: Is it me?

PIERRE LUIGI: No, no. It's me. When I love a woman, something always happens to my teeth. Once, I was almost married but the bad luck got in the way.

ANNA: What happened?

PIERRE LUIGI: I almost married the most beautiful girl in Cohabamba. Maria Belen, flowers bloomed when she walked in to a room. We had a wedding with five thousand white carnations and incense...lots of incense.

ANNA: So, you were married?

PIERRE LUIGI: I said I had a wedding. The priest, Padre Gustavo, was a holy man, but old with cataracts. He got carried away with swinging the incense holder and he hit me in the mouth before the vows. That's how I lost my teeth.

ANNA: How horrible. What did you do?

PIERRE LUIGI: The only thing I could do, I ran away. Maria Belen looked at me and roared with laughter. I had never seen her look like that before. My grandmother followed me out of the church. She said I could only break the bad luck if I left Cochabamba. Then she gave me some cash and her dentures.

ANNA: And those were the ones I found?

PIERRE LUIGI: Yes. It's too weird, right? I think I will leave now.

ANNA: Pierre Luigi, don't go. We lose things, so we can find new things.

PIERRE LUIGI: I'm not sure it's so easy, Anna. Some things can not be replaced.

ANNA: What things, Pierre Luigi?

PIERRE LUIGI: Big things. Things you can't put in your hand.... All my life I dreamt of the sea, Anna. Mostly I dreamt of fish. Sometimes I was the fish. Even before I almost got married, I knew I would leave Bolivia, because at night I dreamt only of the sea. And then...I finally got there. Anything was possible, I could be anyone. I became Pierre Luigi. Pedro Luis and all his bad luck was gone... But you take your country with you, I am now Pierre Luigi, but at night alone in my bed, I am still Pedro Luis. I speak many languages, but now I dream only of Bolivia, in Spanish.

ANNA: You should go back. It's your home.

PIERRE LUIGI: I don't know if home is a place anymore. I'm a little bit of everything now, like a *tapas*.

ANNA: Do you think another person can be your home?

PIERRE LUIGI: I hope so.... Is that what Dr Bob is for you? He is a wonderful dentist and a wonderful man too. Do you still love him, Anna?

ANNA: That's a difficult question.

PIERRE LUIGI: Believe me, it was hard to ask.

ANNA: Growing up, I never felt at home, I always felt like I was just passing through, that the mountains outside my window were too large to understand. I also dreamt of the sea. Sometimes I was a sea shell in my dreams. Bob pulled me out of that sea shell and made me see myself. He made me feel I could do or be anything, But, Bob is not my home anymore. I'm homeless.

PIERRE LUIGI: Let me be your home. Anna, I think you found my teeth, so you could find me. I have something for you. (*He hands* ANNA *a package*) Take them Anna, cut them up, throw them away, whatever, I want you to have them.

(ANNA *opens the package. It is* PIERRE LUIGI's *dentures. The same dentures that were in* ANNA's *exhibition.*)

ANNA: Thank you Pierre Luigi, thank you. (*She kisses* PIERRE LUIGI.)

PIERRE LUIGI: Everything O K with the teeth?

ANNA: They're perfect. But I can't accept these, they brought you to Europe.

PIERRE LUIGI: Please, they were *mi abuela*'s, maybe she brought us together from heaven. Anna, do you think you could possibly be Mrs Pierre Luigi? I don't have a ring. Take the teeth instead.

ANNA: Can I take the teeth and promise to consider your offer. I need some time. You see, I'm changing what I'm doing in my work, I want to experiment with stone again and my head is full of ideas.

PIERRE LUIGI: Time? O K. Stone, garbage, whatever you do is beautiful. *(He kisses her.)* Where will you go next?

(PIERRE LUIGI and ANNA keep kissing each other through these lines.)

ANNA: Here.

PIERRE LUIGI: Me too. Everyday I will ask you.

ANNA: What about your job?

PIERRE LUIGI: I have no job. I left. I have a little money, maybe now is the time to open a fish restaurant. *(He stops kissing ANNA. Very serious)* Anna.

ANNA: What?

PIERRE LUIGI: Do you like fish?

ANNA: I love fish. *(They kiss again.)* And I am inviting you to a big fish lunch. I'll meet you at the *taverna* in a minute.

PIERRE LUIGI: So, you haven't said no?

ANNA: Yes, I haven't said no.

PIERRE LUIGI: I am known for my stamina.

ANNA: Good.

PIERRE LUIGI: Please do not disappear again.

ANNA: I'll try not to.

PIERRE LUIGI: I won't move until I have your word.

ANNA: You have my word. I won't go anywhere until after lunch.

PIERRE LUIGI: Well, that's something .

ANNA: Encouraging, Pedro Luis?

PIERRE LUIGI: *Demasiado.* Almost. I am almost happy.

(PIERRE LUIGI exits singing, Busco El Mar. *Silence.* ANNA *looks at the sea.)*

ANNA: To saying yes to museums and to muses old and new, to eternal cities and cities I have yet to see, to finding what I've lost and knowing what I've found. And to a long, long lunch.

(She pulls back her arm to throw the teeth into the "sea.")

(Blackout)

(The sound of the teeth hitting the water)

END OF PLAY

EL OTRO

Octavio Solis

ABOUT THE AUTHOR

Octavio Solis is a playwright and director living in San Francisco. His works
MAN OF THE FLESH, PROSPECT, EL PASO BLUE, SANTOS & SANTOS,
LA POSADA MÁGICA, and DREAMLANDIA have been mounted at the
Oregon Shakespeare Festival, the Dallas Theater Center, the Magic Theater
in San Francisco, South Coast Repertory, the San Diego Repertory Theater,
the San Jose Repertory Theater, Teatro Dallas, Latino Chicago Theater
Company, La Compania de Albuquerque, Teatro Vista in Chicago, El Teatro
Campesino, and Thick Description in San Francisco. Solis has received an
N E A 1995-97 Playwriting Fellowship, the Roger L Stevens award from
the Kennedy Center and the Will Glickman Playwright Award for SANTOS
& SANTOS, a production grant from the Kennedy Center Fund for New
American Plays for DREAMLANDIA at the Dallas Theater Center, the
1998 T C G/N E A Theater Artists in Residence Grant, the 1998 McKnight
Fellowship grant from the Playwrights Center in Minneapolis and the
2000-2001 National Theater Artists Residency Grant from T C G.
His collaborative project with playwright Erik Ehn, SHINER, mounted
in June 1999 by the Undermain Theater in Dallas, is his most recent
production. Solis is a member of the Dramatists Guild and New Dramatists.

EL OTRO was first workshopped through H P P in August 1997. The cast and creative contributors were:

CATARINA .... Mara Hoguín
ROMY .... Ruth Livier
LUPE .... Armando José Durán
BEN .... Jesus Mendoza
NINA .... Raquel Salinas
EL CHARRO .... Gregg Daniel
ALMA .... Denise Blazor
POLO .... Ruben Garfias
ROSS .... Christopher Setherols
OFFICER .... Hal Landon Jr

Director .... Diane Rodriguez
Dramaturg .... John Glore

EL OTRO was originally commissioned by Thick Description Collective. It premiered on 25 July 1998. The cast and creative contributors were:

ROMY .... Maria Candelaria
LUPE .... Octavio Solis
BEN .... Johnny Moreno
NINA ....Mónica Sánchez
EL CHARRO .... Rhonnie Washington
ALMA .... Tessa Konig-Martínez
POLO ....Joaquin Aranda
ROSS ....Rod Gnapp
OFFICER ....Michael Torres

Director .... Tony Kelly
Scenic design .... Elizabeth Mead
Lighting .... Rick Martin
Costumes .... Julie Slinger
Music .... Vincent Montoya & Tattooed Love Dogs
Dramaturgy .... Karen Amano

EL OTRO was also given a staged reading by the Public Theater in the New Works Now Festival 1997.

CHARACTERS & SETTING

ROMY
LUPE (GUADALUPE)
BEN
NINA
EL CHARRO (EL CHARRO NEGRO)
ALMA
POLO (APOLONIO)
ROSS (COWBOY)
OFFICER
ANASTACIO (*played by* BEN)

Time: the present, on a Monday.

Place: El Paso, the border, El Otro

ACT ONE

(ROMY *emerges from the darkness. The shadows of two men loom large behind her.*)

ROMY: La Romy knows the way she knows the way it goes sun yanked out by the roots at dawn *y en la noche* buried in the ground like an old bone that's how long we got that's all it takes to live...

(*A* MAN's *voice, singing softly.*)

MAN: *Eres miá para siempre*
Aunque vengas del vientre
De tu madre

ROMY: ...barely time enough to love *casi nada* la Romy knows the way it goes *más que nada* you come you kiss and die that's the *cuento* only story we got time to tell 'cause there it goes there goes my sun...

MAN: *Ese vicio, esa hambre*
estos huesos, esta sangre
son del padre

ROMY: ...he's leaving his Romy and she's ready to die she's taken all day to die and there it goes up toward the blue above us, the sun the sun over Romy and these two *babosos* in the parking lot of the Hidden Valley Shopping Center who don't feel the fire that Romy feels...

MAN: *Cuando mi peor enemigo*
Es el más conocido
No vale la pena amar
Hay que morir o matar.

ROMY: ...but Romy knows she knows the way and she's about ready to take it...

(LUPE *stands beside her.* BEN *in army uniform appears opposite them.*)

LUPE: Are you him?

BEN: Yeah.

LUPE: Where's she?

BEN: Watching *Good Morning America*. She gave me the keys and said pick her up.

LUPE: Is that uniform supposed to impress me?

BEN: No.

LUPE: 'cause it don't.

BEN: Good.

ROMY: It don't impress me neither.

BEN: Nobody asked you, kid.

LUPE: *Trucha*. That's my kid you talking to, freak.

ROMY: I can take him.

BEN: Give her a birthday kiss and let's go. C'mon, Romy, your mother's waiting for you at the house.

ROMY: Uh-uh. Ain't goin' back.

BEN: Romy...

(LUPE *strides up and plants his face almost against his. He smells him.*)

LUPE: Two eggs, over easy. Chorizo with onions. Wheat toast, margarine, coffee, low fat milk.

BEN: You got a good nose—

LUPE: Cheap cherry lipstick. Tall glass of pussy juice.

BEN: That's about enough, Lupe.

LUPE: You going down on my wife, Sarge? She what you have for a fortified breakfast every morning?

BEN: She's not your wife anymore. And I'm not a sergeant.

LUPE: What's his name, sweetheart? What do dog turds like this go by nowadays?

ROMY: Ben.

LUPE: Benjamin. I got a question for you. When does a wife quit being a wife? When she says? When he says? When the court says? I always thought it was when a life quit being a life, *ese*.

BEN: It was over long before I showed up, man. Ask the kid. You were outa their lives months before.

LUPE: I don't question that. It's love that mystifies me. It must got the properties of water. Sometimes ice, sometimes its a gas, sometimes its all wet. Is that clever? Fuck me, I don't mean to be clever. It don't become a man like me to use wit on a fool like you.

BEN: Are you gonna wish her a happy birthday or what?

LUPE: You're no fool now, though. Vato's husband number two.

BEN: This is your last chance. After today, you don't see her no more.

ROMY: Don't make me go with him, *Apá*. He's a loser.

LUPE: He's your new father, baby.

ROMY: I don't care. I hate him.

LUPE: She hates you, friend.

BEN: She'll get used to me.

ROMY: Make me go with him and I'll kill myself.

LUPE: Shit, she's starting to sound like me. You better take her off my hands, Ben, before she really makes some trouble.

ROMY: NO! FUCK HIM! I'M STAYING WITH YOU!

BEN: Romy, don't start. We gotta get you ready for school.

ROMY: DON'T TOUCH ME, CHUMP.

LUPE: *Romelia Maria. Pórtate bien, mijita, o te doy tus chingazos.*

ROMY: *Si, Papi.*

LUPE: She's yours. Watch your fingers.

BEN: What you tell her?

LUPE: Be cool or be kicked in the teeth. (*He kneels and faces* ROMY *to make his goodbyes.*) Oye. Lemme see your eyes. (*He peers into them.*) *Ay te watcho, mijita.* Take care of your mother and don't be such a fuckin' pain to her. Remember these things: the razor in your sock in case you ever need to hitch a ride somewhere. Don't ever drink outa someone else's beer unless you helped pay for it. Always, always, speak Spanish to spite your teachers. And if this doofus walks by in his underwear in front of you, report his ass. Is that the lip? Don't give me the lip. Quit it, c'mon, I got you a present. (*He searches his pockets for it.*) Shit. Hold on. It's gotta be in my car.

(*He goes, leaving* ROMY *crying with* BEN.)

ROMY: *Como duele* Romy says what a hurt to see someone you never gonna see again and since when he ever look her in the eye when except to say goodbye gotta figure out a way to die gottagottagotta be gone gottagottagotta be gone

(LUPE *returns.*)

LUPE: Damn, Romy, I don't know what to say. I had a present for you, but I musta left it at the *chante. Orale,* Ben, think we could take ten minutes to go by the house—?

BEN: We'll wait for you.

LUPE: No way, man. Come along. We'll go in my car. Ride with me, *ese.* I'm not so bad a guy as Nina makes me out.

BEN: Once you're done, I'm supposed to go straight home.

LUPE: Ten minutes. Just a couple blocks. I'll drive us there and back. It's her present, man.

BEN: Ten minutes?

ROMY: I'm not sitting next to that chump.

LUPE: Shut your ass. *(To* BEN*)* Ten minutes, dude.

ROMY: Then la Romy *y los dos babosos* in the car and then her in the back seat and them in the front and then seeing El Paso streak by like bad laundry and then she hears the doofus saying....

(All three in the car)

BEN: And then I told Nina I thought it was harsh for the court to strip your visitation rights; you're entitled to see her at least once a year.

LUPE: Nina told you about me?

BEN: Not really.

LUPE: Then how do you know what I'm entitled to?

BEN: Well, you're her father, aren't you? *(No reply)* Anyway, I hope the last visitation you got to spend together was worthwhile.

LUPE: *Simón, cabrón.* Tell him what all we did on your last visit, honey.

ROMY: We went to Dairy Queen.

LUPE: Awesome shit those parfaits.

ROMY: And then we went to the movies.

LUPE: Some kickboxing thing.

ROMY: And then we saw those people.

LUPE: She kept me company while I drove around and scored a couple deals.

BEN: A couple deals?

LUPE: A little this, a little that. I got some exceptional medication people are talking about.

BEN: What kinda medication?

LUPE: NASA of the mind. Show him, Rome.

*(*ROMY *shows him the bag.)*

BEN: Now I get how come the courts stripped your visitation rights.

LUPE: Don't worry about her, Benny. I brung her up right. What's our motto, honey?

ROMY: Just say no.

LUPE: What else did we do? Oh yeah! We keyed this guy's car and shot his dogs for cheating a friend out of some bricks for his patio. Dogs, man, they don't know when to give up the ghost. It was kinda funny.

BEN: Ha ha.

ROMY: And you know what this Romy knows the way she's got it right in her lap the way out of the story she sees it now *hijola* these little buds of peyote these dream givers she could eat em and quietly join all those other suns that ever set so she puts a few buds *en su* pocket and eats one and begins to feel it break slow like a secret like a little black secret

LUPE: Did you hear something?

BEN: No.

LUPE: Something whizzed. I felt it whizz right by us, shooom, right through these open windows, this wee chunk a righteousness. Shoom, right under our noses, didn't you feel it?

BEN: Maybe it was a bug.

LUPE: I need to see this guy.

ROMY: And then we stop in front of this house.

(ROSS *the cowboy comes out, his ear bleeding profusely.*)

ROSS: Hey, Lupe! *¿Como te va, buey?*

LUPE: Damn, Ross, what the fuck happened to you?

ROSS: Nothin'. It's nothin'. Who's the soldier boy?

LUPE: Friend of mine. Ben from Fort Bliss. Are you okay?

ROSS: Yeah, yeah. I'm fine.

LUPE: Your ear looks pretty bad, white boy.

ROSS: It's fine. I feel like a million.

BEN: What are you talking about? You're bleeding all over yourself.

ROSS: Loop, is this guy, like, trying to make a point or something? 'Cause if he's trying to make a point, he should come right out and make it and not sit on his fucking hands all day.

LUPE: No, shit no, nothing of the kind.

ROSS: I don't appreciate smart ass sergeants.

LUPE: He's cracking a joke. *Un chiste.*

BEN: And I'm a private first class, for your information.

ROSS: You must be frying in that uniform. Listen, I'd ask you all in but things are a bit of a mess in there.

LUPE: I don't mind. Let's break open some sixes.

ROSS: Things are a real mess. I couldn't let you in, Loop. It's way too messy for the eyes of innocents.

LUPE: Whatever you say, Ross.

ROSS: So what you got, buddy?

LUPE: Premium boogie, no fat, all natural ingredients.

ROSS: Vacu-packed for freshness?

LUPE: For your chewing satisfaction.

ROSS: Awright. Come around side of the house.

(They go.)

BEN: You really shoot those dogs?

ROMY: He did, not me.

BEN: Your *mamá's* concerned about you.

ROMY: Crock.

BEN: We care about how you feel.

ROMY: More crock.

BEN: We're ready to help you adjust.

ROMY: *Ese, no seas tan mamon.*

BEN: What?

ROMY: What kinda Mexican are you? You don't even know Spanish. Man, you're embarrassing.

BEN: Romy, I want to work this out. It doesn't have to be this ugly. We're trying to do right by you.

ROMY: Then how come nobody checked with me? How come nobody asked me if I wanted a doofus in the house?

BEN: That's not my fault. Your mom shoulda told you. It doesn't matter anyhow. I would've married her no matter what you thought.

ROMY: Then why should you care now?

BEN: *(Touching her shoulder)* Romy, I—

(ROMY violently recoils from his touch.)

ROMY: Don't you fucking touch me! Pervert!

BEN: I was...I....

(The lights change, casting an eerie glow on BEN.)

ROMY: And then everything's water and she looks at Ben and Ben stares at the sun and then looks back at La Romy with a fierce whiskey spilling out his eyes and whispers in another voice...

BEN: *Eres...mia.*

ROMY: ...the voice of the bad stranger who been messing with my sleep showing up in my dreams in tatters of blood and muck

(The lights resume as LUPE *and* ROSS *return.)*

LUPE: Thanks a lot for waiting up, Ben. Ross ain't no loose honky, he's a stand-up guy. He's the Boss Ross. Right, *ese,*?

ROSS: You don't got a tarp in the trunk, do you, Loop?

LUPE: Sorry, man. What for?

ROSS: My house is in a grievous state. Damn place has turned to hell on me. Gotta clean up. Do a midnight dump-run.

BEN: And take care of your ear.

LUPE: More army humor.

ROSS: I will take care of my ear, sir. Your benediction is gonna make me right. Cuz a you I have the balm to make my pains holy. Cuz a you I'ma have me a SPECTACULAR day! *(He takes a prescription vial and crams his mouth with pills.)*

BEN: What do you mean cuz of me? What is that shit he's taking?

ROSS: Sir, my poor decrepit ass is shittin' gratitude for you. I just hope the *Charro* knows how fuckin' good his angel is.

ROMY: The *Charro.*

BEN: Who's that? What *charro?*

*(*LUPE *raises his shirt, revealing an array of tattoos. Prominent is a large tattoo of a* Charro *in black.)*

LUPE: *El Charro Negro*, Ben. Got to be.

ROSS: Pray for me, sir. Pray that I get a tarp before nightfall.

LUPE: Check with my ex, Ross. She'll fix you up.

*(*ROSS *goes.)*

BEN: Can we go now?

LUPE: You must be roasting in that thing.

ROMY: And you know what? I'm feeling a tingle come tinglin' up my feet tinglin' like when you get up too fast and the blood rushes to catch up with you and you see little holes in the air. And with this tingle comes a music and I see the back of Lupe's head as he drives on and on and on and on...

BEN: What happened back there? Why was he thanking me? Why was he bleeding?

LUPE: You asking too many of the wrong questions, bud. Just know that Ross respects you now.

BEN: What did you tell him?

LUPE: I told him you were taking over. I told him you were sleeping in my place. Was I outa line? Tell me if I was, Ben.

BEN: That looked like a gunshot.

LUPE: Probably was.

BEN: I got that address memorized.

LUPE: Bitchin.

BEN: This kid doesn't need to be seeing stuff like that.

LUPE: I'm with you there.

ROMY: And you know what: I'm there too.

(Lights change. LUPE's apartment. LUPE points and goes.)

LUPE: Make yourselves at home. I gotta take a leak.

BEN: Where's all the furniture?

ROMY: He don't got none.

BEN: Where do we sit, on the floor?

(She does. He sits beside her.)

BEN: Hey, back at that house. I didn't mean anything by that.

ROMY: Why don't you go fight some war and die so we can scratch your name on that dumb wall?

BEN: I understand how you feel. Nobody wants to break up a family. Even a rotten one like yours. But nothin's comin' between your *mamá* and me, girl. She's my wife. And with or without you, we're gonna have us a baby soon—

ROMY: That's gross!

BEN: Don't get me wrong. I like you fine. But I want my own kid, too. A baby to start us off clean, bless the house, someone to—

ROMY: Replace me.

BEN: That's not what I was gonna say.

ROMY: You go try and make a baby with her. Just watch it close, cuz I'll take this razor and slit that baby in its sleep, I swear to God I will.

BEN: I wonder, how much of your Daddy are you?

LUPE: *(With a beer in each hand)* Fully fifty percent. Least thass what I been told.

BEN: A little early in the day for me.

LUPE: If you're serious about taking on this spitfire, you'll need it.

(BEN takes the beer.)

LUPE: Sorry about the digs. Sold everything last week and chucked the rest in the dumpster out back. Kept nothing but my old Zippo lighter. I used it to keep time to all her pretty songs.

BEN: Nina sings?

LUPE: Pipes just like Vikki Carr. She serenaded me all the time.

ROMY: Did you find it?

LUPE: What?

ROMY: My present.

LUPE: No. It's around here. Go look in the kitchen.

(ROMY goes, grumbling to herself.)

BEN: Can I borrow your phone to call Nina?

LUPE: Just cut off the service. Relax. I'll get you back to your car. Where do you hail from, soldier?

BEN: Chicago.

LUPE: Cool.

BEN: Second generation. Working-class Mexicans from Pilsen.

LUPE: We must look like hicks to you. Why'd you join the service?

BEN: I dunno. I got tired of living on the dole. I needed some discipline in my life. Army's a good place to start. The chain of command is clear, P F C to God. Why are you asking me all this? We should be going back.

LUPE: I'm not done with my beer, pal. Tell me how you met my wife at the cafeteria.

BEN: I like chili-cheeseburgers: hers are awful good. I like a certain kind of woman: she's that kinda woman. What can I say? In a town where I don't know a soul and people don't talk much, it was nice that she was nice.

LUPE: Yeah.

BEN: Nina in that funky white uniform and her little name tag. She gave me a new lease.

LUPE: So wassup with you and my daughter?

BEN: What do you mean?

LUPE: How come she call you a pervert?

BEN: What are you insinuating?

LUPE: I'm not insinuatin' shit. I'm saying I heard both of you back at Cowboy's. Wassup with you? She what you come to my house for, Ben?

BEN: Lemme tell you one thing, buddy, before you jump to any more conclusions. I didn't know about this kid. I never heard two words about her until after I proposed to Nina.

LUPE: You expect me to believe that?

(ROMY re-enters.)

BEN: I don't care what you believe. The fact is in all the times I went out with her, not once did the name Romelia pass her lips.

ROMY: You're a liar.

BEN: It's the truth. She was a free and single woman so far as I was concerned and your little ass never came up. Not till after we got the rings. I'm willing to raise her as my own but not how that you're suggesting. So don't even go there, Lupe, okay? Let's get back to my car.

LUPE: Lemme find that present first. (He goes.)

BEN: Fuckhead.

ROMY: La Romy sitting there staring at the wall feeling her momma's denial start to seep through the cracks and then she see that old lady coming already feel her pressure she's coming she's about to—

(An old woman, ALMA, enters, furtively. She becomes very distressed when she sees BEN.)

ALMA: *Ay Dios Santo, fuente de todo bien, aqui aqui, mi dulcisimo hijo, mi dolor mas profundo,* all my prayers answered, all my benedictions given truth, here, here, he breathes, he walks, witness to my shame, *Oh corazón abierto para ser refugio de las almas, recíbeme!*

BEN: Yes? You know this lady, Romy?

(ROMY shakes her head. ALMA is visibly rattled.)

BEN: Are you looking for someone, ma'am?

ALMA: *(Speaking in a hushed voice) Dios mió. Dios mió. Dueño de mis dolores.*

BEN: Ma'am?

ALMA: Face so pale, eyes so pure, still the boy we knew. Do you know who I am? *¡Los bienes del mundo, los renuncio todos!* There are lies which come true and nights with opened veins. Numbers on the palm of the hand and little bones in the clock. Ants in my water and regrets I daily light candles for. *Ticka ticka tick.*

BEN: Are you with some church or something?

ALMA: It is the time, *mijo*, which picks us. The sins ripen. Fall at our feet. Open up like ulcers. Proclaim our souls to hell. For our crimes, *Anastacio*, forgive us.

ROMY: Who?

ALMA: *(Turning to* ROMY*)* And you! You who deliver us. *Santísima flor.* For you, *virgencita*, on my knees, on my knees for you, I will receive your host. *(She thrusts* ROMY's *hand into her mouth.)* Hm. Hm. You are my sacrament.

*(*LUPE *enters, sees her, and seizes her by the collar.)*

LUPE: You! What are you doing here! Get your ass away from my daughter, bitch!

ALMA: ¡*Perdon, perdon!*

LUPE: Shut up! Ben, I'm disappointed in you.

BEN: What, she came in, I didn't know what—

LUPE: Are you all right, baby? She hurt you?

ROMY: No.

BEN: Who is she?

LUPE: This hag? This disgusting crone? She's my maid. Alma the fucking maid. She comes here every Monday to clean the house for me.

BEN: What's there to clean?

LUPE: Tell him.

ALMA: The floor, the walls, the sink in the kitchen, the vegetable bin in the refrigerator, the toilet bowl, the windows-

LUPE: What did you tell him? Tell me what you told him.

ALMA: *Nada, señor.* Not a thing. I just wanted to see.

LUPE: Alma, you sick cow, who do you think this is? Tell me who the fuck you think this is.

ALMA: *No sé.*

LUPE: This is Ben from Ft. Bliss. Ben from Chicago. What the fuck is your last name?

BEN: Cortez.

LUPE: Benjamin Cortez.

ALMA: *Mucho gusto, Señor Cortez.*

LUPE: Now what did you tell them? What did you say? Didn't I make it clear that you were to stay and wait at the ranch? Don't you know you

almost ruined everything? What kinda fuckin' maid are you anyway!
(He produces a handgun, which he levels at her head.) I OUGHTA BLOW YOUR
DAMN HEAD OFF!

BEN: Whoa! Lupe! What are you doing?

LUPE: This domestic is an incompetent, Ben. A pervert who don't know the
first thing about raising children in a positive environment!

BEN: Put the gun down, man!

LUPE: I've had it with her excuses!

ALMA: *¡No, señor, por favor!*

LUPE: I pay her well, Ben, don't I pay you well, and all these years I kept her,
even when I was broke, I kept her because I thought I should depend on
something, I thought she might give the world some credibility, Monday
comes, maid comes, Monday comes, maid comes. But now I'm not so sure
the routine makes any sense now. Mondays are starting to feel like a bitch
to me. Maybe if I do away with the maid, Mondays won't come. That would
suit me fine. What do you think, Alma?

(ALMA urinates on herself, creating a small puddle.)

LUPE: Get a mop.

(BEN starts to go.)

LUPE: Not you. You.

(ALMA goes.)

LUPE: She's the maid.

BEN: You gonna put that away?

LUPE: Thought you were accustomed to seeing firearms in the Army, Ben.

BEN: Put the gun away or I'm gonna have to kick your ass.

LUPE: Whoa. Hubby number two grows some balls.

ROMY: Is that my present?

(ALMA returns with a mop and starts cleaning up her mess.)

LUPE: What? No, honey. This ain't even loaded. Check this out.

*(He aims at the floor and slowly pulls the trigger. A nasty click sends a shudder
through ALMA.)*

LUPE: See?

ROMY: Where's my present?

LUPE: I dunno, babe. Alma, have you seen...?

ALMA: No *señor.* But it can only be at one place.

LUPE: Where?

ALMA: *Al otro lado.*

BEN: Where?

ROMY: The other side.

ALMA: *Allí en el rancho estará.*

BEN: What *rancho* is she talking about?

ALMA: You know what *rancho, mijo.* It's where you belong, Anast—

LUPE: Shut your hole! *(Keeping his gaze on* ALMA*)* What have you heard about me, Ben?

BEN: What do you mean?

LUPE: What have you heard on the street? Have you heard like, that Lupe, *ese,* he's bad news, he's into some shit, like, he's killed some kid or somethin', *ese.* Have you heard that?

BEN: No.

LUPE: Have you heard anything about me killing a woman?

BEN: No.

LUPE: Me neither.

ROMY: *Apá,* I want my present.

LUPE: What you thinkin', Ben?

BEN: Let's get her present.

LUPE: Alma, go back to where you were. And stay put.

ROMY: *Pero La Romy* can't stay put in her own head cuz the little buds are starting to break up inside her and slowly Mom slowly come up from her bowels slowly come up from the belly of her girl one seed at a time Mom how could you pull this shit you denied me to that chump Mom how could you...

(As she speaks, the others recede into the darkness and NINA *emerges, coming toward her in a slow sweeping glide.)*

NINA: Romy...

ROMY: Mom...

NINA: *Mi gatita...*

ROMY: *Ay, Amá...*

*(*NINA *bursts forward, a large bruise under her right eye.)*

NINA: Don't you come near me! Don't you dare come dragging those shoes into my house! Lookit you, girl! What is that!

ROMY: Horseshit.

NINA: *Pos* take your shoes off! Take them off! *Valgame,* where in this crummy neighborhood did you get horseshit from?

(ROMY *sits to take off her shoes.*)

ROMY: A horse. Damn, quit being such a mom.

NINA: You quit being such a smart mouth. Don't wipe your hands on me, girl. Damn, I come home from work and not a minute's rest!

ROMY: — Hey! What happened to you?

NINA: *Nada.* Other shoe.

ROMY: Your eye's all swoll up!

NINA: I don't want to discuss it right now.

ROMY: D'you two fight again?

NINA: I said, I don't wanna discuss it.

ROMY: I can't believe it. What did you tell him that he did this to you?

NINA: I told him don't hit me. Now, what horse are you talking about?

ROMY: The one in Mr Tovar's backyard.

NINA: The Tovares? The Tovares have a horse? Are you sure?

ROMY: I heard it whinny this morning. So when I got home from school, I got on my Keds and went to see.

NINA: You went to their house? The socks.

ROMY: (*As she takes them off*) To the alley *atrás.* I climbed up the corrugated fence he keeps there, but I couldn't see it. So I jumped over and landed in this big ol' pile of *caca.* But there it was.

NINA: You saw it?

ROMY: *Amá,* it was a young colt. This skinny thing with legs like willow branches and this white hanky stain right on its nose. He made this little snort and shook its head to one side and clopped in place like it was ready to run.

NINA: Did you get close?

ROMY: I couldn't move 'cause he was staring right at my kneecaps, but he came to me, *Amá.* He came slow and let me touch him.

NINA: *Mija,* that's a trait you get from me. I had this way with horses too. They'd come to me like I was one of them. Their hides rippled when I ran my hand across their backs. I learned to love when I learned to ride.

ROMY: You rode horses? When did you do that?

NINA: Way before you were born, kid. Did Mr Tovar catch you?

ROMY: No. I felt someone watching me the whole time, though. So I split.

NINA: Don't be jumpin' into people's yards. It's trespassing. Mr Tovar, especially.

ROMY: How come we never see them? How come they never come out or nothing?

NINA: They're sad people, *mija.* They gave up all their horses years ago when they lost their only boy.

ROMY: How come they got that colt now?

NINA: That's what I'd like to know. Hose off. You stink.

ROMY: I can't. You got the sprinkler on.

NINA: Then do what I woulda done, stupid.

ROMY: What.

NINA: Run through it!

(She dashes into the shower of the "sprinkler" screaming and laughing as ROMY *follows suit.)*

ROMY: IT'S COLD!

NINA: IT FEELS GOOD!

ROMY: YOUR UNIFORM!

NINA: THE HELL WITH THAT!

ROMY: LET ME GO! I'M GETTING WET!

NINA: GOOD! CLEANSE YOURSELF!

ROMY: ¡ANDALE! ¡AMÁ!

NINA: ALL RIGHT! ALL RIGHT!

(They run out and stand by their shoes, panting with delight. ROMY *finds a small note* NINA *dropped by the sprinkler.)*

ROMY: And you know what from Ama's soul a petal fall inside the ring of water a note of secrecies and La Romy see it pick it and save it for no reason why.... *(She puts it away, unseen by* NINA.)

NINA: I'm not letting him in the house again, Romelia. I told him. This is the last time.

ROMY: He's my *Apá*.

NINA: I can't be married to that man no more. *No más.* C'mon.

ROMY: What.

NINA: I'm not drinking by myself. One beer. A toast to the new colt on the block. But first... *(Turning to the 'sprinkler')* One more walk through the water.

(NINA slowly courses through the invisible rain, feeling the cleansing drops on her face. ROMY watches her go.)

ROMY: La Romy sees you Mom and sees something scared hurt something hidden from even you *Amá* and you know what you wish you could hose yourself off hose off years of shit but it won't wash off that white uniform you wear...

(BEN and LUPE enter. LUPE holding his shoes and socks in his hands.)

LUPE: You ready, babe?

ROMY: Uh-huh.

BEN: Hold on a minute. What's going on? What are we doing?

LUPE: We're crossing the river, Ben.

BEN: What for?

ROMY: To get to the other side, stupid.

BEN: Hey, they got bridges for this last I heard.

LUPE: They're not available routes for me anymore. See what I'm saying? Take your shoes off and roll up your pants.

BEN: I don't think this is legal, Lupe.

ROMY: We should leave him here.

LUPE: Ben, the Law is an outmoded thang. It's just an excuse to make people do what they don't want to do. Shit, the Law's even moved into my bedroom. Laid down these fuckin' rulings that don't make no sense. Custody, property, restraining orders, it's all bullshit.

BEN: I'm not letting you take her across.

ROMY: Why not?

BEN: Because you could drown, you idiot.

ROMY: Pffft.

BEN: Yeah, you say that now.

LUPE: It's not deep in this part. Trust me.

BEN: No way.

LUPE: *Oyeme*, Benjamin, what's the deal here? Are you establishing the chain of command? You pulling rank on me, babe?

BEN: There is no present for her, is there? I'm not doing it at her expense.

ROMY: I don't know how you even think you can be my Dad. You don't got the guts to cross the damn river cuz you ain't no real Mexican.

BEN: I'm Mexican. I got Mexican blood in me.

ROMY: Don't go foolin' yourself, Ben.

BEN: I'M A MEXICAN, GODDAMMIT!

(A Border Patrol OFFICER *leaps out, aiming his flashlight at them.)*

OFFICER: Did I hear someone say Messican?

ROMY: Oh-oh.

BEN: Hey, how's it goin'. We were just leav—

OFFICER: Stay right where you are, brother. Don't make me chase you down.

BEN: Whoa, take it easy. I'm trying to tell you, man, they wanted me to go with them across the river—

OFFICER: Really. To that side.

BEN: Isn't that crazy? They wanted to cross right here.

OFFICER: You sure it wasn't the other way around? You didn't just swim from that side to this?

BEN: C'mon. Do we look like illegals? *(To* LUPE*)* Clear things up with this character and let's get the hell out.

LUPE: *¿Cómo?*

BEN: Tell him, Lupe.

LUPE: *¿Qué díjo este buey?*

ROMY: *No sé. Creo que ya nos chingamos, Apá.*

BEN: Aw, cut it out! Talk English, both a you!

LUPE: *No hables así, mijita, o te doy por la madre.*

ROMY: *Si me pegas, te pego partás pero más fuerte.*

BEN: We're American.

OFFICER: I heard Messican.

BEN: C'mon, the uniform, I'm an enlisted man. Wanna see I D?

OFFICER: That would be helpful.

*(*ROMY *starts to run. The* OFFICER *aims his gun at her.)*

OFFICER: *¡ALTO! ¡NO SE MUEVA O LE DOY UN BALAZO POR LA CABEZA!*

BEN: SHIT! ROMY! WHAT THE FUCK ARE YOU DOING! DON'T RUN!

(ROMY *freezes.*)

LUPE: *Por favor, señor,* no keel my leetle chile. *¡Es mi hija!*

OFFICER: EVERYONE! On the ground! Now! You too, *jovencita!*

BEN: Do as he says.

(*Everyone lies flat on their stomachs. The* OFFICER *frisks the men for weapons.*)

OFFICER: So what's the motivation, sergeant? Don't like the pay in the Army? Feel you gotta diversify by takin' on wetbacks?

BEN: I'm not a coyote. And they're not illegals.

OFFICER: Uh-huh.

BEN: The girl is my step-daughter, the man is her father. He's trying to get me to wade across to Mexico. And I'm not a sergeant.

OFFICER: (*Finding the bag full of peyote*) Well, hi-de-hi-hi-ho.

BEN: Oh fuck.

OFFICER: What are these for, sergeant, your allergies?

BEN: I have nothing to do with that.

OFFICER: (*Finding the gun*) How about this? (*No reply.*) All right. *Quítese la ropa, por favor.*

BEN: Say what?

OFFICER: Start stripping.

BEN: What for?

OFFICER: Just do it.

BEN: Lupe. Say something. Tell him you're American.

LUPE: *Soy Americáno.*

OFFICER: Peel.

(*They strip to their shorts.*)

OFFICER: In all my ten years on the Border Patrol, never ever have I come across anyone trying to sneak from the U S side to the Messican. That's a good one. Why would anyone give up living in the richest country on earth and go live in that shitpot? What could possibly be there that can't be had here?

LUPE: Maybee chee ees ded.

OFFICER: Whut?

LUPE: Ded. Joo cahn dress her op in jools an fine closs an put mucho make-op on her fase. Joo can get een bed weeth her an mahke sex weeth her an mahke beleef dat chee ees good an muy linda, but joo canna fool joorsef. Chee ees a rotteen corpse an chee duzznt eefen know joo are der. Cos la *verdad, señor,* ees dat chee ees ded to joo an maybee alwaz has bin.

OFFICER: Are you talking about America?

BEN: He's talking about his ex-wife.

LUPE: We haf too go bahck, *señor.* We canna leef in dee same box weef da ded. *Tenemos que devolvérnos.*

OFFICER: I can't let you go.

LUPE: *¿Por qué no?* It ees our right.

OFFICER: But it's our job, too, to protect the border from—

LUPE: To keep us out, dat ees joor yob. To send us bahck ees de same ting.

OFFICER: Well, one sure for sure: I don't much see the difference between Messican and Merican now. Alla you look like wetbacks to me.

LUPE: Dat ees what we are. *Mojados.* Eliens. Whatefer border wi cross.

OFFICER: I hate this job. I really hate it. I tell Lucille, Lucille, this job is the sickest job there is. To have to pick up them poor people and haul them to the station like strays to the pound, it's terrible. And to see in their eyes that terror. And to deal with that on a daily basis, cutting people's hopes off right at the knee, right as soon as they set foot on the levee, to bag 'em right there and knock 'em back across, it's terrible. I go, Lucille, I'm a barb wire fence with Ray-bans. She just stares back at me like I'm not even there. I hate this damn job. *(Tossing their clothes back to them)* You wanna go back, I can't stop you.

LUPE: *Vámonos.*

BEN: You're letting us cross? Are you crazy?

OFFICER: Get.

ROMY: Thanks, mister.

OFFICER: *Señores,* if I see you on this side again, I'll perform my duties to the letter and you'll be sorry for it.

LUPE: Joo weel be doeen us a faybor. *Gracias.*

(LUPE and ROMY go as BEN yells at the OFFICER.)

BEN: You can't let us go! You can't! That girl could drown in that water!

OFFICER: She seems to be fordin' it all right to me.

BEN: Oh shit! ROMY!

(BEN *runs off after them, past* ROMY *who stands downstage. The* OFFICER *takes* ROMY'*s shoes and goes.*)

ROMY: And then we're toe-deep then ankle-deep then knee-deep in water that is more mud than water and it feels good to La Romy and then you know what swooosh we're deep like that I see two heads in front of me bobbin' and chokin' an' swooosh La Romy starts to go under and under is thick black syrup with old tires swimmin' and bottles and tennies and La Romy feels a bog crammin' in her mouth goin' down her lungs like a big foot goes in a sock and swooosh I can't see a thing but I think a Mom I think a her I think I'm drownin' but I think a her my Mom I see her my Mom MAMÁ!

(*Lights change.* NINA *appears. She seems to be waiting.*)

NINA: I hear you, baby. (*She turns around and calls loudly.*) COWBOY! COWBOY, I KNOW YOU'RE IN THERE! GET YOUR ASS OUT HERE RIGHT NOW! I'M GONNA CALL THE COPS, ROSS! I MEAN IT! GET OUT HERE!

(ROSS *enters, really stoned, his wound cursorily dressed with a bandanna.*)

ROSS: Hi, Nina. I didn't hear ya. The waffle iron was on.

NINA: Jesus Christ. What the hell happened to you?

ROSS: Me and Marie. You know how we mess around. It was a accident.

NINA: Oh shit. Marie! Ross, what have you done? Is Romy in there? You got my little girl in your house?

ROSS: No, no, Nina, listen, you can't go in, you can't, they're not here, they're not!

NINA: They were here, though, right? That's what you're saying, right?

ROSS: You wouldn't have a tarp, would you?

NINA: Listen to me, Ross. My man was supposed to be home with Romy hours ago. I been everywhere looking for them. Nobody's seen them and nobody's seen Lupe. Nobody knows shit. But he's got *mija* and my new guy and you're the only one I know who can help me. Now where the fuck did they go?

ROSS: Dunno. You know Loop, movin' target. Boy, these pants are finished.

NINA: Ross, goddammit, I'm talking to you!

ROSS: Hey, take it easy!

NINA: How long we known each other, Cowboy? How many times you come to my house and cry on my shoulder about your girl? How many bottles been passed between us? We're losers, *ese*, *puros* amateurs when it comes to love, takin' care of our *gente*. We deserve what's coming to us. But not my *mija*. She's got nothing to do with this. If he hurts her, if he so much as touches her, we're all fucked for life.

ROSS: If I only had a tarp, I might....

NINA: I don't have a goddamn tarp, Ross!

ROSS: You checked the trunk? *(She looks at him, then goes. Pause. She returns dragging a large tarpaulin.)* Lord in fuckin' heaven.

NINA: How did this end up in my car, Ross?

ROSS: It's perfectamundo.

NINA: When did you and him dig this up?

ROSS: A few days ago. Can I have it?

NINA: Where are they?

ROSS: I used to bust horses, you know. A ranch out by Abilene. I would get up at five, eat cold beans out of a can, and take the meanest horses and ride 'em till they broke. Took pride in my bloody boots. It was a damn good livin'. But you just can't treat a woman like that, can you?

NINA: No, you can't, Cowboy.

ROSS: They got spirit won't quit till they do. *Chíngao.*

NINA: I told that girl to leave you. Poor thing loved you too much.

ROSS: I'm sorry.

NINA: Where are they?

ROSS: I used to bust horses, Nina. Did I ever tell you that?

NINA: Take this thing in there and clean up your mess and do what you have to do. And this time don't miss.

(ROSS drags the tarp off. NINA holds back tears.)

ROMY: Mamá don't cry the reeds sway and rattle in the green-black current that carries me along the rows of wildflowers and alfalfa that witness my sinkin' don't cry I see my dyin' is a pretty one if here is where I die among the yellow fleshy bubbles of gathering foam with the soft muddy floor sucking my feet under and the sky all asunder and you know what Mamá the water tastes like skin like a man invading my mouth his whole self slipping in my shell like the tiny crayfish in the rushes no Mamá don't cry just hear and don't cry.

NINA: I hear you, baby.

(She goes. Lights change. ROMY falls to her knees, out of breath. LUPE and BEN stagger on, wet, cold, panting, their clothes drenched and muddy in their arms.)

BEN: Oh my god! Oh my god! Jesus Christ!

LUPE: That was some ride! Yeah! That's the way to live! Goddamn!

BEN: I thought you said it wasn't gonna be deep!

LUPE: That's the river, *ese,* the river, she one treacherous bitch! Ha!

BEN: That water was twenty feet at least! It was spinning us around like twigs! We coulda drowned!

LUPE: Like I said, Ben, that was some ride! You gotta be ready, you gotta keep the blood red, the fists clenched, the teeth grit down, 'cause now we're on the other side, *cabrón!* WOOO!

BEN: Uugh. I smell like shit.

LUPE: *Este río tiene la mierda de dos países.* Transamerican cesspool.

BEN: What am I gonna tell my C O about my uniform?

LUPE: Fuck your uniform! When are you gonna learn, brother? The army don't mean shit here. God ain't no American and he don't wear no uniform and he don't give a shit about P F Cs. We're on the Other, man! The Other!

BEN: This is crazy.

LUPE: You're catchin' on. How are you, sweetheart?

ROMY: Okay.

BEN: What do you mean okay? You nearly went under, you brat.

LUPE: He's right, Romy. We almost lost you. *De chiripada este cabrón te salvó.*

ROMY: Him?

LUPE: He dragged you ashore by the scruff, didn't ya, ace?

BEN: You were swimmin, fine, but at some point, you just quit and let yourself go. What was I gonna do, let you sink?

LUPE: The fact is, he saved your ass.

ROMY: I guess you're thinkin I should thank you.

BEN: You don't have to.

LUPE: It was a sight, babe. He had you one arm around your neck, and he was holding your head up, and his face was real near to yours and his hand, you know, kinda rode down over your breast, and *mano,* it was a sight.

ROMY: Is that true?

BEN: Dammit, Lupe, what are you doing?

LUPE: *Nada,* Ben. Just trying to find us a place where we can watch the moon pus up in the sky without the chiggers crawling up our ass.

ROMY: Were you really trying to feel me up?

BEN: I was keeping your stupid head above water. You're gonna get hypothermia if we don't get you out of those clothes and into some warm place.

LUPE: Sit down, relax, commingle.

BEN: Fuck you. *(He goes.)*

LUPE: I feel sorry for you, Rome. Your father's a nerd.

ROMY: He's not my father.

LUPE: Hey, I'm clownin' you. You know damn well who your old man is. You wanna be rid of him? I can do that, you know. You want me to do that?

ROMY: No.

LUPE: Then what? Are you pissed at me? Huh?

ROMY: No.

LUPE: *¿Cómo esta tu mamá?*

ROMY: I spend the whole weekend with you and this is the first you ask of her.

LUPE: How is she, I said.

ROMY: Better. She ain't sittin' up in the kitchen all night smoking cigarettes or talkin' to herself in the mornings and wipin' those red puffy eyes. She's not alone in the evenings. She's actually starting to look younger.

LUPE: So this soldier makes her happy?

ROMY: I guess.

LUPE: That's too bad. Your *mamá* and me were made for each other, you know.

ROMY: Oh sure. You hardly showed your face and when you did you were drunk and you trashed the house and took Mom's money and made fun of her food like she couldn't do nothin' right and you never took us out to dinner even, *Apá!* Mom couldn't keep any friends 'cause they were afraid of you. And junkies were always callin' for you or if it wasn't them it was the police, and then she said you hit her. Yeah you were made for each other, all right.

LUPE: You *are* pissed at me.

ROMY: You don't have to go, *Apá*. You can change.

LUPE: I have. I've gotten worse.

ROMY: You can't let this guy be my father. You're my father.

LUPE: I dunno, babe.

ROMY: You are! I know you are!

LUPE: Lissen to me, you little cunt. You keep the fuck away from me! I don't want shit to do with you! You should've stayed with your mother while you had the chance! You got me all wrong! I ain't your father! I never been your father!

(He turns away as BEN *enters carrying a rolled up old quilt.)*

BEN: I found this. It's filthy but it's dry.

(He places it on ROMY'S *shoulders. She shrugs it off.)*

BEN: What's wrong? What happened?

LUPE: She's touched by your goodness, Ben. Such a heart a gold, I just wanna cut it out and put it by the dice on my dashboard.

*(*BEN *places the quilt over her shoulders and turns to* LUPE.*)*

BEN: What you tell her?

LUPE: Nothing she don't already know—

(Suddenly ducking, forcing BEN *down with him.)*

LUPE: Heads!

BEN: What is it?

LUPE: Didn't you see it?

BEN: What, another bug?

LUPE: Ain't no bugs, Ben. This is a bullet.

BEN: A bullet? I didn't hear no gunshot.

LUPE: Why would you? It's not meant for you. *(To* ROMY*)* Did you hear it?

ROMY: Nope.

*(*NINA *enters in her robe.)*

ROMY: And then La Romy feel another chemical vision riding on the back of bad memory she don't say nothin' as Mamá come from that day past when I was sleepin' in my bed

NINA: Hey, deadweight.

LUPE: Yeah?

NINA: You gonna watch T V all night *o vas a venir a la cama?*

LUPE: Where's Romy?

NINA: Sleeping in her room. Or trying to. She's keeps having these nightmares about some man trying to grab her. Comes out of the earth and grabs her.

BEN: She told me there wasn't ever any heat between you.

LUPE: There wasn't.

NINA: Well?

LUPE: Nina, why is it what when I look at you and see the flesh of your lovely tits peekin' through your blouse by the little cup at the base of your neck and then I catch a whiff of the sweet oil of your sex, why is it that when I start to get it up for you, I am overwhelmed with this numbing guilt?

NINA: 'Cause you're a Catholic.

BEN: She said you hate her more than anything in the world.

NINA: Don't you love me anymore, Lupe?

LUPE: I do.

NINA: Maybe that's what you feel guilty about.

LUPE: The lengths I went to. Things I did.

BEN: What did you do?

LUPE: Unspeakable things.

NINA: Then don't speak them.

(They kiss.)

NINA: How's your guilt now?

LUPE: Harder.

(They kiss again.)

ROMY: And then in bed La Romy hear them thumping away thumping away thumping away heaving gasping scratching making that messy sex that always scare her cuz how could La Romy have come from that noise that rage that desperation and how come she didn't just dissolve in the shower that they take after and how can all of that mean love how can it possibly mean love.

BEN: Was there ever a time that you opened up to each other?

LUPE: No.

NINA: Can I be real honest with you, Lupe?

LUPE: Sure.

NINA: Back then, when you did what you did, and washed that bat in the river, I was crazed with fear.

LUPE: So was I.

NINA: But you know what? It turned me on. To see what you would do for me. Kill a man for me. Fuck. Is that sick or what?

LUPE: Pretty damn sick.

NINA: Nobody loved me like that. Nobody went that far. I just didn't know I was worth that.

LUPE: You still are, babe.

NINA: Uh-uh. These days, I don't feel like much of anything. Even sex with my old man feels like adultery.

LUPE: What's your point?

NINA: You're fucking someone else, aren't you?

LUPE: If I was, you think I'd tell you?

NINA: I would.

LUPE: Okay... Are you?

NINA: You're gone for days sometimes weeks at a time without a word and just like anyone else I'm a woman who wants. I ain't gonna stand around and wait for you to show. It's lonely in this damn house and I get tired of hearing myself pine.

LUPE: Who is he?

NINA: Nobody.

LUPE: You bring him in this house?

NINA: I still got scruples.

LUPE: Here, lemme wipe them off. *(He slaps her.)*

NINA: FUCK YOU, LUPE!

LUPE: Shit. What am I doing? Nina...

NINA: Uh-uh. Back off.

LUPE: I'm sorry.

NINA: *(Taking out the same gun seen before)* Kiss your ass goodbye, Loop.

LUPE: Nina, don't be dense.

NINA: You won't stay and you won't stay away. I won't have strangers hitting me. Romy, the older she gets, the more she adores you. The bigger shit you become the more she likes it. It's gotta stop, Lupe. Right now.

LUPE: Gimme that thing.

(She fires it. Huge bang. LUPE flinches.)

LUPE: *Pendeja.* You missed.

NINA: Uh-uh. My bullet's just taking the long way around. Get the hell outa here.

(He turns away. She goes.)

BEN: She told me she once fired a gun at you. Was that true?

LUPE: Na. Nina likes to dramatize things.

ROMY: And then you know what La Romy shivers at the nearness of lead and pees where she sits out of fear and coldness...

BEN: Assholes never told me the desert could get this cold.

LUPE: Who?

BEN: Officers at Fort Bliss. Yeah, right, Bliss. Nothing to do in this town but find a place to get outa the sun. Nintey-six degrees is mild. The thing that really gets me is how the nights get so wicked cold. Just when you start to be grateful for the evening, this desert chill sets in. Then another scorcher by nine o'fucking clock. The worst conditions for a man who likes to know where he stands.

LUPE: Baby, I'm sorry. *Se me metió el Diablo.*

ROMY: My stomach hurts.

(A moment, then ROMY rushes into LUPE's arms. They hold each other tightly. A shaft of light pierces the dark.)

BEN: What's that?

ROMY: ¿Apá?

(LUPE faces the source of the beam, and sings robustly.)

LUPE: *Perla de mi vida*
No me dejes solo aquí
Prefiero el infierno
Al mundo frío sin ti!

(An OLD MAN with a flashlight comes up to him.)

OLD MAN: *(Planting his circle of light on one of his tattoos)* ¿Qué significa eso?

LUPE: Serpent. For the sin of Envy.

OLD MAN: And this bleeding rose?

LUPE: Is for the sin of Lust.

OLD MAN: And this knife?

LUPE: The sin of aggravated assault.

OLD MAN: *Eres maldito, Lupe.*

BEN: Does he know you?

LUPE: This is Polo. My gardener. He tends to my crop.

BEN: He must've known we were coming. You must've known.

LUPE: Crink in the shorts of Time, Ben. His incident got together with our incident and made coincident. Kinda like with you and Nina.

POLO: This is him?

LUPE: Ben from Fort Bliss.

(POLO *stares intensely at* BEN *then turns to* ROMY.)

POLO: She don't look so good.

LUPE: That's cause she's coming under his custody.

BEN: Romy, you got a fever? Let me feel you.

ROMY: Keep your hands to yourself. I'm fine.

LUPE: Let's get the fuck outa here.

ROMY: And then La Romy the two babosos and the old man Polo like the game like the Italian guy who went to China we're all crammed in his old pick-up and La Romy is sitting on my *Papi's* lap and for no reason at all but maybe night I start to cry

LUPE: I see the lip. No lip, Rome.

BEN: Where exactly are we going?

POLO: *El rancho.*

BEN: What *rancho*? Where is it?

POLO: *Allá.*

LUPE: We're on the Other, man. Didn't I tell you?

POLO: *El Otro.*

ROMY: What's your problem?

BEN: I'm itchy. All over.

LUPE: Don't scratch. You'll rip the bodies off but leave the heads inside and get infected.

BEN: What are you talking about?

LUPE: Ticks. They were all over the blanket you brought. I got them too.

BEN: Aw...SHIT.

LUPE: It's okay, *ese.* We're almost there.

BEN: My head, my arms, my balls...

LUPE: How come you ain't scrubbing?

ROMY: I didn't get bit.
And you know why 'cuz in her blood she got the poison her exit weed spreading wide on her now and then La Romy see the old white stucco

walls gleaming even on this moonless night and she see the heehaw of the donkey come flying through the air covered in cornspit and she know we're there

POLO: *¿Quieren frijoles?*

LUPE: *¡Orale!* Pot a beans and tortillas for the starchy farts, Ben! Eat while I look for my Romy's present.

BEN: Fuck her present! I want to go home! I'm covered with ticks!

(LUPE *embraces him, lifting his feet off the ground.*)

BEN: What are you doing!

LUPE: We're mingling bloods, *ese!* Trading these little eight-legged whores and filling their fat little stomachs full of the wine of you and me and making you and me *CARNALES* inside them! BROTHAHS!

BEN: We're infested, you crazy fuck!

LUPE: Chill. I know how to get them off. Follow me.

(*They go.* POLO *enters with a bowl. He sits and watches* ROMY *as she staggers to the ground.*)

ROMY: I don't want it.

POLO: You have to eat. You the only good thing that's ever come out of that man.

ROMY: He said he wasn't my father.

POLO: Consider yourself lucky.

ROMY: I wish he was different. If *Papi* was more like Ben, I could like take him home and make us a family again. Leave that doofus here.

POLO: (*As* ALMA *enters and quietly stand upstage, unseen*) Tell me about the doofus.

ROMY: He came outa nowhere. All of a sudden he's married to *Amá* and I don't even know him. He walks in wearing this uniform like it entitles him to me.

POLO: Ben is his real name?

ROMY: Yeah. I guess.

POLO: Has he ever said the name *Anastacio*?

ROMY: No. But the maid has. Alma the maid. How come?

POLO: *Come tus frijoles.*

(POLO *joins* ALMA *and they go. In another space,* LUPE *and* BEN *enter a corral.* LUPE *carries a bottle in each hand.*)

LUPE: Time for our ablutions, sergeant.

BEN: Our what?

LUPE: *(Proffering one of them)* Take it. It'll kill the ticks. *(Taking his shirt off)* Its mescal. The old man makes it from the *agave* in his garden. Take your shirt off.

BEN: What for?

LUPE: They're going start laying eggs on you.

(BEN *takes his shirt off. They rub themselves down with the liquor, occasionally swilling from their bottles.)*

LUPE: I can see what she likes about you.

BEN: What are you gonna do, now that you're cut loose?

LUPE: Cut loose, I guess. What are you gonna do?

BEN: I dunno. I got some ideas.

LUPE: How do ya like the brew? Fermented in oblong casks of dried oak and hammered tin, then buried in the earth like a dead man.

(LUPE *offers his back.* BEN *rubs mescal into it.)*

LUPE: What are you thinking?

BEN: What if I was you.

LUPE: What if you was?

BEN: I don't know how I'd live with myself. I don't know if I could ever give up on my woman, but I know for damn sure I'd never give up on my child.

(BEN *offers his back.* LUPE *starts to rub the stuff on.)*

BEN: What if you were me?

LUPE: Bitch, I'd probably kill myself.

BEN: Nina appreciates what I am. The first time she brought me to her house. It was quiet.

(NINA *enters as* LUPE *slips back.)*

NINA: Dark. Night.

BEN: She kept the lights out and brought me to the bedroom.

(She touches his shoulder.)

LUPE: On my bed?

NINA: Not on the bed. The floor.

BEN: Can we turn some lights on?

NINA: Shh. No.

LUPE: Why you whispering?

NINA: Just be quiet. Sit. Here.

BEN: What's this?

NINA: Piquante. And a bag of chips. And these. *(Rubbers)*

BEN: What's going on?

NINA: You start.

BEN: I'm not into chile, Nina.

NINA: You have to. If you're here to say what I think you're going to say, you have to.

BEN: Is it hot?

NINA: Four alarm.

BEN: Did you bring water?

NINA: Straight up. *Dale.*

(He dips a chip and bites it. During the following sequence they eat chips in hot sauce, getting progressively burned.)

NINA: Do you think you know me, Ben?

BEN: I think I do.

NINA: Have you been looking for me all your life?

BEN: Yes.

NINA: 'Cause I sure been waiting for you all of mine.

BEN: I'm not complicated, I don't ask much of life, except a good job, good weather, a good woman.

NINA: You're a good man.

BEN: I would've stayed a virgin if I knew I'd meet you this soon. But it was that or a bullet through my head. Between dying and loneliness, there's no contest. Dying's quicker.

NINA: *Es la pinchi verdad.*

BEN: I knew you were out there, I knew I'd find you, at a time meant just for us, but I never knew it would be this good.

NINA: You haven't once touched me. You haven't once asked me to bed.

BEN: I don't wanna fuck you. I've done fuck. Fuck is what bodies do. I want to make love. Don't you see?

NINA: What would you do for me, Ben, what would you do?

BEN: Anything, anything.

NINA: Would you die for me (yes) would you surrender your life for me (yes) would you give up your soul (yes) would you be poor (yes) would you still want me the way I am?

BEN: No matter what.

NINA: You are a dream, *cabrón*. Something out of my past. I don't deserve you.

BEN: Kiss me, Nina.

(They kiss.)

NINA: *Ay*, Benjamen, if you knew my trials, my years of silence, my sentence of guilt and hunger, all the times I wished myself dead, all the times I did die in that man's arms in our bed, all those times I prayed for evil shit....

BEN: What evil shit.

NINA: I prayed never to get pregnant and all the times I did, I prayed to God he'd flush those babies out of my body. I prayed for them to die before they saw light of day, and my god, oh my god, how they died, they all died, little babies...and something else....

BEN: Shh. Nina. Don't cry. Shh.

NINA: No, I did something else, I have to tell you—

(He drinks the contents of the jar. He burns.)

BEN: I wanna marry you. I wanna take care of you, give you the love you need, I wanna be with you for life and give you children. Look, rings, honey. I got the rings.

NINA: You really want me?

BEN: I'm serious as all shit. I sold my car, my bomber jacket, and my mother's Saint Christopher medal for this. I'm bound to my choice with gold, Nina. Fourteen fucking carats.

NINA: First there's something you have to know.

ROMY: Mom.

BEN: Who's that?

NINA: That's another thing we gotta talk about.

BEN: Who is that?

NINA: My Romy.

BEN: *Your* Romy?

ROMY: Mom.

NINA: If you've always known me and you've always been waiting for me, you've been waiting for her, too.

BEN: I need a glass a water.

(NINA *takes the rings and goes.*)

BEN: Do you hear me? I need a glass of water, Lupe! My throat's on fire! (*Silence*) Lupe?

(LUPE *appears with the bat.*)

LUPE: You don't need water.

BEN: What are you doing with that?

LUPE: You need Louisville. (*He viciously smashes the bat on the ground by him.*)

BEN: HEY! What's going on, Lupe?

LUPE: You tell me. Smartass fucking sergeant.

BEN: I'm not a sergeant—

LUPE: Don't you think I know that! Don't you think I noticed your bones?

BEN: What?

LUPE: The same fine bones in the face. Same high-tone look in the eyes.

BEN: Where's Romy? Romy, get your butt over here now!

LUPE: You're not taking her. She ain't yours to take.

(BEN *starts to run but* LUPE *smashes his leg with the bat, dropping him.* LUPE *grips his head in a vise.* ROMY's *body jolts with a vision.*)

ROMY: And all a sudden La Romy feel her *corazón* swell up like a gourd to receive the *cuento* that bedevil my Dad and make hell inside him...

LUPE: (*Holding him tightly*) You never know when to quit, do you! The past too horny to stay past! Well, I seen you! I seen the two of you!

ROMY: ...two shapes standing in the dark...

LUPE: Making out like dogs right in this corral!

BEN: NO!

LUPE: And I seen what you look like!

ROMY: ...a thin boy pale so pale you see the green stems of his veins spread along his arms fragile but unafraid of life...

BEN: Stoppit! Man!

LUPE: In the arms of my goddamn bride!

ROMY: ...a young girl a living heart smooth skin big dark eyes the boy kissing love-notes on her shoulder blade...

BEN: NINA*!*

LUPE: BUT I TOOK CARE OF YOU THEN, DIDN'T I DIDN'T I!

ROMY: ...a devil aiming death at the boy the boy's veins bulging his face red his eyes clenched with tears and blood gathered in his mouth...

BEN: FUUUUUCK!

LUPE: I caught you full in the temple, motherfukkah, the mole rushed out your nose and POW I heard the crack of bone and teeth and Nina gasping and me cussing and *pinche* Louisville just keep on finding fractures. Boom. Boom. Boom.

ROMY: Nothing but a black and shiny mess where his pretty face was, all open blood and muscle and the nightsky smeared with clouds...

LUPE: I did it once, I can do it again!

BEN: WHO THE FUCK AM I SUPPOSED TO BE? WHO!

ROMY: And the last thing La Romy see is horses and a name come to her in a mouthful of blood...

LUPE: *Anastacio*!

(LUPE *drops* BEN *to the ground and stands over him.*)

LUPE: You and me, we got business, we got hell, we got shit there ain't no word in English for, we got the *rio*, the sewage, the liquor, the *chile*, El Paso and the Other Side, parasites and *penitencia*, mescal and parfaits, death and daddyhood, we got it all between us, *carnal*, and its fuckin' time we settled that sin.

(ROMY *raises the bowl to drink when a brilliant light introduces* EL CHARRO, *awesome, ominous, dressed in the glittering finery of the Mexican cowboy. His spurs clink as he steps forward and raises the broad brim of his sombrero.*)

EL CHARRO: *Dónde está el baño.*

(*Blackout*)

END OF ACT ONE

ACT TWO

(ROMY *and* EL CHARRO. *As before. Still. Harking the changes to come. Distinct Mexican accordion ballad plays eerie gyrations punctuated by ghostly barking and shrill cries.*)

ROMY: And then everything's water and she looks at Ben and Ben stares at the sun and then looks back at La Romy with a fierce whiskey spilling out his eyes and whispers in another voice *Eres mia* the voice of the bad stranger who been messing with my sleep showing up in my dreams in tatters of blood and muck

(*Around them an effusion of grotesque images flash in nightmare color:*
LUPE *viciously smashing the bat down on the tarp.*
Torrents of blood, bloodletting, and gore
Equine shadows soaring overhead
POLO *trudging past, a heavy casket on his back*
NINA *enters with a gun.*
She aims it.
ALMA *sucking on the fingers of the hands.*
It fires with a tremendous roar.
All the images disappear.
Except for ROMY
In the far distance, the neighing of a single horse
EL CHARRO *finally takes a step to clink his spurs and utters:*)

EL CHARRO: *La cuenta, por favor.*

ROMY: Hey. You.

EL CHARRO: *La cuenta.*

ROMY: Are you Death?

EL CHARRO: *Dónde está la playa.*

ROMY: I just wanna know: Are you Death?

EL CHARRO: *Soy Charro.* I'm *el Charro Negro.* Exile. Mister *Penitente.*
The guilty conscience of my poor misbegotten land. I'm Death, all right.

ROMY: Then make yourself useful. Help me to die.

EL CHARRO: What you want to die for?

ROMY: Livin' ain't worth the trouble. Too much pain. I seen a terrible thing in my head that can't be true, and if it is, all the more reason to die.

EL CHARRO: What you got there?

ROMY: Peyote in my bean soup.

EL CHARRO: Spicy.

ROMY: I wanna eat it but I can't.

EL CHARRO: You ain't done your penance is why. You gotta purge your sins.

ROMY: How do I do that?

EL CHARRO: You turn to me. Get on your knees. Roll back your sleeves. Hold this spoon.

(She does all this. EL CHARRO sits before her.)

EL CHARRO: Keep it very still. *(He pours a small black goop on the spoon then turns a lighter on under it.)* Now freely confess.

ROMY: I hate my mom. I hate her for bustin' us up. I hate her for not makin' the effort. But mostly right now I hate her for makin' like I never existed.

EL CHARRO: She denied you?

ROMY: Uh-huh.

EL CHARRO: Like Peter at the cock's crow. Go on.

ROMY: I hate my *Apá*. He's acting real strange to me. Him, too, he said he wasn't my dad, wasn't ever my dad, then he takes it back. Fuck his ass, I say. Seems like nobody wants me, except...

EL CHARRO: Yeah?

ROMY: Ben. But he's a nerd. Don't even know *jalapeño* from *serrano*, he's so white.

EL CHARRO: So?

ROMY: So I can't be with him. How come you're dressed like that?

EL CHARRO: And this terrible thing you've seen?

ROMY: I dunno. A man getting killed. My Dad doing it. *Amá* there with them. That's a dream though. Peyote yankin' my chain. What's with the get-up?

EL CHARRO: It's my vestment, it's how I been stamped. This is how you die. *(In one motion, he undoes his belt and straps it around her forearm. He produces a thin blade, dips it into the serum in the spoon and applies a tattoo to her arm.)*

ROMY: Ow. What are you doin'?

EL CHARRO: This is how your daddy and me met. I remember the day. Juarez in the spring. Birds singing. Flowers blooming. Dogs lapping up blood of a knife fight. He walked into my dementia. Wanted someone to confess to. So he had me branded on his side for company. Poured his damned soul out to me. Keeps me *au courant* on all his mortal sins. There.

ROMY: What is it?

EL CHARRO: A wee horsey. If you wanna die, ride that pony down.
(He takes ROMY'*s hand and they move across the dark.)*

ROMY: And then La Romy feel him tug her chemical heart down down follow that sun down to where it goes when it goes down at night and she know this man will lead her there

(The BORDER PATROL OFFICER *appears, sitting on the river shore with the gun and Romy's shoes cradled in his arms.)*

ROMY: I know that buttface.

EL CHARRO: I figured. He's got that pinched anality round the mouth.

ROMY: What's he doing here?

EL CHARRO: Doubt if even he knows.

*(*NINA *comes on behind him.)*

ROMY: *Amá!*

EL CHARRO: Whoa, girl. She in her own space now.

NINA: That's my gun.

OFFICER: What?

NINA: That's my gun you got.

OFFICER: I disarmed...some desperados.

NINA: And that's my girl's shoes. What are you doing with her shoes?

OFFICER: They went in.

NINA: Here? Did they reach the other side? Did she make it? Did you see her make it?

OFFICER: I saw them go in. I saw the current carry them around the bend. After that, it was just water.

NINA: And you let them take her.

OFFICER: She wanted to go.

NINA: And you let her go? What's the matter with you?

OFFICER: I'm lost. My compass is all thrown. What's north, what's south. I'm all froze up in this damn hole and everythin's spinnin' around. I can't move!

(NINA *feels the earth at his feet.*)

NINA: Oh no. Oh my god.

OFFICER: What is it, lady? Where am I?

(NINA *addresses* ROMY, *whose presence she senses.*)

NINA: This is where he lay, baby. This is where for thirteen years he hid from the world and kept it guessing.

ROMY: Who?

OFFICER: I can't lift my damn feet. It's like I'm dying inside.

NINA: It is a night of eruptions, *mija*. All I see is a bat blowing a million specks of blood all over me, my dress, my face catching all the spatters. I feel sick and I throw up on the gravel and just then I feel another eruption inside me like a light coming on! I feel it! A pressure. A promise. Sweeping from the pit of my gut to all my bones and vessels. Eyes turn to grey and I hear horses.

ROMY: *Amá*, what happened? What did you do?

NINA: I only wanted to see his horses.

OFFICER: I never caught anyone sneaking southaward. Yearning for the other side. It threw my compass. The whole world's turned on us. Black is white, white, black, death life, life death, Donny Marie, Marie Donny. What the hell am I guarding! A line! A dadburn line in the water!
¡Alto alto! ¡Un balazo por la cabeza!
¡Me need ver tu passaport!
¡Muy impassaportante!
Your no *hombre, por favor!*
¡Aqui se habla inglés! Pais de los muertos, land of deceased, home of the braves *de* Atlanta, *mi casa es su* frickin *casa!*
¡Bienvenidos!

NINA: Always dead men giving us pause. Grabbing us by the ankles every time. Least I have a chance to keep my girl clear. Wherever she is.

ROMY: Right here.

NINA: I can't lose her.

ROMY: You don't hate me?

NINA: I don't.

OFFICER: You don't what?

NINA: I don't want her to die. (*Turning out*) ROMELIA! DON'T YOU BE DEAD, GIRL! DON'T YOU DARE HAVE SUNK TO THIS RIVER BOTTOM! I still need you around, baby, it's not finished, please, honey, be alive, it's not finished. *(To the* OFFICER*)* Dump that gun in the *rio* and go home, border fool. *(Taking the shoes, she starts slowly stepping toward* ROMY*.)*

ROMY: What is she doing?

OFFICER: Are you going in?

NINA: If I make it across, that's where I'll find her. If I go down, that's where she'll be.

ROMY: No, Mamá! Go back! Go back!

NINA: Romy, little shit, I'm coming.

ROMY: It's deep! You're gonna drown! Go back!

NINA: *Sigo en tus pasos, baby. Voy donde tú vas.* Right behind you.

ROMY: No! Go back!

NINA: Life or death, *Amá* is on the way. *(She continues wading in a circle around* ROMY *with her shoes held high over her head.)*

EL CHARRO: Your mama's fearless, girl. Taking danger in the mouth.

OFFICER: *(Calling after* NINA*)* If you drown, miss! Miss, if you drown, could you wash ashore on the Messican side? Then I'll know which side is which! *(He wanders off.)* Alto. Alto.....

(They watch as she makes her slow march across the river.)

ROMY: Oh fuck. Where she going?

EL CHARRO: Somewhere kneedeep, waistdeep, neckdeep, souldeep.

ROMY: Is she dead, Charro?

EL CHARRO: Dead's a relative term in El Otro. When people die, they become story, and when stories die, they become myths, and dead myths become tattoos. I'm a purgastory thirteen years and half a crime old. Suffice to say I'm what's left of an old myth. And that's what he's gonna be.

*(*LUPE *steps out carrying a roller attached to a long pole, a paint pan and a tarp. He stands before* NINA*.)*

EL CHARRO: A man with more faith in his heart than his heart had in him and thereby a rift between them. Exile been his home address. You, child, slipped in the mail slot.

NINA: *Voy donde tu vas. (She traverses the stage like water and goes.)*

ROMY: Is that my dad?

(He paints an invisible wall between him and ROMY*.)*

ROMY: What are you doing, Apá?

LUPE: Pressing paint. Pressing white paint into the walls of white people, *mija*, it gets me to thinking, what a bitch it is to be good and what a bitch when you ain't. And you know what, working this roller like a hoe on the wall, *mija*, my mind comes to you, before you even show your little brown ass, I see you not a boy 'cause what do I want with a boy, a boy would most likely turn out like his father, but a girl, my god, a girl might just turn out like her mom.

(POLO *and* ALMA *enter behind him.*)

LUPE: That would suit me fine. *¿Y sabes qué?* Your name comes to me. Romelia. Thinking up your name is the last good thought I'll ever have.

POLO: Guadalupe.

LUPE: *¿Si?*

POLO: Are you Guadalupe Madero?

LUPE: That's me. How did you get in?

POLO: *Señor,* I am Don Apolonio Tovar and this is *mi señora,* Doña Alma.

LUPE: *Para servirle.*

POLO: *Señor* Lupe, you'll excuse me if we come without notice but—

ALMA: —Do you know where your wife is?

LUPE: What do you mean?

POLO: *Señor,* we are respectable people. We came from Sinaloa where four generations of Tovares made their reputation with horses, the breeding, raising, training of good quarterhorses—

ALMA: Do you know where your *puta* is?

LUPE: My wife is home. What the hell is this about?

POLO: *Señor* Lupe, we have a ranch not far from here full of quality stock, and with the help of our son we plan to—

ALMA: Our plans are *mierda*! Our boy is with her, *pendejo*, open your eyes! Open your eyes, you idiot, they are doing each other like dogs!

LUPE: *Mentiras.*

ROMY: Lies!

POLO: Believe it. Our son and your wife.

ALMA: *¡Como perros!* Go see. See if she's home. See if she's waiting for you in your bed. See if she's there! *¡Baboso! ¡Idiota! ¡Te pone los cuernos y ni te das cuenta!*

LUPE: How do you know this?

ALMA: WE SEEN THEM, YOU STUPID!

POLO: It's not the first time. We tried to stop them once before. We tried to reason with him. She's not for you, *hijo*. She's a married woman now. She could bring disgrace on us all, Anastacio.

ROMY/LUPE: Anastacio.

POLO: But he won't listen. He wants to be with her. This cannot happen. We have plans for him at the ranch. Everything comes to breeding.

LUPE: I can't believe I'm hearing this.

ROMY: Then don't, *Apá*!

ALMA: God is my witness, the *Virgen Santa también*, that little bastard walked out on me! Left me talking to myself! My own little *puto* and he treats me this way! God is my witness, he is not having her another night!

LUPE: What do you want me to do?

ALMA: What do you think?

POLO: This very night, they're running away. She is leaving you, Señor Lupe. Stop them. Talk to her. Remind her of her vows.

ALMA: Keep your bitch in your own house and tell her to stay away from our son.

LUPE: But what if—

ALMA: There is no if, *baboso*! Are you a man? *¿Eres Mexicano?* Do what you have to do.

POLO: We thought you should know.

(They leave.)

ALMA: *Centro de mis amores por toda la eternidad no quiero Señor resistir mas...*

(LUPE somberly takes the roller off the pole and rests it in the paint pan.)

ROMY: *Apá...*

LUPE: No, baby.

ROMY: *Apá*, you don't have to listen to their shit. You know *Amá*'s good.

LUPE: Yeah. Real good.

ROMY: Don't do it.

LUPE: Don't do what.

ROMY: Don't go over there.

LUPE: Where am I going, Romy?

ROMY: Ranch.

LUPE: What am I doing once I get there?

(ROMY hesitates.)

LUPE: Tell me, honey. What is it they expect me to do and you think I already done? 'Cause I'm confused, I'm so fucked up, I don't know which end is up. What do I do, Romy?

ROMY: Go home.

LUPE: I can't do that.

ROMY: Please, Dad.

LUPE: Someone has to stop them.

ROMY: Then talk to her. Tell her you love her. She'll stay if you tell her that.

LUPE: She's a whore, baby.

ROMY: She's good. Forgive her.

LUPE: I would. But it just ain't my style. *(He starts to head out.)*

ROMY: PLEASE, APÁ! DON'T KILL HIM!

LUPE: Is that what I do? What do I use? A gun? Knife? The bat in the bed of my truck?

(ROMY reacts to the last suggestion.)

LUPE: Thass it. *Pinchi* Louisville. Be a Mexican they said. Well, baby. I'll bring down our culture on that brother. Watch me. *(He twists and wrenches the tarp in his hands.)* I'll roll him up in this. He'll lie rolled up in tarp three feet under river silt. Won't he. *(He gathers his things into the tarp and rolls it up.)*

ROMY: Apá, I love you.

LUPE: What was the name I gave you?

ROMY: Romelia.

LUPE: Oh yeah.

EL CHARRO: Romelia Maria.

LUPE: Hell of a name for retribution.

(He goes.)

EL CHARRO: There he goes.

ROMY: What's goin' on, *Charro*? I feel like I'm making this shit happen! But how? How? I never knew this, did I? How could I know it?

EL CHARRO: There are things our bodies know before we do. Little secrets rolled up and slipped in the flutes of our bones. Mystery loves, mystery griefs, longings so private that we act on them before we even feel them.

ROMY: I feel them again.

EL CHARRO: *El Otro.*

ROMY: All asudden everything's all bony the trees the walls the moon all got bones showing through their skin and even time is all bony and then La Romy see the dogs...

(Eerie barking and howling of dogs. ROSS enters, his whole left side drenched in blood, dragging the rolled-up tarp.)

ROMY: ...the big ol' dogs *Apá* shot circling around eyes bald fangs bared sense of smell all gone their bodies thin as shadows and then she see the dead walking...

ROSS: Kid.

ROMY: The Cowboy...

ROSS: You don't wanna look in there...

ROMY: All pasty faced...

ROSS: Not for the eyes of innnocents...

ROMY: Bleeding out his head...

ROSS: That's a burden for grownup fools like me to tug and drag on.

ROMY: Ross what are you doin'? Get your ass to a hospital, man.

ROSS: Too late for that, kid. My medulla oblongata took a shotta penitent lead.

ROMY: Huh?

EL CHARRO: Blew his brains out.

ROMY: What you pull shit like that for?

ROSS: Cause a love. Love that don't know when to quit. Love that goes too far. You can't treat someone you love like a horse, you know.

ROMY: What are you talking about, Ross?

ROSS: I'd rather accuse than excuse her. I'd rather kill than lose her. I lose her anyways. What remains is the remains.

ROMY: What's that smell?

ROSS: My bodily functions ain't what they were. Nothing ain't.

ROMY: Wait, Ross. Hold on. *Esperate!*

(ROSS goes.)

ROSS: You can't treat someone you love like a horse. You can't. Too messy for the eyes of innocents but you're innocent no more. No more.

(ROSS staggers out. EL CHARRO and ROMY silently regard the rolled-up tarp for a moment.)

EL CHARRO: That tug you feel in your soul is hunger. Hunger's what passes for gravity in *El Otro*.

(NINA *enters and regards the tarp.*)

NINA: *Muchacho bravo. Querido.* How am I going to live without you....
(*She takes a razor from her sock which she places against her throat.*)

ROMY: No. *Amá.* Rolled up inside of you, a seed of me there. Feel me? Feel me?

NINA: I do.

ROMY: Open that vein and I die. And you never see me. And I never grow. And I never get to feel your love, or hear your lullabys, or keep you up nights with my crying—

NINA: I could do without that.—

ROMY: —And I never get to know what school is, and never get that ten-dollar bill from your purse, and never feel what walking through a sprinkler with you is like—

NINA: What ten-dollar bill?

ROMY: Mom, forget it, you never missed it, anyway.

NINA: You've been through my purse?

ROMY: *Amá*—

NINA: You've been through my purse, *caraja*!?

ROMY: Get off my back, *esa*! How else am I supposed to know you, what kinda person you are, what secrets you keep? You won't tell me squat! I figure you out by the kleenex you keep, the lipsticks you wear, by the little things you collect, the coupons, matchbooks, sticks of gum, and those little notes to yourself.

NINA: Notes?

ROMY: You write little poems and prayers to me, Mom.

NINA: I do?

ROMY: Little songs wrote out of need and fear. Valentines scribbled in these tiny letters with such passion, *Amá*, like they were wrote down with that razor. Here. (*She takes out a slip and passes it to* NINA.)

NINA: *Tus susurros y tus besos*
Del sabor de aceituna
Como golodrinas vuelan
Al cuerno de la luna.
(*She cries softly, putting the razor away.*)

EL CHARRO: All I gotta say is...you owe that lady ten bucks.

ROMY: I saved her, Charro, didn't I? Didn't I save her?

EL CHARRO: Not from the hurt that never goes away but gets polished by the tears into a smooth little peachpit of woe. But what you care about living, anyway? Ain't you decided on dyin'?

ROMY: Well, yeah, but...

EL CHARRO: You're not having a change a heart, are you?

(LUPE enters.)

LUPE: Nina...

NINA: No.

LUPE: Nina, *ven.*

NINA: Get away from me.

LUPE: It's all over. He's gone.

(He approaches her. She stands and points the razor at him.)

NINA: I don't know you! *¡Animal!* I don't want anything to do with you! I'll kill you if you come near me. I swear I will.

LUPE: You want me dead? Then go ahead. Put an end to it now. Do it!

(LUPE steps into range. Nina, aiming the razor, sings.)

NINA: *La risa de mi Amánte*
Resuena en mi pensamiento
Es la musica de mi soledad
Es todo mi alimento.

LUPE: This love that razes men to the ground.

NINA: We're doomed, Lupe. *Bien chingados.*

ROMY: And then he touch her. And then she feel it. And then he kiss her neck. And the sickness in her and the hate in her and the fear rush to the place he kiss and an amazing thing happen....

NINA: I kiss him.

ROMY: And the hate in him and the fear and the sickness in his heart rush to his hands draw her close and an amazing thing happen...

LUPE: I want her.

ROMY: Not forgiveness but desire overwhelm their bodies now bound forever by this death, desire like a crime moving growing for thirteen years and then an amazing thing happen....

NINA: I'm going to have a baby.

LUPE: His or mine. His or mine.

NINA: Mine.

(LUPE *carries her up and starts slowly out.* NINA *sings softly as they drift off.*)

NINA: *Tus susurros y tus besos*
Del sabor de aceituna
Como golodrinas vuelan
Al cuerno de la luna.

EL CHARRO: Don't you think she sounds like Vikki Carr?

ROMY: Is this what death is, Charro? Hearing things I don't wanna hear. Seeing people cut each other up? Lookit them fools, ese. Sucking up to their own pain. Seems to me that living's just another way of dyin'. You just... feel it more.

EL CHARRO: Maybe you should verify that with the one man who's nigh on to his mythhood by now. He's right there, all rolled up in his meat burrito death, Rome.

(ROMY *eyes the tarp and, grabbing one end, with a single heave unscrolls it.* BEN *rolls out, his body completely caked with mud and offal.*)

ROMY: Ben?!

(*He opens his eyes and slowly rises to his knees. He speaks as* ANASTACIO, *in the voice which sang at the beginning.*)

ANASTACIO: *muchos días*

ROMY: Say what?

ANASTACIO: *he estado muchos días....abajo.*

ROMY: Wait, you're talkin' Spanish.

EL CHARRO: He has so many days...been down. Primroses and rye have sunk their roots in him.

ROMY: Anastacio?

EL CHARRO: In pieces. Fragments you can fill a gourd with.

ANASTACIO: Where is she?

ROMY: Who?

ANASTACIO: She was here a moment ago. I had her in my arms. Have you seen her?

ROMY: No.

ANASTACIO: *¡NINA! ¡NINA! ¡NO TE VAYAS SIN MI! ¡NO ME DEJES SOLO! ¡TENGO FRÍO!*

ROMY: She's not here.

ANASTACIO: Can you tell me where she is? *Una muchacha* with brown eyes. We played checkers, counted headlights by the levee at night, rode horses. Do you know her?

ROMY: Yeah. At least I thought I did.

ANASTACIO: She wouldn't leave without me. She's waiting for me. She knows I'm going with her. NIIIIINA!

ROMY: It's too late. She's gone.

ANASTACIO: *No, no puede ser.* I have my bags. We're running away. I told my father so. Didn't I?

EL CHARRO: You did, son.

ANASTACIO: We were in the corral at night. Seeing my horses for the last time. *Mis caballos sementales.* Restless hide. Then blood in my mouth, breach in my temple. And then...then...

ROMY: Yeah?

ANASTACIO: Nothing. This room called longing where I wait and wait and wait. I miss something and I don't know what. I feel my eyes water and I don't know why. I can't move. A millon mouths inside me, none of them crying for Jesus. I slip from one memory to another fainter memory to one that is barely dust and still the dust proclaims me anastacio.

ROMY: That's 'cause you're dead.

ANASTACIO: Then it doesn't matter now. It's up to you.

ROMY: Me?

ANASTACIO: Your eyes, the way the tears give them color, heat. Here in the shape of your face, the way the lips make that little rose. *Eres de Nina. Tú, mijita.*

ROMY: She's my mother. My name's Romy.

ANASTACIO: Then I'm not dead, after all.

(He reaches his hand out and grabs her. She recoils.)

EL CHARRO: Love what you can, Romy. The days decompose.
(He lightly caresses her cheek.)

ANASTACIO: When you see your mother, tell her my wounds still call her name. Tell her they blame her for none of it.

ROMY: But my dad. It was him that smushed your head in. He busted you up.

ANASTACIO: Your father is blameless. He never hurt anyone. His only crime was love.

ROMY: Huh?

ANASTACIO: When its time,you'll see that. You'll know him. Bones in the clock. Ticka ticka tick. I'm cold.

ROMY: Anastacio...

(The light darkens. LUPE enters, bat in hand.)

LUPE: Having a bad night, honey?

ROMY: Apá...

ANASTACIO: Light slips away. Sockets darken.

LUPE: Is that bad man creeping in your sleep again?

ROMY: He said you didn't do it. How can that be?

ANASTACIO: *Eres mía. (He rolls himself up in the tarp and is still.)*

ROMY: Didn't you beat him dead? Didn't you say so? How can he say my father is blameless?

LUPE: No one ever is. *(He swats the rolled tarp in front of him with the bat.)*

EL CHARRO: Now we're dyin'.

ROMY: What you doin', *ese!*

LUPE: Making the bad man in your dreams go away. *(He smashes the tarp with the bat.)*

ROMY: STOP IT! Fuckin' cut this *pedo* out!

EL CHARRO: Can you feel your own Romy soul turning to ash and mold?

LUPE: Don't look at me like that, Romy! Judgment is a thing I do not take lightly. *(He bludgeons the tarp viciously.)*

ROMY: What are you doin', Ap!

EL CHARRO: Feel yourself steeped deeper than any sun ever gone feel the little crumbs of life drifting and the light going all tarblack and cold?

(Light dims around them till they're hardly visible.)

LUPE: Kid, I'm just trying to be your dad. *(He turns skyward and yells.)* GET YOUR INK READY, *CHARRO*! WE GOTTA *PACHANGA* TONIGHT!

(The place explodes with dangling strings of colored Christmas bulbs, bathing the place with eerie garish light. Present, somber and still, are ALMA, and POLO. EL CHARRO has vanished.)

LUPE: Check it out!

(Suspended high over their heads, a multicolored piñata of a horse, which POLO controls by rope, ceremoniously descends.)

LUPE: There it is, *mija*, descending from on high, over the *corral de los Tovares*, your fucking present! See the sign the flying horse clopping at the air above like a reckoning! A *caballito, pochita*! Filled with the sacraments of the flesh! Aaayy-aayyy! (*He shouts and laughs and dances like a madman under the pinata, slamming the bat on the ground.*)

ROMY: In the half-dream of the *corral La Romy* hear the braying of the dead the wheeze of flesh against bone sigh against moan hell against home *y las maldiciones corren and rien como caballos*

LUPE: Woooo! This night you gonna do it! This night with this bat you gonna join your daddy! Do what Daddy done! Bust open the *pinche* shell of our lie and shower us with penance! Manna, baby! Wooo!!

ALL: Happy Birthday, Romelia! *¡Feliz Cumpleaños! (Etc)*

LUPE: *¡Viva Romelia Patronesa de los Malditos!*

ALL: *¡Viva Romelia!*

ROMY: *Apá.*

LUPE: Wassup, babe?

ROMY: Where's Ben?

LUPE: He's goin' through his changes, honey. Vato needs to be himself.

ROMY: We have to find Ben.

LUPE: What's the hurry, *pochita*? He'll show his ass in time. Right no El Charro Negro tells me we need to get in the spirit of things. Handtruck me some of that grog! We need to be anointed, by god! (*He guzzles from a bottle of mescal.*) *¡Orale!* Check out the *jefita*. It's grabass-time for our little Romy and the old sow's lighting candles like its Lent. I remember when she wasn't so pious! Who you praying to, *esa*?

ALMA: *La Virgen de Guadalupe.*

LUPE: Thass my namesake! Ask her who she favors in the Cowboys game. I got some *feria* running on that show.

POLO: Let's do this, Lupe. *Esta piñata* weighs a ton!

LUPE: Hang on to it, Apolonio! What's your problem, horse breeder? Don't know how to rope 'em in? LOWER THE GODDAMN THING!

(ALMA *ties the bandanna over* ROMY's *eyes.*)

LUPE: *Y hechale las Mañanitas.*

(POLO *and* ALMA *sing as* LUPE *places the bat firmly in* ROMY's *hands and slowly twirls her about.*)

POLO/ALMA: *Estas son las mañanitas*
Que cantaba el Rey David

Hoy por ser día de tu santo
Te las cantamos a ti

Despierta mi bien despierta
Mira que ya amaneció
Ya los pajarillos cantan
La luna ya se metió

LUPE: This game is all about the woes of the world. The way we purge and appease ourselves with *sangre*. Played right on the border between the riches of bliss— *(Kisses her)* —and desertion. Up from the heavens strung on a wire, the shape of all our *desmadres*, coming down slow like a ufo. A child's game, Rome, but like all children's games, it cuts deeper than we see. *(Placing the tip of the bat on the head of the horse)* One good whack, *mijita*. All the woes of this world turn to candy.

(ROMY searches blindly for the piñata. *POLO makes it weave and dance around her. Everyone is breathless in anticipation. She wobbles feebly about.)*

LUPE: *Orale. Dale madre, mija.*

POLO: C'mon, Romy. You can do it.

ALMA: *¡Pégale!*

POLO: *¡Fuerte!*

LUPE: C'mon, Romy! Show 'em what you got!

(ROMY winds up, swings, and misses.)

LUPE: FUCK!

ALMA: *Andale*, Romy, hit it! One good shot and *it's over!*

POLO: Absolve us, Romelia!

ALMA: Give us back our son! *(She swings with a cry and misses again.)*

LUPE: Goddammit! What's the matter with you!

ALMA: C'MON, YOU STUPID BRAT, SWING!

POLO: *¡YA VIRGEN YA! ¡DALE MALDÍTA!*

(LUPE maneuvers the piñata *till it is right in front of her.)*

LUPE: NOW! *(She stops and turns her blindfolded head askance.)* What are you waiting for? Now! Hit it!

POLO: Guadalupe, this is crazy! Forget this *piñata*! Show us where he is!

ALMA: *¡Mijo!* Anastacio! Come out, son! This is me! Your mother!

POLO: We're here, boy! Show yourself!

ROMY: Whiffing candlesmoke and dung and crude unearthed liquor
La Romy hear a voice but cannot tell which voice it is and which she
should obey and wonder how much death is already in her keyhole.

(She rips off her blind, goes to the tarp and pokes it. It unscrolls and BEN,
drenched in the same slime of before, gashed and bruised, falls out.)

BEN: YAAAAAAAAAHHH!

ALMA: *Dios santo!*

LUPE: There he is. The damn guest of honor.

*(*BEN *pulls on the halter around his neck and turns his bloodied face to the group.)*

BEN: You fucks...

ALMA: Is this him? *¿Es él nuestro hijo?*

POLO: What have you done to him, Madero?

LUPE: Just cured him a little, you know, like you cure meat.

ROMY: Ben?

LUPE: No, baby. This is Tovar.

BEN: No...

POLO: *Anastacio Mario Enrique Tovar.*

ALMA: So many years, so many days, waiting. Nights with open veins.
Ants in my water. God and this devil bring you back.

BEN: I'm..I'm....

POLO: Good to have you back, *hijo.* It's been a long time.

ALMA: We're sorry for the way we treated you. Forgive us for telling him.
We didn't know what he'd do.

POLO: Its our fault he made you leave. *Perdonanos.*

BEN: *(Pushing them away)* I don't...know you...

LUPE: Don't be saying that. Don't pretend shit never happened. You know
what you did. You brought it on yourself, broda. You banged my old lady.
Ruined my life. Gave us the *mal ojo!* You do it every goddamn night, every
time I look at my girl's face, and I see your *pinchi* eyes looking back. You
know what that does to a man? Separates him from his own balls, that's
what it does. And now here you are again, in a fuckin' uniform, no less,
and I'm supposed to roll over and die. Wassup with that? *(He takes the
bat from* ROMY.*)* This time, Tovar, you are giving Romy up to me.

BEN: No...

LUPE: Tell her she ain't yours.

BEN: Romy...

(LUPE *pokes him with the bat.*)

ALMA: Lupe! NO!

ROMY: Dad, what are you doing?

LUPE: You don't want her! Say it!

BEN: Let's go home.

(LUPE *pokes him again.*)

ALMA: Ayy!

POLO: *Ya no le peges, Madero!*

LUPE: She's not yours. Tell her you give her up!

ROMY: Say you hate me, Ben! Say you don't want shit to do with me! (*He prods him again.*)

BEN: The choice isn't mine, it's yours.

ROMY: Mine?

BEN: You're a year older now. A big girl. Big enough to make up your own mind. You don't have to deal with lies anymore. I'm not your father. He is. But lying rolled up in that tarp I learned something. I'm not afraid to die. I feel like we've been there already. You and me. So what the hell. Lemme die for you one more time, Romy.

ROMY: What?

BEN: (*Extending his bloodied hand toward her*) Eres mía.

(NINA, *enters, soaking wet, her uniform muddied and torn, with* ROMY's *shoes in her hands.*)

NINA: The last thing he said. You are mine.

ROMY: *Amá...*

LUPE: Babe.

NINA: Ben, you alright?

BEN: No.

ROMY: I knew you'd make it. I knew it.

NINA: Put the bat down, Lupe.—

LUPE: Remember this *corral*, Nina?

NINA: This ain't Tovar, Lupe.

LUPE: Got Tovar in him, though. Check out the bones. The pretty polished temple.

NINA: Tovar's dead, Lupe.

ALMA: *¿Cómo?*

POLO: *¿Qué dice?*

NINA: *Señor y Señora Tovar,* I'm sorry, my ex- has grievously misled you. We both have. This is my husband, Ben from Fort Bliss.

BEN: I don't even know who the hell Tovar is.

ALMA: He told us our son was hiding in Chicago. He said that he wanted to come back to us.

POLO: All we had to do was atone, he said. Do all these *pendejadas* for the girl and Anastacio will come!

ALMA: You are him! Tell us you're our boy!

BEN: I'm sorry.

POLO: Then you lied to us?

ALMA: Where is he? What have you done wih him?

NINA: Where is he, Lupe? He's not where we buried him.

ALMA: WHERE IS OUR SON!

(ROMY *grabs the bat from* LUPE, *turns to the piñata and pounds the bat down with all her might. It smashes and a steady stream of old dusty bones, ash, and rotting frays of cloth come tumbling out in a small pile.*)

ROMY: This was my father.

NINA: We killed him, Romelia. *Dios nos perdone. (She goes to the bones.) Muchacho bravo, mi Tovar, mi prieto,* we knew each other before we even met deep in that place quicker and crueler than heart brain or will. Barely a man, Romelia, but I was barely me. They tried to tear us apart by sending him south, and I married Lupe. But can another man take up the work the first one abandoned? Lupe is the price I paid for losing hope. Because Anastacio came back, taller, straighter, darker, with the light hotter in his eyes for me, and I knew it before he even saw me beyond all hope but not beyond desire. *En el ritmo de nuestro cuerpo lo vi:* tears on his face and I wiped them with my hand and they were ice cold.
And here he is, *mija,* sitting in our mess, our *desmadre.* Not the same man, but mine just the same.

BEN: Why didn't you tell me?

NINA: I almost did. But I was afraid to lose you.

ROMY: Is that why didn't you tell me?

LUPE: You knew. Deep in your own body, you knew the *cuento*. And you knew it had to end this way. *(He grabs the bat from* ROMY *and stalks toward* BEN.*)*

ROMY: *Apá*, wait. You can't do it. He stuck it out, he went the distance. Not 'cause you led him like a dog, not for Mom. But for me. Me.

LUPE: So?

BEN: *(Realizing it as he teeters on his feet)* So Hubby number two grows some balls. Hubby number two feeling like home in *El Otro*. Fuckin' *rio* washed me of my whiteness Fuckin' ticks kissed my welcome back *Agave* thickened my *pinche* tongue and your goddamn bat bruised my brownness on. Bam! Bam! Bam! private first class benjamin cortez that man you think I am he's part of me now his blood and my blood blended but no sir uh-uh I do not die like that I will not be so easily dead I have me a mission that mission is father and father say you are my daughter I promised I would see you home and by God almighty
I
Will
See
You
Home.

LUPE: Have it your way, sergeant. *(He arches back to swing the bat.)*

ROMY: He's not a sergeant, Apá.

(Pause)

LUPE: What?

ROMY: He's a private. First class.

LUPE: I see.

ROMY: It can't be the same. I can't live with you now. But that don't mean you ever stop being my dad. We never lose that, ever, Apá.

LUPE: *Simón.*

ROMY: You said thinking me up was the last good thing you'd ever do.

NINA: Put the Slugger down, Lupe.

LUPE: What do I have to do to be your father?

ROMY: Let me go.

(He nods soberly. Then he winds up to strike ROMY. *The bat freezes in midair.* EL CHARRO *enters, with his silver-tipped finger following the trajectory of the bullet.)*

EL CHARRO: And out of the vanishing point where border meet border in the wish and never was of sun and dark and real and bones one eye of Romy see a teeny ball of lead heading straight this way and with her other eye see the best part of her Dad the one quarter inch of pure that never know sin open up its mouth to receive to admit to recognize and a wizz go past her face and the teeny ball is received and recognized and understood and then you know what:

LUPE: ¡*PUTA VIDA!* (*He drops the bat, sighs hoarsely, and falls to his knees.*)

ROMY: ¡*APÁ!*

LUPE: *Que la chingada.*

BEN: What's happened?

NINA: I told you, *ese.*

LUPE: Fuck.

NINA: I told you it'd catch up with you. It was just taking the long way around.

(EL CHARRO *takes out his tattoo kit. He tears* LUPE's *shirt off and straddles his back like a horse.*)

EL CHARRO: Now you ripe for some new ink, brother.

LUPE: *Me rompió el corazón, Carlos.*

BEN: I don't believe it.

ROMY: *Charro,* what are you doing, *ese?*

EL CHARRO: Finishing what I started. Here will go a big *corazón* broken open by love and a bullet. You stay with your *mamá.*

LUPE: Do as he says, Rome.

ROMY: You can't take him! He's my dad!

LUPE: *Romelia Maria, pórtate bien o te doy tus chingazos.*

NINA: He means it, baby.

BEN: We better get her out of here.

(*She goes.* LUPE *sinks gradually into* EL CHARRO's *arms.* ALMA *goes to* ROMY *as* POLO *empties the crate of mescal.*)

ALMA: *La vida no vale no vale nada santa virgen señora sagrada tus hijos todos son condenados,* all the sons of Adam all damned all damned forever. (*She kicks* LUPE.) *Demonio.*

POLO: Romelia, we saw you in our yard with the colt. If you want, you come by anytime to see that pony.

(ALMA *and* POLO *place the bones into the empty coffin crate.*)

LUPE: All the good I had left in my life.

NINA: She needs a real father, *viejo.*

LUPE: Plees enjoy yoor affair weet thee beauteefool cadaver, *señor.* Lyeen weet her may kill joo, but also joo may breeng life bakk to her. Now, fuck off.

ROMY: Shitty the way I wailed on you, Ben.

BEN: Just keep my ass away from Mexico. It's a sick and filthy place fulla twisted people and as close to hell as I ever want to come.

NINA: I'm sorry you feel that way, honey, 'cause this ain't Mexico.

BEN: What?

NINA: We're still in Texas. You swam across the river at the point it heads north and the border goes west by fence.

BEN: Holy Crap! All this whole time I been in the States? Then where the hell is *El Otro* supposed to be?

EL CHARRO: We know where it is, don't we, Lupe?

LUPE: *Ya pélense.* You're gonna miss *Good Morning America.*

NINA: *Ay te watcho, loco.*

EL CHARRO: *(As the others start to go)* Next time you're in *El Otro*, Romy, look me up: I may be lucid.

(ROMY starts toward LUPE, but his singing halts her.)

LUPE: *Ay mamacita no te vayas*
Que no ves que te quiero más que nada
Si te vas, te hecharé de menos
Y después te hecharé a la chingada.

(She turns and leaves with NINA and BEN. POLO and ALMA wheel the coffin crate off for burial.)

LUPE: If you wanna go, Carlos, don't lemme stop you.

EL CHARRO: I ain't goin' nowhere. Not till you pony up your penance, brother. *(Muttering in his ear)* La cuenta, por favor. La cuenta.

(He continues tattooing as LUPE looks toward the first glimmer of dawn. ROMY returns.)

LUPE: Is that the lip? Don't be giving me no lip now.

ROMY: ...not the real Romy but La Romy of his mind come back and look with love on her *Apá* and feel the hole in his back and the fissures in his heart long enough to believe he can take it back to say the words he's never said say them now *Apá* there's time there's air there's a ghost of me here to hear you...

LUPE: It ain't my style, sweetheart.

(ROMY caresses then kisses his forehead. LUPE groans.)

ROMY: Your present.

...and then La Romy she leave to catch up with herself sitting in Polo's truck with Amá on one side and Apá Ben on the other tearing down the dirt road that lead to the paved street that lead to the interstate that take them like wind take the desert pollen to their rightful place the house already booming with the hollow music of *Good Morning America*...

(Tableau. Slow fade to black)

END OF PLAY

REFERENCES TO SALVADOR DALI MAKE ME HOT

José Rivera

ABOUT THE AUTHOR

José Rivera's plays THE HOUSE OF RAMON IGLESIA, THE PROMISE*, EACH DAY DIES WITH SLEEP, MARISOL, GIANTS HAVE US IN THEIR BOOKS*, MARICELA DE LA LUZ LIGHTS THE WORLD, CLOUD TECTONICS*, THE STREET OF THE SUN, SUEÑO, SONNETS FOR AN OLD CENTURY, REFERENCES TO SALVADOR DALI MAKE ME HOT, and LOVERS OF LONG RED HAIR have been produced at Manhattan Class Company, the Ensemble Studio Theater, Circle Rep, Los Angeles Theater Center, La Jolla Playhouse, Hartford Stage Company, the Magic Theater, Berkeley Rep, Actors Theater of Louisville's Humana Festival, the Joseph Papp Public Theater, Denver Center Theater, the Group Theater, the Alliance Theater, the Goodman Theater, the Eureka Theater, Playwrights Horizons, Santa Fe Stages, South Coast Rep, the Mark Taper Forum, and Merrimack Rep Theater, as well as Mexico's Centro Cultural Helenico, London's Orange Tree Theater, Singapore's Action Theater, Toronto's Theatre Pass Mireielle, Scotland's Travers Theater, Puerto Rico's Teatro La Taller Camandula, France's Theatre de Folle Pensee, and the national theaters of Sweden and Norway. Honors include an Obie award for Outstanding Play (for MARISOL), a Kennedy Center Fund for New American Plays grant (for STREET OF THE SUN), a McKnight fellowship, grants from the N E A, the Rockefeller Foundation, the Fulbright Commission, the Berilla Kerr Foundation, the Whiting Foundation, and Sundance. In 1991, Rivera co-created and produced the critically acclaimed T V series *Eerie, Indiana*. Rivera is currently working on commissions for South Coast Rep (BRAIN PEOPLE) and the La Jolla Playhouse (ADORATION OF THE OLD WOMAN).

*Published by Broadway Play Publishing Inc

REFERENCES TO SALVADOR DALI MAKE ME HOT was first
workshopped through H P P in June of 1999. The cast and creative
contributors were:

MOON .... John Ortiz
COYOTE .... Richard Coca
CAT .... Svetlana Efremova
MARTÍN .... Sol Castillo
SAM .... Victor Mack
GABRIELA .... Camilia Sanes
BENITO .... John Ortiz

Director .... Juliette Carrillo
Dramaturg .... John Glore

REFERENCES TO SALVADOR DALI MAKE ME HOT received its world
premiere on 28 January 2000 at South Coast Repertory, David Emmes,
Producing Artistic Director, and Martin Benson, Artistic Director. Pacific
Life Foundation was the honorary associate producer. The cast and creative
contributors were:

MOON .... Robert Montano
COYOTE .... Victor Mack
CAT .... Svetlana Efremova
MARTÍN .... Wells Rosales
GABRIELA .... Ana Ortiz
BENITO .... Robert Montano

Director .... Juliette Carrillo
Scenic design .... Monica Raya
Costume design .... Meg Neville
Lighting design .... Geoff Korf
Composer and sound designer .... Mitch Greenhill
Dramaturg .... John Glore
Stage manager .... Randall K Lum
Production manager .... Jeff Gifford

REFERENCES TO SALVADOR DALI MAKE ME HOT was developed with the assistance of the Mark Taper Forum (Gordon Davidson, artistic director), the Ensemble Studio Theater West (Curt Dempster, artistic director), The Joseph Papp Public Theater (George C Wolfe, producer), the Relentless Theater Company (Olivia Honegger, artistic director), Duke University, and South Coast Repertory (David Emmes and Martin Benson, artistic directors).

Special thanks to Julia Edwards, Jo Bonney, John Ortiz, Camilia Sanes, Jeff Storer, Jessica Hecht, Jerry Patch, John Dias, Mervin P Antonio, Zannie Voss, Michele Vazquez, Maricela Ochoa, Iona Brindle, Ruth Livier, Oscar Agueyo, Jesus Mendoza, Stefan Olmsted, Adam Rosenblatt, Dana Parker Bennison, Imoh Ime Essien, Adam Saunders, Joel McCauley Jr, Chris Schussler, Laura K Lewis, Julio Monge, Tony Torn, Danyon Davis, Carlo Alban, Timothy Huang, Shirley Fishman, Richard Coca, Sol Castillo, Sue Karutz, John Iacovelli, Doc Ballard, and Nephelie Andonyadis

CHARACTERS & SETTING

MOON, *the moon in the sky,* GABRIELA'*s friend (doubles as* BENITO
COYOTE, *a wild one*
CAT, *a fat one,* GABRIELA'*s pet*
MARTÍN, *a Latino of fourteen,* GABRIELA'*s neighbor*
GABRIELA, *a Latina, late twenties, an Army housewife*
BENITO, *a Latino, early thirties,* GABRIELA'*s husband, a soldier*

Time: Shortly after the Persian Gulf War

Place: Barstow, California

ACT ONE
GABRIELA'*s backyard. Night*

ACT TWO
GABRIELA'*s kitchen. 7:00 A M*

INTERMISSION

ACT THREE
GABRIELA'*s bedroom. Night*

ACT FOUR
GABRIELA'*s backyard. 7:00 A M*

"And I'll sleep at your feet,
to watch over your dreams."

—Lorca, BLOOD WEDDING

The play is dedicated to my soldier-brothers,
Julio, Charlie, Tony, and Hector.

ACT ONE

(Barstow, California. Night)

(A cement-covered backyard. A wooden fence upstage. Cactus. Birds of Paradise. Large spiny-edge aloe)

(Beyond is the desert surrounded by low, barren mountains)

(The MOON, standing on an old refrigerator, plays the violin: something lush and sentimental.)

(A female CAT and a male COYOTE regard each other warily.)

COYOTE: *You don't trust me.*

CAT: *You're transparent.*

COYOTE: *You smell like soap.*

CAT: *You smell like shit.*

COYOTE: *Shit's natural. Remember natural?*

CAT: *You're full of secrets and worms.*

COYOTE: *You don't even know
what fresh blood tastes like!*

CAT: *Hunted!*

COYOTE: *Brainwashed!*

CAT: *Unloved!*

(The COYOTE howls with laughter.)

COYOTE: *Unloved? I'm free! I am myself!*

CAT: *Deluded.*

COYOTE: *And how do I keep my freedom?
I don't worry about their love.
Their clinging, petting, hurtful...*

CAT: *Jealous too!*

COYOTE: *Love with chains and collars attached.
Love with no purpose to it,
no reproduction, no passion.*

Love predicated on obedience.
Love with violence implied.

CAT: *You have no idea how good it is.*

COYOTE: *You think everything they do is good.*
You seen what they done to my desert?
The way the mountains
are so nicely carved up—
such beautiful scars!—
oh, the pretty bomb craters!—
those sexy switchblade cuts
in the flesh of the land!
What kind of drugs
do they put in your food?

CAT: *How cold does it get at night, Coyote?*
How hard is that desert mattress?
What's in that darkness?
What's it like to live
in a world full of enemies?

COYOTE: *Fun. Easy.*

CAT: *The reason for the terror*
in your eyes...?

COYOTE: *That's lethal energy you see in my eyes, Cat.*

CAT: *Scavenger energy.*

COYOTE: *A hunter's gaze.*

CAT: *Bone-picker energy.*
You let the real hunters
do the killing:
let cars do the killing.
Then you come along,
tail between your legs,
sniffing around for the leftovers,
all weasely and cautious,
licking up the cold blood
and competing with the flies
for the juicy bits.

COYOTE: *Disinformation!*

CAT: *Oh, such honor.*
Nature at its best.
Majestic, awesome nature!

COYOTE: *You wouldn't survive a day—.*

CAT: *You're not even smart enough*
to be a dog.
What exactly are you?
Half-rat? Half-mole?

COYOTE: *Not a single cold night!*

CAT: *Poor me, with a home,*
protection from the sun,
good eats, lots of toys:
Gabriela gives me everything.

COYOTE: *Toys and regular meals*
have made you fat.
Blunted your instincts.
Why don't you come out with me?
Right now: do what I do for one night.
No home, no petting,
no flea collar, no place to hide.
You couldn't do it, could you?

CAT: *I don't have to prove a....*

COYOTE: *Prove it to yourself.*
Twenty-four hours in the wild.
I'll take you to the desert.
I'll take you hunting—
lots of prey, natural enemies to dodge—
you'll learn to look
at your precious Gabriela
from a real animal's point of view.

CAT: *I take one step out of this yard,*
you and your little posse gang-attacks me!

COYOTE: *You have my word.*

CAT: *Bet you'd love that...eating me.*
Tasting my round, warm meat.
Domesticity has made all my fat
soft, easy and wet with juice.
I can see the saliva forming in your mouth
right now.

COYOTE: *That all you see?*

CAT: *After you've swallowed my*
moist outer layers—
you can chew my heart muscles
and give your jaws a real workout.
Take you all night to eat my thighs.

COYOTE: *Saliva's dripping down*
and something else is coming up.

CAT: *Not really.*

COYOTE: *Oh yeah.*

CAT: *What a pig!*

COYOTE: *You ain't never been laid*
by a wild animal, have you?

CAT: *Is that what all this has been about?*

COYOTE: *Like you didn't know!*

CAT: *Barbarian!*

COYOTE: *In the wild we really know how to love.*
In the wild we do it under the savage sky,
get dirt in our eyes,
wet the ground with our funky juice.
It's not very pretty but it's effective.
You scream so hard your ancestors hear you.
It's not even sex, it's beyond sex,
beyond bodies, come on Cat
animal on animal.
I'll knock you around so hard
all nine of your lives will have orgasms.

CAT: *...All nine?*

COYOTE: *Then you'll bear little coyote-cats—*
tough mutant sons-of-bitches
who love the taste of blood
and the chase and the moonlit night!

CAT: *I can't do that—I'm fixed.*

COYOTE: *Fixed! Fixed!*
Oh, the beautiful English language!

CAT: *Answer is No!*

COYOTE: *Aw, I wasn't going to beg!*
This is me begging!
(He begs for sex.)

CAT: *Of course you're begging.*
You know what's in store for you.
Nobody loves like a house cat.

COYOTE: *What do I have to say?*
What do I have to promise?

CAT: *Let me see.*

COYOTE: *A little lick? A sniff?*
Wet the edge
of my tongue with your—?

CAT: *What about some information?*
What happened to Pinkie Lefkowitz?

COYOTE: *Pinkie who?*

CAT: *Neighbor. Male.*
Persian. Light brown,
long tail, weakness for grasshoppers.

COYOTE: *Don't know a thing about that!*

CAT: *Pinkie's been missing two days, Coyote.*

COYOTE: *Why are you asking me?*

CAT: *What about Climber Rodriguez?*
Missing a week! Any clues?

COYOTE: *You watch that tone of voice!*

CAT: *All the neighbor-cats've been disappearing*
beginning with the first day
of your arrival in Barstow!
Making dirty war on my people!

COYOTE: *(Laughing) You hate war, huh?*
War makes you comfortable, Cat.

(A fourteen year old Latino boy, MARTÍN appears at the fence. He looks at the yard through a telescope.)

(The MOON notices MARTÍN, snickers.)

MOON: *Aw, look at the little perv—*
back for more ...

MARTÍN: *She better be so naked tonight!*
(Seeing the COYOTE)
A coyote! And me without a weapon!

(The COYOTE continues to beg for sex. He's shameless.)

(The CAT refuses.)

MOON: *(To MARTÍN) Give it up, little boy,*
she's outta your league.

MARTÍN: *(To the MOON) But Gabriela's my religion.*
My altered state of grace.
I look at her ass and I hallucinate.

But what if I was born too late?
I'll be forever in exile.
Forced to watch from a distance
and contemplate what never
could have been.

MOON: *(To* MARTÍN*) You want me to kick your ass?*

(The backdoor opens.)

*(*GABRIELA, *a Latina of twenty-seven, wearing sweatshirt and sweatpants, walks into the yard.* GABRIELA *holds a 9 millimeter.)*

GABRIELA: *Enemies! Enemies!*

COYOTE: *(Seeing the weapon) Holy God! (He tries to hide.)*

GABRIELA: *Who's out here?*
I'll shoot.

CAT: *Just me, Gabriela!*

GABRIELA: *I heard voices.*

CAT: *Put the weapon down,* nena,
and go back inside.

GABRIELA: *Who's out here with you?*
Vampires? Are there vampires?

COYOTE: *(To* CAT*) Don't tell her about me, please—.*

GABRIELA: *They say vampires are buying up houses*
all over Barstow.
They say vampires are well-organized.
They've filed down their teeth.
They smile without fear of detection.
They gain your trust.
You invite them over for barbecues.
You go to movies together.
You cuddle during the scary bits.
You unzip their flies.
Then you close your eyes
and they sink their miniature fangs
into your unprotected psyches
and drain the blood from your mind
until you're one of them.

CAT: *Really, Gabriela, you need to get laid.*

GABRIELA: *I heard voices.*

CAT: *When does Benito—?*

GABRIELA: *That's voices—plural.*

CAT: *(A glance at the* COYOTE*) Eh—no—it's just me and the moon.*

GABRIELA: *The moon? The distant moon?*

COYOTE: *Bless you, gentle, sexy Cat!*

GABRIELA: *I've been looking up*
at the night sky for months.
Watching the watchful moon.
Noticing the stars.
Before you're born, I wonder,
as you looked around,
and took inventory of the womb...
did it look like this?
Did you see the moon and stars in there?
Floating bits of fire—
maybe the nutrients from your
mother's bloodstream—
looking like constellations
against the deep, deep black
of your mother's night sky?
What do you say, Moon?
What's the good word tonight?

(The MOON *laughs.)*

MOON: Ay Dios, *those pajamas!*

GABRIELA: *They tell me headhunters*
have been elected to all the schoolboards, Moon!

MOON: *It's a jungle down there.*

GABRIELA: *I knew it.*
That's why I have this!
(She fires a shot in the air.)

MARTÍN: Una pistola!

MOON: *What a woman!*

GABRIELA: *Behind every tree is a dark spirit,*
a hungry one, and they watch me
through my bedroom window
and I want these spirits to know
I am armed and considered dangerous.

MARTÍN: *(To the* MOON*) Something's wrong.*
She ain't naked.
She's been naked, every night

for six weeks, soon as the sun goes down,
walking back and forth, back and forth,
and you could see everything.

GABRIELA: *I've taken measurements.*
When we first moved here
each of these cactus trees
was twenty feet from the house.
Then one night I heard curious sounds.
I walked out here and thought I saw
the cactus trees moving toward me.
I ran inside and got a tape measure—
and sure enough! Fifteen feet!
"Get over here, Benito," I shouted.
And Benito came and took measurements
and told me I was crazy
and went back to sleeping
and snoring and gyrating in the bed
and dreaming of Miss Panama
and Miss El Salvador
and Miss Teen Puerto Rico
and I sit out here
and watch the cactus trees
inching closer and closer to my house
concealing dark spirits,
secret-keepers and heart-breakers.
Yesterday I measured the trees.
Ten feet! Ten feet exactly!
What's it going to take to make
Benito believe me?
Why does he think I make it up?

MARTÍN: *(Frustrated) She's gonna talk all night!*

MOON: *(To* GABRIELA*) In the house to your right*
an insomniac is looking through
old photo albums.
Her eyes trace memories back
to their original moments:
birthdays, first kisses, a young boyfriend
who wanted babies right away.
The photos excite faded pathways
in the brain where old ghosts
are too tired to haunt.
She runs sleep-deprived fingers
over black and white surfaces,
trying to feel the skin

of that old boyfriend.
But the photographic paper yields nothing.
There are only secrets here.
The moment before the photo was taken
and the moment just after:
these moments are exiled
to those parts of the brain
reserved for all the forgotten things.
And this poor girl, nonsleeper,
re-enacts her nightly journey
toward understanding her past...
and every night,
inexplicably powerful currents
turn her away.

GABRIELA: *Poor girl.*

MOON: *In the house to your left*
an old man watches his old wife sleeping.
She breathes slowly
and he holds a mirror to her mouth.
A little cloud assures the old man
that she is alive.
He thinks of the day they first made love,
a sweet October day thousands of miles
and hundreds of seasons from here.
He had never held a body
so rich with dreams
and she had never held a body
so hairy and full of feral hunger
and that first night,
a night without food or sleep,
as she lay in his exhausted arms...
he reached for a mirror
and put the mirror to her mouth
and she breathed on it—
proving to this young disbeliever
that she was indeed alive
and not a dream,
a woman and not a fabulous invention.
And now the old man is afraid
of life without her
and keeps a small firearm in his house
and he checks his wife's dutiful breathing
and knows what to do in case it ever stops.

GABRIELA: *Poor old man.*

CAT: *(To the* MOON*) Stop telling her those morbid stories*
or she'll never rest!

GABRIELA: *Poor girl, poor old man:*
poor people everywhere!
(She starts to sob.)

(The MOON *puts his violin down and comes down from the sky.)*

(As the MOON *gets closer to the ground, the* COYOTE *howls in pain.)*

COYOTE: *OH GOD IT HURTS!*
IT HURTS MY BODY SO MUCH!

CAT: *Stop that hideous noise!*

COYOTE: *THE MOONLIGHT!*
IT HURTS SO BAD!

*(*MARTÍN *covers his ears in pain.)*

MARTÍN: *That noise freakin' irritates.*
Drives me crazy insane!

(The COYOTE *howls even louder as the* MOON *gets closer to the backyard.)*

CAT: *(To the* COYOTE*) Why don't you stop that?*

COYOTE: *(Weakened) The light of the moon—*
is sharp like daggers—
cuts into my skin—
ricochets in my nerves—
that's why coyotes howl!

(The MOON *enters the backyard.)*

(The COYOTE *passes out.)*

(The CAT *goes to the* COYOTE*.)*

CAT: *Coyote? Coyote? (She holds the* COYOTE*.)*

MOON: *(To* GABRIELA*) There, there, Gabby.*

GABRIELA: *(To the* MOON*) Oh, you didn't have to*
come down here to—.

MOON: *But I wanted to.*

CAT: *(Angry, to the* MOON*) Look what you did!*

GABRIELA: *Just an overly-sentimental*
gun-toting Army housewife.

MOON: *(To* GABRIELA*) They say from the tears of women*
are civilizations made.

GABRIELA: *They really say that?*

MOON: *No, not really.*

GABRIELA: *Then why did you get my hopes up?*

MOON: *Shakespeare called me inconstant.*

GABRIELA: *I see why.*

MOON: *I never recovered from that!*
The bastard!

GABRIELA: *It's easier knowing ahead of time*
when you're bullshitting me.

CAT: *Coyote? Speak to me!*

(No response from the COYOTE. *The* CAT *cries.)*

GABRIELA: *(To the* MOON*) Have you ever danced*
with a woman holding a gun?

*(*GABRIELA *and the* MOON *dance.)*

MOON: *From the tears of women*
comes mathematics sonatas
table manners the zipper
the merengue editorial pages
county fairs guitar strings
lipstick and the fables
of Jorge Luis Borges...

GABRIELA: *You're trying to get into*
my shorts, aren't you?

MOON: *(Faster, more excited) ... brain surgery pickles*
Macondo Chartres Cathedral
the double play Bukowski tostones
and "Two Pieces of Bread
Expressing the Sentiment of Love."

GABRIELA: *(Gasps) Ay! References to Salvador Dali*
make me hot!
(She kisses the MOON *passionately.)*

(The CAT *kisses the* COYOTE *passionately.)*

CAT: *(To* COYOTE*) Those are very soft lips*
you have for a wild animal.

GABRIELA: *(To* MOON*) Those are very soft lips*
you have for a celestial object.

MARTÍN: *A strange transformation*
is taking place as I watch Gabriela
dance with the lucky moon.

I came here tonight to see
a naked woman,
and hopefully see her thing.
But I'm bathed in the light of the moon
and as I listen to the words
of that gorgeous, spied-upon creature,
I'm changed completely.
The little boy who wanted
a cheap thrill is dead.
In his place, out of his cold remains,
rises a young man full of mature,
virile desire: a young man
in love with love!
(He jumps down into the yard.)

(GABRIELA *talks to the* MOON. *She and* MARTÍN *speak in sync.*)

GABRIELA/MARTÍN: *I (wanted/want) to touch (Benito's/her) skin*
because I (wanted/want) to learn something.
Not about the temperature of (his/her) body.
Or how soft the hairs on (his/her) thing are.
Touching (his/her) skin (had/has) to do with...
testing the vibrations...
down past the glands and mute corpuscles...
down where bones talk
and the human body hums with music...
I (wanted/want) to find out
if we're tuned the same way.
What's the pitch of (his/her) soul?
Can I hear it if I tried?
Will I ever be able to sing along with it?

MARTÍN: *(To the* MOON*) I think she wants my ass.*

GABRIELA: *But Benito's little dick-brain...*
always interprets my touch
as nothing but a touch!
"Does this mean you wanna do it tonight?"...
"No!" I'd say—
Jesus!—he never understands...

MARTÍN: *A-ha! They're incompatible!*

GABRIELA: *The idea of me exploring*
the notes and chords of his soul,
frankly, never occurred to the man.

MOON: *(To GABRIELA)* *Yes, actually, I do, actually,*
I, yes actually, yes, I do actually
want to get into your shorts.

MARTÍN: *(To the MOON)* *Get in line you big stupid rock!*

GABRIELA: *I don't know what's happening in his mind.*
The dreams of my husband are a mystery to me.
What secrets have abducted my husband from me?
Was it the war?

MOON: *(To MARTÍN)* *I'll kick your ass, punk!*

GABRIELA: *What's funny is people always say,*
if you want mystery, go to the moon.

MARTÍN: *He ain't mysterious.*

MOON: *(To MARTÍN)* *You little—.*

MARTÍN: *He's been explored too much.*
Too many little nasty footprints
and American flags all over him!

MOON: *I'll knock your block off—.*

GABRIELA: *I say the deepest secrets*
and the most confusing mysteries
aren't on the moon,
they're in the heart of the person
who lies next to you in bed every night.
Whole worlds go spinning around
their little orbits in there,
major civilizations
with their own alphabets
and food rituals
and ancient tales of love and woe
rise and fall in there—
and you can't get in there
to see for yourself.

MARTÍN: *I'll let you in,*
mi vida, mi luz, mi alma!
(He pushes the MOON away from GABRIELA.)

GABRIELA: *(To MARTÍN)* *Who the hell are you?*

MARTÍN: *Name's Martin.*
Martin del Cuerpo Grande y Peludo.
And the moon can't love you like I can,
mi cielo, mi corazon, mi sangre
mi *extra-big sized box of Cocoa Puffs!*

GABRIELA: *What are you? Twelve?*

MARTÍN: *Fourteen,* mi amor.
And growing.
I have new hair
about to happen all over my body.

GABRIELA: *I have a husband.*
Six-foot-six?
Two-eighty-five?
Owner of this and other firearms?

MOON: *(To* MARTÍN*) What do you mean I can't love her*
like you can?

MARTÍN: *(To the* MOON*) You're incontinent.*
Shakespeare said.

MOON: *"Inconstant" not "incontinent,"*
you little fart!

(The MOON *and* MARTÍN *fight.)*

(The MOON *takes the gun from* GABRIELA *and pistol whips* MARTÍN.
MARTÍN *falls hard.)*

GABRIELA: *(To the* MOON*) Look what you did!*
You're supposed to be romantic.

MOON: *I did it for you.*
How romantic can you get, mujer?

GABRIELA: *(To* MARTÍN*) Kid. Hey kid.*

MOON: *(To* GABRIELA*) Does this mean it's over—?*

GABRIELA: *(To the* MOON*) Just get out of my face, all right?*
(She tries to revive MARTÍN.*)*

(With a piece of chalk, the CAT *draws the outline of the dead* COYOTE *on the*
concrete.)

(The dejected MOON *starts to go back into the sky.)*

MOON: *I shouldn't get involved with people.*
I should just watch.
That's what the moon does best.
Watches and witnesses—
then silently reports to you
through your dreams,
whispering nightly in your ear,
hoping to give you a fighting chance
in this hard, carnivorous world.
Yes, Gabby, the trees are indeed closing in on you.

Your visions of vampires and zombies are true.
And your husband's mind and heart
seem to have been kidnapped from you, poor girl.
So listen to the shadows, nena.
Pay attention to the lines between the lines.
That's the only way you're going
to survive out here,
at the edge of nowhere.
(The MOON *is back in the sky.)*

*(*GABRIELA *holds* MARTÍN.*)*

GABRIELA: *Poor Martín.*
For you love is a mystery and a poem.
For me it's bad habits
and tricks that don't work any more.

MARTÍN: *(Semi-conscious) ...I'm gonna die an old man*
who ain't never touched a woman's thing...

GABRIELA: *It's bones and hair and musky smells*
and a lot of ambiance that fades
with the daylight...
I don't know whether to love you
for your illusions
or smack you soundly
with the flat side of a shovel.

MARTÍN: *(Semi-conscious) ...when they buy virgins*
they say the grass
never grows on the grave...

GABRIELA: *I have no way of knowing*
what I'm going to do tomorrow
when Benito comes home.
The house will seem too small.
He'll cry and shout in his sleep
as the truth fights to get out
while he dreams.
When I ask him about it,
he'll deny, deny, deny.

MARTÍN: *(Semi-conscious) Sleep with me.*

GABRIELA: *The person I've chosen*
left his body at the house
while his mind and soul travel
the solar system for love and laughs.
I wonder if I can get him back.

I wonder if I want him back.
I wonder if I care anymore.

MARTÍN: *(Semi-conscious) I know you want babies.*

GABRIELA: *(A sad laugh) I'll sleep with you.*
But this is not
what you had in mind.

(GABRIELA *lies on the ground next to* MARTÍN. *They're not touching.)*

MARTÍN: *(Semi-conscious) Finally.*
In the arms of a woman.

GABRIELA: *Tomorrow morning is going to bring changes.*

MARTÍN: *(Semi-conscious) It's better than I ever imagined.*

GABRIELA: *Big, hurling, great, awful changes.*
I'm ready, Martin, are you?
I'm ready to make it happen—
and I'm ready for whatever happens to me.
Let it come.
Let the awful and beautiful changes come.

(GABRIELA *and* MARTÍN *fall asleep side by side.)*

(The MOON *plays the violin, something sad.)*

(The COYOTE's *soul leaves its body.)*

(The CAT *is astonished by this.)*

(The violin plays as the lights fade to black.)

END OF ACT ONE

ACT TWO

(Seven A M. GABRIELA's *kitchen. Refrigerator, sink, stove, kitchen table and chairs.)*

*(*BENITO, GABRIELA's *husband, a Latino sergeant of twenty-nine, in full desert camouflage uniform, stands surrounded by duffel bags.)*

*(*GABRIELA *wears very tight cut-offs, tank top; she's shoeless.)*

(She and BENITO *haven't seen each other in six weeks.)*

BENITO: Where were you?

GABRIELA: Backyard.

(They kiss briefly.)

BENITO: What's in the—?

GABRIELA: Slept there.

BENITO: Bed on fire?

GABRIELA: Just did, that's all.

BENITO: Huh. What's the coffee situation?

GABRIELA: As you wish, master.

BENITO: Call me master a lot, I really like it.

*(*GABRIELA *makes coffee.)*

GABRIELA: You lost a shitload of—.

BENITO: God bless them M R Es.

GABRIELA: Nice circles under the eyes.

BENITO: Ain't slept in forty-eight.

GABRIELA: *(Re: her haircut)* You're looking at me like I'm...

BENITO: You didn't mention the—.

GABRIELA: Bored. You hate it.

BENITO: Ages you—but just a little—hardly nothing!—five or six years, max!

GABRIELA: *(Can't help but laugh)* House passed inspection *without* your help, you owe me ten, you fuck, and here's your gun.

(BENITO *hands* GABRIELA *ten dollars as* GABRIELA *hands* BENITO *his 9 millimeter.*)

BENITO: Not "gun"—"weapon." Your gun hangs between your legs.

GABRIELA: Nothing hangs between my legs, sergeant.

(BENITO *eyes her up and down with great male appreciation.*)

BENITO: 'Cept me. Gabby. Oh, squeeze-able, eat-able, good-to-the-last-drop...

GABRIELA: I got a question. It's gonna sound, like stupid, but anyway: did you see the moon last night?

BENITO: *(Still on* GABRIELA's *body)* ...better than pogey-bait...

GABRIELA: Did you see the moon last night? I really gotta know this, Benito... *(She looks at him like his answer will decide everything.)*

BENITO: The moon? Why on earth is a working man looking at the moon for?

GABRIELA: Oh, forget it...

BENITO: The moon wearing a dress? Jerking itself off?

(GABRIELA *ignores him and opens the refrigerator.*)

GABRIELA: We're outta milk.

BENITO: Like maybe that's why they call it the Milky Way. The moon whacks off and comes all over the sky and *that's* the Milky—.

GABRIELA: Benito. That's gross.

BENITO: Who cares about the stupid—?

(GABRIELA *starts to leaves.*)

GABRIELA: I'm going out, pick up some milk...

BENITO: Now?

GABRIELA: Cigarettes too, master?

BENITO: Stop calling me master, wench!

GABRIELA: Well, if you don't wanna come into the milk container and pour *that* in your cof—.

BENITO: What is your God-given problem?

GABRIELA: *(Trying to leave)* Two minutes won't kill—.

BENITO: But I just got back from the field!

GABRIELA: Take a nap while I'm—.

BENITO: And how come there's no milk?

GABRIELA: Okay, I'm going....

BENITO: What're you doing all day? It's the first. I'm back today. It's been today since like forever.

GABRIELA: I use milk. It runs out. I didn't go shopping. Why?

BENITO: Too busy with the lesbian hair—?

GABRIELA: Too busy boning that cute Mexican boy lives next—.

BENITO: That little fag?

GABRIELA: That "fag" helped me out while you were gone—.

BENITO: *Cono*, girl, you are like...I don't know what...

GABRIELA: Yeah, well, welcome home.

BENITO: Feel welcomed too. It's been forever since I got kissed serious or groped around here—and the first thing you want is, you see my face, you're out the door! *(He goes to the refrigerator, opens it.)* There is nothing in here. It is a desert in here.

GABRIELA: Okay, Christ, I'm going...

BENITO: An empty fridge! That's like apocalyptic even!

GABRIELA: It's just a refrigera—.

BENITO: Ice cube trays full of sand. Not even a beer. *(He checks cabinets, drawers.)* Catfood, catfood, catfood. What—? You mad at me or something? Mad at little old Benito for something he ain't got clue one what he did?

GABRIELA: Not exactly mad and learn *English*, please.

BENITO: "Not exactly?" Now that strikes terror. *Oye.* We're starting over. Re-starting the clock back. *(He exits and re-enters.)* Hi honey, I'm home! Back from the field. From two hundred cancer-making degrees. From boredom so perfect and rare it lacks a name. From nothing good to look at but the backsides of doorknobs with their thumb up their ass, and farm boys so interbred they can't tell a M16 from the gun between their legs.

GABRIELA: *(Can't help but laugh)* Why are soldiers such children?

BENITO: Better haul that face over here, *coño!*

(BENITO grabs GABRIELA and kisses her. This kiss evolves rapidly and he's all over her. He tries to unzip her pants and take off his clothes during the following.)

GABRIELA: For a guy who ain't slept in forty-eight—.

BENITO: *(Taking off his shirt)* Missed you like a sad broken son-of-a-bitch.

GABRIELA: Sorry I'm like the dragon lady from hell, but I got—*Benito*—when I'm sleeping, I get—what are you doing?

BENITO: *(Stripping fast)* Thought since you ain't seen a man in a month and a half, you'd like to see what a man looks like.

GABRIELA: I got my period today.

BENITO: Hey I'm liberal. Anyway, you think I'm afraid of a little blood?

GABRIELA: Like living with the author of the Song of Songs, I swear.

BENITO: *(Working her zipper)* You call Costco...?

GABRIELA: Just give me a minute to catch my breath...

BENITO: *(Working her zipper)* ...tell 'em you're out sick today...?

GABRIELA: Maybe let's get to know each other first?

BENITO: *(Working her zipper)* Why?

GABRIELA: Pull that zipper any lower and I'm yelling rape.

BENITO: *(Thinks it's a joke)* You're so funny.

GABRIELA: BENITO I'M FUCKIN' NOT *FUCKING* WITH YOU!
(She pulls away, pulling up her zipper, shaking, fighting for control.)

(BENITO looks at her a cold, long moment.)

BENITO: I walked into some other dude's nightmare, *hija,* 'cause you ain't you.

GABRIELA: ...You know the cat's missing?

BENITO: When I'm home from the field we leave words and other debris at the door, then close the motherfucking door!

GABRIELA: Did you hear what I said about the cat?

BENITO: Ain't the pussy I'm interested in right now...

GABRIELA: *Ay, Dios,* man, God, shit: go play with yourself!

BENITO: Is it my fault you got the Ass of Heaven?

GABRIELA: How many ways I gotta tell you I'm not some strip-artist whore-bitch you picked up in some German night club—?

BENITO: Then don't wear those shorts!

GABRIELA: Clawing at me like I'm a piece of twenty-five dollar street trash—.

BENITO: You know where I can get it for twenty-five? Dang! Point the way, girl!

GABRIELA: And it's hot. I wear shorts 'cause we live in Barstow and it's *July?*

BENITO: Okay, *nena,* that was a joke, I will not claw you, I will respect you, 'cause you are the farthest thing on earth from a twenty-five-dollar-German-whore-bitch-street-bitch-German-thing, really, I tell you the God's honest.

GABRIELA: Don't even try to mock me—.

BENITO: Though half the company's probably already in bed with their old ladies.

GABRIELA: Their old ladies are sex slaves and I'm not.

BENITO: *My* bad luck!

GABRIELA: You wanna hear about the cat or not? *(She starts cleaning: washing dishes, wiping down counter tops, etc.—she's obsessive.)* I got home from school last night. I call her. Nothing. Then all night I'm hearing coyotes setting up camp under my window, whole *posses* of 'em, like, I don't know, like, like...

BENITO: *(Can't believe he's being ignored)* How come with you everything's gotta be like something else? Why can't shit just be what it is with you?

GABRIELA: *(Ignoring him)* ...like they opened up an asylum full of coyotes and they all parked their crazy asses in my backyard last night for a convention of the insane.

BENITO: Oh, that's clear, thank you.

GABRIELA: I think they ate my cat. One you gave me for my birthday?

BENITO: Maybe I'll get that milk—.

GABRIELA: The cat's devoured. Mind's all like—Christ: no!—thinking of her maimed to death by wild animals chewing her. And I think it's gotta mean something. There's no coincidences, Benito. I decided I let too much of life walk past me unwatched. That life is fulla signals that teach you shit. And I've been blind like I didn't wanna know. So I'm thinking that something like this doesn't happen for no reason, the cat, and I'm pondering what those reasons might be and asking myself: what other signs of important things have I been missing lately? You know. About us. And shit that's going on.

BENITO: *(Making a shopping list)* Beer, milk, bullshit remover, strap-ons—oops, scratch the...

GABRIELA: This desert...that's the thing, Benito...it's like, like....

BENITO: Wait, I'll do it. It's like...a nuclear beast ate up the whole world with all its flaming teeth and left nothing for us but the deep-fried leftovers in the Tupperware of Human Shit.

GABRIELA: Benito. Try being in this house—*alone.*

BENITO: Loneliness is your choice, *nena.*

GABRIELA: No one chooses this!

BENITO: If you didn't look down on all my buds and their wives who tried hard to make friends with you and found it impossible.

GABRIELA: Those Barbie Dolls your buddies are saddled with? Those wooden pieces of perpetual blow job machines—?

BENITO: This language is offensive. Period.

GABRIELA: I tried making friends. But it's a scientific fact: the brain can only gossip and talk about soap operas for so long before it starts to puke on itself. Or maybe I just got tired spending my afternoons with those girls, with cucumbers in our mouths, practicing blowjobs.

BENITO: You were getting a valuable lesson!

GABRIELA: *Benito* ... The desert is quiet. Nothing in it moves. It looks almost gentle. So you think, damn, if nothing in it moves, maybe it's safe for you. You can go take a walk in it. You can lie on the ground and stare at the moon.

BENITO: *Ay*, this moon crap again...

GABRIELA: Shakespeare called the moon inconstant, Benito.

BENITO: And I care!

GABRIELA: But that not-moving, you know, it's a mirage. It has its ways, the desert, that it knows how to...consume you. So many ways to get you tricked. So you trust it. Stupid you: you go out and coyotes jump your ass and eat you. The sun bakes you. The night-cold freezes blood. The bigness of it scares your heart and makes it stop. Okay—so then you *don't* go outside. You're stuck *inside*—over at the friggin' Costco or the commissary on post or a sorry-ass movie in Victorville with the Barbie Dolls. But then everyone you see in the dark air conditioning's like...vampires sizing you up for the next dinner. Strangers make you feel small and stupid. Couples with their fancy fingers all inside each other's pants remind you your old man's not around. On the movie screen is life all full of big blood and sex and people making perfect funny jokes every time. Like to remind you nobody really laughs in your world when you're alone. And that's what my life has been like, Benito, okay? And you know what? It really sucks! It's really a shitty thing to do to a person!

BENITO: So what are you telling me? Tell me what you're telling me and stop telling me the other shit you're not telling me.

GABRIELA: They stick you in a war. I don't see you for a year. I finally get you home *moments*, it feels like, not enough time to take your temperature, get used to your smell or know why you cry in your sleep—boom!—we're shipped to the desert and you're off to the field again!

BENITO: This is my job we're talking about here, right? What are you saying about my job?

GABRIELA: I'm saying fuck your job, okay?

BENITO: That's telling me something. I'm telling you: not to worry about the desert, in a year it's Germany.

GABRIELA: Oh, *that's* a step up—.

BENITO: WELL WHAT AM I SUPPOSED TO DO?! WILL YOU TELL ME THAT?! DAMMIT TO FUCKING HELL ON *EARTH*, GABRIELA!

GABRIELA: Don't yell at—.

BENITO: I am in the—what? Let's read aloud the little tag here on my...sez— ARMY! I am in the Army. In the Army you travel. That's what the Army is, homegirl! A great motherfucker of a travel agency. And they don't recommend all nice and sweat-free: THEY ORDER YOU! One year it's Germany where the whole country is full of Germans, and I'm sorry but we tried to get rid of the Germans, but dammit, the Germans didn't want to go! Then the next year it's the desert. Oh, the desert's hot! It's boring! Full o' vermin! The Army wives never finished pre-school. Pain in the ass! But in case you didn't notice, your car runs on oil and there's this place where oil comes from and everybody wants a piece of that sucker but if you want a piece of anything on God's goofy earth you gotta display the size of your *cojones,* and oh my God, the Middle East is in a desert!

GABRIELA: I know where the damn—.

BENITO: *(On a roll)* We train soldiers in the art of desert warfare—where?— in the desert! *Ay Dios mio!* I go out to the field for weeks at a time—why?— 'cause they pay me to! I don't like it. I don't want it. But I didn't feel like cutting pineapple the rest of my life in some Puerto Rican Plantation of Death. I told you I'm staying in the Army twenty years and retiring at the ripe old age of thirty-eight, pocket a full pension and never for a second sweat the money shit for as long as I have life, never. Told you that our first date, running out of that bar with skinheads chasing us. I got nine years left on the meter, Gabby. More than half the way there. So the next nine years, *nena,* is Germany or the desert, Germany or the desert, snow or sand, Nazis or knuckleheads, back and forth like that assuming war don't break out and I'm not protecting goat-herders in Somalia! That's the trip you signed on to take. Are there any questions, Private?

GABRIELA: No sir. *(She pours all the coffee she just made down the sink.)*

BENITO: You gotta stop acting like you know more than everybody.

GABRIELA: I do know more than everybody.

BENITO: Then keep it to yourself, 'cause, you know what, it's boring, okay? It's a turn off.

GABRIELA: *(Laughs)* Oh, *that's funny!*

BENITO: Everything you say and do reflects on me—.

GABRIELA: Turn off? I'm the one that's off.

BENITO: You get into a car accident, it's *my* rates that's go up. You break the law, it's *my* rank that's busted—.

GABRIELA: My eyes, my senses—*off*. My ideas *off*. My—oh fuck it—now we're just going in circles here. Talking in and out of the same three sentences as if like more words means more communicating. Ain't that a joke? Let me get that milk. *(She goes for her car keys.)*

BENITO: You got no clue of my life's insanity out there—'cause I make this army shit look easy. Look graceful. That's why you don't know jack how fucked it is.

GABRIELA: What're you bitching about?

BENITO: The last three weeks in the field, for me, I got my ass stuck in Star Wars, Gabby, okay? That's where I was. *Inside.* Behind a *desk*. In front of a *computer screen*. I went outta my mind. I'm going to the Captain, going, Sir, I wanna be outside. If I'm gonna play G I Joe I wanna be out in an M1A1 or jumping out of a chopper or blowing expensive stuff up, not in a goddamn *building* with *air* conditioning. But no. Captain rules. So I'm in Star Wars now.

GABRIELA: Why don't you give me one good clue—?

BENITO: It's like this. The desert floor is covered big time with sensors connected to satellites tracking every piece of moving hardware we got out there—Abrams, Cobras, A P Cs—our side and the bad guys. So the grunts and gun bunnies go through their combat simulations, right?, and on a computer in this building called Star Wars what happens in the field is monitored in real time. So I gotta watch this computer screen and see how the battles go. That's what I did for weeks of my life I'll never get back.

GABRIELA: That's cause for bitching? You're sitting in air conditioning!

BENITO: Gabriela, I don't wanna sit. Sitting is for *officers*. For *points*. A man does not sit when he *works*.

GABRIELA: Yeah, but, think, you could, maybe there's training here you can pick up, you know, learn a, you know—.

BENITO: Skill? That I can use in the "real world"?

GABRIELA: It saves on your body and you don't have to wreck yourself...

BENITO: Just waste away like some puke college professor—.

GABRIELA: I just don't think you should be like some common foot soldier—.

BENITO: I am no common anything, okay?

GABRIELA: I just think this shows the Captain—.

BENITO: What? Wants to get his prep school lips around my joint? He pulled me out of a line of men. This has nothing to do with me at all.

GABRIELA: So what are you afraid of?

BENITO: Go shoot yourself.

GABRIELA: No, I'm asking you something—.

BENITO: No, no, no, no, I know how the mind is working now, it's so obvious, Gabby, c'mon. "Benito hates to use his brain. Benito don't know a good thing when it's staring straight into his baboon face!" You know what I had to do? Watch men doing their work. A man watching other men work. All day long. Then I had to write a "narrative description" of all the things the men did while they worked. So I'm in front of a half-billion dollars of pure high tech and with two little chopstick fingers I take a half hour to type out three sentences and I can't spell half the words I have to write. That's my job.

GABRIELA: But nobody shot at you, did they?

BENITO: *Coño!* It's like you *want* me to be an officer.

GABRIELA: You get more money—.

BENITO: Officers are assholes.

GABRIELA: But if *you* were an officer, *you* wouldn't be—.

BENITO: My friends would *think* I was an asshole and that's the same—.

GABRIELA: Why are you so afraid of being better? I don't understand it!

(BENITO *throws his arms in the air and sits at a kitchen chair, facing downstage, his back to* GABRIELA.)

BENITO: What did I do? What did I do? Huh? I just want you to take your top off!

GABRIELA: *(Sarcastic)* Stop you're getting me so horny.

BENITO: Damn, I'm, like, out there, in no man's land, pretending to have war except all the hardware is more real than me, but the conflict is a game, it's fiction, and that's my job and I come home to you, all beautiful, like what you see after death and the angels greet you in the morning, and you hope, you know, God allows sex with the angels in Heaven maybe once in a while if you're extra good around Christmas, but everything between us is real war, honey, and it's getting old real fast, baby, I'm telling you. *(He closes his eyes and they stay closed during the following.)*

GABRIELA: I keep having these dreams. I don't know what they're telling me. They seem so real. Am I losing it?

BENITO: *(Eyes closed)* Think we agree the answer is yes.

GABRIELA: There's so much going on with you you don't want to talk about.

BENITO: *(Eyes closed)* Nothing's going on. I just got back from the field. You don't know me. I don't know you. Happens every goddamn time I come home...

GABRIELA: But this time it's the first time you were in the field since the war and I'm like all outta practice being your wife....

BENITO: *(Eyes closed, sleepy)* ...we'll get over it, like we always....

GABRIELA: ... and I'm having dreams every single night and all of them want me to test you...

BENITO: *(About to fall asleep)* Stop. Just stop with that. Don't tell me no more about dreams. It's your usual freak out, when I come home.

(Silence from GABRIELA for a second.)

(BENITO falls asleep in the chair.)

(GABRIELA takes off his boots.)

GABRIELA: Jesus, I forget how much space you take up. And you got a smell. Soon you'll be leaving pubes on the tile. And, like, if I think things now— am I gonna know which thoughts are mine 'cause they're mine or they're mine 'cause you put them there....

(MARTÍN enters holding a large cardboard box.)

MARTÍN: Where's my reward, woman?

(GABRIELA sees her cat inside the box.)

GABRIELA: I was ready to call the fucking morgue!

MARTÍN: Found her surrounded by coyotes all salivating and doing the humpy motion with their torsos.

GABRIELA: *(To cat)* Better not catch no rabies, you!

MARTÍN: *(Re: BENITO)* No one's worried about the noise level?

GABRIELA: He'll sleep for seven straight, I swear, *days. (She puts the cat in another room.)*

MARTÍN: I'm going to the store, you want anything?

(GABRIELA gives MARTÍN money.)

GABRIELA: Ten for the cat rescue: now go.

MARTÍN: You saying you don't want me around no more?

GABRIELA: I'm saying my old man's back from the field and has a limited sense of humor when it comes to who he thinks wants to fuck me.

MARTÍN: I'm only saying I know you want babies. I'm old enough to get you pregnant.

GABRIELA: Get out of my house before I kill you!

MARTÍN: I wouldn't ask you to serve me. I can wash my own *ropa*. I would bring you hot *huevos* in the morning. Read the *periodico* to you. Put your *pelo* up in bobby pins. Keep your *piso* waxed. Your *cocina* full of canned creamy soup and Cocoa Puffs. Okay, *nena*?

GABRIELA: Out, please.

MARTÍN: I don't need to be big and strong. I can handle your nightmares if you tell them to me. I love a house full of singing and fresh desert air. I'll even tolerate your cat. Don't answer right away, Gabby. But think about it.

GABRIELA: Please don't do this to me, Martin. (MARTÍN *gives* GABRIELA *a kiss on the cheek and goes.*)

(GABRIELA *looks at* BENITO *a long moment, watching him sleep. She comes downstage of him and sits cross-legged on the floor, facing upstage. She takes off her top, exposing herself to* BENITO, *who continues to sleep.*)

BENITO: *(Sleeping)* Gabby's having dream....

(*Lights begin to fade. It seems to become night in the kitchen. Upstage, the* CAT *and* COYOTE *appear, watching.*)

GABRIELA: ...her dreams are full of broken moonlight, Benito...her dreams are full of moist sex and the dirty smell of sweat...her dreams level civilizations and make them grateful for chaos and heavy breathing and whirlwinds...

BENITO: ...Gabby's having awful dreams....

(GABRIELA *holds herself and tries hard to keep from crying and* BENITO *sleeps and the lights go to black.*)

END OF ACT TWO

INTERMISSION

ACT THREE

(That night)

(GABRIELA's bedroom. On the walls: photos of tanks, BENITO's military citations, a poster of Salvador Dali's "Two Pieces of Bread Expressing the Sentiment of Love," a black velvet unicorn poster. Military swords are displayed over the bed's headboard. A stack of books and a telescope next to the bed.)

(The light of the MOON comes in through upstage windows.)

(There are occasional maddening offstage howls of coyotes.)

(BENITO lies in bed, fast asleep, bootless and minus the web gear, but otherwise dressed as he was at the end of ACT TWO.)

(GABRIELA lies at his side, dressed as she was in ACT TWO. She holds a mirror to BENITO's mouth, watching his breath clouding the glass, leaning close to him.)

(BENITO cries in his sleep. He sounds like a wounded coyote. He thrashes. Alarmed, GABRIELA shakes BENITO awake.)

(BENITO wakes with a gasp. Without looking or thinking he takes a swing at GABRIELA.)

(GABRIELA instinctively pulls back and BENITO misses. He's disoriented, breathing hard.)

BENITO: *Never*...never wake me up like that, *nena,* if you don't want your teeth on the floor.

GABRIELA: *(Shaken)* I'm sorry. I forgot. It's been a while, remember?

BENITO: Shit; shit; that whacked my nerves up pretty bad. It's the same day?

GABRIELA: I'm not sure what's the day.

BENITO: You okay? I didn't—?

GABRIELA: Some instinct in me remembered you been doing that since the war.

BENITO: Everything's swirling in this room, *carajo.* Must be all the drugs I don't take but wish I did.... *(Groaning, he unsteadily gets out of bed and goes to the offstage bathroom.)*

(GABRIELA talks to the offstage BENITO as he takes a leak.)

GABRIELA: You were talking in your dreams.

BENITO: *(Offstage)* I never dream.

GABRIELA: Everyone does. It's only human.

BENITO: *(Offstage)* I ain't only human. I'm human-plus.

GABRIELA: I heard you making noises. Like something was coming outta someplace in you, someplace down and low, like where your bones talk.

BENITO: *(Offstage)* This just in: bones don't talk.

GABRIELA: *If* they did. You cry in your sleep too. So quiet maybe only a bat could hear it. So secret, too, the air that brings it up from inside you hardly makes a scratch in the mirror I held all day long to your mouth, 'cause I was afraid you were dead sometimes.

BENITO: *(Offstage)* I'm so glad to know that.

GABRIELA: *(More to herself)* It's kinda screwed up: of all the parts of the body, only the brain gets the power to speak. I'd love to know what your stomach thinks.

(BENITO comes in from the bathroom.)

BENITO: My stomach thinks you're mental. Other organs have their own viewpoints on this.

(During the following, BENITO strips down to his boxers—a not-so-subtle striptease for GABRIELA, who does her best to ignore him....)

GABRIELA: *(Trying to change the mood in the room)* ...Okay, here's what I don't get. How come in eleven years in the Army I never heard you or any of your pinhead friends say one honest patriotic thing?

BENITO: *(Stripping)* I love my country. It's the people in it I hate.

GABRIELA: Makes me laugh to think of you risking your life for a bunch of tree huggers.

BENITO: *(Stripping)* Immigrants, welfare queens...

GABRIELA: Welfare? C'mon! What was the house in Germany we didn't pay for? That pumped-up car? That ain't taxpayer money being wasted?

BENITO: Taxpayer's getting a lean, mean fighting machine—with a nice ass.

GABRIELA: Who can't stop crying in his sleep like an infant baby.

(BENITO gets into bed.)

BENITO: Every soldier does that. It's nothing. Justifies the combat pay.

GABRIELA: If it's nothing what's the big crime in telling me?

BENITO: ...And how come there's sand in here?

GABRIELA: You think, oh your mind's this distant private place, what happens in there only happens to you—but it happens to me, too—.

BENITO: It's gotta lighten up in here or I'll mistake this bed for the bottom of Death Valley.

GABRIELA: I tell you every passing thing that hits my mind, Benito.

BENITO: *(Sarcastic)* And it ain't as boring as scrubbing a barracks' floor with a Q-tip.

GABRIELA: Oh. It's my job to entertain you, huh? And if I don't do my job, I might as well do something else tonight. *(She gets out of bed and starts changing her clothes.)*

BENITO: What are you doing?

GABRIELA: If I hurry, I can catch the second half of my class.

BENITO: Tonight? You're going to school—?

GABRIELA: It's been tonight since about forever.

BENITO: You always quit your classes when I'm home from the field. That's been the deal—.

GABRIELA: But I really like this one. It's astronomy. It makes me aware of the fucking universe, okay?

BENITO: Gabby, for crying out loud—.

GABRIELA: *Exactly* what you been doing all day in your sleep. Driving me crazy with the sound of pain that's busting your gut. Making me wonder what's in there, thinking the worst, holding my breath for an answer getting *zero*. You want me to stay? Give me a husband that's more than a body in my bed, okay?

BENITO: You need this from me? You really need to know?

GABRIELA: You need it more than me.

BENITO: *Oyeme, nena, por Dios,* it was...nothing. A thing. I did a thing, after the ground war I never told you about. Messed my head a little. Now get back in—.

GABRIELA: *(Getting her telescope)* School's an hour one way, I'll be back in—.

BENITO: Maybe *you* get something outta pulling barbed wire out of a person, but the person *doing* it *suffers.* We like to put pain to *rest.*

GABRIELA: Silence never rests nothing.

BENITO: The *balls* you have! Dang! *(Beat)* The war was over. We were pacifying little towns left and right and the ragheads had these big time curfews, like they couldn't assemble more than three of them on a street corner, if they did it's, boom, automatic arrest, no questions asked, off to Saudi Arabia and them in their monkey-language all pissed off at you. So the scene's all pacified and I'm just hangin' with a couple of treadheads

contemplating playing spades on the downtime, it's *that* mellow—when—
some idiot—fires a rocket at the A P C I'm standing next to and blows a hole
in it the size of Kuwait and decimates one of my corporals. And I'm telling
you, I'm tripping. I'm like insane over this event. I'm stomping around the
desert like baby Godzilla, cursing the little Persian freaks and I got wild,
Gabby, you know what I did? The war is over and you know what I did?
I called for fire. I'm the F O out there and I get on the horn and I call an air
strike and I leveled a town. Precision-guided munitions fell by the ton on a
little town 'til every shack, every Mosque and shithouse where people lived
their tortured camelshit lives got turned to dust and wind 'cause of me.
After the bombs stopped falling a place that used to be on a map got
de-mapped from earth and that happened 'cause they pissed off an
American soldier. They pissed off the man in your bed.

(GABRIELA looks at BENITO, then goes to hold him.)

GABRIELA: Oh, my baby...I'm so sorry... *(She kisses BENITO.)*

BENITO: Gabby...

GABRIELA: ...just think it's better...you let this out of you...you won't be
hunted in your sleep by the death of your friend no more....

(BENITO looks at GABRIELA.)

BENITO: What death?

GABRIELA: Your corporeal. You must've lost your shit when he died.
No wonder you—.

BENITO: Uhm—he didn't *die*, Gabby.

GABRIELA: He didn't? What do you mean he—?

BENITO: Got *wounded* is what.

GABRIELA: Like—near-fatal? Lots of blood?

BENITO: His hand—.

GABRIELA: Got blown off?

BENITO: They blew off his fingers!

GABRIELA: Wait a minute. A village in Iraq for a—?

BENITO: Very important fingers!

GABRIELA: You leveled it 'cause one of your buddies got a *pinky* wound?

BENITO: We evacuated them *first*, Gabby.

GABRIELA: You let them out before the bombs fell?

BENITO: *Most* of them anyway.

GABRIELA: Some people stayed and died?

BENITO: Ones that didn't *listen*—.

GABRIELA: Women and children—?

BENITO: I can't control what happens in the mind of a raghead. Did they go? Some did. Others not. In a war...

GABRIELA: Which was over, you said.

BENITO: In a rural pacification program...

GABRIELA: I hate your job. I really do. That's all I'm saying here.

BENITO: Swear, *nena,* you are unlimited in your ballbusting gifts! I'm trained to respond: what could I do?

GABRIELA: Not call the air strike?

BENITO: You weren't there. You don't know. We didn't know. We were in a *situation,* Gabby, blood, tension, enemies, heat, howling pain, adrenaline surge could give the Vatican a hard-on...

GABRIELA: You never do shit like that.

BENITO: It bothers you, we'll call an Army shrink.

GABRIELA: Is it crazy if I don't like to think of you as a killer? If I don't like when they take my husband and make him kill?

BENITO: *Way* outta line, Private—.

GABRIELA: You hate it too! You do! *Inside,* you do! If you didn't, you wouldn't cry every time you close your eyes—.

BENITO: I do this thing—you're right, I hold it in—'cause I'm afraid to disturb you—okay, *este*—we got off on the wrong foot this morning, let's communicate—let me give you every growling demon inside me making all the noise that keeps me up at night, and I say, girl kill this fucker for me, 'cause I can't, bury this creature 'cause it's torturing me, and you go and put on fangs and torture me some more.

GABRIELA: You don't sound tortured. You sound proud you erased a town and wrote your name in that dust—but I don't believe it. I think it's a lie you tell yourself so you can survive the army.

BENITO: Sure about that? Maybe I liked watching the bombs fall.

GABRIELA: Don't say that, you didn't like it, Benito.

BENITO: Fine! I'm boycotting telling you anything serious anymore!
(He gets out of bed and starts to straighten up the room, sweeping, etc.)

GABRIELA: That's cool 'cause you know what I did when you went to war I boycotted telling you about?

BENITO: You had an affair with an Iraqi.

GABRIELA: I had an affair with a guy named Muhammad.

BENITO: That better be an allegory of speech.

GABRIELA: I took a class in Bamholder on Arabs. I read about Islam.
I didn't know jack about those people, but I thought—.

BENITO: Hey. How do you clear an Iraqi bingo room? Yell B-52.

GABRIELA: I thought: he's going out to kill them, then I wanna know who
they are. I learned about this orphan Muhammad, who believed in Jesus
and humility and created a kneeling prayer 'cause his people were too
proud to kneel to their God and he thought that was bullshit. An angel
grabbed him by the nuts and said: "recite!" And he recited and didn't
stop for twenty years and practically invented his people's language
when he did.

BENITO: I'm getting your library card burned on national television and
the country will cheer.

GABRIELA: I thought—if I learned something about those people you're
dropping "precision-guided munitions" on, I could respect them, and my
respect, maybe, would balance out what you were doing, in a karma way.

BENITO: A karma way. Giving aid and comfort to the enemy—.

GABRIELA: Nobody got any aid or comfort as I thought of you risking your
ass for nothing.

BENITO: Freedom ain't nothing! Freedom ain't nothing! Freedom ain't
nothing!

GABRIELA: How do you bomb a town to make it free?

BENITO: That's *enough* of that! It's *over*, Gabriela. Good guys won. Good guys
come home. Good guys pick up where they left off.

GABRIELA: It's never over. Spoken or not, a soldier takes his battles with him
everywhere he goes. You taught me that.

BENITO: Not tonight: no. Tonight we're exempted from all shit. Tonight
nothing gets through to us. (*He gets back into bed and kisses* GABRIELA.)

GABRIELA: Benny, I'm not trying to bust your balls...I just wish I had the
words...for all the *thinking* I've been....

BENITO: At the edge of the bed, the soldier is just a man again.

(*Before she can stop him,* BENITO *pulls* GABRIELA *closer.*)

BENITO: Tonight we're taking inventory. Reading all the pages on this fine
book of photographs. Maybe we'll remember why we're here. What's this?
(*He points to the scar on* GABRIELA's *knee. This is an old game of theirs.*)

GABRIELA: That was the morning I fell off the roof of my house playing Super Puerto Rican Girl and I caught the corner of a fridge we kept outside, with my knee.

BENITO: A beautiful jagged mess. Like your mind. This? (*He kisses her scar and points to her thigh.*)

GABRIELA: That was the afternoon my brother thought it'd be radically cute to plunge a fish hook bone-deep in my thigh. Repeatedly.

BENITO: Remind me to remove his thorax for him. (*He kisses her scar and touches her arm.*)

GABRIELA: The night *Abuela* thought it'd be a howling pisser to stick the burning buttend of a Marlboro here and see how high I'd jump.

BENITO: Serious need for a lobotomy, that bearded old bitch, for hurting you in any way, shape, or form. That's my real job. To hurt what hurts you. (*Sees a scar he's never seen before*) What's this?

GABRIELA: Oh. Mexican kid next door asked me to play touch football and I slipped and cut myself.

BENITO: He changed your body! Who said your body's supposed to change, huh? (*He starts to kiss* GABRIELA.)

(GABRIELA *pulls away ever-so-slightly.*)

GABRIELA: Tell you what else I don't get. How, like, a feeling, which is made of nothing, gets made part of your body—you know? Why would a doubt make a burning hole in your stomach or a lump in your throat heavy as a man?

BENITO: Swear you use words like some people use razor wire and guard dogs.

GABRIELA: You know you get mean when you're impatient?

BENITO: I'm human and male so fuck me.... (*He grabs her around the waist and kisses her stomach.*)

(GABRIELA *is frozen.*)

GABRIELA: In Germany it was all that cold....

BENITO: ...and what are you doubting...?

GABRIELA: ...cold like when you're abandoned by God. Cold like the fingers of a baby's corpse. Cold that fucks you and gives you a virus. Then it's you in boiling Iraq. I imagine you naked in the desert...captured by the enemy... and, no, they don't kill you right away, they take their time...until you scream out your mother's name when they've found your softest places and learned how to dismantle you and put you back together any old way they feel like it. And me waiting, sucking in rumors like life-saving air: washing dishes, cleaning, polishing the car, reading, pacing, smoking, crying, punching holes in the walls, puking.

BENITO: High maintenance.

GABRIELA: I hated falling asleep 'cause of the dreams. In my dream: I get your body after the war. You can't move. I can't figure out why. You open your mouth for me. I put my hand down your throat. My whole arm goes in. Your skin is see-thru so I watch my hand groping the things in your stomach. There's little round rocks in you, smooth, like from a beach, and I pull these outta your stomach by the fistful but you don't get better. Not 'til I'm reaching deeper in your bowels and pull out the rusted nails and burning bits of shrapnel that were in there and they cut my hand to pieces but I don't stop until I pull them all out of your body.

BENITO: Do I get better?

GABRIELA: Never know. I wake up.

BENITO: There's a way, Gabby, to make all that go away. To wake up forever. Don't fight me, *nena*. I missed you. I was ready to kill myself without you. These hands don't just pull triggers and evaporate life. They have other jobs besides counting dead. These are good hands. You know that from experience. You know I can fix every bad dream in your head. Okay? I can cure this insanity you have if you let me turn your brain off for a night. Turn off this river of words that keeps drowning us... *(He kisses her.)*

(GABRIELA pulls away.)

GABRIELA: It won't turn off. I can't do it. *(She puts on jeans and a shirt and shoes.)*

(BENITO watches her, motionless.)

BENITO: You still going to that class?

GABRIELA: *(Shaking her head no)* I'm leaving. You.

BENITO: You're leaving. Me.

(GABRIELA packs clothes.)

GABRIELA: I have some money from Costco I saved up, I'll take the little car, I'll live in Victorville, or Los Angeles, or Vegas, I don't really know at this....

BENITO: You only think you're leaving me.

GABRIELA: I ain't slept in that bed since you left for the field—.

BENITO: Come back in the bed, please.

GABRIELA: —for six weeks I slept in the backyard, half-hoping those coyotes'd eat me.

(BENITO gets out of bed and grabs GABRIELA roughly.)

BENITO: The fuck you're leaving! Let's see you leave if I don't let you.

GABRIELA: *(Pushing back)* Don't push me, okay? I'll kick your ass!

BENITO: You're gonna kick *my* ass?

GABRIELA: Kick it all the way to Baghdad!

BENITO: You got somebody else? Little La Raza boy-toy next door?

GABRIELA: Please. Do I look that stupid to you?

BENITO: Friggin' great news, Gab!

GABRIELA: I thought—I'm so stupid and this proves it—I thought: no, I can't leave while you're in the field—you come home to an empty house—so out of *fairness*, a sense of *justice*, I'll make you see I'm drowning in the sand and the cold—.

BENITO: *Ay Dios! Ay Dios!* These words!

GABRIELA: —and maybe you would see it, clearly, finally—.

BENITO: When did you put on all these clothes I never seen before?

GABRIELA: —and think that you could, for me, for my life, leave the Army, turn your back and leave this shit—.

BENITO: It's so unfair! When I go to the field, I need for you *not to change!*

GABRIELA: —I could finally, finally see what it was like to be married to you in a different way—

BENITO: One crudely stupid selfish woman—.

GABRIELA: Not in an army town, where everybody's armed like the end of the world. Not smelling like tank fuel. Not playing God. Not one of us living a life the other can't understand anymore. But it's never gonna happen is it—?

BENITO: No—there's no—there's no—no—no—no!

GABRIELA: Then if it's no, I can't stay....

BENITO: One total messed-up mental case...

GABRIELA: And who wouldn't get like that? I got no real education, Benito, 'cept what I scrape together from night schools. Got no life-long friends. Got no experience but friggin' temp work 'cause of all our moving. I'd like to actually maybe be something someday better than working at Costco all my life. I'd like to make more than minimum wage before I'm thirty-eight. If you could just—listen—walk away from this life, *mi cielo,* and I know that would be so hard for you...

BENITO: You can't decide shit like this in secret.

GABRIELA: ...but if you quit the Army I can forgive it all—so fast!—I could wake up from the nightmare: the war, everything...

BENITO: This some kind of gruesome test?

GABRIELA: ...and go to where we can both go back to school—.

BENITO: Me and school? Are you cracked? I read at a fourth grade level, you wanna know the absolute.

GABRIELA: I know it feels unfair of me, and you love the Army...

BENITO: You're leaving 'cause I don't read books enough? Don't know about astronomy and Allah and Salvador Dali?

GABRIELA: ...and I wanna love what you—.

BENITO: You think I'm common, but I'm not. I jump out of planes. I climb mountains. I swim the ocean. I know martial arts. I can survive in the middle of nowhere with nothing but shoe string and a mirror. I can take apart an M16A2 and put it back together blindfolded. I speak three languages. I met the Secretary of Defense. I defended an oppressed country against naked *aggression*. I was in history. Is none of that any good anymore?

GABRIELA: Of course it is—but it cost one of us a whole life. I worked my ass off so you could play G I Joe with your friends.

BENITO: You didn't get nothing back? You had parents wanted to haul your ass to Alcatraz. You had intimate knowledge of the juvenile *penal* system.

GABRIELA: And I ain't been perfect. There were times I stopped trying—.

BENITO: A house, a car, insurance, shelter, love, you get love, because I stupidly, ridiculously, fanatically love you—you get that?—you see that in the plus column? Should I repeat? It's the love, stupid!

GABRIELA: I want to change—.

BENITO: I'm sorry I love you and the Army. I'm sorry I have two loves. But one, you might notice, is inanimate. Ain't got a soul. Can't really compete.

GABRIELA: It's doing not-so-bad, I think!

BENITO: What you really want is for me to like literally attach myself surgically to the hip—.

GABRIELA: I'd love that.

BENITO: Well here's the big Geraldo newsflash, *nena*: I can't give it. One hundred percent of me? Not available in any store.

GABRIELA: I give it to you. Every day. Because I have no other love, Benito. You're my army. You're my family. You're my religion.

BENITO: Then that makes you better than me. You'll be decorated accordingly. But me, I need to be—don't even think of laughing— someplace, whatever, that's my privacy: where you can't go.

GABRIELA: This just in: I know.

BENITO: I get that private thing in the field sometimes. When I'm out there, I sometimes can feel—all the previous wars. Feel them in my body. My chest. No wonder that's where they put the medals. Out there training, before they stuck my ass in Star Wars, I tried to even feel, you know, Korea in me, even Vietnam. Men doing impossible things together. Men agreeing.

GABRIELA: Men, men, men...

BENITO: With codes and rules on how to be. Instead of all the chaos puked on the world by eunuchs with no code and no rules—all pussywhipped and worried about exchange rates, being weekend warriors, playing their mind games on the weak: just sliding from moment to moment like there was no absolutes for valor and manhood and freedom.

GABRIELA: You joined the Army 'cause you were poor.

BENITO: And I ain't poor no more. And I don't just mean the Grand National parked outside. I mean in me, my mind: the war on poverty ended and I won it.

GABRIELA: Benito. All that's true for you but it's not true for me.

BENITO: Did a fine job fooling me all these years. Guess I hallucinated all the nights we had: playing cards with my friends, and you're drinking beers, telling dirty jokes, your hand on my knee, big, big laughter—.

GABRIELA: We were drunk half the time!

BENITO: You told me you wanted eight kids with me.

GABRIELA: I thought I did.

BENITO: No, you didn't *think* you did, you *did.* Looked me in the eye. Sometimes the tears falling, fat as snakes, your fingers around my stick so tight you almost broke it, eyes on fire, you whisper so low and sexy: "I love you, baby,"—you said that!—"so much, I want to have eight kids with you." The pants come down. The legs get wrapped around my neck. Do I disbelieve that now? Was it a lie? Are you lying now? Were you crazy then? Are you crazy now?

GABRIELA: I was eighteen when I said that about the babies. Before we knew I couldn't. Before the war changed you.

BENITO: The war didn't change me. It changed you.

GABRIELA: And I don't think you're common. I don't think I'm smarter than you. I knew if you wanted to, you could be anything. It's fear that makes you run from your mind, Benito.

BENITO: You don't deserve to have a house. You don't deserve security.

GABRIELA: *Cono*, that is so lame it's not even—.

BENITO: Oh fuck it, fuck it! Man, what is wrong with me? Standing in this bedroom begging you to stay with me? I don't have to beg no damn woman for no damn thing in the world. You have decided—before I even got home. So great. So that's the message handed down from the Supreme Court, on the day of my return from busting my hump for her, the day of reunion, the day of new honeymoons and second chances. You've *assaulted* me with this shit. You've hit me right between the eyes, *nena*. It'd be better to just take my sidearm and let the bullets do the talking. I don't beg. A man does not beg. You go find what you're missing. Read every book in the world. 'Cause right now we're oil and water, a train wreck, and you know what? Thank you, baby. This was good. Saved us a lot of time. I now have more time to watch T V. *(He puts on clothes.)*

GABRIELA: What are you doing?

BENITO: You know what? You're wrong—I don't run from my mind, I don't, I live inside myself, where there's no way out, and I see what I do. I see what I put you through, for years.

GABRIELA: Could this be a whiff of a hint of a shadow of saying "I'm sorry"?

BENITO: You said you'd forgive everything if I left the Army: that means forgiving ain't impossible. That's what I want. Forgive me and hold on until I can retire in nine years. You can do it, private. The war was a fluke. There will not be another one in my life. I'll do everything I can to get orders for anyplace on earth but Germany or the desert. I'll volunteer for Star Wars. I'll suck off the captain. I'll learn to type. Just don't make me rip my life in half and erase eleven years of it 'cause then I'm dead for sure, Gabby. *(He has to keep from crying. He pushes his emotions down, way down.)*

GABRIELA: Why do you gotta be so convoluted?

BENITO: 'Cause I'm not supposed to make it easy for you to break my heart.

GABRIELA: Like I made it easy for you?

BENITO: I'm gone. I'll be on post. You decide if you wanna be here when I come home tomorrow morning. We'll try the homecoming again, if you want. But really think about it. Think about me. Don't do anything until you think about me. (BENITO *leaves the room.)*

(GABRIELA *collapses into bed and thinks about everything.)*

(COYOTES *howl.)*

(GABRIELA *falls asleep.)*

(Blackout)

END OF ACT THREE

ACT FOUR

(Early morning. The backyard. A hint of sunlight over the east threatens the darkness.)

(The MOON is faint, weak, low in the sky, softly playing the violin.)

(The COYOTE'S GHOST and the CAT stare at each other in wonder.)

(MARTÍN and GABRIELA, not touching, sleep side-by-side. GABRIELA is wearing sweatpants and sweatshirt.)

CAT: *(To the COYOTE'S GHOST) I thought you were dead, Coyote.*

COYOTE'S GHOST: *(To the CAT) I'm a ghost.*

CAT: *I thought I'd never see you again.*

COYOTE'S GHOST: *I'm a memory.*

CAT: *A vivid one—my body remembers!*
A difficult one too.

COYOTE'S GHOST: *I'm a dream.*
I'm not really here.

CAT: *I know. I miss you.*

COYOTE'S GHOST: *You were right not to trust me.*

CAT: *I didn't know what to*
think of you at first.

COYOTE'S GHOST: *I wanted to hurt you.*
To teach you to be wild.
Then kill you quick—
and eat you
and not give a shit.

CAT: *Then the moonlight stabbed you*
and ripped you off,
and there was nothing
I could do about it.
And with your passing,
all my hopes for a wild ride
in the endless night seemed to end.
But you're back!

COYOTE'S GHOST: *Am I?*

CAT: *I don't have to miss you anymore.*

COYOTE'S GHOST: *Why do you stare at me?*

CAT: *You're transparent!*
It's so cool!

COYOTE'S GHOST: *I can't even smell you.*

CAT: *Coyote, I'm hot.*

COYOTE'S GHOST: *I can't smell anything.*
What kind of hunter will I be?

CAT: *Smell me and you'll know.*

COYOTE'S GHOST: *My appetite for blood: gone!*

CAT: *There are other kinds of smells.*
Other kinds of hunger.
An infinity of tastes.
And ways to satisfy.

COYOTE'S GHOST: *What are you thinking, Cat?*

CAT: *Thoughts! Wild ones! (She yowls in heat and grief.)*

(MARTÍN wakes up.)

MARTÍN: *(To the MOON) After my pistol of love*
found its target and
exploded with love-shrapnel
inside her, and sent her mind
to the dizzy edge of the universe,
where it sat and wondered
what the fuck hit it...
she fell asleep.
Mission accomplished!
I am now a man.
Seeds are planted.
Other men notice my manhood
and are suddenly afraid.

MOON: *(Bored, sarcastic) ...So hide your daughters, people.*

MARTÍN: *SO HIDE YOUR DAUGHTERS,*
PEOPLE!

(GABRIELA wakes up.)

GABRIELA: *I just had the strangest dream....*

MARTÍN: *I think I got you pregnant.*

GABRIELA: *Then you have the only sperm*
on earth that crawls across cement,
burrows through cotton panties,
and grows flowers in barren sand.

MARTÍN: *Ask the moon what I did!*

MOON: *(Weak) At night, love can't*
hide from me.
My light penetrates.
When virgin blood and
virgin seed hit the sheets,
I'm there,
counting the droplets.

GABRIELA: *(To the* MOON*) Delightful job you have.*

MOON: *(Weak) It's a living.*
But, now, my time is almost over.
Gotta go to bed.
My sister the sun is
impatient and pushy.

GABRIELA: *In my dream: cats don't talk.*
Refrigerators are indoor appliances.
The moon doesn't play the violin.
On the moon, sunlight cooks the land
and there's zero romance and no sound.
Dreams don't get born there.
Some day the moon will be landfill,
people think.
So the moon watches,
with indifference,
as the earth rises
out of its bleached horizon,
all soft and blue,
like a marble covered in tears.

(The MOON *yawns, gets dimmer.)*

MOON: *Yeah, whatever.*

GABRIELA: *But what if I'm still dreaming?*
What if none of us wake up?
What if we go on like this:
dreaming and sleeping, dreaming and sleeping,
until we're like boxes-within-boxes
and there's no way out?

MOON: *Adios,* Gabby!

GABRIELA: *(To the* MOON*) Before you go,*
explain my dream to me.
I couldn't recognize Benito and me.

MOON: *It's a dream about soul mates.*

GABRIELA: *Who never agree? Who misinterpret?*

MOON: *You two go deep.*
So the wounds go deep.
You give a person so much,
you rearrange them.
You re-write them.
He's your creation.
You're his.

GABRIELA: *Was it all a mistake?*
Was it all hormones
and sweaty fingers?
Beer and pot and sucking each other?
Was it the uniform?
Was it the jokes he told
and the food he cooked?
Was it just youth?
Why didn't I take more pictures
of those days?
Why can't I remember
them better?

MOON: *(Weak) Too tired to think...*

GABRIELA: *My parents went from one island,*
Puerto Rico, to another island, Long.
They bought a little house
and never left it.
No interest in the horizon beyond.
I was losing my mind,
so I stole beer and blouses
from local establishments.
My desperate mami
shipped me to cousin's,
in South Carolina,
where I ran wild,
sneaking into all the bars,
looking for the lucky young man
to donate my cherry to.
Do you remember how we met?

MOON: *A bar. A wild October night. A melee.*

GABRIELA: *Fists flying, American G Is*
drunken rednecks.
Benito and other recruits
on the floor getting nailed
by local skinheads.
I pulled him to his feet
and ran out of the bar with him
before it really got ugly.
Saved him. Held him.
Brought him back to his own body.
To his future—away from his virginity.
I was fifteen years old.
Our futures mingled—
it was sweet and reckless...
we were each other's
drugs and cigarettes...
we floated in and out of dreams
that both of us wrote...
wide-eyed, breathing fast,
hands like fish,
enough soft skin to cover
the earth ten times over,
turning from solid to liquid,
many liquids, many smells,
no waking up, ever.

MOON: *(Fading) ...fading...*

GABRIELA: *Who wouldn't get married*
under those circumstances?
Who wouldn't assume
that passion—and tenderness—
could last forever?
Who could have predicted
the changes in the body and the spirit?

(The MOON *starts to set.)*

MOON: *(Fading) ...don't turn to me*
for precise answers, Gabby...
I'm a reflection of a reflection...
I'm a co-dependent satellite...
not even confident enough
to be a planet...
and what you ask about...
are intangibles...
there will always be things

you can't know about each other...
there has never been a machine
made to x-ray the heart
and reveal its secrets,
except for poetry...
and I'm way too tired
to deal with poetry tonight...
Shakespeare called me inconstant...
"that nightly changes in HER circled orb"...
even got my gender wrong...
the motherfucker...
but I guess I am...
that's as close to precise
as the moon can get...

MARTÍN: *(To the* MOON*) I wish you'd leave already!*

MOON: *(To* GABRIELA*) ...everything you do*
will seem like a mistake...
for a very long time to come...

(Using his telescope like a gun, MARTÍN *takes aim at the* MOON.*)*

MARTÍN: *Bang!*

(The MOON *disappears. More sunlight)*

GABRIELA: *(To* MARTÍN*) Boy, you need to go.*

MARTÍN: *But I'm your man.*
And you stole my virginity.
You owe me something for that.

GABRIELA: *Sun's coming up.*
Benito comes home from the field
this morning, seven A M,
must be close to that,
I suggest you disappear, muchacho.

MARTÍN: *I'm only saying*
I want to spoil you—
on a cellular level.

GABRIELA: *Child, I'd break you in two.*
I'd send you screaming for the exits.
I'm doing you the biggest favor
of your life right now.

MARTÍN: *Then give me back my virginity.*

GABRIELA: *I'll give you back your virginity.*
(She kisses MARTÍN *passionately.)*

MARTÍN: *The giving was better than the taking!*

(The MOON appears, his head just barely visible.)

MOON: *I'm up here—*
not getting anything from anybody!
(The MOON disappears again.)

GABRIELA: *You're a sweet kid, Martin.*
You don't belong in this town.
We have that in common.
You kiss good.
I could get into visiting you
every afternoon after school
and distracting you
from your math homework
and totally messing up your chances
for college.
I could see going crazy in your bed
and burning your house to the ground
with the two of us
taking long baths together
and drinking so much beer
we'd both have comas for a week.

MARTÍN: *I'm searching for the downside*
to all this.

GABRIELA: *I can see you getting*
more and more dangerous, Martin.
I can tell by looking in your eyes:
you're the type
that falls in love real easy.
That plans babies
after the first conversation.
Like somebody I know.

MARTÍN: *You think...other girls*
see the same danger as you?

GABRIELA: *You broadcast it through your eyes,*
like leprosy.

MARTÍN: *Are you saying I'll never get laid?*

GABRIELA: *Not with me,* muchachito.

(MARTÍN looks at GABRIELA, angry, it's like his entire personality has changed.)

MARTÍN: *I gotta go.*
There's nothing here.

Nothing here I want.
You hear me?
Nothing here I want!
Nothing here I want!

GABRIELA: *Take it easy, Private...*

MARTÍN: *This whole thing is bullshit!*
And I don't want any more of you
playing with my head,
you cutting my nuts off,
you doing psycho-brujeria-witchcraft on me.
I'm glad we never got involved, bitch!
I'm glad I broke your heart!

GABRIELA: *Did I miss something here...?*

(MARTÍN *starts to go over the fence.*)

MARTÍN: *This is my life:*
I rent porn.
I shoot coyotes at night.
I harass faggots.
I steal my relatives' weapons.
I take target practice on the moon
and every day I get
closer and closer to manhood
and I worry how the world will crush me—
and if I don't touch a woman's thing soon,
will I finally go berserk
and blow you all away?
(He is gone.)

(GABRIELA *shoots the gun three times into the sky, getting the* CAT's *attention.*)

CAT: *(To* GABRIELA*) What are you going to do today?*

GABRIELA: *Today I'm going to have both*
my eyes sucked out of my face
and replaced with the eyes
of a teenage Persian slave girl.

CAT: *Cool.*

GABRIELA: *I will grow some fruit today*
in my womb.
I will recite the Holy Koran.
I will change into
Salvador Dali's foreskin
and fuck a red-haired soprano.
I will collect severed egos.

I will organize the red ants
that live in the garage and
teach them to milk each other
so I never run out of milk
for Benito's coffee.
I will melt time.
I will call Muhammad collect
and gossip about his homeboy Jesus.
I will drink a hummingbird's saliva
drop by little drop
and stare into Benito's eyes
and try to read his mind
and wonder if we still
love each other
and if I can't figure it out
I think the thing I have to do
is devise a gruesome test.

CAT: *A gruesome test! I like that!*

GABRIELA: *The first night we met,*
as we ran from the bar and the cops,
into the night...
there was a wicked moon in the sky,
smoking a Cuban cigar,
playing a mandolin with
thirteen-and-a-half strings.
Benito stopped to look at the moon.
The skinheads were gaining on us.
He said it looked so cool tonight.
I didn't even notice it
and he made me notice it.
I realized I like a man who notices
the moon even with skinheads
coming closer and closer.
I thought that was brave and thoughtful.
I thought that was manly and kind.
He asked me if I was an angel.
He wondered if God would let him fuck me.
I can forgive everything
if I know for sure
he's the same man I saved from peril.
So I'll ask him about last night.
Did he see last night's moon
or has he stopped looking
at the sky forever?

(The sound of a car entering the house's garage.)

CAT: *Guess who.*

*(*GABRIELA *opens the refrigerator. It's full of sand.)*

GABRIELA: *(Nervous) Outta milk!*
I'm getting weird déjá vu.
I meant to go last night to the commissary
but I thought I heard the trees
getting closer to the house.

CAT: *Oh, he'll believe that one!*

GABRIELA: *Got nothing to wear*
but cut-offs.

CAT: *He'll see you like that*
and think: horny housewife.

GABRIELA: *This can't be like other times.*
I have to think about Benito.
I have to make him see that we're looking
at a train wreck...
(She starts to exit into the house.)

CAT: Nena, *wait! What do I do*
if my lover's a ghost?

GABRIELA: *Fuck him anyway, Cat.*
(She enters the house.)

(The CAT *and the* COYOTE'S GHOST *look at each other.)*

COYOTE'S GHOST: *Do you trust me?*

(The CAT *approaches the* COYOTE'S GHOST *and breathes deep.)*

CAT: *Ay! You smell like air!*
You smell—like heaven,
like a graveyard on a cloudy day.
You smell like transformation, hope, prayers.
You smell like a whisper.
Let's do something right now.

COYOTE'S GHOST: *How long will I last with you?*

CAT: *Before we lose our courage?*

COYOTE'S GHOST: *How long do I really have?*

CAT: *Before the deceptions start?*

COYOTE'S GHOST: *And the fights to the death.*

CAT: *And the madness.*

COYOTE'S GHOST: *How long can we possibly last?*

CAT: *Before we have to test*
each other's love?

(*The* CAT *and the* COYOTE'S GHOST *approach each other. The* CAT *dances with the* COYOTE'S GHOST, *as we hear, and possibly see...*)

BENITO: *Where were you?*

GABRIELA: *I was in the backyard.*
I slept there last night.

BENITO: *Something wrong with the bed?*

GABRIELA: *I just did, that's all.*

BENITO: *Is there any coffee?*

GABRIELA: *You lost a lot of weight.*

BENITO: *God bless that Army food.*

GABRIELA: *And nice circles under the eyes.*

BENITO: *Ain't slept in forty-eight hours.*

GABRIELA: *You don't like my haircut....*

BENITO: *Makes you look older—*
but not too much—
five or six years at the most!

GABRIELA: *The house passed inspection,*
without your help, you owe me ten,
and here's your gun.

BENITO: *Don't say "gun"—it's a "weapon."*
Your gun hangs between your legs.

GABRIELA: *Nothing hangs between my legs, soldier-boy.*

BENITO: *Except for me. Gabby.*
Oh, squeeze-able, eat-able,
good-to-the-last-drop Gabby...

GABRIELA: *I have a question.*
It's going to sound stupid,
but I have to ask you.
Did you see the moon last night?

BENITO: *...better than pogey-bait...*

GABRIELA: *Did you see the moon last night?*
I really have to know this, Benito.
I really have to know.

(Lights to black as GABRIELA *awaits* BENITO'*s answer and the* CAT *and the* COYOTE'S GHOST *dance slow and hot and tight.)*

END OF PLAY

WATSONVILLE: SOME PLACE NOT HERE

Cherríe Moraga
Music by John Santos
with Gilberto Gutierrez

ABOUT THE AUTHOR

Cherríe Moraga is the author of numerous plays including SHADOW OF
A MAN, which won the Fund for New American Plays Award in 1991 and
HEROES AND SAINTS, which earned the Pen West and Drama-Logue
Awards and the Will Glickman Prize in 1992. This year her plays were
collected in a new volume entitled *The Hungry Woman: Five Plays by Cherríe
Moraga* (Albuquerque: West End Press). Two other recent books include a
collection of poems and essays entitled *The Last Generation* (Boston: South
End Press, 1993) and a memoir, *Waiting in the Wings: Portrait of a Queer
Motherhood* (Ithaca: Firebrand Press, 1997). Ms Moraga is also a recipient
of the National Endowment for the Arts' Theater Playwrights' Fellowship
and is the Artist-in-Residence in the Department of Drama at Stanford
University.

WATSONVILLE: SOME PLACE, NOT HERE was initially commissioned and developed by Brava Theater Center of San Francisco. It was presented as a staged reading at the following theaters: the Brava Studio Theater on 1 May 1995, directed by Tony Kelly; the Traveling Jewish Theater, produced by Brava Theater, on 5-6 June 1995, directed by Amy Mueller; the John F Kennedy Center for the Performing Arts in Washington DC on 19 February 1996, directed by Amy Mueller.

WATSONVILLE: SOME PLACE NOT HERE was first workshopped through H P P in August 1995. The cast and creative contributors were:

DOLORES . . . . Angela Moya
JUAN . . . . Vic Trevino
CHENTE *et al* . . . . E J Castillo
SONORA . . . . Evelina Fernandez
AMPARO . . . . .Lupe Ontíveros
JO-JO . . . . Fidel Gomez
LUCHA . . . . Olivia Chumacero

Director . . . . José Luis Valenzuela
Dramaturg . . . . .Jerry Patch

WATSONVILLE: SOME PLACE NOT HERE had its world premiere on 25 May 1996 at the new Brava Theater Center in San Francisco, under the artistic direction of Ellen Gavin. The cast and creative contributors were:

DOLORES VALLE . . . . Lee Garay Toney
DON ARTURO/CHENTE/MONSIGNOR MENDEZ . . . . Gary Martínez
(Roberto Varea Gutiérrez after May 30)
JOJO . . . . Peter Gómez
AMPARO . . . . Tessa Koning-Martínez
LUCHA . . . . Minerva García
JUAN CUNNINGHAM . . . . Jesus Mendoza
SONORA . . . . VIVIS
MUSICIAN-STRIKERS . . . . Francisco Herrera & Lorena de la Rosa
GUADALUPANAS, STRIKERS, RAPPERS & DANCERS . . . . Veronica Arana,
Cat Callejas, Raquel Haro & Nigel Toussaint

Director . . . . Amy Mueller
Sets . . . . Shevra Tait
Lighting design . . . . Lonnie Alcaraz
Sound design . . . . Rona Michelle
Costumes . . . . Gail Russel
Stage manager . . . . Liz Murtaugh
Original musical compositions . . . . John Santos & Gilberto Gutiérrez

WATSONVILLE is a recipient of the Fund for New American Plays Award, a project of the John F Kennedy Center for the Performing Arts, with support from American Express Company, in cooperation with the President's Committee on the Arts and Humanities. Also thanks to Theater Communications Group's National Theater Artist Residency Program which helped support this project. T C G is the national organization for the American Theater, and is funded by The Pew Charitable Trusts.

NOTES FROM THE PLAYWRIGHT

The story of WATSONVILLE is pure imagination, based loosely on three actual events that took place in a central Californian coastal farm worker town by the same name. Those events include the cannery strikes from 1985 to 1987, the 7.1 earthquake of 1989, and the appearance of the Virgen de Guadalupe on the face of an oak tree in Pinto Lake County Park in 1992.

Many of the images, ideas and cuentos in the play grew out of interviews I did with various residents (mostly Mexican immigrant women) of Watsonville. Their stories have been excerpted, adapted, and re-configured in order to develop the fictionalized characters of the play. Any resemblance the characters bear to actual individuals is purely coincidental.

About the language:

One of the major challenges in the creation of WATSONVILLE was how to best represent the various languages the townspeople would use. The majority of the immigrant Mexican population in the real town of Watsonville speaks a beautiful fluent Spanish. (Most of the interviews I conducted took place in Spanish.) An occasional English word enters the conversation only when there is no exact Spanish equivalent. Spanish is the private and public voice of this Mexican community, its voice of prayer, of passion and of protest. To have that voice truly resonate in this play, at least seventy percent of the dialogue should have been written in Spanish.

So, in many ways, even the language of WATSONVILLE is a fiction, one writer's attempt to communicate to a larger multi-cultural audience something of the Mexican immigrant experience, filtered through her own Chicana (i.e. Mexican, U S-born) imagination.

The languages in WATSONVILLE, the play, occur along the full spectrum from Spanish to English. Those characters who in real life would be Spanish-only speakers employ a greater and more fluid use of Spanish in the play. (Spanish phrases are interwoven to retain the "sabor" and sensuality of the original Spanish). On the other end, the mono-lingual and/or dominant English-speakers may at times speak entirely in English. My hope is that this balancing act between the two languages ensures both cultural authenticity and accessibility to a new (more broadly-defined) American audience.

CHARACTERS & SETTING

DOLORES VALLE, *cannery worker and Guadalupana, late fifties*
DON ARTURO, DOLORES' *husband, seventy*
JOJO, LUCHA's *fifteen-year-old son*
AMPARO, *cannery worker and community-organizer, early sixties*
LUCHA, *cannery worker and mother of two, early thirties*
CHENTE, *shop steward at cannery, early fifties. Played by actor playing* DON ARTURO
JUAN CUNNINGHAM, *half-breed, ex-priest and community organizer, early forties*
SONORA, *physician's assistant at community clinic, early forties*
MONSIGNOR MENDEZ, *played by actor playing* DON ARTURO

Also: STRIKERS, GUADALUPANAS, DANCERS, & RAPPERS

The time: the on-going present, with the future just around the turn of events, the turn-of-century.

The place: Watsonville.

The Set: In Spanish, the word "pueblo" means both "town" and "people." The set for "Watsonville" most closely reflects the latter definition, a setting for "a people"—a Mexican immigrant worker, Indio-Catholic people—where private property is the land on which they work, represented by chain-linked and barbed-wire fences and corrugated aluminum walls. Still, as Mexicans of Indian descent, el pueblo remembers the land as belonging to no one but the earth itself. To that end, the cannery, the kitchen, the union hall, the picket line, the park, the hospital, the warehouse—in short, all the action of the play—is housed within the circle of a grove of aging oaks. The central image of the play is Dolores' altar, always candle-lit and sainted, which opens through a window to the oldest and tallest oak of the grove. Here, miracles take place.

This play is dedicated to the Mexican women workers of Watsonville and for Bárbara García, amiga-activista, in gratitude.

ACT ONE
"LA HUELGA"

(There is the trumpet call of a lone mariachi.)

(Elder female voice in the darkness) "Nos vamos a poner en tus manos, Espíritu Santo, para que nos ilumines, y que todo esto, que va a sacar de Watsonville esta muchacha, sea un beneficio, sea una historia tan linda."
Una Guadalupana de Watsonville.

(In the darkness, a lone mariachi trumpet plays tema.)

Scene One

(Late afternoon in November. The eve of Día de los Muertos. Danzón on the record player. DOLORES opens the refrigerator, its light washes over her face. She wears a calavera mask, an apron and housedress. As the music rises, she begins to dance with her imaginary partner. Very elegant. A "great love" is leading her around the sala floor. After a few minutes, she hears DON ARTURO entering from the offstage bathroom. She rushes to the record player, turns it off, removes the mask. DON ARTURO wears a cleanly-pressed guayavera. He has a cigarette in his mouth and a constant cough. He turns on the Spanish station at low volume, sits and watches it, occasionally sipping from a pint of mescal. DOLORES has crossed to the kitchen table. She wraps a tray full of enchiladas in foil. She ties a ribbon around it. In the upstage room is an altar to La Virgen de Guadalupe. It is illuminated by candlelight.)

DON ARTURO: Somone's gointu come and steal those enchiladas right off of her grave.

DOLORES: Es el Día de los Muertos. No one's gointu to steal them.

DON ARTURO: You think anybody cares what holiday it is? People are hungry! I bet you somebody's going to sneak in at night and clean-up every Mexican grave en el cementerio.

DOLORES: Pues, por lo menos, she knows I tried.

DON ARTURO: She don't know not'ing. She's dead.

DOLORES: *(To herself)* One of these days, when I get enough money, I'm gointu move Cerezita to San Francisco, so she can be with her brother.

DON ARTURO: Ay, muy cozy. Who gives a damn where you are, when you're dead. You think it matters to them?

DOLORES: Cerezita quiere mucho a su hermano.

DON ARTURO: Están muertos ¿no entiendes? No les importa a ellos what their graves look like, who's laying next to them, what comida you put on top of their tombstone.

DOLORES: ¿Qué sabes tú? What do you know about their feelings? Dead or alive, you never cared nothing for your children. If you did, maybe Mario and Cerezita would still be alive right now.

DON ARTURO: Oh sí, I told my son to be a maricón. I told him, "Toma, hijo, traga este veneno, suck it down your throat and up your culo!"

DOLORES: Y la Cerezita?

DON ARTURO: Bueno...

DOLORES: *(After a beat)* My world is black with you. You make everything ugly. Lo peor posible.

(There's a knock on the door.)

DON ARTURO: No contestes. I don't wannu see nobody right now.

(Another knock)

DOLORES: ¿Eres tú, JoJo?

DON ARTURO: Díle que se vaya.

DOLORES: *(Whispering)* Cállate tú. You know he comes on Tuesdays to help me. *(She goes to the door.)*

DOLORES: Pásale, hijo.

(JOJO enters carrying his backpack and a small paper sack.)

JOJO: Hola, Doña Lola. I brought you limones from our trees. *(He hands her the bag.)* Buenas tardes, Don Arturo.

(DON ARTURO grunts, turns his attention to the T V.)

DOLORES: *(Taking out a lemon)* ¡Son grandotes!

JOJO: We got a whole orchard full in our backyard.

DOLORES: Te lo creo. I saw your sister con su limonada stand out there on Main Street. *(She pours the lemons out onto the table.)*

JOJO: It's really my stand. Elenita works for me.

DOLORES: You take after someone I know.

JOJO: Nah, my Mom would never *give* away potential profits.

DOLORES: Verdad.

(JoJo has taken out a small writing pad and a pen from his backpack, sits down at the table. DOLORES goes to the refrigerator, takes some pills.)

JOJO: Anyway, Elenita's good for business. People buy more from little kids. *(Beat)* I'm ready.

DOLORES: ¿No quieres un vaso de leche?

JOJO: No, gracias.

DOLORES: I just buy it for you kids. We don't need milk no more. We're done growing.

JOJO: Gracias, Señora. No tengo sed.

DOLORES: Bueno una fruta?

JOJO: No...

DOLORES: *(Bringing over the bowl of fruit)* Toma. ¿Si quiera una manzana?

JOJO: Okay. Gracias. *(He takes the fruit, sets it down by his writing pad.)*

DOLORES: Bueno ¿listo?

JOJO: Sí.

(He takes the pen in his hand. As DOLORES dictates, JOJO.)

DOLORES: *(Dictating)* Mi querida hija, Cerezita.

DON ARTURO: Estás loca ¿sabes?

DOLORES: Espero que esta carta te encuentre bien.

DON ARTURO: You expect her to answer you from the grave?

DOLORES: *(To JOJO)* You can put it into English, mijo. She reads English better. ¿Qué iba a decir yo...?

JOJO: *(Reading)* "I hope this letter finds you well."

DOLORES: Bueno. *(Dictating)* La situación en mi trabajo está peor.

JOJO: *(Writing)* "The situation...at work is...getting...worse."

DOLORES: Hoy recibimos un notice—

JOJO: "Today...we received...a notice—"

DOLORES: Que otra vez nos van a cortar nuestro sueldo—

DON ARTURO: ¿Qué dices?

JOJO: They're gonna cut your salaries again?

DON ARTURO: ¡Ya nos 'stamos muriendo de hambre!

DOLORES: Sí. By one dollar, twenty-five cents.

DON ARTURO: ¡Ladrones!

JoJo: Wow. *(Writes)*

DON ARTURO: Why dint you tell me?

DOLORES: ¿Para qué? You going to go out and get a job?*(Dictating to* JoJo*)* Ya sabes que es casi imposible—

JoJo: "You know...that it's almost...impossible—"

DOLORES: De vivir con lo poco que gano.

JoJo: "To live...on the little...bit...I make."

DOLORES: Tu padre todavía no 'stá trabajando—

DON ARTURO: You keep me out of this!

JoJo: " Your father—"

DON ARTURO: If I got something to say to her—

JoJo: "Isn't working—"

DON ARTURO: I'll tell her myself!

DOLORES: Hay rumores—

JoJo: "There's rumors—"

DOLORES: Que va a haber huelga.

DON ARTURO: ¿Cómo qué huelga? ¿Es la verdad?

JoJo: You're going on strike?

DOLORES: No sé. There's a lot of talk en la canería.

DON ARTURO: *(To* DOLORES*)* No te vas a meter tú en esas cosas!

JoJo: Is my mom gonna strike, too?

DOLORES: Bueno, toda la companía, dicen.

DON ARTURO: ¿Me oyes? Los sindicatos son corruptos. They just use the workers nomás.

DOLORES: *(To* DON ARTURO*)* ¿Qué sabes tú?

DON ARTURO: Yo sé mucho. I seen the same thing in México. The unions come in and fill your head with ideas and then when things go bad, they dump you por otra causa.

DOLORES: *(To* JoJo*)* I don't remember where we were.

JoJo: You were talking about going on strike.

DON ARTURO: Es pura política. Los obreros son los títeres de los sindicatos!

DOLORES: *(To* JoJo*)* I think we finish the letter some other time, hijo.

JoJo: Sí, señora.

DON ARTURO: That's what happen to me in the mines.

DOLORES: *(To* DON ARTURO*)* And that was a hundred years ago! *(Putting some fruit in a plastic bag)* JoJo, toma esta fruta para tu hermanita.

JOJO: Gracias. *(She escorts him to the door.)*

DON ARTURO: *(To* JOJO*)* And you tell your mother que she better stay out of this strike business if she wants to keep food en tu estómago.

DOLORES: JoJo doesn't gottu say nothing to his mother. She's not your wife.

DON ARTURO: That's her problem. Le falta un hombre para mandarla.

DOLORES: *(To* JOJO, *softly)* Andale, mijo. He doesn't know what he's saying.

DON ARTURO: Oh sí. Su madre se cree muy independiente. I even seen her at the bars by herself con otras divorciadas.

DOLORES: *(To* JOJO*)* Don't pay no attention to him, hijo. Está tomado nomás. *(Gesturing that he's been drinking)* Nos vemos mañana, mijo.

JOJO: Hasta mañana.

*(*JOJO *exits.* DOLORES *turns around, glares at* DON ARTURO.*)*

DON ARTURO: *(Suddenly sheepish)* ¿Qué? ¿Qué? I'm just telling the truth.

DOLORES: She's the boy's mother.

*(*DOLORES *takes her rosary out of her pocket and crosses to her altar. Large image of la Virgen de Guadalupe is illuminated by candlelight. She begins to pray. Tema rises softy in the background.)*

DOLORES: Te necesitamos, Virgencita de Paz. Tú sabes que con unos anuncios buenos muchas gentes van a despertar. *(Pause)* Porque ya sabes que estamos dormidos.

*(*DON ARTURO *crosses himself guiltily. Lights fade with the illuminated image of la Virgen on the altar lingering for a few moments. The silouette of an oak tree emerges from behind the image, leaves stirring slightly in the breeze.)*

Scene Two

(The next day. Sounds of a working cannery in the darkness. LUCHA *and* AMPARO *are working the broccoli line with other workers. The lunch whistle blows. They freeze. Then they remove their work gloves, grab their lunches and cross together to the cannery lunch room.* LUCHA *is quite "dolled-up," which is how she appears throughout the play, full make-up, stylish heels (when not on the line) and colorful outfits. Not tacky, but definitely lively. Lights rise on the cannery lunch room. As* LUCHA *and* AMPARO *sit down to eat their lunches,* DOLORES *joins them.)*

LUCHA: On the night shift me dijeron que la Cookie, the forelady, she stood outside the bathroom con un stopwatch...to see how long it took each worker to do her business.

AMPARO: No me digas.

DOLORES: *(Overlapping)* ¡Qué bárbaro!

LUCHA: Then she told them that from now on they could only go to the toilet on their break.

DOLORES: She expect everyone to hold it that long?

LUCHA: So, on their ten-fifteen break, eighty-five women line up all at the same time to go to the bathroom. It took them almost two hours before everyone got back to work. By then it was time to punch the clock.

(Everyone cracks up.)

AMPARO: *(Laughing)* ¡Ay, la Cookie musta been so mad!

LUCHA: When you gotta go, you gotta go.

AMPARO: It's not right that you can't even go to the bathroom when you haftu.

DOLORES: Hay mucha presión.

AMPARO: Yo soy rápida para trabajar, pero the quota they're asking of us is too much.

LUCHA: *(Looking into her compact)* Ay sí, this job is giving me wrinkles.

AMPARO: I don't wannu hear nothing about las arrugas. Ya tengo el mapa de Michoacán en la cara. El desierto, montañas rocosas, arroyos por todas partes.

DOLORES: Ay, Amparo, no es tan vieja.

AMPARO: *(To DOLORES)* Are you gointu eat ese burrito, comadre?

DOLORES: Sí—

(AMPARO snatches it from her.)

LUCHA: *(After a beat)* Did you see? They took Margie off of "set-up" and put her back onto la linea.

AMPARO: That means somebody on la linea, just got kick out the door.

DOLORES: Esa new girl, Sarita...y su cuñada...

LUCHA: Margie told me que los patrones are losing money, that they're going to have to close down the company and move it to México.

AMPARO: They're trying to scare you ¿no entiendes? So you'll go along with this new cochino contrato.

LUCHA: Yo sé.

AMPARO: Did you see your check this week?

LUCHA: ¿Cómo?

AMPARO: Look at it. You, too, comadre.

(CHENTE *enters, carrying a Coke. The women take out their paychecks from their aprons, examine them.*)

AMPARO: Chente!

CHENTE: ¿Qué tal, Señoras? (*He starts to sit down next to* LUCHA, *giving her the coke.*)

AMPARO: (*To* CHENTE*)* Síentate aquí. I wanna show you something.

(*He sits next to* AMPARO.)

CHENTE: ¿Qué pasa?

AMPARO: Mira. (*She takes out her paycheck from her pocket.*) This is my pay for two weeks.

CHENTE: And...

AMPARO: It's more than it's supposed to be.

LUCHA: El mío también.

CHENTE: No se quejen. Maybe you worked some overtime that you....

AMPARO: No, mira. They didn't take out my union dues.

(CHENTE *examines the check stub.*)

AMPARO: It's eighteen dollars.

CHENTE: Tienes razón. (*To the others*) Are your checks the same?

LUCHA: Sí. Es igual.

CHENTE: ¿Dolores?

DOLORES: Sí. It's eighteen dollars too much.

AMPARO: ¿Qué significa, Chente?

CHENTE: I guess they figure if you get a bigger check in your hands, you'll be happy. No questions asked.

LUCHA: Pues, yo tengo mis preguntas.

DOLORES: No entiendo.

CHENTE: Shea, the owner. He knows we've been meeting. They say he's trying to squeeze out the union.

LUCHA: ¿Cree que somos pendejas? Does he think we'll just go along with them for a lousy eighteen dollars a month?

CHENTE: Miren, let the other mujeres know. See if their checks are the same. I'm going to call the union office and tell them to keep their doors open late tonight. Everyone should go down there and pay their dues as soon as they get off work.

LUCHA: Chente, va a haber huelga?

CHENTE: They want another forty "take-aways," vacations, sick leave, seniority, you name it.

AMPARO: *(To* LUCHA*)* Prepárate. We're going to strike.

Scene Three

(Mid-morning. A few weeks later. In black out. Voices can be heard shouting. "¡Huelga! ¡Huelga! ¡Huelga! ¡Huelga!" Lights rise to strike in full swing. DOLORES, AMPARO, LUCHA, CHENTE, and JOJO as well as other strikers stand in front of the "Pajaro Valley Cannery." There is a bus bench on the corner; traffic can be heard in the distance. The strikers break out into song.)

HUELGUISTAS: *(Décima Alegre)*
"Vamos juntos que la unión
mucha fuerza nos dará
y nadie nos quitará
la fuerza de la razón." *(Repeat last two lines)*

(One passerby honks her horn in support. The strikers respond.)

LUCHA: ¡Qué viva la huelga!

HUELGUISTAS: ¡Qué viva!

"La justicia en la balanza
mas pareja debe ser
para el hombre y la mujer
derechos y no esperanza. *(Repite)*

(The song ends and the strikers gather round to form the "audience." The stage becomes an agit-prop stage set. Someone unrolls a sheet-like curtain that reads, "Teatro de las Bravas." From behind it, emerge LUCHA and AMPARO who wear shower caps, aprons and over-sized gloves. LUCHA wears a sign saying "obrera" and AMPARO wears one saying "veterana.")

(Acto)

(The workers stand shoulder to shoulder, simulating a cannery assembly-line. They "chop, sort, pack.")

OBRERA: Oye, veterana. How many fingers chu got left now?

VETERANA: Déjame ver, obrera. *(Counting)* Todavía tengo three tall ones on the left hand. Y en la derecha, tengo... *(Counting)* ...un medio dedo in the middle, a half a pinkie, y un pedacito de pulgar. ¿Y tú, obrera?

OBRERA: Bueno, yo...yo soy *(Shaking out her fingerless gloves)* ALL THUMBS!

(They crack up. The FORELADY *and* MRS OPRIMIDA *[Indicated by a signs and played by* JOJO *and* DOLORES, *respectively] enter the acto.* MRS OPRIMIDA *uses a cane. She is quite ancient.)*

FORELADY: There's too much socializing going on. The only talking I should hear is you ladies training Mrs. Oprimida.

OBRERA/VETERANA: ¡Bruja!

(A satirized cumbia comes on as LA VETERANA *and* OBRERA *proceed to train "*MRS OPRIMIDA." *The workers' pace begins normally then gradually quickens to the point of the ridiculous.)*

VETERANA: They want the first cuts a certain size, five or six inches...

*(*FORELADY *prods them on.)*

FORELADY: ¡Andeles! ¡Andeles!

OBRERA: And la prómixa persona cuts it again según los pedazos que quieren...

FORELADY: Con las dos manos! Use both your hands!!

VETERANA: Luego más después pasa por donde it gets cooked.

FORELADY: Move those hands! ¡Rápido! ¡Rápido!

OBRERA: You pack it en cajas and then you weigh it....

VETERANA: And you got to be ready que all the boxes get filled.

FORELADY: ¡Andeles! ¡Andeles!

OBRERA: And then you send the boxes to be wrapped again y ya van al freezer.

FORELADY: You're laggin' ladies!

VETERANA: Los restos, they put through un molino—

OBRERA: And they grind it up and that gets weighed and empacado también.

MRS OPRIMIDA: *(Cutting herself)* ¡Ay!

(Cumbia stops abruptly)

OBRERA: ¿Qué pasó?

MRS OPRIMIDA: Me corté.

VETERANA: ¿Mucho?

(The women gather around her. The dialogue overlaps.)

MRS OPRIMIDA: No sé.

FORELADY: What's the matter? Why did you stop working?

MRS OPRIMIDA: Traigo el guante puesto.

OBRERA: She cut herself.

VETERANA: Pues, quíteselo.

FORELADY: Déjame verlo.

MRS OPRIMIDA: *(Removing the glove.)* ¡Ay, puedo ver hasta el hueso!

FORELADY: It's down to the bone!

(For a moment, everyone stands around stunned.)

FORELADY: That's not a sign for the rest of you to stop working. ¡Miren! That broccoli is piling up.

VETERANA: ¡Pero mira la sangre que viene!

FORELADY: I'll tend to her. *(They still don't move.)* You heard me! Back to work, all of you. *(Pulling MRS OPRIMIDA off by hooking the cane around her neck)* It's because everyone's too busy socializing and not paying enough attention to what they're doing. That's why accidents happen....

(They exit. The women start to go back to work.)

OBRERA: *(Beneath her breath)* Vaca fea.

VETERANA: ¡Eh, obrera! Don't "agonize." Organize!

OBRERA: ¿Qué quiere decir eso, Veterana?

VETERANA: *(Throwing off her gloves)* I mean, Ya Basta! It's time we go on strike!

OBRERA: *(Shouting out to the audience)* ¡Qué viva la mujer obrera!

ALL: ¡Qué viva!

(End of Acto)

(Everyone begins shouting ¡Huelga! ¡Huelga! ¡Huelga! as the song resumes and the actors remove their signs and costumes.)

Viva la unión, viva la unión
que no nos podrán negar
que tenemos la razón. *(Repite)*

(Mid-song, there is the sound of a bus approaching. One by one, the strikers stop singing as they catch sight of the bus.)

JOJO: *(Crossing to* LUCHA*)* Mom, mire.

(As the bus stops, they all stand together in shocked silence.)

LUCHA: ¿Quiénes son?

AMPARO: They're esquiroles.

CHENTE: Scabs.

LUCHA: ¿De dónde viene?

CHENTE: They're from Salinas.

DOLORES: *(Softly)* Dios mío.

AMPARO: And we're har'ly two weeks on the line.

JOJO: Where'd they get 'em from?

CHENTE: Los files, the bars, the airport...dondequiera.

*(*LUCHA *suddenly rushes toward the bus.)*

AMPARO: Lucha!

LUCHA: *(Screaming at the bus full of scabs)* ¡Pinches Cabrones! ¡Vendidos! ¡Hijos de la chingada! ¡Se venden por unos! ¡Unos pinches pesos!

JOJO: *(Starting toward her)* Mom!

CHENTE: *(Stopping him)* No! Déjala. She's right.

JOJO: But—

CHENTE: *(Suddenly sobered)* Once scabs start coming in, this strike could go on forever.

(Blackout)

Scene Four

(Eight weeks into the strike. JUAN *and* CHENTE *sit at a local taquería, drinking coffee.)*

JUAN: I don't know, Chente. I'm working three other projects right now. This tenants' rights organization in San Francisco, the gang prevention project, the—

CHENTE: But this is different. With a strong support committee, the strike could be won in a month...two at the most.

JUAN: That's what you say now.

CHENTE: Cunningham, you don't know these women.

JUAN: I know a few.

CHENTE: Then you know you ain't gonna find a more dedicated bunch. Most of these ladies sleep no more than five hours a night. They work in the canneries y en su tiempo libre, they're out there en los files con el pepino, la mora, la manzana.

JUAN: Yo sé.

CHENTE: In between time, they feed their husbands, limpian la casa, raise their children and even their grandchildren.

JUAN: So, then why do you think they can stay with this strike?

CHENTE: Are you kidding? They're primed for it. They know how to take care of each other, how to cook cheap and for a lot of people, how to share babysitting, the carpools, every kind of resource.

JUAN: Bueno pues, si ya están preparadas—

CHENTE: Te digo, their comadre system is intact. It's just a question of getting them to believe they can win.

JUAN: Can they, Chente?

CHENTE: *(After a beat)* Claro que sí. *(He checks his watch)* Vámonos. The ladies are probably waiting for us.

(As they rise, the lights crossfade to the strike support committee meeting. AMPARO and LUCHA are standing around a coffee machine.)

LUCHA: Once we get our jobs back with our raises y todo, I'm not going to be stupid like before. I'm going to start saving my money.

AMPARO: ¿Qué vas a hacer con el dinero, Lucha?

LUCHA: I figure I can put me a little business someday. Mis hijos me pueden ayudar. I'll call it, "Lucha's Tamale Parlor." I saw the name one time en San Francisco.

AMPARO: Buen idea.

LUCHA: Last week, my kids and me fuimos a Santa Cruz, con una olla de tamales. Ni tenían carne los tamales. Puse queso y chile nomás. I charge a dollar-fifty a cada uno. In two, three hours we sold the whole pot of tamales and we came home with seventy-five dólares en el bolsillo.

AMPARO: You can't beat that.

(DOLORES enters.)

AMPARO: *(Teasing)* ¡Qué milagro!

DOLORES: No empieces, Amparo.

AMPARO: Pues, the way you talked on the phone I dint think we'd see you here.

DOLORES: *(To* LUCHA*)* Es mi marido. He's like a broken record that's scratching into my brain...all day long. "Where you going? ¿Con quién andas?"

LUCHA: ¡Qué gacho!

AMPARO: *(To* DOLORES*)* You're obligated to do your hours on the picket line. That's it. If you don't want to come to the meetings after this, está bien.

*(*JUAN *and* CHENTE *enter.)*

CHENTE: Buenas tardes, Señoras. Look who I brought with me.

AMPARO: *(Softly)* I don't believe my eyes.

*(*AMPARO *rushes to* JUAN*, embraces him.)*

AMPARO: Father Juan! What are you doing here?

JUAN: Ay, Doña Amparo. ¡Que gusto verla!

*(*DOLORES *doesn't move.)*

DOLORES: *(Softly)* Padre.

(He goes to her, extending his hands to her. She takes hold of them.)

JUAN: It's been a long time, no?

DOLORES: Sí. Mucho. *(Pause)* You look so different...con barba—

AMPARO: Y sandalias. You look like a hippie, Padre. Where's the priest's collar?

JUAN: It got a little too tight for me, Doña Amparo.

AMPARO: Bueno, I never thought it fit you too good anyway.

DOLORES: ¿Qué quiere decir eso?

JUAN: I left priesthood, Señora. It's been about...well about eight years. Soon after...McLaughlin.

DOLORES: Ya no es cura.

JUAN: That's right. I'm no longer a priest.

(There is a pause.)

DOLORES: Oh.

JUAN: And how is Don Gilberto? You couldn't drag him to the meeting?

AMPARO: He pass away, Father...Juan. Not too long ago.

JUAN: I'm...sorry.

AMPARO: He went peaceful-like.

(Another pause)

CHENTE: Bueno, I want you to meet Lucha Lerma.

JUAN: Hello.

LUCHA: Halo.

CHENTE: You'll be working with her and Amparo—

AMPARO: Espérete un momentito. I think maybe I miss something.

JUAN: I know it's a kind of a shock—

AMPARO: Pero ¿qué está haciendo acá, en Watsón?

JUAN: Well, I—

CHENTE: He's the person who's going to help us with the support work
for la huelga.

AMPARO: That's you?

LUCHA: An ex-priest?

JUAN: Yes.

AMPARO: I can't believe I'm seeing you.

DOLORES: *(Softly)* Ni yo.

(There is an awkward pause.)

CHENTE: Okay, everybody, siéntense. We need to get down to business here.

(They all sit down, exept JUAN)

CHENTE: Go 'head, Cunningham. Why don't you start by telling them a little
bit about your work?

JUAN: Okay—

CHENTE: Tell 'em about the cells, Cunningham.

JUAN: Yes, well, the idea is to form small groups, como pequeñas células,
desiminadas por toda la comunidad.

LUCHA: ¿De dónde es, Señor?

JUAN: Yo soy de Sanger, en el valle de San Joaquín.

LUCHA: Your family, ¿eran campesinos?

JUAN: Algunos. We moved to Los Angeles when I was still a boy.
My mother raised me by herself. She was a factory-worker.

AMPARO: She's checking out your credentials, Padre...digo, Juan.

LUCHA: *(Overlapping)* Quiero saber. I got a right to know.

CHENTE: Lucha, this is about a larger strategy. We're already two months
into the strike and the owner is still refusing all of our demands. The scabs

are coming in by the hundreds, así que parece que this strike could go for a long time. We've got to get a bigger base of support.

LUCHA: *(To* JUAN*)* ¿Es comunista, Señor?

JUAN: No, I wouldn't call myself that.

LUCHA: ¿Marxista? ¿Leninista?

JUAN: I—

LUCHA: *(Sarcastically)* "¿Representante del partido de la liberación revolucionaria de los de abajo?"

CHENTE: Ya, Lucha.

JUAN: *(To* LUCHA*)* No, you're right. You have a right to know what I'm doing here.

*(*LUCHA *glares at* CHENTE.*)*

LUCHA: ¿Ves?

JUAN: *(To* LUCHA*)* I won't lie to you. I am a professional organizer. I've come to Watsonville to help this strike get off the ground. He trabajado con la juventud, las uniones—

LUCHA: Are you from the Teamsters?

JUAN: No. But I—

LUCHA: Who pays your bills then?

CHENTE: Lucha!

*(*SONORA *enters, watches from the door.)*

LUCHA: Pues ¿qué quiere decir "professional organizer?" He works for somebody.

JUAN: Yes, I...it's an...organization. There's a fund. Some of us...well, we have ties to organizations throughout the Southwest, México, Honduras, Guatemala—

LUCHA: ¿Qué's eso...Guatemala? I just want to feed my children right here en Watsón.

JUAN: I want you to feed your children, too.

SONORA: He's an ACARista.

LUCHA: ¿Qué?

*(*CHENTE *motions to* SONORA *to come in.)*

SONORA: Asociación Cristiana para Acción Revolucionaria

CHENTE: This is Sonora Robles, la directora of La Clínica para el Pueblo.

SONORA: Hello.

CHENTE: Most of you know her already. Pásale, Sonora. Have a seat.

(SONORA *takes a seat next to* DOLORES, *greets her.*)

LUCHA: *(To* SONORA*)* Go on with what you were saying.

SONORA: About the ACARistas? They are a group of ex-priests...Jesuits...who have left the Church. They were liberation theologians.

DOLORES: ¿Ningunos son curas?

SONORA: No, but they're still involved—

JUAN: In liberation.

SONORA: Yes.

JUAN: It's true that I used to be a priest. If I wanted to hide that, I wouldn't have come to a place where...two women whom I greatly admire know my history. *(He indicates* AMPARO *and* DOLORES. *Small pause)* In a certain way, I came because of these two women. I only spent a few years in McLaughlin, but—

AMPARO: But he dint leave until we had burn down every pinche vineyard in that pueblo.

JUAN: And it still didn't stop the growers. They just moved their pesticides and their cancers to some other unsuspecting town. *(Pause)* Ask these women what they got in compensation for the loss of their homes, their health... *(Looking to* DOLORES*)* their children?

DOLORES: *(Softly)* Recibimos nada.

JUAN: That's what I'm fighting. Owners who try and convince you that poison is food and slavery is a job.

AMPARO: That's for damn sure.

JUAN: I'm not here to do anything against you. We have the same goals. First: maintain the strike. Get the community mobilized for food and clothing drives, fund-raising, and shared child-care. We picket banks, grocery store chains, brussel sprout fields, any place we can make an impact. We organize demonstrations, boycotts, and major publicity campaigns. I mean national campaigns! Second: negotiate with the cabrones and win.

AMPARO: ¡Adelante!

CHENTE: ¡Eso!

JUAN: Now, you all have to decide whether or not you'd like the support of the organization I represent. I'll respect your decision, whatever it is.

CHENTE: ¿Quieres decir algo más, Lucha?

LUCHA: No.

CHENTE: Entonces, can we go ahead and talk about forming the support committee? *(To* SONORA*)* You came for that reason ¿no, Sonora?

SONORA: Yes...I'm... sorry I got here late.

CHENTE: Bueno—

SONORA: Chente, I'd like to say something antes de que continuemos.

CHENTE: Go 'head.

SONORA: Quiero anunciar que la clínica will provide free health care to all the huelguistas y sus familias for the duration of the strike.

(Applause all around)

SONORA: *(To* JUAN*)* You talked about mobilizing the community?

JUAN: Yes.

SONORA: Well, I just left about a dozen Hell's Angels outside la clínica with a van-load of cheese and milk for the strikers' families.

DOLORES: ¿No son esos drogadictos?

SONORA: Ah, Doña Lola, they drink a lot of beer! Y, pues ni modo, they want to support the strike!

AMPARO: Está bien.

CHENTE: *(Overlapping)* ¡Sí, todos juntos!

(Pause. Everyone looks LUCHA.*)*

CHENTE: *(After a pause)* ¿Bueno...Lucha? ¿Tienes mas preguntas?

LUCHA: No. Sigan con la discusíon.

Scene Five

(Weeks later. SONORA *is speaking on a cellular phone. Her hair is down, hanging over her shoulders.)*

SONORA: I'm not gonna discuss this now. I got to get to the picket line.... Get over it, Selena.... Get over it. It's my work. There's nothing more to talk about. I want your stuff out, it's pretty simple.... Just come and get it... You can use Marta's truck.... She will.... This week... Any time while I'm at work.... Right, I don't want to see you, Selena.... It's been six months, for chrissake.... No, I'm tired of having your shit in my basement, that's all. Don't the girls miss their stuff?... Yes, there's all kinds of toys down there.... *(Pager sounds. She turns it off.)* It hurts, Selena. Don't you get it? I miss the

girls.... Listen, if you don't come this week, I'm movin' the stuff out myself.
I know plenty of kids who could use.... No, I'm not bringing it to you....
No, I don't want to see you. Do you hear me, Selena? I don't.... *(Dial tone.
She looks at the receiver.)* Shit. *(She puts phone into her coat pocket, checks the
number on the pager and dials.)*

(Crossfade to the sala of DOÑA DOLORES. DOLORES *is staring out the window as if
in a trance.* JOJO *stands at a distance from her, holding medicine.)*

JOJO: Doña Lolita? *(No response)* Doña Lolita? C'mon, take your medicine.

*(*DOLORES *does not respond.* SONORA *can be seen through the window, coming up
toward the house. She knocks on the door.* JOJO *answers it.* SONORA *enters,
carrying a small medical bag.)*

SONORA: *(Softly)* How long has she been like this?

JOJO: Since I paged you. She's just been staring out that window.

SONORA: Doña Lolita, are you waiting for someone? JoJo tells me you
haven't been taking your pills.

DOLORES: *(Beat)* I dreamed with my daughter this morning.

SONORA: Cerezita.

(She motions to JOJO *that he can leave. He exits quietly.)*

DOLORES: *(Turning to her)* I fell asleep praying, boca arriba and she came to
me with wings at the foot of my bed.

SONORA: Like an angel?

DOLORES: Sí. Un angel tan bello.

SONORA: Why don't you sit down on the couch? Let me check your blood
pressure. It'll only take a minute.

DOLORES: ¿Sabes que? When I first saw you come up the walkway, I
thought you were my Cerezita. I thought you were a bird broke out of
her cage with arms and legs like wings. *(Pause, studying* SONORA*)* Es el pelo.
My baby had long hair like yours, "her beauty mark," I used to say.

SONORA: I didn't braid it. I—

DOLORES: And then one day, she lost all her hair, and she left me in a cloud
of smoke. Poof!

(Beat)

SONORA: ¿Qué 'stá cocinando?

DOLORES: Caldo.

SONORA: Huele bien.

DOLORES: Es el ajo. That always makes a kitchen warm. Maybe like a dog, Arturo will stick out his nose and find his way back home from the bar tonight.

SONORA: Just follow the garlic trail. *(She has crossed to the stove, ladles the soup into a large bowl, places it on the table.)* You're serving the soup already? Won't it get cold?

DOLORES: La comida's got to be on the table when my marido comes home. *(She folds a napkin and puts a large soup spoon over it.)*

DOLORES: He always uses the big spoons, las grandotas. He doesn't like the cucharitas. He says it's like eating with a toothpick. I say, it looks like he's eating with a shovel. Pero así le gusta. That way, he says, he gets it all down at once. Albóndigas, verduras, caldo...all in one spoon. He gets a little bit of everything.

SONORA: Doña Lolita, I'm not leaving here til I've heard your heart, at least.

DOLORES: It won't tell you nothing you don't already know. Did you know I lost my daughter?

SONORA: I...yes.

DOLORES: Arturo will come in without warning, de prisa, wanting to eat and I won't be ready. That's how angels come to you, too, without warning...at the foot of your bed. *(Beat)* Do you want this soup, hija?

SONORA: It's for your husband.

DOLORES: It's getting cold. I'm going to lay down. Over there on the sofá. Let me look at you eating, it would be nice to look at someone eating mi caldo de albóndigas.

SONORA: Can I check you afterwards? Do you promise?

DOLORES: Te lo prometo. *(Pulling out a chair for her.)* Hard as the times are, I still got enough to make my caldo y compartirlo con mi Doctora. Gracias a Dios.

(SONORA sits.)

DOLORES: *(Beat)* Arturo wants me to leave the strike. He says that I'm a puppet...that I don't think for myself.

SONORA: Then we're all puppets, Señora.

DOLORES: He left here so mad. *(Beat)* You want a different spoon? ¿Una cucharita?

SONORA: *(Sitting down)* No, this is fine.

DOLORES: Bueno. Cómetelo.

(SONORA begins to eat. DOLORES watches her.)

DOLORES: Ay, sí. You hold that spoon just right. My daughter never held a spoon. She couldn't.

SONORA: Está bueno, el caldo.

DOLORES: Gracias. Es el cilantro. También pongo una gotita de limón right before I put it in the bowl. Finish your soup, mija. I'm going to close my eyes for a few minutes. *(She crosses to the couch, pulls a worn serape over her. She prays softly)* Oh Virgen Inmaculada de Guadalupe! Madre del verdader— *(And falls asleep.)*

(Lighting transition. The altar in the corner of the room grows bright with the image of Guadalupe. The oak grove appears in the background. SONORA rises and crosses to it, her figure silhouetted in the moonlight. DOLORES awakens to the distant sound of sirens and gunshots.)

DOLORES: ¿Hijita? ¿Eres tú? *(Rising, spying SONORA's figure through the altar window)* ¡Corre, hija! ¡Corre!

(SONORA turns to look at DOLORES, then walks off into the darkness. DOLORES crosses to beneath the shadow of the oak.)

(Música Indígenaón #1 rises softly. A single oak tree is illuminated, standing out from the rest. There is a sudden chilled wind. DOLORES's robe stirs in the breeze. She draws the rebozo closer to her. Blackout)

Scene Six

(Three months into the strike. AMPARO, LUCHA, SONORA, and JOJO are on the picket line. There's a back beat coming out of JOJO's boom box. JOJO begins to rap. The STRIKERS cheer him on.)

JOJO: "It was nineteen hundred and ninety-six
and patroncito tried the same ole trick,
cuttin' back wages of moms and dads
saying "Four twenty-five that ain't so bad."
Raza, ...Rise Up!"

LUCHA: ¡Andale, hijo!

AMPARO: Go, go home boy!

JOJO: "So Chisme started on the broccoli line,
'va a haber huelga, if y'all don't mind.'
Carmen and Lupe and Yolanda, too.
Todos juntas, they were all too through."
"Raza"

ALL: "Rise Up!"

(Cutting them off abruptly)

JOJO: That's as far as I got.

ALL: Ah!

SONORA: *(Rappin')* "Now we're movin' into week number twelve and... the food bank...something...something is stocking up its shelves."

AMPARO: Suena bien.

JOJO: Yeah, but you gotta make it all fit right.

SONORA: Well, I almost did.

LUCHA: *(To JOJO)* Write something about the scabs.

(LUCHA and SONORA continue down the picket line.)

JOJO: *(Jotting down some notes as he and AMPARO cross to picket line upstage)* "Scabs comin' in...scabs comin' out." *(To AMPARO)* What rhymes with "out?"

AMPARO: Doubt.

(JUAN and CHENTE join the picket line downstage right. LUCHA is within earshot.)

CHENTE: I came to the United States for the first time in 1958 through the Bracero Program. I was just kid, really. 'Bout JoJo's age. In those days when you crossed the border, they'd take your clothes off, fumigate you...like an animal.

JUAN: God, I can't imagine going through that.

CHENTE: It's hard. You just pretend in your mind that you're someplace else. *(Small pause)* Then in 1962, I migrated legally. Been with Pájaro Valley Canning ever since.

JUAN: That's a long time.

CHENTE: Almost thirty-five years. The union's been with me the whole time. I got my G E D and started climbing right up the ladder.

LUCHA: That's cuz you're a man!

CHENTE: You could go back to school, Lucha. Dicen que nunca es tarde para comenzar.

LUCHA: When do you want me to start my college career, Chente? After la guardia, I go to los files to make a horseshoe of my body until the sun goes down.

CHENTE: ¡Hijo! They don't call you "Lucha" pa'nada!

(She ignores him, keeps walking on down the line.)

JUAN: She's pretty hot under the collar.

CHENTE: And few other places, too, I think. *(He laughs at his own joke.)* Pero, she's one of the most go-getter womans you'd ever wanna meet, always working, hustling, but still keeps herself up real nice. *(Pause, observing her)* I like that in a woman.

JUAN: ...And your wife?

CHENTE: Hey, don't get me wrong, Cunningham. I love my wife. Pero... I'm no saint.

(They cross upstage to the line. Stage right LUCHA *takes out her lunch.* SONORA *is picketing nearby.)*

LUCHA: The scabs will be coming out for their lunch break pretty soon. We should eat before they do.

SONORA: You go 'head. I'll keep up the line.

LUCHA: The line está bien covered.

SONORA: Bueno...I didn't bring a lunch.

LUCHA: Véngase. I'll share mine con usted. I got plenty.

SONORA: Gracias, no. I...I'm not hungry.

LUCHA: ¿Qué es? Anorexic? *(Laughs)*

SONORA: No, I'm just not that organized. I forget.

LUCHA: I thought you were the organizer. You don't got any kids, do you?

SONORA: No. Not really.

LUCHA: Por eso. Cuando tiene hijos, you organize every minute of your life. *(She eats in silence for a few moments. Appraising* SONORA*)* Está muy flaquita, not like the rest of the bunch here.

SONORA: I—

LUCHA: And we should all be huesos by now, after so many months con la huelga y cuando nos dan unos pinches seventy-five dollars a week nomás. Pero no. Seguimos siendo panzonas!

SONORA: No 'stá gorda.

LUCHA: Miente. *(Holding up a tamal)* ¿Segura? ¿Tiene chile verde...? I made them special.

SONORA: What's the occasion?

LUCHA: I don't know. *(Laughing)* Maybe for going four month without a man.

SONORA: Gracias, no.

(Suddenly, there is the sound of a car driving by and screeching to a hault. LUCHA *and* SONORA *watch the scene in the distance. A bottle is thrown and someone shouts out an obsenity at the strikers.)*

JUAN: Hey, what the hell're you doing?

CHENTE: *(Overlapping)* ¡Cobardes!

(The car takes off, wheels screeching.)

LUCHA: ¡Cabrones!

(There is a pause.)

SONORA: Do you ever get afraid, Lucha?

LUCHA: ¿De qué?

SONORA: La violencia. Maybe losing the strike.

LUCHA: I dont' think about losing, I think about winning.

SONORA: Yeah, but are you ever afraid?

LUCHA: Fíjese. If we got the guts to come here por el desierto como mojados, we got the courage. Hasta que les ganemos. ¿Verdad?

SONORA: *(Smiling)* Sí. *(Beat)* Where you from, Lucha?

LUCHA: ¿Yo? Ay, de un pinche rancho. Tres horas al pueblo.

SONORA: What pueblo?

LUCHA: Coalcomán, Michoacán. *(Teasing)* You never heard of it?

SONORA: *(Teasing back)* No. We didn't get too much Mexican geography in school.

LUCHA: Well you must of learned something. Es doctora.

SONORA: I'm not a doctor exactly. I'm a P A, a Physician's Assistant.

LUCHA: Pero tenía que asistir a la universidad ¿no?

SONORA: Sí.

LUCHA: I'd like that for my daughter, for her to become something special, to go to college, estudiar.

SONORA: Of course.

LUCHA: But she doesn't like to read. My son loves it. JoJo even reads the back of the cereal box for breakfast. La niña dreams nomás.

SONORA: How old is she?

LUCHA: Ten.

SONORA: When I was that age, I just dreamed, too.

LUCHA: Yo no. I thought only boys could dream. I ask God, decía a veces, "Ay diocito, ¿por qué me hiciste mujer? Why didn't you make me a man instead?"

SONORA: I know that prayer.

LUCHA: But I didn't really want to be a man, I only wanted the same chances. Por eso, vine al norte.

SONORA: For more "opportunity."

LUCHA: Sí, for my children. Los niños aquí tienen toda su mesa completa de comida. They can go to school, pueden mejorarse. Even if los padres tienen que trabajar como burros.

SONORA: *(Sarcastic)* The American dream.

LUCHA: What's wrong with that?

SONORA: Nothing. I just don't believe in it.

LUCHA: Cause you don't have to, you already live it. I see you come and go from the meetings. You live free.

SONORA: Free.

LUCHA: Sí, free. Aunque es mujer, you don't got nobody telling you what to do.

SONORA: I'm forty-two-years old, Lucha.

LUCHA: And Dolores is almost sixty. Look at the life que lleva la pobre.

SONORA: And were both mexicanas.

LUCHA: No digo que no conoce prejuicio.

SONORA: No?

LUCHA: Mire. I see a lot of people come through town to give us help. It seems like every person got something they want to bury or dig up here en Watsón.

SONORA: I've been here ten years, Lucha. Watsonville is not a political phase for me.

LUCHA: No quiero decir que—

SONORA: La clínica started in an apple shed. We had nothing. We were giving people check-ups from right out of los files, hanging sheets up with clothespins for privacy. We'd see fifty kids a night...and after that, their parents.

LUCHA: Sí, pero...¿por qué, Watsón? Con la educación que tiene usted, you could do anything...go anywhere?

SONORA: I don't like "anywhere." I like it here.

LUCHA: Bueno, sí hubiera tenido su educación, you wouldn't find me with the dirt under my uñas or chopping up my fingers on some assembly line. I'd move to a big city like Los Angeles or San Diego, I'd dress up con stockings and lipstick every day of my life, and I'd work in a clean place without a pinche time clock to punch.

SONORA: Yeah, but it'll be different for your children.

LUCHA: Ojala.

SONORA: No, I mean maybe when your kids get the education you didn't, maybe they won't want that office job in L A.

LUCHA: Bueno, they could—

SONORA: Maybe they won't be able to forget that dirt under your fingernails.

(LUCHA *looks at her nails, then back at* SONORA.)

LUCHA: *(After a pause)* Tal vez, but I know I'd like to forget it.

Scene Seven

(Fall. Early evening, many months later. Lights rise on several scenes at once. JUAN and SONORA are working at the strike office. SONORA sits before a computer. JUAN writes in a notepad. Across town at the cannery, a striker with guitar sings solo of longing. He and the other strikers appear in silhouette against the setting autumn sun. It is a somber photograph of resistance. At the Valle home, DON ARTURO sits in front of the t.v. with a remote in one hand and a beer in the other. DOLORES prays before her altar. She lights a candle, moving her lips softly.)

HUELGUISTA: *(Décima)*
"Mi patria es pura riqueza
pero esta mal repartida
en el campo allá no hay vida
solo miseria y tristeza.

Cuando a crecer uno empieza
ver que al norte todos van
y no quedando otro plan
me fui de la tierra mía
y hoy no sé si vuelva un día
ay dios, a mi michoacán."

(DON ARTURO keeps changing stations. Clips of sit-coms, gameshows, talk shows, a spanish-language variety hour, etc. Canned laughter. A news anchor comes on.)

NEWSCASTER: Well, in spite of yesterday's Columbus Day blizzard, the weather looks bright for Republicans here in Washington, Liz. The surprisingly swift passage of Senator Casanova's bill, #1519, cracking down on illegal immigration, met with little to no resistance from Democrats. The bill effectively bars employment, education and health services to all illegal aliens and their children. The Florida hispanic senator was all smiles—"

(DON ARTURO *changes the station. A Mexican drama comes on as* LUCHA *and* AMPARO *cross from the picket line to the Valle home. The singer continues in the background.*)

HUELGUISTA: "Por tener un mal gobierno
nuestra patria mexicana
el campesino no gana
vive como pobre eterno

Y El Norte es un infierno
mas si se gana esta guerra
vive mejor que en su tierra
porque se halla la manera
y en México aunque uno quiera
al campesino se encierra."

(AMPARO *and* LUCHA *appear at the door of* DOLORES' *house.* AMPARO *knocks.*)

DON ARTURO: ¿Qué? ¿Quién es?

(LUCHA *nudges* AMPARO *in the ribs.*)

AMPARO: Amparo. Venimos...digo vengo por Dolores.

(DON ARTURO *slowly pulls himself out of his seat.*)

AMPARO: ¿Arturo? Quiero hablar con Dolores.

(DON ARTURO *ignores them, gets another beer.*)

AMPARO: *(To* LUCHA*)* No contesta. ¿Qué vamos a hacer con éste.

LUCHA: *(Pounding on the door loudly)* Don Arturo, ¿Está Dolores? We got a meeting tonight.

DON ARTURO: Está rezando. She's praying for all you viejas y sus pecados!

LUCHA: *(To* AMPARO*)* Es un sangrón. I don't know how Dolores puede soportarlo.

AMPARO: *(Sarcastic)* Religion. *(Pounding with more force now)* ¡Compadre, soy yo! ¡Por favor, ábreme la puerta!

DOLORES: *(From her altar)* ¿Quién es, Arturo?

DON ARTURO: ¡Son tus amigas comunistas!

DOLORES: ¡Ay, tú!

(DOLORES *goes to the door.* DON ARTURO *stands at the refrigerator drinking the beer.*)

DOLORES: *(Opening the door)* ¡Ay, lo siento! A él no le gusta tener visita.

LUCHA: Venimos por tí nomás.

DOLORES: ¿Para qué?

AMPARO: To go to the meeting.

(The women enter.)

DOLORES: Amparo, how many years you know me?

AMPARO: No sé. Mas de trienta.

DOLORES: Thirty-five years and you're still trying to change me?

AMPARO: I'm not. Now Lucha's working on you. She doesn't know no better.

LUCHA: Dolores, you heard the news.

DOLORES: Sure. I couldn't sleep all night on account of it.

AMPARO: It's the story of our lives, comadre, not that many years ago. Imagínate...without our green cards where would we be at right now?

DOLORES: Yo sé.

AMPARO: Even the children born here won't be able to go to school, ni ver a un doctor, ni—

LUCHA: This bill could kill la huelga. If the workers get divided between who's legal and who's not, we'd be almost a year on the line para nada. *(Beat)* We got to get all the mujeres to the meeting tonight. We got to confront the union.

DOLORES: ¿Por qué?

LUCHA: To take a stand against the bill.

AMPARO: So far the union's said nothing. When I talked to Juan, me dijo que—

DOLORES: I don't trust him no more, Amparo.

AMPARO: Juan?

DOLORES: He's changed too much. Ahora anda a los bars—

LUCHA: ¿Qué importa si...?—

DON ARTURO: I told her I saw him at the bar. She makes a big deal about it.

DOLORES: *(To AMPARO)* You remember before he could hardly get down a beer? *(She takes a long swig.)*

AMPARO: Juan está muy dedicado a la huelga.

DON ARTURO: She doesn't want the man to be a man, she wants him to be a saint. She don't live in the real world.

DOLORES: Go back to your televisión. Es lo único que sabes hacer.

DON ARTURO: She 'spects a man to be un angel, living en las nubes...

AMPARO: *(To* DON ARTURO*)* Compadre, ya!

DON ARTURO: No me mandes. I'm not your child. *(He exits.)*

AMPARO: ...Comadre.

DOLORES: I got nothing to fight for now. I got no more kids.

AMPARO: And when you had kids, you were too busy protecting them—

DOLORES: I lost them anyway.

LUCHA: Fight for my kids, Dolores.

DOLORES: *(After a beat)* It's not my business to be en los meetings, Lucha. I'd rather be on the picket line or packing the food baskets. There, all the womens speak the same way, "How is your kid doing in the junior high?" "Who's going to bring the frijoles para el fund-raiser?" I understand that...mejor que "the working-class struggle." A veces I look inside myself to see if those words touch me someplace...some place que tiene corazón *(Touching her heart)* y me siento fría. I feel completely cold inside.

(LUCHA grabs DOLORES' rebozo off the back of the couch, hands it to her.)

LUCHA: Not me. I feel on fire.

(Soft fade on Valle home. Full rise on strike office as JUAN crumples up a piece of paper in disgust and tosses it into the wastepaper basket.)

JUAN: I don't know what to write. I can't pretend. If this bill becomes law, the strike's dead.

SONORA: Write that.

JUAN: I can't write that. They need enouragement. They need—

SONORA: Dreams?

JUAN: Maybe. That's better than despair. *(He lights up a cigarette.)*

JUAN: I still don't see how they could really enforce a national law. It'd be a bureaucratic nightmare.

SONORA: No? Read this. *(She hands him a newspaper, points to a paragraph)* Right out of the Casanova's mouth.

JUAN: *(Reading aloud)* "The enforcement of the law would begin in labor camps and food-processing plants throughout California, moving on to the garment industry in towns and cities along the Mexican border, including Los Angeles. Since the majority of illegal aliens—"

SONORA: Please...stop. This wasn't supposed to happen.

JUAN: What?

SONORA: *(Small pause)* Juan, I came of age in 1970.

JUAN: And?

SONORA: And it gave me a very skewed view of reality. *(Beat)* In '68, my brother's dragging me over to Garfield High School to go barricade the East L A streets with our bodies. I went from the "school walk-outs" on a weekday to grape boycotts on the weekend. Standing out there in front of the Safeway passing out U F W leaflets and bumper stickers. *(Pause)* Then in 1970, I am kissing Teresa Treviño, a verifiable brown Beret, behind the loud speakers at the Chicano Moratorium.

JUAN: That was your political awakening?

SONORA: That's how I remember it. I don't know what was beating louder, my heart or the bass of the conjunto on the stage.

(JUAN smiles.)

SONORA: I never thought things would go this way. Always imagined that each year of my life would bring us all closer to—

JUAN: To what?

SONORA: I don't know.... Equality. Is that naive? A little piece of land and a little peace of mind for everybody.

JUAN: That's a lot.

SONORA: I guess. *(Pause)* Then in '76, after a decade of marches, and boycotts, and door-to-door canvassing, and school lunch programs and self-help groups, I'm booted out of MeCHA for being a dyke and there's a whole women's movement (white as it was) to break my fall—

JUAN: So, you're gay, huh?

SONORA: Is that a problem?

JUAN: No. I—

SONORA: Good.

JUAN: I just wasn't...sure.

SONORA: Really? Since the strike got started, you can read it on the walls of most public buildings.

(JUAN snubs out his cigarette, returns to his typewriter.)

SONORA: So, Juan...what were you doing in 1970?

JUAN: *(Pause)* I was reading Paul Tillich under the shade of the seminary live oaks.

SONORA: He was the pervert, wasn't he? The guy with the pornography stash?

JUAN: Yeah, but that came later.

SONORA: If I were a priest, that's what I'd want, to be locked up in a library somewhere, studying the "great thinkers." Yeah, give me monkdom, Gregorian chants all day and night.

JUAN: Do you have any idea how monasteries smell?

SONORA: Oh please...

JUAN: *(Teasing)* Do you realize how little monks wash, brush their teeth, change their underwear...?

SONORA: Another fantasy bites the dust. Truth is, all this anti-immigration mess... it's escape fantasies I'm having, not the hermitage.

JUAN: Where to?

SONORA: I don't know. Some place not here. Some place that doesn't feel like a foreign country.

JUAN: Ironic, huh?

SONORA: *(A touch of irony)* So, where's home, carnal? Where's home for the dispossessed chicanada?

JUAN: I honestly don't know.

(CHENTE *enters very agitated.*)

CHENTE: Do you have the statement ready?

JUAN: No, I'm still working on it.

CHENTE: What did you write? Let me see. *(He pulls the paper out of the typewriter.)*

JUAN: It's not done.

(CHENTE *scans it briefly, then crumples it up.*)

CHENTE: No, we got to let them think there's nothing to be concerned about.

SONORA: But there is!

CHENTE: The bill's passage means nothing. The law's unconstitutional. The courts will rule that.

JUAN: We can't count on that—

CHENTE: We got to convince the huelguistas that they must go on with the strike no matter what. We have to make them believe that we believe, that this is no wrench in the works. That—

SONORA: If this bill really becomes law, the strike goes down the toilet. Half of the workers don't have papers. They'll have no legal right to their jobs.

JUAN: *(To* CHENTE*)* But if we can get the union's support, get them to make some public statement that they are not in accord with the law—

CHENTE: You expect the union bosses to go to jail for the huelguistas?

JUAN: No, I mean only to say that they oppose the spirit of the law.

CHENTE: We got to be realistic here. We've got to find out who's legal, who isn't.

SONORA: What?

CHENTE: Really get a sense of the numbers and let the union know. Maybe it's fewer than we think. Maybe the loss of a few workers won't—

SONORA: You can't do that.

CHENTE: I didn't say turn them in, I said just find out cuantos son ilegales.

JUAN: And panic everyone? No, we'll just wait and see. We'll just tell the strikers they've got to wait and see—

(Lighting transition. Spot on JUAN *as he continues speaking, then full rise on Strikers' Meeting.* AMPARO, DOLORES, *and* LUCHA *are present.)*

JUAN: We all have to just wait and see.

LUCHA: A la chingada...wait and see! Los gringos are not waiting to see. I went to get on the bus yesterday en Santa Cruz. The bus driver stop and let on everybody else and then when I tried to subirme al autobus, me dijo que he didn't have to pick me up, that he didn't have to give service to no wetbacks. He just shut the door on Elenita and me and he just drove away.

JUAN: But he doesn't know si eres legal o no.

LUCHA: I got el nopal estampado en la frente, that's all they need to know.

JUAN: Then report him, Lucha.

LUCHA: To who? The I N S? *(She walks away, disgusted.)*

SONORA: Lucha's right. The fall-out's already coming down. If this law is upheld in court, lots of workers won't have jobs, even if we were to win the strike. Neither the union nor the cannery is going to break the law to protect the undocumented workers. The government will put sanctions—

CHENTE: We're getting way ahead of ourselves here.

AMPARO: Pero, no es justo. We all go out on strike together. ¡Todos juntos! No solamente la gente con sus papeles.

JUAN: You're right, but—

AMPARO: Esta ley me da mucho miedo. I didn't have to suffer, como muchos otros, la desgracia of coming here ilegal. But I suffer the same consequences. En eso de nada me servían los papeles. From the beginning—

CHENTE: The union is with you. Haven't they stuck with you this whole year? The most important thing is we keep up the momentum, that we show the union and the community that we are a united front, that we aren't afraid of these anti-immigrant measures, that—

DOLORES: *(Feeling suddenly overwhelmed)* No me gusta. It's too hot. Va a haber un temblor.

AMPARO: Anytime it gets over eighty degrees, she always thinks it's an earthquake coming.

DOLORES: Por lo menos, la naturaleza don't got no prejudice. She hits everyone and she don't ask for your green card to shake you hasta los huesos.

AMPARO: *(Half to herself)* Tiene razón la mujer.

(A silence falls over the room. Outside a lone striker with guitar holds up the picket line. He plays softly, con una tristeza, in the background. DOLORES crosses to her kitchen, sits. She fans herself with a union pamphlet. SONORA and the other women join her at the table. Lighting transition.)

SONORA: ¿...Doña Lolita?

DOLORES: *(After a pause)* Yesterday, on my way home from la guardia, I heard the news about the law they make against nosotros mexicanos. I got so sick I went right to bed. Así que this morning, bien tempranito, I go out to get the clothes on the line. I forgot about them the night before. And my son's tee shirts were still there...I had washed them to give...para tu JoJo, Lucha.

LUCHA: Gracias, Señora.

DOLORES: I figure he's big enough for them now. Y allí estaban colgando como white ghosts with their arms all stretched out en la neblina. Fue una mañana muy gris. By the time I got all the clothes down and folded, I saw the sun coming out, peaking up over las lomas. It was so orange, it was almost red y la luz, bien fuerte.Y luego it passed over the top of the hills and spilled its light all across los files. De repente everything was covered en luz. I turn my eyes away, it was so bright. Y miré p'arriba un pedacito de luna. The moon look like a small smile in the sky, un poco chueca.

(The guitar begins to rise again very gradually.)

Y por alguna razón, I thought of México así, desapariciéndose. Que mi México es la noche, la oscuridad, the place of dreams. And I saw the sun como el norte, stealing our dreams from us. El sol era brillante y maravilloso pero México was fading from its light.

LUCHA: And now the light is going to burn us out completely with its laws

DOLORES: Eso fue lo que pensaba yo.

(The lights and sound of guitar gradually fade out.)

Scene Eight

(Three months later. A cold and wet January morning. LUCHA *stands on the street in front one of the gates to the cannery with her picket sign.* AMPARO *and a few of the other strikers can be seen in the distance, holding up the line. Suddenly* JOJO *enters, goes to his mother, grabs her by the arm, starts pulling on her.)*

JOJO: C'mon, Mom, they're coming. I saw the bus waiting for them over there at the K Mart.

LUCHA: No. Go home if you're afraid.

JOJO: I'm not afraid.

LUCHA: Son esquiroles.

JOJO: They don't care, 'amá. They just wanna work.

LUCHA: Well, so do I. I just wanna work, también. I been just wanting to work already for fifteen months. Aren't you tired of the food baskets?

JOJO: Yeah.

LUCHA: Seeing your mamá stand in front of the Safeway and beg for donations?

JOJO: Yeah.

LUCHA: Digging through a stack of old clothes to find a damn pair of pants for you to wear to school?

JOJO: Yeah, yeah.

LUCHA: Seeing your sister with patches in her dresses?

JOJO: You know I'm tired of it.

LUCHA: Pues, I'm tired, too. I'm tired of the pinche landlord always on my back...que la renta, y que la renta...y que cuando vas a trabajar. Every scab bus you see means another month on the picket line for your mother.

(There is the sound of a bus approaching in the distance.)

JOJO: Mom, the scab bus is coming.

LUCHA: Good, estoy lista.

JOJO: 'Amá!

LUCHA: Vete, ya. Go stand on the other end con Amparo.

JOJO: No. I'm staying with you.

LUCHA: Then stay out of the way.

(As the bus pulls up, LUCHA *comes downstage to meet it.* JOJO, AMPARO, *and the strikers look on. They are stunned.)*

AMPARO: ¿Pá dónde va tu mamá?

JOJO: She's gonna talk to the scabs.

AMPARO: She's going on the bus?

JOJO: Yeah.

AMPARO: ¡Ay, Dios!

(Sound of bus door swinging open. LUCHA *walks down the center aisle of the audience, as the center aisle of the bus. She passes out fliers about the strike and the anti-immigration bill. Actual fliers regarding a current-local concern affecting Latino/people-of-color can be employed here.)*

LUCHA: *Yo tengo 15 años en los estados unidos.* I came here alone, without a husband and I worked in the grapes in the Central Valley. También trabajé, picking cotton a mano, dragging the sack y a mi bebé recién nacido. Quizás en ese tiempo you saw algún americano wearing a cotton shirt que yo pizqué.Una camisa muy bonita, muy blanca, and made with the cotton that I picked. Y después acá en Watsonville, I've worked en las canneries, packing todo el proceso de comida. ¿Para qué? So that us inmigrantes could fill the gringos' table con comida.
Gente, no vaya a trabajar. En esta canería, they had us working como esclavos. If you go in there to work today, you'll be hurting us. Es verdad que you get a day's pay, pero ¿qué pasará mañana? They'll do the same to you as they done to us. If you don't go in, we can negotiate a contract and later you can come in as real workers, también. Los patrones son americanos. he people they are exploiting es nuestra misma raza. La gente mexicana.

*(*LUCHA *watches as we hear the sound of the bus door closing and the bus pulling away. A smile comes over her face as the strikers all cheer and wave "Adios." Suddenly there is the sound of tear gas bomb being tossed and exploding. Smoke fills the air. Screams and the muffled voice of the police. The crowd disperses. Blackout)*

(In the darkness, the brutal sounds of a physical assault are heard: heavy blows to a body with fists and sticks, grunts of pain, the distorted voices of young males, shouting obsenities. They are full of rage and violence. Police sirens interrupt the beating. The stage becomes a maze of spinning red and blue police lights. An ambulance can be heard in the distance, speeding across city-blocks. DOLORES *appears. She stands in the oakgrove, wearing a rebozo around her shoulders. The colored lights whirl dizzingly about her. Then as the light of the midnight moon rises behind her, the sirens and police lights fade. The wind blows.* DOLORES *draws the rebozo more tightly to her.)*

DOLORES: Virgencita, how many more faces can death wear? Tonight La Muerte put on the clothes of the gringo and beat my JoJo into the ground. He can't wake up. Without your touch, Madre, JoJo can't wake up.

(The wind begins to rise. Sound of sea birds in the distance.)

DOLORES: Mi Virgen, te ruego don't take our son from us. *(Pause)* ¿Qué quieres de mí? *(Pause, she extends her hands)* Enséñame el camino and I'll walk that road, te prometo. Just don't take the boy! You can't have the boy! *(Suddenly full of rage)* Wake him up! ¡Te mando!

(The sound of the wind begins to take on the resonance of a choral of female voices becoming increasingly distinct as it rises in volume. A procession of women, dressed in a ghostly white, enter and slowly approach the largest oak in the grove. DOLORES looks on, frightened, awed. The women's faces appear to be covered by a white gauze-like mask, except for one. Her face remains in shadow, yet bears a faint resemblance to SONORA. She cradles a bundle in her arms.)

VOICES: *(Chanting)* Chihuacóatl, Quilaztli, Tonán, Centeotl, Centeotlcihuatl, Xilonen, Teteoian, Chicomecóatl, Citlalicue, Chinipa, Yoalticitl

(The light of the crescent moon passes onto DOLORES' face.)

DOLORES: *(Over the voices)* Virgencita ¿me hablas?

VOICES: *(Chanting)* Coatlicue, Teotenantzín, Tlaliyolo, Toci, Tonantzín, Guadalupe, Madre.

(The voices continue their incantations. The glow of the moon drops into the leaves of the oak.)

DOLORES: Tonantzín, why do you call me Mother?

(Its branches are washed in the light as is the faint impression of la Virgen de Guadalupe in the center of the tree. The figure shimmers iridescent. DOLORES falls to her knees.)

DOLORES: ¡...Mi hija!

(The women retreat in slow procession, just as they had entered.)

(The image of la Virgen in the tree intensifies. A powerful wind smelling of the sea passes over DOLORES. The song of pelicans and other sea birds fill the air. There is the slight tremor of an earthquake. Blackout)

END OF ACT ONE

ACT TWO
"LA APARICION"

(Female voice in the darkness) "A great portent appeared in heaven: a woman clothed with the sun, with the moon under her feet, and on her head a crown of twelve stars. She was pregnant and was crying out in birth pangs, in the agony of giving birth."
The Book of Revelation, 12

Scene One

(Weeks later. Late-winter, 1998. A Bolero *plays on the record player.* DOLORES *is cutting lemons on the kitchen table.* JOJO *is squeezing the cut lemons into a pitcher. He has a bandage around his head and his arm is in a sling.)*

JOJO: That's what Ghandi did.

DOLORES: ¿Quién es Ghandi?

JOJO: An Indian revolutionary.

DOLORES: ¿Un indio?

JOJO: Not an Indian from here, from India. He'd fast until he got what he wanted.

DOLORES: What did he want?

JOJO: Justice.

DOLORES: Justice.

JOJO: For poor people. He wanted people to make their own clothes with their own cotton and use the salt from their own oceans to sell. He wanted them to be independent.

DOLORES: Did he die, too, like Cesar Chavez?

JOJO: Yeah, but not from fasting. Even Cesar didn't die exactly from fasting. He just went to sleep one night in Arizona and never woke up.

DOLORES: That's a nice way to go.

JOJO: But the newspapers said that all that fasting he did in his life wore his heart out.

DOLORES: *(After a pause)* Oh.

JOJO: *(Beat)* You sure you wanna do this?

DOLORES: How did the Hindu die?

JOJO: Ghandi?

DOLORES: Sí.

JOJO: Some one shot him. Another Indian.

DOLORES: That's how it usually happens ¿qué no? Your own people hurt you the most.

JOJO: I guess. *(Showing her the half-full pitcher of lemon juice)* Is this enough?

DOLORES: Debe ser...for today.

(She pours water into the juice, takes a long drink. JOJO watches her.)

JOJO: How long you going to do this, Doña Lola?

DOLORES: Until I get what I want.

(Black out)

Scene Two

(Days later. Strike warehouse. LUCHA, AMPARO and SONORA are packing boxes with food items. In the background, DOLORES can be seen speaking in low whispers to JOJO who records what she is saying into a small torquoise book.)

SONORA: That oak grove is sacred. The Ohlones Indians buried their dead out there.

AMPARO: "¿Holones?"

SONORA: Ohlones. They worshipped oak trees.

AMPARO: You think Dolores is worshipping a tree?

SONORA: No. I mean, it doesn't matter. To her, she's worshipping la Vigen.

AMPARO: No te entiendo, Sonora.

SONORA: Miren, tengo una amiga, Dakota...es india, she knows about the history from here.

AMPARO: ¿Y qué dice?

SONORA: Well,... I was living with someone for awhile and she had two little girls.

LUCHA: ¿Con quién vivías?

SONORA: No la conoces. Anyway, when she moved out, she left a lot of stuff behind, especially a lot of the girls' toys. So, I just moved it all into my basement.

AMPARO: Sonora, ¿qué tiene que ver esto con Dolores?

SONORA: I'm getting to that. Anyway, I finally got Selena to come and pick up her stuff.

LUCHA: ¿Es mexicana?

SONORA: ¿Quién? ¿Selena? No, es filipina.

AMPARO: Ay, Lucha ¿qué importa la raza de la señora?I want to hear the story!

SONORA: Well, for every night after that, I'd hear all this racket like there was someone down in my basement moving furniture around.

AMPARO: Sería un racoon.

SONORA: No. Every morning, everything was in the exact same place.

AMPARO: ¿Qué fue entonces?

SONORA: So my friend, Dakota, comes over and she's looking at the big oak outside my kitchen window and she says to me... "The Ohlones are buried out there. They miss those children's spirits in those toys."

LUCHA: ¡Qué mentiras!

SONORA: "You need to make an offering." So, I did some prayers and burned some sage—

AMPARO: ¿Qué es eso... "zage"?

SONORA: Una yierba. I never heard a peep in my basement again.

AMPARO: So, you think la Virgen is one of these Holones.

SONORA: Well, not exactly, but I just think Dolores found a holy spot.

LUCHA: ¿Qué opinas tú, Amparo?

AMPARO: Bueno, I know she's not lying. I know she believes la Virgen spoke to her.

LUCHA: Pero dice ella que she saw her...de carne y huesos, que la virgen apareció entre muchas mujeres, dressed just like us...bueno like you, Amparo...como una cannery worker.

AMPARO: Gracias, Luchita.

LUCHA: Y la Virgen left her estampa on one of the trees.

SONORA: You can see it right there on the face of the trunk.

AMPARO: ¿Fuiste tú?

SONORA: I had to go.

AMPARO: Yo no. I'm not going. I'm scared. If I really see la Virgen, it's going to scare me.

SONORA: They already got a line of gente out there praying to the tree, bringing ofrendas. You should see it. Rosaries hanging all over it, pictures of people's loved ones...flowers and velas everywhere.

LUCHA: *(To SONORA)* So, you believe.

SONORA: I believe there's something out there. You can feel la fuerza, even if it's just the faith of the people.

LUCHA: Tú sabes mejor que yo, Amparo, Lola's not all there all the time.

AMPARO: Yo sé que ha sufrido mucho.

LUCHA: Exacto. She's got a lot of problemas. So she sees what she needs to see.

(CHENTE enters with JUAN.)

LUCHA: I worry, though, que it's going to pull la gente away from la huelga.

AMPARO: Juan. ¿Qué cree usted? What you think the Church is gointu say about la aparición?

JUAN: I don't know what the Church will do. But, I know what I think and I agree with Lucha. It's a distraction.

(The men help the women stack the boxes.)

LUCHA: Now is not the time to escape into the heavens. The rosary's not going to get us our jobs back. Necesitamos más acción, más—

CHENTE: I don't know. Maybe la aparición is a good thing, to believe in something—

LUCHA: I believe in god, but I don't believe in praying away our troubles.

CHENTE: I didn't say that, Lucha. But if la aparición can bring people together, especially when we're on the brink of losing what faith we got left.

AMPARO: It's this damn law. Everybody's walking around holding their breath, wondering what's gointu happen.

CHENTE: Pero también es que we been over sixteen months with the strike and—

JUAN: And we're still at an impasse with the cannery.

CHENTE: People need something to keep their confidence up. Anytime you got numbers, that gives you strength. You can't go wrong with that.

JUAN: That's true. Maybe we can use this apparition—

AMPARO: No. You don't use not'ing. You either believe that is la Virgen on the tree or you don't. That's all there is to it. If you believe, go down on your knees and try to listen to what she got to tell you about where we're supposed to go next. If you don't believe, pues 'stá bien. Jus' go on with your work like you was doing already.

(Silence falls over the room.)

Scene Three

(A week later. LUCHA's *home.* SONORA *and* JOJO *sit together,* JOJO's *schoolbooks spread out in front of them.* JOJO *still wears a few small bandages; visible signs of the beating a few months passed. Sound of T V sitcom in the background.)*

JOJO: Have you ever looked into a gringo's eyes real close-up?

SONORA: I...guess.

JOJO: They got nothin' inside 'em. Nada. You just look into them and it's like...there's nothin' there. It's like somebody just squeeze the brown outta their eyes and took their soul.

SONORA: Not all gringos have blue eyes, JoJo.

JOJO: Those punks that beat me up did. They were empty inside. You could see it in their eyes, Sonora.

SONORA: ...Yeah.

JOJO: *(Beat)* They knew my Mom's name.

SONORA: They did? But why didn't you say—

JOJO: I was afraid. I didn't know what she'd do. I was afraid she'd get hurt.

SONORA: ...Yeah.

*(*LUCHA *enters with two beers.)*

LUCHA: ¿Ya terminaron?

SONORA: *(Suddenly)* It gets easier once you get to geometry.

JOJO: Thanks, Sonora. Algebra's kickin' my butt. *(To* LUCHA*)* Sonora's smart, Mom.

LUCHA: Es doctora. Debe saber algo de "math."

SONORA: A physician's assistant, te dije.

LUCHA: Sí, sí, but it's too long to say. *(To* JOJO*)* Bueno, go in there and watch T V con tu hermana. Quiero un poquito de tiempo con Sonora antes de que se vaya.

JOJO: All right. See ya.

SONORA: Later, JoJo.

(He exits. LUCHA hands SONORA a beer.)

SONORA: You gotta great kid. You raised him good, Lucha.

LUCHA: I think he raised himself mostly...or maybe we just grew up together.

SONORA: Nah, he admires you.

LUCHA: He defends me. Anyway, gracias por ayudarlo. Once JoJo pass the eighth grade, that's about as far as I could go with the homework.

SONORA: He's gonna do fine. Besides, it was fun, I've kind of missed it.

LUCHA: ¿Qué?

SONORA: The kids I used to live with...helping them.

LUCHA: Selena's children?

SONORA: ...Yes. How—?

LUCHA: Is that who you called when you came in?

SONORA: Selena? God, no. That's long over.

LUCHA: Entonces tienes otra novia.

SONORA: Who? Marta? ...my lover?

LUCHA: No sé.

SONORA: She's just a friend. She paged me.

LUCHA: Oh. *(Beat)* Why didn't you tell the mujeres en la huelga que eres lesbiana?

SONORA: I didn't think I had to. Why didn't you tell them you were straight?

LUCHA: No juegues conmigo.

SONORA: I'm not playing with you.

LUCHA: It hurt me.

SONORA: What?

LUCHA: Que everyone knew, menos yo. I see all the time lots of women around you. Filipinas, negras... But I don't think nothing of it, then I feel like a pendeja cuando Amparo tells me. ¿No tienes confianza en mí?

SONORA: I trust you, Lucha. I just am who I am. I thought it was obvious. I'm not hiding anything. If you didn't know, I wasn't hiding it.

(Pause)

LUCHA: Do you sleep with all those women?

SONORA: Who?

LUCHA: All those mujeres you hang around with.

SONORA: *(Enjoying it)* Some. Not always. Most are friends.

LUCHA: Friends.

SONORA: Friends.

LUCHA: No entiendo. When a man and a woman are together, he's got men friends and the woman's got woman friends. The other way, it's too confusing. How do you know who is who? How do you know when to be celosa?

SONORA: Oh, you know. Always trust your instincts.

LUCHA: Your instincts.

SONORA: Bueno...it's just like men and women, you can always tell when something's going on.

LUCHA: How can you tell?

SONORA: Well, I...people flirt.

LUCHA: They flirt.

SONORA: Yeah, they tease each other and smile a lot. *(Smiling)*

LUCHA: No, it would make me crazy. Every woman could be your lover.

SONORA: Well, not every woman.

LUCHA: You're making fun of me.

SONORA: I'm not making fun of you.

LUCHA: You are. Your eyes are laughing at me.

SONORA: You started it!

(Black-out)

Scene Four

(A month into DOLORES' fast. Lights slowly rise on the oak grove and sacred tree. DOLORES and the Guadalupanas sing "Desde el cielo," accompanied by guitar. They pray in the background as JUAN enters.)

GUADALUPANAS: Virgen preciosa, te rogamos y te pedimos, traigas la paz y prosperidad a esa comunidad pacífica, a nuestro hogar, Watsonville querido.

(Moments later, AMPARO approaches JUAN standing at a distance from the tree.)

AMPARO: ¿Por que viniste, Juan? To see how you could use la Virgen for your strike campaign?

JUAN: I'm sorry, Doña Amparo. Sometimes, my political fervor gets ahead of me.

AMPARO: It used to be religious fervor.

JUAN: Are you reprimanding me? You who once told me that religion was no more than an insurance policy for.... How did you put it?

AMPARO: For peepo too scare to face up to the real sinners.

JUAN: And...now?

AMPARO: I still think that, pero...la verdad es que...after my husband die, I feel different about...things. I believe more.

JUAN: I understand.

AMPARO: No, not like I go to Church more or follow all the rules so much, pero es mas que—

JUAN: What?

AMPARO: Bueno...que I know that there's something more than...lo que vemos con los ojos. I don't know what, but a'lease I know que...I believe in the dead now. *(Pause)* Gilberto talks to me, Juan. I hear him as clear as you and me. And that change my opinion about a lot of things. I understand Dolores' ghosts.

JUAN: You've changed, Doña Amparo.

AMPARO: ¿Crees que sí?

JUAN: Yes, you're...softer now.

AMPARO: Ay, por favor, don't call me soft.

JUAN: No, no. Don't worry. You're still tough as nails, but—

AMPARO: But what?

JUAN: I just didn't think I'd ever hear you defending religion.

(DOLORES has crossed to them. She is visibly weak from her fast.)

DOLORES: *(To JUAN)* And I didn't think I'd see you rechazándola.

JUAN: Señora Valle.

DOLORES: Have you rejected God, Juan?

JUAN: I think that's between me and my God, Señora.

DOLORES: Entonces tiene fe todavía.

AMPARO: Lola.

JUAN: I have faith.

DOLORES: ¿Verdad?

JUAN: Sí, faith in what my hands can build, where my feet can take me. Faith in what I can see and touch and make manifest...right here on this ground.

DOLORES: Yo no. On the ground, I got nothing to hold onto. Yesterday, I see Amparo go to the picket line, she's got her pockets filled with pierditas.

AMPARO: Lola—

DOLORES: I know what the stones are for and my heart turns to stone.

JUAN: You'd rather see her tear-gassed by the police?

AMPARO: That's not what she's saying, Juan.

JUAN: Then what is she saying?

DOLORES: *(Turning to the Virgin's image.)* ¿Puede ver a la Virgen, Juan?

JUAN: I see an image that appears to have the shape and color of La Virgen de Guadalupe. Yes.

DOLORES: ¿Es todo?

JUAN: Bueno...I see the faith of the people.

DOLORES: ¿No lo toca a usted? If you read it in your books, will it touch you then? Does your heart go on fire when you read?

JUAN: I don't know what you mean.

DOLORES: The tree is the beginning, Juan. It's the beginning of everything. It makes the paper you read for your revolutionary ideas, for la biblia you used to carry under your arm todos los días.

JUAN: *(Beat)* Piel de Dios.

AMPARO: ¿Cómo?

JUAN: Skin of God. What los indios called the bible the first time they saw it.

DOLORES: Pues, allí 'stá. One of the huelguistas me dijo que she try to take solamente un pedacito from the bark, and it bleed.

AMPARO: ¿Verdad?

JUAN: *(Not believing)* Señora.

DOLORES: I only have them write down what they tell me, Juan. Mire.
(She opens the small turquoise book, points to the page, gives it to him.) Léalo...

(He looks away.)

DOLORES: Hazlo, Amparo. (Passes the book onto AMPARO) ágina doce, donde dice "Clara Olivares."

AMPARO: *(Labored)* "Cuando traté de quitar la corteza del arbol sagrado—"

JUAN: That's enough.

DOLORES: You don't believe it happen.

JUAN: I believe your book says it happened.

(She takes the book back from AMPARO*)*

DOLORES: There was blood on the knife. Piel de Dios, Juan. That bark is the skin of god. *(Pulling him toward the tree)* Touch the skin, Juan Cunningham.

JUAN: *(Pulling away from her)* No! *(Beat)* Why did you ask me to come here, Señora Valle.

DOLORES: *(After a pause)* Because I want you to bless the tree con una misa.

JUAN: A Mass? But the parish is against this.

DOLORES: Mire. No soy tan estúpida. I know what those priests in their fancy church think of us, que somos locas, campesinas brutas.

JUAN: ¿Entonces...?

DOLORES: I'm not asking those priests, I'm asking you.

JUAN: I'm no longer a priest.

DOLORES: You are to God.

JUAN: Please, Señora Valle, tiene que entender—

DOLORES: No, I don't got to understand. No puedo entender que God gives you this gift and you spit on it.

JUAN: I can't...I don't believe.

DOLORES: *(After a beat)* Why do you come back into my life? To torture me with your words, with your eyes?

AMPARO: Comadre.

DOLORES: They're like dark mirrors every day in my face.

JUAN: I'm not here to torture you.

DOLORES: Then what...?

JUAN: I—

DOLORES: If you have rejected God, don't keep my daughter's memory in prison with you.

JUAN: Prison?

DOLORES: *(Tenderly)* You were my daughter's novio.

JUAN: Her groom? What are you—?

DOLORES: You went into that fil together.

JUAN: ...Yes.

DOLORES: She was a bride, vestida de blanco. She died for God.

JUAN: She died for change.

DOLORES: Era una santa.

JUAN: She was a hero.

DOLORES: Is that what they teach you in your revolutionary books? To take the God out of everything?

JUAN: I know what I saw. There was no god out there.

DOLORES: No quiero saber lo que vió.

JUAN: Fine. *(He starts to walk away.)*

AMPARO: Juan, no se vaya.

(He stops. Turns around, looks at AMPARO, *then to* DOLORES. *Their eyes lock.)*

JUAN: Señora Valle, your daughter was a martyr. She knew she'd never come out of that vineyard alive. She knew it better than I. Her death was a protest against the same people who crippled her at birth. Why is that so difficult to accept?

DOLORES: You don't accept it. You're angry all the time.

JUAN: You're right. I can't accept it. I tell you, I saw the way she died. And it has marked me indelibly, more than any priestly vow.

AMPARO: Juanito.

JUAN: No. *(His eyes still have not moved from* DOLORES*)* She wants to know, Amparo!

AMPARO: Lola?

(There is a pause.)

JUAN: By the time Cerezita and I were in the middle of the vineyard...we got separated. I still don't know how. There was so much smoke, and...in the distance...the flames had climbed as high as the pecan trees. I remember looking up at them...a wall of giant flaming torches. And then I got hit... in the gut. I didn't even realize the growers were shooting at us. But the next thing I know, I'm on the ground. I don't know how long I was there. The fire was just sucking up the fields all around us like a magnificent tidal wave, just drowning everything—all that poison into this great ocean of flame. I figured I was drowning, too. *(Pause)* And then suddenly, the smoke cleared and—

DOLORES: And?

JUAN: I see Cerezita. *(Pause)* Someone had torn the cloth from her head. And they had stuck her...the head...onto a thick grapevine post—

AMPARO: ¡Ay, Dios!

JUAN: They had forced the post through her mouth and had hung the veil like a sign around her neck. And on it, in blood...her blood, they had written the words: "THOU ART WRETCHED." *(Pause)* And then I understood—

AMPARO: What, Juan?

JUAN: How profoundly those men...with all their land and all their power... hated us. And I knew that they would do anything...anything not to know their hate was fear. *(Pause)* And I knew I would never be afraid again. Not even of God.

(DOLORES faints.)

Scene Five

(A few days later. Simultaneous scene. DOLORES' home and the Diocese Office. JUAN sits before MONSIGNOR MENDEZ who sits behind a large desk. Cross-stage, JOJO sits at DOLORES's kitchen table. DOLORES lies on the sofa, covered by a serape. She sips from a glass of water. There is a pile of lemons on the table. She is visibly weaker, as she dictates to JOJO who writes in the turquoise book.)

JUAN: Well, there are many versions to the story.

MONSIGNOR: So, I've heard.

DOLORES: Yo sé lo que ví.

JUAN: "Era una mujer humilde," she told me.

DOLORES: Una campesina valiente, vestida de blanco.

JUAN: Dressed like herself, except all in white. She smelled of the sea, she said.

DOLORES: Llevaba una cuna.

JUAN: And she carried a cradle.

MONSIGNOR: A Madonna figure.

DOLORES: Pero, estaba vacío.

JUAN: Well, no. There was no child in it.

MONSIGNOR: Strange.

JUAN: Around the Virgin's head was a crown of stars.

DOLORES: Tenía una corona de muchas estrellas y letras que formaban—

JUAN: With letters forming words, but she couldn't understand them.

DOLORES: Palabras extrañas.

MONSIGNOR: They were illegible?

DOLORES: Pero yo no sé leer.

JUAN: No, she couldn't read them.

MONSIGNOR: What do you mean?

JUAN: She doesn't know how.

MONSIGNOR: Oh...oh.

DOLORES: Pero yo recuerdo un número bien claro.

JUAN: But she distinctly remembered the number...seventy-seven with an X.

DOLORES: Setenta y siete con equis.

JUAN: Well, monsignor. You know to what that refers.

MONSIGNOR: No, what?

DOLORES: The priest at the Church tole me that the numbers meant—

JUAN: Why to the New Testament, Sir.

DOLORES: Que tengo mucho coraje contra mi esposo.

JUAN: When Peter asks, "how often do I forgive those who have sinned against me? As many as seven times?" Christ answers, "not seven times, but seventy-seven times."

DOLORES: *(To herself)* It's true I blame him...que two of my children turn out...different.

MONSIGNOR: Yes, yes. Now I know.

DOLORES: *(To* JOJO*)* Don't write that.

JUAN: You see this woman, she's full of rage, Monsignor. She's suffered a great deal.

DOLORES: Y de repente la virgen se desapareció entre un multitud de mujeres.

(Lights fade on the kitchen.)

JUAN: Her husband is an alcoholic. He hasn't held a job in years. The priest over at Saint Patrick's tole her it was a message, that she must open her heart, forgive her husband his offenses.

MONSIGNOR: Good advice, I'd say.

JUAN: But that's all the Church ever tells these women.

MONSIGNOR: ...So?

JUAN: Do you remember the words of the Virgin Mary when she says—
"The mighty will be put down from their thrones.
And the lowly will be lifted up in their place."

MONSIGNOR: Yes. "And the hungry will be fed." Is this another test?

JUAN: "And the fat and over content will be sent away empty."

MONSIGNOR: I know the passage, Mr Cunningham.

JUAN: Well, those are the words of an angry woman, sir. Not some passive long-suffering santa.

MONSIGNOR: Mr Cunningham, what's evident to me, merely by the little you've told me is that...well...this was a private revelation. It may do the woman some good on a personal level, but in terms of something larger—

JUAN: It may be personal, Monsignor, but it's left a public mark. Politically, it could mean—

MONSIGNOR: Oh, I've seen that marking.

JUAN: You have.

MONSIGNOR: Well, pictures. I sent my aid. You know as well as I do that that impression could be anything. Go to any other oak of its kind and you'll see a dozen possible Virgins of Guadalupe, Black Madonnas, Niños de Atoche, San Martíns.... Tell a person what to look for and the eye will shape it. My aid said the image appears in two other places on that same tree.

JUAN: Yes.

MONSIGNOR: People see what they need to see. This woman, she's only trying to draw attention to herself.

JUAN: But she's fasting—

MONSIGNOR: This fast of hers is no more political than this apparition.

JUAN: She's fasting against the anti-immigrant bill, Monsignor. That's more than the Church is doing.

MONSIGNOR: Did you come here to insult me?

JUAN: No, sir. It's just that she's getting weaker daily. Her condition could become critical.

MONSIGNOR: Then stop her, if you want to help her.

JUAN: I don't want to stop her. I want to give her and those strikers praying in that oak grove some kind of hope. The Church's blessing could do that.

(There is a pause.)

JUAN: Monsignor?

MONSIGNOR: She's a lonely woman, you said that yourself. The Church can't hop on every train that comes into the station. Now if you'll excuse me, I have an appointment.

(MONSIGNOR *begins gathering up papers on his desk, stuffing them into a briefcase.*)

JUAN: I know Señora Valle, Monsignor. She feels it a *manda* to share what she has witnessed, a *carga* I know she'd rather not carry. Hasn't she carried enough...? The burden of nearly a decade of working twelve-hour shifts at a cannery that is on the verge of dismissing her without a cent of compensation.

MONSIGNOR: Tell it to your ex-Jesuit compañeros, Mr Cunningham.

JUAN: Two dead children. One from AIDS, the other deformed from pesticides—

MONSIGNOR: Wait a minute. Isn't this the same woman from that Valley town—

JUAN: McLaughlin.

MONSIGNOR: Who claimed her daughter was la Virgen?

JUAN: Yes, but—

MONSIGNOR: And you expect the Church to believe this woman now?

JUAN: That girl was murdered, I witnessed it myself. The Church was no where to be found then, either.

MONSIGNOR: It is you, not I, Mr Cunningham, who have abandoned the "Church of the Poor." I am still a priest.

JUAN: Yes.

MONSIGNOR: And, unlike you, I know there is protocol to follow concerning these matters. Lourdes, Fatima, La Virgen en El Tepeyac, these have survived the tests of decades...centuries.

JUAN: But, what crime is there in meeting with Señora Valle and giving the tree the blessing she seeks?

MONSIGNOR: Because any action on the clergy's part is tantamount to sanction. We might as well proclaim that we believe that the face of Jesus really did appear on a burnt tortilla in some farm worker's breakfast in Texas and that Guadalupe announced her presence in the rear bumper of a Chevy in East Los Angeles. It's ludicrous. (*Slamming shut his briefcase.*) Now, as I said, I have an appointment—

(*He indicates the door,* JUAN *rises.*)

JUAN: One thing I know for sure. Whatever was moving in the collective hearts of the people of this town was just waiting to come out. Whether that apparition originated with God, the pure exhaustion from the strike or the absurdity of this anti-immigrant bill, it doesn't matter. The people in this town want some change, Monsignor. And I'm going to see that they get it, with or without your support.

(JUAN *starts to walk out. Stops*)

JUAN: You're wrong, Monsignor. I may have abandoned the Church, but I have not abandoned the poor.

(JUAN *exits. Crossfade back to* DOLORES' *kitchen.* AMPARO *enters the kitchen with an empty shopping bag. She crosses to the refrigerator and opens it. A mound of lemons tumble out. She begins stuffing the lemons into the shopping bag.* DOLORES *looks on from the sofa in shocked amusement.* JOJO *stands next to her.*)

DOLORES: ¿Qué 'stás haciendo? Don't take my lemons! (*Pulling herself up from the couch*) No son tuyos.

(*They struggle over the bag, stumbling over the lemons rolling all over the floor.*)

AMPARO: I'm not gointu let you kill yourself.

DOLORES: Hice una promesa a la virgencita.

AMPARO: Did you promise to kill yourself?

DOLORES: It's not your business.

AMPARO: Dolores! ¡Síentate!

(DOLORES *sits down right on the floor.*)

AMPARO: JoJo, I don't know why you listen to her above everybody else? Can't you see how sick she's getting?

JOJO: It's better she's eating lemons than nothing, isn't it? (*He gets another bag, starts picking up the lemons.*)

DOLORES: You shouldn't blame the boy.

AMPARO: No, I should blame you. No sé, comadre. I've know you for thirty-some years, and I still don't understand you.

DOLORES: What are you going to do with my limones?

AMPARO: I'm going to drink them.

DOLORES: ¿Cómo?

AMPARO: I'm going to follow your way. I'm going to squeeze them into some water, poner una cucharita de azúcar and I'm gonna drink 'em. I'm gointu follow your way because I can't change you from your way.

DOLORES: No, Amparo. (*She puts the last of the lemons into the bag.*)

AMPARO: Tú dices que la Virgen wanted a sacrifice. Pues, nobody likes to eat better than me. And for as much as I like to eat, it's probably worth three people on a hunger strike.

(JOJO *laughs.*)

DOLORES: You don't have to do this, comadre. It's my own prayer.

AMPARO: Yo sé. I do it anyway. Just to keep you company. *(To* JOJO*)* Go on home now, hijo, I'll stay here con Dolores until Sonora gets here. We're going to watch you like a hawk, m'entiendes?

JOJO: Are you really gonna fast?

AMPARO: Yeah, but I'm not gonna keep my mouth shut about it.

Scene Six

(The next day. The strikers are preparing for a fund-raiser. JOJO *is hanging a sign that reads: "PACHANGA/PARTY. EXPAND THE STRIKE TO THE FARMWORKERS. "* SONORA, LUCHA, *and* JUAN *are setting up chairs, the mike system, etc.* CHENTE *has just entered.)*

JUAN: *(To* CHENTE*)* Our thinking is that it's time to move the strike out to the fields, to the farm workers.

CHENTE: But the farm workers aren't on strike.

JUAN: But we're not gonna win this thing without farm worker support. We expand the strike to include every aspect of food production in this region. Farm workers, cannery workers. We boycott the grocery stores—

CHENTE: That's a mistake. It'll put too much pressure on the union.

LUCHA: It's supposed to put pressure on los patrones!

CHENTE: I'm a week outta town and the support committee votes this in?

SONORA: The union is ready to throw in the towel, Chente.

JUAN: They're ready to concede almost everything to Shea: health benefits, senority, the cut in pay.

CHENTE: That's because the strike's gone on too long. It's straining the union's resources.

SONORA: And what about the huelguistas' resources? Every day another striker comes in with an eviction notice.

JUAN: With the farm workers out on strike at the peak of the season, we'll all win! In two weeks tops, everyone will be back to work with better contracts! In the long run, the union saves money!

CHENTE: It's too big of a risk.

LUCHA: And you're too big of a gallina. *(Coming along side of* JUAN*)* Listen to Juan, what do we got to lose?

CHENTE: *(Eyeing them both)* The support of the Union.

LUCHA: ¡Adió! But they don't got a union without workers!

JUAN: You yourself told me we needed a more aggressive strategy.

CHENTE: Sí, pero there's got to be another way.

SONORA: Like what?

CHENTE: Bueno, I know we don't like to talk about it, but as long as those scabs keep coming, the strike isn't even making a dent in the cannery's output.

SONORA: That's the union's lame excuse. Those scabs aren't doing the quantity or the quality of work trained workers can.

CHENTE: Still, as long as they got workers to replace us, we don't got a leg to stand on.

LUCHA: I stand on my own two feet. *(To* CHENTE*)* That's what everybody in this room needs to be doing.

(There is a pause.)

JOJO: *(Softly)* ...Mom?

LUCHA: Sí, hijo.

JOJO: Doña Amparo went on the hunger strike with Doña Lolita.

JUAN: She did?

JOJO: Yeah, she started yesterday.

LUCHA: *(After a beat)* Then, I think we should join, too. Dolores needs our support. She can't do it alone no more. Time is running out for her.

SONORA: And for the huelguistas. Any day now, the courts are gonna rule on #1519.

LUCHA: Verdad. Either the union is going to dump us cuz half of us are ilegal or we dump the union because we won't accept their concessions.

SONORA: Either way we need a Back-up plan.

CHENTE: What? Starving ourselves to death?

LUCHA: It's better than giving into them, no?

JUAN: Yes, we do it along with a farmworker strike.

SONORA: Look at the impact Cesar Chávez had at one time because of his fasts.

CHENTE: This is not 1968!!

JUAN: No, it's 1998! You see any improvement?

(There is a pause.)

SONORA: Bueno, I'm down for the fast, but tonight we party, right?

JUAN: Right!

LUCHA: Eso!

(Lighting transition. "Banda Music" plays on the jute box. Fundraiser in full party-swing. Dancers enter the dance floor in couples, "quebradito"-style, along side CHENTE and LUCHA. JUAN and SONORA watch them. They sit in a booth, drinking beer.)

JUAN: So, Chente's finally getting his time with Lucha.

SONORA: He aint gettin' shit. I don't even think Lucha likes men.

JUAN: What? You think she's gay? She sure seems to be enjoying herself right now.

SONORA: She likes to dance. And no, I don't think she's gay. Not liking men does not a lesbian make.

JUAN: Thou protests too much.

SONORA: She's straight, Juan. Straight women always gotta keep their dukes up more, that's all.

JUAN: I see you've studied this.

SONORA: Observation nomás. What about you, Juan?

JUAN: What?

SONORA: What do you like? Girls? Boys? Both?

JUAN: Books.

SONORA: Books.

JUAN: Ask Amparo. She thinks I sleep with them. *(Imitating her)* "That's why you don't got nobody in your bed. There's no room."

SONORA: She's right. Books can't keep you warm at night. Nah, I don't believe you. Everybody's got somethin' lurking. C'mon, no secret fantasies? Tú sabes, no dream-life.

JUAN: *(After a pause)* Okay, I'd love to make love to Che Guevara.

SONORA: Get out! Really? But he's dead!

JUAN: Doesn't matter. You're talkin' fantasy, right?

SONORA: Right.

JUAN: Well, that's my fantasy. The oldest one I've had. You had Teresa Treviño and the Chicano Moratorium. Well, I had my revolutionary pressed into the smooth sheets of a paperback.

SONORA: You are too crazy.

JUAN: Always wanted to kiss that Jesus Christ mouth, stare dreamingly into those brooding never-satisfied eyes. Che, the lover.

SONORA: *(Raising her beer in a toast)* Fidel, our Father who art en Cuba.

(They clink their beer bottles.)

JUAN: *(Sadly)* ¡Ay, pobre de Cuba! The only island left in the world!

(They are momentarily nostalgic, then they both bust up.)

SONORA: Now, I'm really depressed.

JUAN: Why?

SONORA: Two queers without a date on a Saturday night.

JUAN: Just queer for the revolution, baby.

SONORA: Well, that's awful!

JUAN: Why?

SONORA: That's as bad as being a priest. I mean it's the same as being a priest. Your religion is Marx, your lover is Che, your Father is Fidel. All thoroughly inaccessible men.

JUAN: *(Laughing)* Pretty pathetic, huh?

SONORA: You need to get laid, Carnal. By somebody! *(Shouting out to the bar)* Somebody help this man out! He needs to get laid!

(They both start busting up again. A "Cumbia" comes on. CHENTE and LUCHA return to the booth.)

CHENTE: ¡Chinga'o! I was getting thirsty. She's wearing me out!

LUCHA: *(Overlapping)* What's so funny?

SONORA: I'm trying to get Juan here a sex life.

CHENTE: Why? You thinking about providing one?

SONORA: No.

CHENTE: *(Giving LUCHA a squeeze)* Cuz I'd like one, too.

LUCHA: No seas grosero, Chente. You're married.

CHENTE: That don't mean I'm dead.

LUCHA: It does to me. *(She takes a swig from her beer, then grabs JUAN's hand across the table.)*

LUCHA: Vente, Juanito. *(To* SONORA*)* I'll show este pochito, como bailamos los verdaderos mexicanos!

JUAN: *(Jumping to his feet)* ¡Vámonos!

SONORA: ¡Orale! But, I'm next, Lucha.

*(*LUCHA *and* JUAN *take to the dance floor.)*

LUCHA: *(To* JUAN, *indicating* SONORA*)* ¡Que brava es! ¿no?

JUAN: No mas que tú.

LUCHA: Pues, gracias.

(They dance, stopping periodically for LUCHA *to give him a pointer.* CHENTE *and* SONORA *look on.)*

CHENTE: Ah, if only I wasn't married for a day.

SONORA: You couldn't keep up with her, Chente.

CHENTE: I could try.

(Suddenly the music changes to a slow number, Latin Pop. JUAN *takes the initiative and brings* LUCHA *into his arms. They dance.* CHENTE *and* SONORA *sit in silence with their beers watching the couple dance. The music and lights fade out.)*

Scene Seven

*(*CHENTE *sits at a desk, adding figures on a calculator.* JUAN *enters, he is livid. He lunges at* CHENTE, *pulls him up by the collar.)*

JUAN: You sonavabitch. You sonavabitch.

CHENTE: ¿Qué chinga'o haces? ¿Estás loco, buey?

JUAN: You turned them in, didn't you?

CHENTE: I—

JUAN: You bastard! You put la migra on them.

CHENTE: Let me explain.

JUAN: How could you do that, man?

CHENTE: Cálmate, hombre, I don't wanna fight you.

JUAN: *(Pushing him away in disgust)* Give up your own Raza to la migra.

CHENTE: They were scabs. They were vendidos—

JUAN: No, they're just people, man, just people trying to make a living.

CHENTE: That's very nice, Juan , pero not too practical.

JUAN: Is it practical to split up families?

CHENTE: I couldn't think about that.

JUAN: Apparently not.

CHENTE: I had to show the union we could win. The union bosses were caving in on us. They weren't going to go for no farmworker strike. All they saw was a strike with no end in sight. They wanted to settle. If we were to have settled this week, we would have lost everything. Everything we'd done for the last eighteen months would've been for nothing.

JUAN: You gonna turn us in, too? You gonna turn the huelguistas in too, Chente?

CHENTE: I wouldn't do that.

JUAN: No?

CHENTE: No!

JUAN: That's right. Why bother when Congress will do it for you.

CHENTE: Listen, Cunningham. I did the right thing. It was a hard decision, but the right one. That cannery has come to a complete halt. Chingao, after that migra raid, ni un esquirol has gone near the place. Have you been down there?

JUAN: Yeah. Nobody's celebrating.

CHENTE: (*After a beat*) Ni modo. They'll be thanking me in a few days. Now we can really begin to negotiate. Te digo, we're holding the cards, camarada.

JUAN: You're a fool, Chente. You think that union is your friend?

CHENTE: Yes!

JUAN: You don't know who your friends are. Where's your heart, man?

CHENTE: Where's your heart? In your pants?

JUAN: What are you talking about?

CHENTE: You know how I feel about Lucha.

JUAN: And...?

CHENTE: I saw how you danced with her the other night.

JUAN: When? At that fundraiser? You danced with her, too.

CHENTE: And you took her home.

JUAN: Ah, Jesus!

CHENTE: I see how she's taking your side on everything now. De repente es Juan aquí...Juanito allá—

JUAN: You're a bigger fool than I thought, Chente.

CHENTE: And you're a faggot.

JUAN: Then you got nothing to worry about now, do you?

(JUAN *exits.* CHENTE *watches him, then crosses back to his desk, sits down, checks his watch, and turns on the radio. Sportscast comes on.*)

SPORTSCASTER: "A win tonight would vault San José into second place."

(CHENTE *takes out a soccer ball and pair of old soccer shoes from under his desk, changes his shoes. Lights rise on* DOLORES *and* AMPARO *in* DOLORES' *house. They are squeezing lemons.* LUCHA *appears at home. She is sewing a patch onto* JOJO's *jeans.*)

SPORTSCASTER: "That's three points behind the undefeated Los Angeles Galaxy. Missael Espinoza, the Mexican mid-fielder from Guadalajara will start. With Espinoza in the lineup, you can be sure there will be a large Mexican crowd at the Spartan Stadium tonight, Beth. Well, that's it for Sports, now back to you ..."

NEWSCASTER: "Well, Sal, we may be seeing a large Hispanic turn-out in front of the federal building tonight as well. Just hours ago, in a unanimous decision, the Supreme Court ruled to uphold Senate Bill 1519,—"

(*Everyone freezes.*)

NEWSCASTER:—a key piece of legislation in Florida Senator Casanova's "American Mission." The law prohibits illegal immigrants and their children from obtaining employment, education, and all social services, including non-emergency health care. The I N S is preparing to send thousands of agents into the chiefly agricultural regions of the California and Texas within the month.

(CHENTE *exits hurriedly. Blackout*)

Scene Eight

(*A neighborhood park.* CHENTE *arrives with the soccer ball.* JOJO *has been waiting for him.*)

JOJO: I thought you weren't gonna come practice with me today.

CHENTE: You heard the news?

JOJO: Yeah...they announced it on the P A at school. (*Pause*) What's gonna happen with the strike, Chente?

CHENTE: I guess we just gotta wait for the Union to give us the word. But it don't look good.

JOJO: That sucks, man.

CHENTE: Well, you can't expect the Union to go against the law for us, vato.

JoJo: Why not? That's what my sister's principal's doing.

CHENTE: What is she doing?

JoJo: Breaking the law. She's gonna keep kids in school until the feds force her to shut the doors. That's what Elenita told me. That they'd have to come and put her in jail first.

CHENTE: That's really something. Is that Mrs Covarrubias?

JoJo: Yeah.

CHENTE: What about the high school?

JoJo: Our principal's a punk, man. He just shut whole school down for now. He said he was trying to prevent "further violence." Shit, we didn't even really wreck nuthin', not compared to how we was feeling.

CHENTE: What happened?

JoJo: I dunno. We were all just kina stunned. After they made the announcement, everyone just stopped and looked around the room at each other. It was like allavasudden we were trying to read on each other's faces who was "legal" and who wasn't. Thinking real quick about who had an accent and who didn't, who dressed like a Mexican, who brought tacos to school...stupid stuff like that. It was crazy the stuff going on in our minds.

CHENTE: Yeah, está bien loco.

JoJo: And then it was like everybody in the class just all of a sudden got scared and really pissed off all at once. And I could see that the teacher was kina scared too, like he didn't know what to expect from us. And without sayin' nothing, we all just got up out of our desks and ran out to grounds outside, and then into the streets. Everyone was shouting and crying and hella pissed off and hurtin'. The whole school was out there. Just kickin' down trash cans, climbin' up on bus shelters, jus' screamin' and hittin' things out of bein' so mad.

CHENTE: *(After a pause)* ¿Mijo?

JoJo: Sí.

CHENTE: ¿Tiene papeles tu mamá?

JoJo: *(Softly)* No, my mom's only got fake papers.

CHENTE: ...Es duro.

(JoJo *suddenly wraps his arms around* CHENTE.)

JoJo: I'm scared, Chente. I don't wanna go back to México. I never even been to México.

CHENTE: I know, hijo. We're all scared. *(Rising, pulling* JoJo *to his feet)* Come on, I'll walk you home. I kina lost my ganas to play.

JOJO: Me, too.

CHENTE: You don't got a school no more and we probably don't got a union. We gotta stick together.

(CHENTE *puts his arm around* JOJO's *shoulder. They start to exit. Black-out.*)

Scene Nine

(*One week later. A Spring morning.* DOLORES *has been on the fast for over six weeks. She is very weak. A soft blue glow from* DON ARTURO's *T V set washe over her figure lying on the couch. She is covered by a serape and prays the rosary. A barrage of crowd sounds, and music of a live telecast of a political rally can be heard. A newcaster comes on.*)

NEWSCASTER: (*Over the din of rally sounds*) Well, Roger, today is May Day and you couldn't ask for a more fitting commemoration of International Workers Day than this. Thousands of people have come out this morning in support of a Wild Cat Strike against Pájaro Valley Canning. Now, for those viewers who don't know what a "wild cat strike" is, the strikers have refused to accept the contract their union representatives have negotiated with the Pájaro Valley. Since the Supreme Court's ruling on the illegal immigrant bill, the Teamster's contract now...uh...by law, must deny all undocumented workers a return to their jobs. This is what the workers are protesting. Hunger strikes in solidarity with the workers and in opposition to the new law have erupted throughout California and the Southwest. As I understand it, Roger, the strike support committee...uh...will be meeting with strikers within the next few hours and...hope to arrive at a final decision on the contract. We'll have more for you then.

(*A montage of music and speeches can be heard [see appendix at the end of the play]. They gradually fade out as the lights crossfade to the oak grove.* SONORA *sits at a picnic table. It is covered with burning velas. She is making tobacco ties.* LUCHA *approaches.*)

LUCHA: I thought maybe I'd find you here.

SONORA: Lucha.

LUCHA: The rally's already started.

SONORA: Allí voy...I just took a little detour.

LUCHA: To pray?

SONORA: ...Yeah.

LUCHA: Is it so hopeless?

SONORA: Bueno...how long can we stay out on strike without a union?

LUCHA: No sé.

SONORA: We might not win this.

LUCHA: No digas eso.

SONORA: You're not tired of fighting?

LUCHA: I've always had to fight. This is nothing new.

SONORA: Yo sé.

LUCHA: *(Snapping back at her)* No, tú no sabes. It's different for me than it is for you. From the time I was a little girl, I've always had to defend myself... whether it was from my brothers, del papá, o en la calle. I've lived con los puños así. *(She puts her fists together.)*

SONORA: You don't have to fight me, Lucha. We're not that different...really. Maybe one of these days you'll believe me.

(SONORA crosses to the tree. She buries a tie at its base.)

LUCHA: *(After a pause)* ¿Qué 'stás haciendo?

SONORA: Burying tobacco ties.

LUCHA: ¿Qué's éso?

SONORA: They're like...little prayers. Dakota taught me.

LUCHA: ¿Pero por qué lo haces tú? You're not an Indian.

SONORA: I've got yaqui blood.

LUCHA: Bueno, any Mexican can say that, pero ya no somos indios. That's like starting all over.

SONORA: *(Beat)* Maybe. *(She grabs an acorn off the ground, holds it up to LUCHA.)*

SONORA: You see this?

LUCHA: Sí.

SONORA: When this holy tree we're standing under is long dead and gone, this little acorn may have grown into a tree as great as this one.

LUCHA: Así que—

SONORA: Así que this acorn is the future, a future you and I will never see. In the same way...this old tree is our history. The very acorn that birthed this tree spilled off of some Momma oak the Ohlones were worshipping five hundred years ago. *(Beat)* Do you have any idea what this place looked like when all it knew was indios?

LUCHA: No.

SONORA: Paradise, Lucha, true paradise. And not like some postcard from Santa Cruz. There were marshes, savannah, redwood forests for days. Elk, antelope, deer, coyotes. And every kind of sea bird imaginable.

(She crosses back to LUCHA, *sprinkles a bit of tobacco in her palm. She presses* LUCHA's *palm closed, holding her fist.)*

SONORA: You put your faith in the workers y...bueno, I...I do, too, pero creo en algo más también. I'm praying to this holy oak cuz it's the only thing that seems right to do right now. Call her Tonantzín, Guadalupe, call her whatever you want. This is as close to a God as it gets for me.

LUCHA: You really see la diosa on that bark?

SONORA: *(Looking straight back at* LUCHA, *big smile)* Oh yes, I see her perfectly clear.

(Their eyes lock. There is a pause.)

SONORA: *(Suddenly, gathering up her things)* Vámonos, let's get to the rally. I think JoJo's got a surprise for you.

Scene Ten

(A political rally. Protesters are shouting. "Wild Cat! Wild Cat! Wild Cat! Wild Cat!" A rap beat comes up over the rally p.a. system. JOJO *stands before the assembly with his "back-ups."* LUCHA *and others look on.)*

JOJO: After many long months on the picket line,
it got harder and harder holdin' up that sign.
Scabs comin' in ...and scabs comin' out,
the Teamsters boys started havin' their doubts.
Raza,

ALL: Rise Up!

JOJO: To try and make matters just a little worse,
Washington's revvin' up its hearse.
Talkin' bout wetbacks "get your butts back home."
Gente knowin' home is in the bones.
Gente knowin' home is in the bones.
Raza,

ALL: Rise Up!

JOJO: Raza Cósmica's our middle name
A veces we don't hear it, 'mid all the profane.
But every-so-often, la Virgen comes down,
dice a su gente, "y'all gather round."
Raza,

ALL: Rise up!

JOJO: Les traigo un mensaje, in case you might forget,
you were here first by the name of Aztec.
Tarahumana, Apache, Yaquí—
Indio bloodlines to name just three.
Raza,

ALL: Rise up!

JOJO: With the strike comin' round to year number two
ladies on the line wanna try somethin' new
"Huelga de hambre" is the battle song
Legal or not, we all belong
we're obreros unidos, one thousand strong.
Raza,

ALL: Rise Up!

JOJO: So, the union's chicke and leaves us flat,
knowin' wetback aint the back to scratch.
But a river's flowin' up and over that skin,
with a force so strong, raza gotta win.
with a force so strong, raza gotta win.
Raza,

ALL: Rise Up!

JOJO: Raza,

ALL: Rise Up!

JOJO: Raza,

ALL: Rise Up! *(Fade out)*

(Music and lighting transition to the Strike Committee nearby. AMPARO, CHENTE, SONORA and JUAN are present.)

CHENTE: Now, I know you all don't approve of what I did with the scabs—

AMPARO: No we don't.

CHENTE: But, regardless of what you think of my tactics, it won us the strike.

SONORA: The threat of the farmworkers coming into the strike, that's what got Shea to concede.

CHENTE: Ni modo. We can have our jobs back.

AMPARO: Some of us can have our jobs back.

CHENTE: All we have to do now is sign the contract. This is the best deal we'll ever get from Shea. You return to work with your full wages, complete health benefits, paid vacation. We should be celebrating. This is a victory for la huelga!

AMPARO: No es una victoria cuando nuestra raza sufre por ella.

JUAN: It's your same old strategy, Chente. Screw all the undocumented workers.

AMPARO: ¡Fuiste mojado! How can you forget that. You came to this country crawling on your belly like every other pobre mexicano!

CHENTE: I don't care lo que opinan de mí! This is where each person's got to think about your own families, your own future. Es verdad que not all of the huelguistas will be able to return to work.

AMPARO: Which child should we give up to the slaughter, Chente? Which one of México's children doesn't deserve a decent living?

CHENTE: How many people could we really be talking about, Amparo? También what good will a job do those workers anyway, when they won't be able to send their children to school or get a doctor to see them when they're sick?

AMPARO: You wait, Chente. A year or two from now and the gov'ment's gointu take away the same rights from legal inmigrantes. Where will you be then? With your green card stuck up your culo.

(LUCHA *enters with* JOJO.)

JOJO: Juan, they're asking for you guys at the stage. You're up next to speak.

(Sudden silence. They all look at one another.)

SONORA: Let's face it. We don't know what we're going to tell these people. We don't know what we're going to do next.

AMPARO: Pero, we're doing everything we can. This hunger strike, even los kids aren't eating. The gov'ment won't let them starve to death?

SONORA: No? We're talking about Mexican kids, Amparo.

AMPARO: Yo sé.

JUAN: *(To* JOJO, *after a pause)* Tell them...tell them we're coming.

JOJO: ...Okay.

(He starts to exit. LUCHA *stops him.)*

LUCHA: No espérete. *(To* JUAN*)* What are you going to say out there?

JUAN: *(After a pause)* I don't think we should do it.

AMPARO: ¿Cómo?

JUAN: I don't think we can tell the huelguistas not to sign.

CHENTE: Now you're thinking.

SONORA: What do you mean?

JUAN: How can we ask the strikers to keep on striking? They're worn out! Marriages are falling apart. Husbands are just walking out on their families. People are sleeping in their cars, for chrissake!

AMPARO: So, now you want us to give up?

JUAN: This Wild Cat doesn't have a chance against a federal law!

LUCHA: What are you going to tell them, Juan?

JUAN: I don't know. I guess...we should tell them...that each person has to follow their own conscience. That... each person has to do whatever their conscience directs them to do.

LUCHA: What is this mierda?

JUAN: What?

LUCHA: ¿Por qué hablas así?

JUAN: Because I—

SONORA: Lucha, maybe Chente's right. Maybe you do need to think of your kids. Without a job—

JOJO: (Anxiously) Mom...?

LUCHA: Don't worry, we won't come begging to you.

SONORA: What?

LUCHA: You're no better than Chente. Things get hard and everybody wants to turn in los ilegales.

SONORA: But how can I ask you to turn your back on a job you struggled almost two years for. I have a job!

LUCHA: Ask me.

SONORA: What?

LUCHA: To stay here, to fight this.

SONORA: To stay here...?

(LUCHA holds SONORA's eyes. CHENTE jumps in.)

CHENTE: You can't take on the whole U S government.

AMPARO: No? What happened to solidarity, Chente?

CHENTE: I'm talking facts here, Amparo, not idealism. You can't eat idealism. You can't pay your rent with solidarity.

AMPARO: And who's paying your rent now, Union-man?

CHENTE: What do you mean by that?

AMPARO: You going back to the assembly line with us once we sign this contract?

CHENTE: No, well...I've been offered—

AMPARO: You got an office job now ¿verdad?

CHENTE: Yes.

AMPARO: ¿Con la unión?

CHENTE: Bueno...sí.

AMPARO: Nice salary?

CHENTE: It's all right.

AMPARO: Pero mejor que what Lucha and me will making on the line ¿que no? Even with all these great benefits we'll be getting.

CHENTE: Lucha? She won't be getting nothing.

LUCHA: Y ¿por qué, Chente? Díme en voz alta en frente de toda esta gente, why Lucha Lerma won't be getting a thing after eighteen months on the picket line.

CHENTE: Because you're illegal.

SONORA: Lucha!

LUCHA: And because I won't open my legs to you.

JOJO: Mom!

LUCHA: Tell him. Tell my son to his face, how you got him to confide in you, Cabrón, so you could turn your back on his mother when she doesn't give you what you want. Tell him how you lied about wanting to help me and my kids out. That you could fix my papers, if I needed. Pues, I needed bad, but not that bad. Mándanos a México si quieres, pero por lo menos regreso con mi dignidad.

CHENTE: *(After a beat)* What's done is done. Those of you who have the proper documents will be allowed to vote on the contract and return to work. Any fraudulent papers and the government hits the company with sanctions and the workers with arrest.

SONORA: *(Aside)* You, bastard.

CHENTE: The rest of you—

AMPARO: The rest of you, what?

CHENTE: You know the law. There's really nothing more to discuss. You boycott this contract vote and everybody loses. *(He exits.)*

AMPARO: *(Shouting after him)* ¡Sin verguenza!

LUCHA: And the rest of you sit around with your hands crossed and wait for La Migra to take you away.

SONORA: It's gonna be a goddamn witch hunt.

LUCHA: Sin trabajos, sin escuelas, sin hospitales, they won't have to hunt at all. We'll come crawling out of the walls, como las cucarachas!

AMPARO: No, mi corazón. *(Going to LUCHA)* Un pedacito de papel no puede separar un pueblo. If they gointu send you back to México, they gointu have to move toda la población mexicana de California. "Solidaridad." ¿Te acuerdas? It's one of the most beautiful words en mi nuevo vocabulario. "Solidaridad." Creo mucho en su fuerza. Nobody's gointu go back to work on the backs of other workers. Who could hold their head up in this town afterwards?

LUCHA: Pero ¿que vamos a hacer?

(There is a pause. Everyone looks at one another.)

JUAN: We continue with the hunger strike. We go back to our original plan and bring the farm workers into the strike. They have even more reason to join us now. There's thousands of undocumented workers out there in those fields.

AMPARO: Es verdad.

JUAN: Legal and illegal, we all stop working. Without workers, there're no profits. Without profits, the growers and cannery owners will be pounding down Washington's door to turn back this law.

SONORA: But we've got thousands of people here right now. They don't know what to do. To vote. To boycott the vote. To vote no. Everybody's all fired up.

AMPARO: Sí. Hay que aprovechar el momento—

(DOLORES enters, very pale and weak. She grabs hold of JOJO.)

DOLORES: *(Softly)* ¿Por qué no hacemos una caminata de rodillas a la Virgen?

SONORA: ¿Qué dice, Señora?

DOLORES: Que we make a *procesión on our knees to the holy tree.*

(JUAN turns away.)

DOLORES: We stop en los files, we pick up los obreros, we go from fil to fil, asking the workers to join us in the strike y en nuestra peregrinación.

LUCHA: You want the mujeres on their knees, Dolores?

DOLORES: Lucha, te digo una cosa. I go down on my knees for God, but not for any man. ¿M' entiendes?

LUCHA: Sí, Señora.

(There is a pause. Everybody looks around at one another.)

SONORA: Pero, Señora Valle, you're not that strong.

DOLORES: JoJo will help me ¿no, mijo?

JOJO: Sí, señora.

DOLORES: We've got to make ourselves un ejemplo. No 'stamos solos.
Está Dios. And the newspapers.

SONORA: She's right, the press is just hanging around, waiting for something
to happen.

DOLORES: Pero tiene que ser una ofrenda sincera. *(To* LUCHA*)* ¿Lucha,
me vas a acompañar o no?

LUCHA: *(After a pause)* Sí, yo la sigo.

AMPARO: I go, too, comadre.

SONORA: Yo también.

DOLORES: ¿Y tú, Juan Cunningham?

JUAN: *(Turning to her)* Go on out there and ask the people to join you.

DOLORES: ¿Yo? No, no sé nada de hablar en público.

JUAN: La Virgen will give you the voice, Señora.

DOLORES: Entonces, you will come with us también, Juan?

JUAN: Sí. La sigo, Señora.

(She looks JUAN *square in the face.)*

DOLORES: Gracias...Padre. *(Extending her hand to* JOJO*)* JoJo, ven.

(Crowd and rally sounds rise again as they cross to the stage area. JOJO *helps*
DOLORES *onto the podium. Lighting transition,)*

DOLORES: *(Standing before the crowd, timidly at first.)* No estoy acostumbrada
a hablar en público...pero...many people have asked me, what did la Virgen
say to you? And I didn't know if or when to say. Ahora sí, I know now is
the time.

(There is a slight tremor. DOLORES *stops.)*

DOLORES: La Virgen 'stá con nosotros. *(Another soft rumbling)* La Virgen de
Guadalupe is our mother, la Virgen de todos, más de los mexicanos. When
we pray, who do we call for...? Pues a la madre, porque desde nuestra niñez
we always knew que la madre is the one who listens to her children, who
cares for her children. Even before God, we call for the mother. Acá en
Watsón la madre has travel thousands of miles to show herself to us, los
mexicanos, to tell nuestra gente que pertenecemos aquí, que we belong here
as much as el gringo. Plant yourself here, dice ella. Like that holy tree, tan

fuerte, tan viejo, tan sagrado, ustedes tienen raíces that spread all the way to México. *(Pause)* Esta ley nueva no vale nada. They think they can kill la huelga with this law pero seguimos siendo huelguistas whether we got a union or not. Seguimos siendo americanos whether we got papeles or not. This land is the same land as México. Todo es América y la Virgen de Guadalupe es la Emperatríz de América, una América unida. *(Pause)* Ahora, mi raza, come with me...on your knees si pueden, para demostrar a la Virgen y a toda américa que somos gente de fe y fuerza.

(Música de la Procesión.)

(DOLORES comes down from the podium with JOJO supporting her. He removes the serape from around her shoulders, folds it in half vertically and lays it down on the ground. The others do the same, laying down Mexican cloth after cloth into a narrow path of color and texture. DOLORES kneels onto it and begins to slowly move herself along on her knees. The rest, in single file, follow her. There is another tremor. As the rumbling increases, the light begins to gradually darken and narrow into a circle on the figure of DOLORES with JOJO behind her. The shadow of the leaves of the sacred oak pass across her face. They begin to tremble ever so slightly, then shake with increasing vigor as the sound of the tremor rises in intensity. Ocean sounds blend into distant female voices chanting in nahuatl.

VOICES: Chihuacóatl, Quilaztli, Tonán, Centeotl, Centeotlcihuatl, Xilonen, Teteoian, Chicomecóatl, Citlalicue, Chinipa, Yoalticitl, Coatlicue, Teotenantzín, Tlaliyolo, Toci, Tonantzín, Guadalupe, Madre.

(The earth begins to quake. Black out. The image of la Virgen in the tree is illuminated for a brief moment. Black-out.)

END OF ACT TWO

EPILOGUE
"EL TEMBLOR"

JUAN: *(Voice in the darkness)* "Then the angel showed me the river of the water of life. A river as bright as crystal, flowing through the middle of the streets of the city. On either side of the river is the tree of life with its twelve kinds of fruit, producing its fruit each month. And the leaves of the tree are for the healing of nations."
The Book of Revelations, 22

"La Madrugada"

(A maze of lights criss-cross, collide and intersect with one another on a dark stage. Sirens can be heard in the distance and the muffled conversation from a police radio. JOJO, JUAN, LUCHA, and AMPARO are huddled around JOJO's boombox in the dawn's light. The voice of a newscaster announces:)

NEWSCASTER: "A major earthquake, registering seven-point-five on the Richter scale, struck the central coast of California. Its impact was felt from Santa Barbara to Sacramento and has left much of San Francisco and Oakland thoroughly devasted. The quake's epicenter was located in the town of Watsonville, which was completely leveled by quake. Reports just surfacing from the area, however, have confirmed that some ten thousand survivors, mostly Mexican residents, were found gathered together in an oak grove in a County Park just outside of town."

(The lights rise onto a make-shift sign that reads: "Camp Milagro." It is dawn, days later. An awe-struck quiet pervades the Tent City. A man stands by the sign, sings softly with a guitar.)

"Allá donde la montaña
se levanta fresca y verde
en la memoria se pierde
como en una telaraña
sentimiento que te araña
cada que al tiempo regresa
que cada día mas te pesa
terminas por olvidarlo
por no tener que llorarlo
cada vez que no regresa."

(JUAN *has been standing beneath the sacred oak, watching the singer from a distance. He turns, looks up at the Guadalupe image.*)

JUAN: It's you, isn't it, Cerezita? The motherless child coming back to mother us all. (*Pause*) The voices in my head have never allowed me peace. You pitied that in me, I remember, how I lived so in my head. But...was it just days ago? I stood in the midst of a moving crowd and could not be spotted apart from it. (*Pause*) I found God, Cere. God in the dissolution of self. God in the disappearance of me into a we so profound, the earth shook open to embrace us.

"Mediodía"

(*Crossfade to Tent City grounds. Noontime.* LUCHA *and* AMPARO *are sitting on a picnic table.*)

LUCHA: ¡Qué vida loca! Nobody gives a damn about who's legal or not now.

AMPARO: Sí, pero it's only a matter of time.

LUCHA: Maybe not. Even those fanáticos fundamentalists right-wingers are scared that all this is a sign from god. Didn't you see the headlines? "Miracle Tree Saves Mexicans of Watsonville."

AMPARO: Well if the earth can open up y tragar all of those gringo "quake-proof" skyscrapers, and they're still not scared, bueno, pues yo no tengo ninguna esperanza para este mundo.

LUCHA: Ni yo.

(JOJO *enters, carrying a large wooden sign.*)

JOJO: (*Beat*) Mom, I finished the sign.

LUCHA: ¿Ya? Let's see it, hijo.

JOJO: (*Holding it up*) I did all the letters by hand.

LUCHA: (*Reading it*) "LUCHA'S MIRACLE TAMALE PARLOR."

AMPARO: Mira nomás.

JOJO: Isn't it cool?

LUCHA: Perfecto, hijo!

AMPARO: ¿Quién te va a comprar los tamales Lucha? Nobody's got a cent.

LUCHA: We'll trade. And the "foot traffic" isn't going to get better than this.

AMPARO: Verdad.

LUCHA: Anyway, I don't got no more time to waste.

(Guitarist plays softly in the background as the lights crossfade to DOLORES *lying on a cot inside a tent structure.)*

"Medianoche"

(Midnight. JUAN *is giving the "Last Rites" to* DOLORES. JOJO, AMPARO, SONORA *[who is attending her] and* LUCHA *look on.)*

DOLORES: Padre, I feel nothing that Arturo's gone. Not even guilty.

*(*JUAN *blesses her.)*

DOLORES: But my children are traveling to me. They got their arms out to me. I see my Cerezita, con cuerpo entero. She holds out her arms like the arms of a tree.

AMPARO: *(Grabbing* DOLORES' *hand)* That's beautiful, comadre.

(There is a pause. DOLORES *takes the small torquoise book from beneath her covers, hands it to* JOJO.)

DOLORES: Toma, hijo.

JOJO: It's your miracle book, Señora.

DOLORES: No, now it's yours.

(He throws his arms around her. She holds him. DOLORES *stretches out her hand to* LUCHA, LUCHA *takes hold of it.)*

SONORA: I think we should let her rest now.

AMPARO: I'll come back and take over for you later, Sonora.

DOLORES: *(Weakly)* The graveyard shift? *(She laughs at her little joke.)*

AMPARO: *(With great affection)* ¡Ay chihuahua, Lola! I still haven't figured you out yet.

(They all file out, exept for SONORA.)

DOLORES: Sonora?

SONORA: Mándame, Señora.

DOLORES: Mañana, a la madrugada...go to the holy tree and thank la virgencita por el milagro.

DOLORES: Se lo prometo, Doña Lolita. I'll go at dawn.

"La Madrugada"

(Lighting transition. It is dawn. SONORA *can be seen coming out of* DOLORES' *tent.* LUCHA *meets her.)*

SONORA: Lucha, what are you doing here? Are you okay?

LUCHA: *(Visibly nervous)* ¿Cómo está, Dolores?

SONORA: She's resting. *(Glancing at her watch)* It's five am. Lucha, what's—

LUCHA: I—

SONORA: ¿Qué te pasa?

LUCHA: I...I brought you this. Toma.

*(*LUCHA *holds out a letter to her.* SONORA *hesitates a moment, then takes the letter.)*

SONORA: *(Tenderly)* Lucha, what is it?

LUCHA: Léela.

SONORA: You want me to read it...now?

LUCHA: Sí.

*(*SONORA *opens the envelope, takes out the letter, begins to read it, as* LUCHA *recites its contents by heart.)*

LUCHA: *(Haltingly)* I learn to write English, for the letter, so maybe better you understand me. I want to talk you the way I hear you talk to other womans. Your voice is more low and you forget where go your hands. You laugh more. I want that you forget like that with me, so we can talk with our hearts. I am no a child. I am a woman who know what she want. Te quiero.

*(*SONORA *looks up at her, holds her eyes.)*

LUCHA: No like sisters. With my sister, Isabel, we sleeped together like angels silence. I no notice her there, but I notice you. You touch me and the place stay forever touch.

(There is a pause. SONORA *looks away.)*

LUCHA: ¿Quieres decir que 'stoy sola? Am I alone in this?

SONORA: No.

LUCHA: Pues díme algo.

SONORA: I don't know what to say.

LUCHA: *(Her voice shaking)* La verdad. Es una cosa muy sencilla.

SONORA: It's not so simple.

LUCHA: ¿Por qué no?

SONORA: It's a beautiful letter. Probably the most beautiful letter I've ever gotten.

LUCHA: Pero you don't feel the same.

SONORA: No, I...it's hard.

LUCHA: No es difícil. It was hard writing the letter.

SONORA: Yo sé.

LUCHA: ¿Por qué te ves triste? Does my love make you sad?

SONORA: In a way...yeah.

LUCHA: Lo siento. I didn't mean to burden you. *(Starts to walk away.)*

SONORA: I didn't say you were a burden.

*(*LUCHA *stops.)*

LUCHA: Mira. No soy pendeja. He sido pendeja con los hombres, y no voy a repetirme el escenario.

SONORA: No eres pendeja.

LUCHA: No?

SONORA: No.

LUCHA: What am I then?

SONORA: Eres guerrera. You're a warrior woman, just like your name says.

LUCHA: "Lucha!" I hate my name. It's a hard name, hard sounds. ¡Chinga'o! You and your words. You have words for everything, everything menos para mi pasión, mi coraje, mi fuego. But I go around trying to choose the right ones. I think si pudiera encontrar las palabras corectas, I could convince you that you love me.

SONORA: No tienes que convencerme. *(There is a pause.)*

LUCHA: Estoy despierta, mujer.

SONORA: Sí, se ve.

LUCHA: ¿Y qué? What do you do with a woman who has woken up? ¿Con una mujer que se 'stá amaneciendo?

SONORA: Ay, Lucha!

LUCHA: *(Mimicking her)* ¡Ay, Lucha! Lucha. ¿No entiendes? I'm sick of being Lucha, of being una madre, obrera, luchadora. Is that all I get to do in this life, fight all the time?

SONORA: No digo eso.

LUCHA: I want to love. Like you. You work and you love. I've seen the women around you. Quiero ser lesbiana como tú. I want to be your lesbiana.

SONORA: Mi—

LUCHA: *(Coming to her)* Lesbiana. Un nombre sensual. Una palabra tan suave, me hace temblar el sonido de ella.

SONORA: *(Softly)* Lesbiana.

LUCHA: Sí.

SONORA: Tú.

LUCHA: Sí.

SONORA: Luch—

LUCHA: *(Pressing her fingers to SONORA's lips.)* No. Ya no Lucha.

(She kisses her. SONORA responds. Lighting transition. Music. LUCHA takes down SONORA's hair, then slowly steps away from her and exits. SONORA stands alone in the sacred grove, her face illuminated in the rising light of the dawn. She prays.)

SONORA: I am going back before the burial
before they lay my town to rest
before blight
before plague
before the final earthquake I am going back
to salvage what is left of my mexicanismo
my womanhood, my honesty going back
into your arms, the arms of my teacher
that is not home, but the place of journeying
transformation, revolución.

I am going back

a la tierra sagrada rising up
through the limbs of the aging oak
and the thick torsos of Redwood mourning
I am going back
to live in those days in resurrection of the past
of the ancient
of the miraculous

I am going back to find my future.

(SONORA crosses to DOLORES' deathbed, stands at its foot. DOLORES sits up at the sight of the illuminated figure before her. SONORA holds out her arms to her. DOLORES stretches out her hand to meet her.)

DOLORES: Mi hija.

SONORA: I grew wings, 'Amá. Flew over the prison walls, and came to you. I heard you were dying.

(The lights gradually fade. There is the trumpet call of a lone mariachi.)

END OF PLAY

APPENDIX

ACT TWO, top of Scene Nine: Rally Clips, Voices from the Podium:

Old Irish Female Immigrant: "I came here as an immigrant in 1923. This country grew rich on the immigrant labor!"

Mexican female striker: "Una vez una policía put his gun at me y me dijo que he shoot me if I didn't leave. Me iba a disparar. Y le dije yo, "Yo tengo cuatro hijos que te van a mantener, but go 'head and shoot me." No me dió miedo, me dió mas coraje!"

White Male Worker: "The rich own the factories, but they don't own us. They can't work those factories without us!"

Mexican Male striker: "Eight-five percent of the workforce are women and to me, if we win this strike, it's because the women won it for us. They're on the picket line day and night, rain or shine, cold or hot... ¡Los hombres no se enfrentaron a la policía. Las mujeres era en frente siempre!

Mexican female striker: Esta huelga para mí es algo fuerte, fuerte. Me ha enseñado a hablar, a defenderme, a decir...No. ¡Ya no! ¡Ya no es justo!

White male lefty supporter: This is apartheid! The economic base of Watsonville is sustained by the Latino workers, but they have no power base!

Black Preacher: "The Book of Revelations prophesized a New Jerusalem. Watsonville is that New Jerusalem, that holy city, where God dwells amongst us! And as promised in the scripture, "God will wipe away every tear...and death shall be no more. Neither shall there be mourning, nor crying, nor pain..., for the former things have passed away."

Mexican female striker: "Los patrones nos hicieron fuertes a nosostros con el matrato que nos han dado. Y ya uno enojado, a ver cuál va a ganar!"

PROTEST & PICKET SIGNS & BANNERS:

Standard (Printed by the Union) Picket Signs:

> Pájaro Valley Cannery
> ON STRIKE
> Teamsters
> Union
> Local 911

Banner at Fundraiser (Act Two, Scene Eight):

> PANCHANGA/PARTY
> EXPAND THE STRIKE TO THE FARMWORKERS!

Banner at the Rally (Act Two, Scene Eleven):

> "HUELGA DE HAMBRE/HUNGER STRIKE"

> "FE, LUCHA, & VICTORIA"
> (FAITH, STRUGGLE, & VICTORY)

> "JUSTICIA, DIGNIDAD, Y VICTORIA!"
> (JUSTICE, DIGNITY, & VICTORY)

Protest Signs:

Stop the Scabs!
Support Immigrant Labor!
¡Viva la mujer o brera!
Stop Anti-Immigrant Violence!
¡Viva la huelga!
¡No nos vencerán!
Stop #1519.
¡No pasarán!
¡Solidaridad!
Solidarity!
No Human Being is Illegal!

LAS CANCIONES
(Songs used in the premiere production)

Himno de las razas, danzón by John Santos. Performed by J Santos and The Machete Ensemble.

Viva de la unión, décima by G Gutiérrez. Performed by musicians and cast.

Mi Patria, décima by G Guitiérrez. Performed by Francisco Herrera.

Flores y la felicidad, bolero composed by John Santos. Performed by Enrique Ramírez (lead vocals), Greg Landau (guitars) and J Santos (percussion, voice).

Oigan compañeros, duo composed by John Santos. Vocals by J Santos and Enrique Ramírez.

Buenos días paloma blanca, canción tradicional. Performed by Musicians and "Guadalupanas" (Veronia Arana, Cat Callejas, Raquel Haro and Nigel Toussaint).

Desde el cielo, canción tradicional. Performed by Musicians and "Guadalupanas" (Veronica Arana, Cat Callejas, Raquel Haro, and Nigel Toussaint).

Sabrina, cumbia composed by John Santos. Performed by Enrique Ramírez with J Santos.

Raza, Rise Up, lyrics by Cherríe Moraga. Performed by Peter Gómez and his "Back-ups" (Veronica Arana, Cat Callejas, Raquel Haro and Nigel Toussaint).

Como en una telaraña, fandanguito composed by Gilberto Gutiérrez. Performed by Francisco Herrera.

La Huelga de Watsonville, music & lyrics by José Luis Orozco. Copyright 1988. All rights reserved. Used by permission. Performed by Musicians and Cast.

The Women of Watsonville, during Wild Cat Strike Rally, composed and arranged by Pat Wynne.

HISPANIC PLAYWRIGHTS PROJECT HISTORY

1986
ONCE REMOVED by Eduardo Machado
CHARLEY BACON AND HIS FAMILY by Arthur Giron
BIRDS by Lisa Loomer

1987
THE PROMISE by José Rivera
PASSION by Ana Maria Simo
BLACKLIGHT by Estela Portillo-Trembley
THE DEATH AND LIFE OF LUIS RODRIGUEZ by Bernardo Solano
MIDDLE GRAY by Sam Garcia
THE JUDAS GOAT by Alfred Lopez

1988
BANG BANG BLUES by Charles Gomez
EVERY THING IN ITS PLACE by Rafael Lima
BROKEN BOUGH by Lynette Serrano-Bonaparte
IMAGENES by Bernardo Solano
SIMPLY MARIA by Josefina López
THE IMMACULATE SALVATION AUTO BODY PARTS STORE by Rafael
  Melendez

1989
MY VISITS WITH M G M (MY GRANDMOTHER MARTA) by Edit
  Villarreal
SHADOW OF A MAN by Cherríe Moraga
MAN OF THE FLESH by Octavio Solis
YOUNG VALIANT by Oliver Mayer
THE LADY ARCHITECT AND THE KING OF TILE by Roberto Athayde
TRAFFICKING IN BROKEN HEARTS by Edwin Sánchez

1990
PROSPECT by Octavio Solis
FLOORSHOW: DOÑA SOL AND HER TRAINED DOG by Edwin Sánchez
A DREAM OF WEALTH by Arthur Giron
THE NEWS FROM PUERTO RICO by Jack Agueros
SCARLET MACAW by Bernardo Solano
GLEANING/REBUSCA by Caridad Svich

1991
LA ILUMINADA by Octavio Solis
SEPTEMBER 11 by Guillermo Reyes
R AND J by Edit Villarreal

1992
BITTER HOMES AND GARDENS by Luis Alfaro
COCKS HAVE CLAWS AND WINGS TO FLY by Amparo Garcia
KUBA by Roger Schirra

1993
PACIFIC OCEAN by Roger Arturo Durling
I CAN'T EAT GOAT HEAD by Silvia Gonzalez S
THE OLD MATADOR by Milcha Sanchez-Scott

1994
INKARRI'S RETURN by Henry Guzman
CLEAVAGE AND SMOKES by Delores Chavez
STRAIGHT AS A LINE by Luis Alfaro
A ROYAL AFFAIR by Luis Santeiro

1995
UNDER THE WESTERN SKY by Amparo Garcia
WATSONVILLE by Cherríe Moraga
N W W Y P by Carlos A Murillo

1996
SANTA CONCEPCIÓN by Anne García-Romero
ADRIFT by Rogelio Martinez
TRACKS by Edit Villarreal

1997
HOW TO MAKE LOVE TO A MULATTO by Jorge Ignacio Cortiñas
CLAUDIA MEETS FULANO COLORADO by Joann Farías
LA ROMY TAKES A DIVE (EL OTRO) by Octavio Solis

1998
LANDLOCKED by Cusi Cram
THE SINS OF SOR JUANA by Karen Zacarías

1999
REFERENCES TO SALVADOR DALI MAKE ME HOT by José Rivera
ILLUMINATING VERONICA by Rogelio Martinez
LUPE, NOW! by Jonathan Ceniceroz
CUCHIFRITO by Eduardo Andino

2000
HORTENSIA AND THE MUSEUM OF DREAMS by Nilo Cruz
THE END OF IT ALL by Cusi Cram
VIEQUES by Jorge González

COMMISSIONED HISPANIC PLAYWRIGHTS PROJECT
WRITERS

Luis Alfaro
Eduardo Andino
Jonathan Ceniceroz
Jorge Ignacio Cortiñas
Cusi Cram (2)
Nilo Cruz
Joann Farías
Ann García-Romero
Rafael Lima
Rogelio Martinez
Eduardo Machado
Carlos Murillo
José Rivera (3)
Edwin Sánchez (2)
Milcha Sanchez-Scott
Lynette Serrano-Bonaparte
Ana Maria Simo
Octavio Solis
Edit Villarreal
Karen Zacarías